THE PRESE

THE PRESENCE OF LIGHT

Divine Radiance and Religious Experience

EDITED BY *Matthew T. Kapstein*

The University of Chicago Press CHICAGO & LONDON

MATTHEW T. KAPSTEIN is the Numata Professor of Buddhist Studies in the Divinity School of the University of Chicago and directeur d'études at the École Pratique des Hautes Études, Paris. He is the author of *The Tibetan Assimilation of Buddhism: Conversion, Contestation, and Memory* and *Reason's Traces: Identity and Interpretation in Indian and Tibetan Buddhist Thought.*

The University of Chicago Press, Chicago 60637
The University of Chicago Press, Ltd., London

Printed in the United States of America

13 12 11 10 09 08 07 06 05 04   1 2 3 4 5

ISBN: 0-226-42490-1 (cloth)
ISBN: 0-226-42492-8 (paper)

Library of Congress Cataloging-in-Publication Data

The presence of light : divine radiance and religious experience / edited by Matthew T. Kapstein
p. cm.
Includes bibliographical references and index.
ISBN 0-226-42490-1 (cloth : alk paper) — ISBN 0-226-42492-8 (pbk. : alk. paper)
1. Light—Religious aspects. 2. Experience (Religion) 3. Mysticism. I. Kapstein, Matthew.
204'2—DC22   2004001058

This book is printed on acid-free paper.

CONTENTS

ILLUSTRATIONS

FIGURES

PLATES (FOLLOWING PAGE 194)

Plate 9. Right side of the panoramic wall painting of the miraculous world of the Wutai Mountains, completed sometime between 947 and 957 on the west wall of Dunhuang cave 61. Some of the pigments in the panorama have suffered considerable degradation, typically darkening over time. This is especially evident in many of the vertical explanatory labels, some of which are now illegible. Plate 9 shows approximately one-third of the complete painting. Note the three horizontal registers: *Lower register,* On the far right, pilgrims leave the city of Zhenzhou and proceed to the mountain gate on the lower left. Balancing this, on the far left of the full painting (in a section not shown here), pilgrims leave from the city of Taiyuan and enter the mountain gate of the pilgrimage route. *Middle register,* Here we have entered the mountain precincts and see the major monastic institutions, numerous thatched meditators' huts, each of the principal peaks (here, from right to left, are depicted the Eastern and Northern Terrace summits), and many miraculous events, most especially manifestations of light. *Upper register,* The world of spirit forces looms above, with figures descending on multicolored clouds (most of the multicolored clouds in the painting take on the auspicious *ruyi* form). The local dragon spirits clearly are subordinated to Wenshu and his hundreds of assistants.

Plate 10. Detail from the right side of the panorama, showing such features as a hand descending on five-colored clouds, the sector of the mountain territory known as "blue-green lapis lazuli realm," the manifestation of an entire body encased in light (again descending on auspicious clouds), and the appearance of a golden bridge. Note that these events do not go unwitnessed: there are humans—monks and laypersons—inhabiting all parts of this earthly realm.

Plate 11. Northern Terrace summit and surroundings (see also the left side of plate 9). The Northern Terrace is the tallest of the Wutai peaks, at 3,058 meters in altitude, and the weather there can be fierce and unpredictable. Note the Thunder God who descends to the left of the Summit Pool, encircled by his drums. The Northern Terrace has special associations with dragon kings, probably because of the frequent rain, snow, and howling winds. In addition to the two pods of dragons descending on clouds, one individual swims in the Summit Pool, and behind him stands a shrine labeled "Hall of the Noxious Dragons." On the lower left of this detail, two monks worship before a stupa of the type generally associated with Aśokan relics—relics of Śākyamuni Buddha said to have been distributed throughout the world by the Indian king Aśoka.

PREFACE

La prima luce, che tutta la raia,
per tanti modi in essa si recepe,
quanti son li splendori a chi s'appaia.

The Primal Light the whole irradiates,
And is received therein as many ways
As there are splendors wherewithal it mates.

Dante Alighieri, *Paradiso,* canto 29.136–38

Among the themes sometimes taken to suggest that there is a universal basis for religious intuition and experience, images of light must hold pride of place. The Law, after all, teaches us that the appearance of light was the first moment in the divine act of creation. The Bhagavad Gītā describes the vision of Lord Krishna, "blazing with the light of a thousand suns." And Buddhist texts refer to the founder's awakening as "radiant light." In mystical traditions, East and West, not only is light ubiquitous, but strikingly precise similarities may be found in altogether different historical and cultural settings. The traditions themselves, in their interplay of convergence and difference, seem to confirm the vision of the whole and its many modes revealed in the *Paradiso* of Dante Alighieri, quoted above with the elegant translation of Dorothy Sayers.

The comparative study of mysticism and religious experience has been enriched during recent decades by a lively debate aroused by scholars who have argued, against the perennialism that had characterized much of early-twentieth-century writing on mysticism, that religious experience is largely a matter of cultural and linguistic construction, and not of context-neutral, universal phenomena. In rebuttal, some have recently sought to challenge constructivism, grounding religious epistemology in experiences that arguably are not contingently constructed, but instead reflect innate capacities of human consciousness and perception. Thus, the claim is sometimes made that we can aspire to locate a "common core," for example, "pure consciousness experience," unifying disparate mystical traditions.

Despite the many excellent contributions to the study of mysticism and religious experience that have emerged thanks to the constructivist-perennialist (or, more broadly, constructivist-realist) debate, from the perspective of those involved in the history and interpretation of particular traditions the conversation sometimes seems to falter by engendering a peculiar dilemma: if religious experience is culturally, historically, or linguistically constructed *throughout*, then it would seem that comparison becomes impossible, because apparent similarities must be reduced to culturally specific constructions that only *seem* to resemble others. On the other hand, if differing mystical traditions are to be nevertheless defined monothetically in terms of a specific universal experience, this must be established apart from all culturally specific constructions, including of course our own, and this is also impossible. In short, it may appear that constructivism and perennialism both undermine the prospects for a significant, comparative study of mystical traditions.

In connection with the present work, however, we find this dilemma to be a false one. It arose in part because earlier twentieth-century studies of mysticism had insisted upon emphasizing what was sometimes called "*the* mystical experience" and thus were often committed, a priori, to the view that a singular essence was to be found concealed beneath mysticism's diverse manifestations. Because the study of historical religious traditions, however, tends to underscore the remarkable plurality of these manifestations, and must take into account many differing types of experience (vision, trance, synesthesia, etc.), as well as a whole range of related matters, including spiritual discipline, theological and philosophical rationalization and speculation, artistic production, and so forth, the entire project of reducing the study of mysticism to the quest for a uniquely determined experience, or even to a small set of determinate experiences, was misconceived. The constructivist position has emerged as a necessary corrective. Equally necessary for the advancement of our understanding of religious experience, however, has been the attempt to indicate that a conception of construction from the ground up, as it were, is not really plausible. What is needed, surely, is a reopening of comparative work on religious experience, but without insisting upon a single "common core," and now fully alive to the dialectical relationship among cultural, historical, and linguistic constructions and the universal possibilities of human experience.

The present collection is offered in the interest of renewing this conversation. We do not wish to privilege or otherwise overemphasize light mysticism among types of religious experience; it has been selected just because it seems as good a theme as any of many others with which to begin, and it affords a useful corrective to the emphasis upon so-called contentless or ineffable experience that has characterized much work on mystical traditions. While we do wish to initiate comparative reflection upon light mysticism in particular, the deeper goal is to advance the larger comparative study of religious experience, above all with reference to the major traditions of late antiquity and the medieval period.

Light is of special interest to us, however, because somehow light *is* special. Light may be either physical or spiritual and therefore is an object both of physics and of religious reflection. It makes possible our sight, and yet it illuminates our dreams, when our eyes are closed and all around us is darkened. "Light" may literally refer to sensory experience, but at the same time it offers one of our most far-reaching metaphors: knowledge is light, its acquisition enlightenment; moral goodness is a guiding lamp, beauty glows, heroic valor is radiant. Indeed, in virtue of light's ubiquity and its pervasion of our categories, it is not always clear to us where one usage begins and another ends. Is the physical light of our world equally a spiritual power? So some have thought. Or may spiritual light glow so forcefully that it becomes an object of physical sight? So others would affirm. Is the equation of light and goodness merely a metaphor, or does it flow from the very first instant of creation, when the deity herself affirmed the goodness of the primal light she had engendered? The studies offered in the present collection give us much to ponder in regard to these and other questions. In the three major parts of this book—emphasizing light in relation to, respectively, the ontology of the divine, the apotheosis of the adept, and the visual culture of religious traditions—"light" is seen to suffuse a broad range of religious phenomena, whose meaning and value vary widely in differing historical and cultural settings, while disclosing important commonalities nevertheless.

Sarah Iles Johnston, writing on early Platonic mysticism in the first chapter of part 1, "The Divine Presence of Light," emphasizes the relationship between the observable properties of light in the physical world and the conceptual properties of the divine. For Iamblichus and other authors she discusses, the natural properties of light both resemble those of the gods and offer a passage whereby the human intellect may approach the divine. The intellectual intuition of divine light is, with quite different emphasis, also a focal point of

Hossein Ziai's contribution (chap. 2), where we explore an epistemological theory favored by Persian mystics from the thirteenth century onward. The theory in question was developed by the twelfth-century philosopher Shihab al-Din Suhrawardī and played a key role in his philosophy of Illumination. Suhrawardī's universe is made up of a continuum of "light" entities, which are distinguished in terms of an equivocal degree of self-consciousness. At the apex of the system, the "Light of Lights" propagates all other lights, forming every sector of the continuum. In chapter 3, Paul E. Muller-Ortega considers one of the streams of Hindu Tantrism in which light mysticism was particularly prominent, the Kashmir Shaivism of Abhinavagupta. He finds in Abhinava's writings an implicit "argument of light," derived not, however, from axioms of reason, but from the phenomenlogy of Shaivite mystical experience.

The second part of the book, "Transformative Visions," begins with Andrew Louth's study of light in the Orthodox Christian tradition. Distinctive here was the apparent tension between the theological assertion of God's ultimate ineffability and the mystical assertion that the vision of divine light is the culminating experience of the path, a tension that was first theologically resolved in the speculations of Maximos the Confessor (580–662) concerning the Transfiguration of Christ. In chapter 5, Elliot Wolfson discusses the metaphysics of illumination that informed the ecstatic theosophy of medieval kabbalah, with special reference to the period of the composition of the *Zohar* in late-thirteenth-century Spain, and focusing upon the interplay of the ontological and phenomenological poles of the light experience. The process of knowing God's light brings about the apotheosis of the mystic, whereby he becomes the light beyond the light, the source of the light wherein the binary opposition of light and darkness is itself overcome. In the following chapter, the present writer discusses Tibetan esoteric traditions in which experiences of light and obscuration play prominent roles. The focal point here is the Great Perfection (*rdzogs-chen*) tradition of meditation, above all its teaching that some adepts who achieve the highest realization attain a "rainbow body" at death. When this takes place, the adept's physical remains dissolve into light and so make manifest the thoroughgoing transformation of the person that had been catalyzed by prior spiritual discipline.

Part 3, "In the Sight of the Eye," considers aspects of light imagery in the visual culture of Asian religions. In chapter 7, Catherine Asher surveys imperial Mughal art and architecture in order to reveal the manner in which the Mughals sought to construct an experience of light reflecting their particular aesthetics of sovereignty. As Asher demonstrates, the light symbolism of the Mughals, inspired in large measure by the Illuminationist philosophy of Suhrawardī, also drew strength from its impact upon the Mughal empire's Hindu subjects. The two chapters that follow study aspects of Buddhism in East Asia, where Indian traditions often played an influential role, but not to the exclusion of religious beliefs and practices relating to light that had first evolved within East Asian cultural milieus. As Raoul Birnbaum shows us in chapter 8, light phenomena in the Wutai Mountains, a region celebrated for its places of pilgrimage, and their traditional interpretation form part of a larger preoccupation with light that is basic to Chinese Buddhist notions of effective religious practice. And in the ninth chapter, Mimi Hall Yiengpruksawan studies the role of light in artistic commissions during the latter part of the life of an important Japanese courtier, Michinaga (966–1027). As she argues, Michinaga was in fact going blind during the period of his preoccupation with spiritual light, and under these circumstances the experience of light must have assumed an especially poignant significance, embodying his aspirations to be sighted and receptive to spiritual vision in future lives.

The threefold division of the book reflects disciplinary distinctions no less than it does substantive differences in the topics considered. Very roughly speaking, in the first section studies of philosophy and the history of ideas predominate, in the second the emphasis is on history of mystical traditions, while the third underscores art historical interests. It will be seen, nevertheless, that these distinctions by no means preclude the delineation of numerous themes of common concern. In the final chapter, the present writer offers concluding thoughts on the studies included here as they pertain to current debates regarding religious experience.

The scope of this book, therefore, embraces many of the key areas relevant to the study of light in relation to religious experience. But the book is not intended to offer encyclopedic coverage of its subject matter, and so it will not be difficult to find topics of importance that are not represented herein. It is the hope of those who contributed to this project only to have addressed a sufficient range of material to inspire fuller reflection on the manner in which light has figured in the constitution of religious ideas and practices and, more generally, to exemplify the need for current research on religious experience to address experiences of sight, sound, and the other senses, to which religious value is ascribed.

* * *

The preparation of this volume has extended over several years and began with two conversations in 1996, with Elliot Wolfson and Paul E. Mueller-Ortega. The upshot of these discussions was a series of panels sponsored by the Comparative Studies Section of the American Academy of Religion in 1997 and 1998. Following this, thanks to the initiative of Elliot Wolfson and the Department of Religion at New York University, a conference entitled "Light, Vision, and Mystical Experience" was convened at New York University in April 2000. Participants on that occasion included the contributors to the present volume, together with Professor Charles Taliaferro (St. Olaf's College) and Professor Matthew Bagger (Brown University). I am grateful to all of those whose efforts facilitated these enjoyable and rewarding events and hope that they will find in this work a suitable gesture of esteem. In particular, I wish to acknowledge with gratitude the encouragement of William Darrow and his colleagues on the steering committee of the AAR Comparative Studies Section and the many and varied efforts of Janine Paolucci and her staff in the Department of Religion at NYU.

For facilitating the publication of this work and guiding it through the press, thanks are due to Alan Thomas, Randy Petilos, and their colleagues at the University of Chicago Press. Erik Carlson's judicious editorial interventions have enhanced the clarity of the text throughout. The Divinity School and the Division of the Humanities of the University of Chicago have generously contributed to the expenses of color reproduction and the preparation of the index. I am particularly grateful in this respect for the encouragements of Dean Richard Rosengarten (Divinity) and Dean Janel Mueller (Humanities).

PART ONE

The Divine Presence of Light

Light came to represent in people's minds the truth of an ideal world of which ours is only a moving model, in which the words "God is light" are a simple statement of fact.

David Park, *The Fire within the Eye*

The experience of light often serves as a bridge between the physical and spiritual planes of our existence. Owing to the intersection of these two domains in and through light, sharp dualities between the physical and the spiritual may be dissolved in interpreting our experiences of light, and perhaps even in the perception of light itself. Physical events are spiritualized for us, and in visionary illumination the real nature of objects seen in the world is disclosed.

If religious traditions have frequently found the presence of the divine to be revealed in light, they have by no means done so in identical ways, though the numerous apparent similarities revealed on the luminous paths they describe seem always to suggest convergences to the imagination. The presence of the divine in the experience of light is one of several key themes unifying the particular studies of religious traditions that make up this book. The chapters in this first section introduce three distinct, but not mutually exclusive, ways in which the nature of divine being has been interpreted in relation to light.

In "*Fiat Lux, Fiat Ritus:* Divine Light and the Late Antique Defense of Ritual," Sarah Iles Johnston examines the relationship between natural light, above all sunlight, and divinity in the Platonic mystical tradition. In the writings of theurgists such as Iamblichus, the conception of natural light's mediation of physical and spiritual worlds is evoked with perfect clarity. As Johnston explains:

By accepting the premise that divinity is a type of light, and by assuming that it behaves like the most familiar sort of light, sunlight, Iamblichus has resolved the conflict between transcendence and interaction. He simultaneously has resolved another knotty issue of the time: the conflict between belief in a single divine principle and an apparent multiplicity of divine forces that are spread throughout the world. He argues that, because it ultimately emerged from a single source of illumination (the Father), divine light remained unified even as it seemed to be dispersed infinitely throughout the cosmos; similarly, all the light cast by the sun remains part of the same whole even as it shines, for example, through a window into a room and illuminates different objects within it.

The Platonic traditions Johnston describes here would play an important role in the formation of later conceptions of the divine light, in late antique and medieval Judaism, Christianity, and Islam. This legacy is reflected in the later chapters of this book that are devoted to aspects of the three monotheistic traditions.

One such reflection may be found in Hossein Ziai's essay "Suhrawardī on Knowledge and the Experience of Light." For this great twelfth-century Persian thinker, light provided a central organizing metaphor, a means to express the unity of being and knowing in which the true essence of things is revealed. But light does not function in Suhrawardī's Illuminationist system as metaphor alone, for in visionary experience the abstract, divine light may also be intuitively disclosed. In Ziai's words,

"Light" must exist at all levels of reality for Illuminationist theory of knowledge to hold, both manifest light (*al-nūr*) necessary for sight and the abstract light (*al-nūr al-mujarrad*) necessary for the visionary experience. Stated simply, it is the Illuminationist theory of the propagation of light that determines how light comes to exist at all levels. The very origin, principle, and nexus of Illuminationist cosmology is the Light of Lights who radiates or emanates "light" because of what it is, and the propagated "rays" reach the entire cosmos. The existence (self-consciousness) of the Light of Lights is not separate from its activity (illumination).

Although, as Ziai makes clear, experiences of light induced through ascetic practice play a fundamental role in this tradition, the Illuminationist theory is by no means offered as a straightforward phenomenological description of the experiences in question. Rather, in a manner analogous to scientific practice, the experiences are taken as evidentiary support for the theoretical elaboration of Illuminationist philosophy. The experience of light is here clearly foundational, but by no means uninterpreted.

In the final chapter of this section, "Luminous Consciousness: Light in the Tantric Mysticism of Abhinavagupta," Paul E. Muller-Ortega introduces us to a tradition that was, so far as we know, independent of the Neoplatonic influences that informed mystical traditions in the medieval West and in the Islamic world. Though Muller-Ortega convincingly suggests antecedents to the Kashmiri Tantric mysticism he considers in more ancient Indian religions, reaching back as far as the Veda, the materials he presents represent a strikingly original iteration of Indian light mysticism. In Muller-Ortega's lucid translation, Abhinavagupta presents this teaching succinctly:

> The essential true nature of all existing things is indeed composed of light, for it is not logically possible that the essential nature of all existing things not be the light [of existence]. And that light is unitary, because it is impossible for that light to become other than what it essentially is. Thus, neither space nor time can sunder its essential unity, because indeed their essential nature is nothing but that light. Thus, the light is one, and that light is consciousness.

Given its stress upon the ultimate identity of light, consciousness, and existence, Abhinavagupta's exposition anticipated aspects of the Persian Illuminationist philosophy of Suhrawardī, who lived roughly two centuries after Abhinava's time. The later historical significance of this congruence of ideas will become apparent in chapter 7 below, Catherine Asher's contribution concerning the imagery of light in the imperial Mughal aesthetics of sovereignty; for the Mughals' appropriation of Illuminationist light symbolism resonated well with facets of the religious life of the Hindus they ruled. The Tantric traditions of India, moreover, in their varied Buddhist guises, would exert a continuing influence upon the formation of esoteric religions throughout Central and East Asia down to the present day.

CHAPTER ONE

Fiat Lux, Fiat Ritus: Divine Light and the Late Antique Defense of Ritual

Sarah Iles Johnston

Describing a mystical experience is difficult.[1] Unions between the human and the divine resist expression precisely because the divine is unlike anything that mortals experience in everyday life—God does not belong in the same category as cars and potato chips. By the same token, anything that can be understood and described with perfect clarity smacks of normal life; abstruseness may help to validate a mystical experience. This is why narrations of mystical experiences so often rely on simile: union with God is "like" being filled with warmth; the sight of God is "like" gazing at a fire. Or, to use Tennyson's words,

Moreover something is or seems,
That touches me with mystic gleams,
Like glimpses of forgotten dreams—
Of something felt, like something here;
Of something done, I know not where;
Such as no language may declare.[2]

There are some mystics, however, who feel compelled to describe and explain their experiences a little more exactly than Tennyson did. Neoplatonic mysticism, which developed in the Greek-speaking world during the first few centuries CE, embraced qualities shared by many other mystical systems, including a tendency toward abstruseness that arose from the belief that God was transcendent and therefore, finally, unknowable. And yet, as a product of Platonic philosophy, it was born into a tradition of investigating the cosmos and describing the relationships amongst the divine and mortal entities who dwelt within it. A Platonist—even a mystic Platonist—could never completely overcome the desire to understand what he was experiencing—nor could he trust his experiences until he understood them, at least in part.

This was particularly so during late antiquity, when the philosophers whom we now refer to as Neoplatonists argued among themselves as to which method of communing with divinity, and thereby improving one's soul, was best. The main dividing line fell between those who, like Plotinus, recommended using only the rational powers of the human intellect (i.e., *theoria:* philosophical discussion and contemplation) and those who, like Iamblichus, believed that rituals were necessary as well. As significant as it was in itself, below the surface of this debate lay even more vital issues. For example, the belief that rational endeavors alone were adequate was supported by, and in turn supported, the premise that human souls did not completely descend from the divine sphere into incarnation, whereas those who believed that ritual was a necessary adjunct argued that souls did descend into human bodies—and thus, that rituals performed in the material world, using material objects, were therapeutic to the soul. Those who espoused rational approaches rejected the material world and portrayed it as a source of pollution; those who embraced ritual believed that even the smallest and lowest portions of the material world were charged with divine power that, when properly deployed through rituals, could improve the individual soul. Each side, interestingly, was able to use statements from Plato's dialogues in support of its views.[3]

In this essay, I will comment on the way in which one group of Neoplatonic mystics, the theurgists, resolved the tension between their belief that divinity was transcendent and their desire to understand their mystical experiences by developing the idea that divinity consisted of fiery light. I will also show how, by doing so, the theurgists were able both to defend the general position that ritual was a necessary part of communing with the divine and to explain how specific rituals worked: in the final analysis, divine light was put to work to save not only the theurgist, but also the metaphysical and soteriological doctrines in which the theurgists believed.

If its broadest implications were explored fully, the topic I have just sketched could fill an entire book. This, combined with the fact that Neoplatonic theurgy in general is a complex subject (made even more complex by the fragmentary nature of some of our most important sources), demands that I focus on only a single aspect of the topic. I will do so by addressing a question that particularly intrigues me and that I perceive to be central to this volume's theme: namely, the manner in which the *observable* properties of light influenced both the development of theurgic mysticism and the manner in which one theurgist defended ritual. As a result, I will have to skim over many of theurgy's central ideas only cursorily; the reader may pursue these further by consulting works cited in the notes. For the same reasons, I have decided to limit myself largely to examining material taken from two of our most detailed sources of information for theurgic mysticism: the *Chaldean Oracles,* poems in dactylic hexameter that supposedly were dictated by the gods to two holy men, a father and son named Julian the Chaldean and Julian the Theurgist, in the late second century CE (hereafter referred to as the *Oracles*); and Iamblichus's treatise *Concerning the Mysteries,* which was written in the fourth century and which was significantly influenced by the *Oracles.*[4] *Concerning the Mysteries* was written in response to the challenge of one of Plotinus's students, Porphyry. Although Porphyry did not completely dismiss the value of ritual, as his teacher had, he challenged Iamblichus to defend its use in the pursuit of higher soteriological goals.[5]

Occasionally, I shall also use materials from some of our other sources for theurgy, including the writings of the emperor Julian (fourth century CE), and two exegetes of the *Oracles,* Proclus (fifth century CE) and Psellus (eleventh century CE). Although the two latter sources must be used with caution, separated as they are from the *Oracles* by three and nine centuries, respectively, the fact that Proclus and Psellus could consult complete copies of the *Oracles* and other, now missing works such as a commentary on the *Oracles* that Iamblichus wrote makes their exegeses important supplements to our knowledge. The emperor Julian's work must be used with caution as well; because he wished to incorporate theurgy into his larger project of reviving "traditional" paganism in the then Christian empire, he sometimes collapsed theurgical ideas together with those from other cults such as Mithraism. Nonetheless, Julian's devotion to the sun as his primary god makes some of his comments on the role of light in ritual important for our topic.

THEURGIC METAPHYSICS

The theurgic identification of divinity and light did not come out of nowhere—the general association between divinity and fire or light was old. Already in archaic Greek literature, for example, gods glowed with brightness: in the Homeric *Hymn to Demeter,* when Demeter throws off her mortal disguise "light shines out from the goddess's immortal skin."[6] Platonic metaphors, such as that of the Cave in the *Republic,* were implicitly built on this association: the transmission of the Good into the material world is represented as sunlight entering darkness.[7] Later Platonists, most notably Plotinus, were inspired by this passage to use images of sunlight as similes, to illustrate the way in which the One transmitted the Good into lower portions of the cosmos or the soul.[8] Heliolatry had entered the Greco-Roman world from the east by the Imperial period; other new religions, such as Mithraism, gave a special place to the sun.[9] But the notions that divinity *was* fire or light and that mortals might somehow interact with or receive it were uncommon in the ancient Mediterranean. In the eastern part of the Mediterranean world, at about the same time as theurgy was developing, the prophet Mani made Light the supreme principle of Good and Darkness the supreme principle of Evil in his dualistic system; Manichaean soteriology, moreover, included incorporating particles of Light into the individual human. There are enough parallels between Manichaeism and theurgy, and especially between their treatments of light, to justify a closer comparison between the two than scholars have offered.[10] But for the moment we must restrict ourselves to the theurgists. Let us begin with a look at the way that identifying divinity and light affected their metaphysics.

The *Chaldean Oracles* referred to the highest divine principle by several names: the Father, the Source of Sources (*Pēgē Pēgōn*), the First Fire That Lies Beyond (*Pur Epekeina to Prōton*), and the Uniquely Beyond (*Hapax Epekeina*) were among them. As the two latter names imply, this divine principle was transcendent, beyond the reach of mortals, *daemones, angeloi* (angels), and even gods.[11] This transcendence was crucial because only by remaining transcendent could the divine principle remain perfect. And yet both the metaphysical and the soteriological doctrines of the theurgists required that the creative and salvific forces of this principle should reach even the lowest realms of the cosmos in some way—if they did not, the cosmos would remain an inert and chaotic mass of physical material, and mortals would have no chance of rising above it.

The theurgists solved this problem by positing that the divine principle, being itself a fire, could penetrate the strata of the cosmos with fiery light and thereby enliven them. Thus, for example, fragment 34 of the *Oracles* says:

From [the Source of Sources] leaps forth the genesis of complex matter.
From there a lightning bolt, sweeping along, becomes less distinct as
It leaps into the cosmic wombs. For from there, all things
Begin to stretch forth wondrous beams towards the place below.[12]

Fragment 37 further describes the Platonic Ideas as flashing (*straptousai*) around in the wombs of the cosmos after having been shot forth from the Father. In the theurgic system, just as in Plato, these Ideas were understood to impose order upon physical material and thus to create the cosmos as we know it. As divine fire or light descended, it also brought to birth and continuously invigorated lesser divinities: gods (the lower rank of whom operated under their familiar Greek and Roman names), *archangeloi, angeloi, daemones,* and heroes. Some of the distinguishing characteristics of these types will be discussed in a later section of this essay; for now, however, I will use the term "divinities" to refer to them collectively (Iamblichus similarly uses the term *theoi* to refer to them collectively at times).

These divinities used the paternal light or fire that they received from the Father to perform their own cosmogonic duties. For example, after Hecate received the paternal light into her womb,[13] she sent forth a light-engendered warmth (*thermē*) that animated the material world.[14] Most importantly for the current topic, the god Aion received the Father's light and passed it on to Helios, who passed it on to the sun; the sun, finally, converted it into sunlight in order to perform his duties.[15]

Iamblichus makes it clear that, even as fiery light descends from the Father, the source of that light (the Father himself) remains separate from and untouched by any of the strata or divinities that his light encounters. Moreover, as each stratum or divinity passes the light further down the line to the strata and divinities below *it,* it too remains separate and untouched. The passage that follows, which is one of Iamblichus's fuller expositions of the idea, specifically addresses the journey of light downward from the realm of the divinities to the material world. It should be noted that although the sun itself receives light from Helios, one of the divinities, and thus is itself a link in the chain of divine emanation that Iamblichus is discussing, here he refers to the sun apart from its role as a link, in order to draw comparisons between its familiar light and the divine light that he is trying to describe:

> [The divine sphere] illuminates certain parts of the cosmos—the sky[16] and earth, sacred cities and regions, certain groves or sacred statues—from the outside, just as the sun irradiates all things with its rays from the outside. Just as the [sun]light surrounds all things that it illuminates, so does the power of the divinities embrace from the outside all things that partake of it. And just as [sun]light is present in the air and yet does not mingle with the air—this is obvious from the fact that there is no light left in the air once the source of light has departed, despite the fact that there is still warmth—so, too, the light of the divinities shines forth separately [from those things that it illuminates] and, being established in itself, proceeds throughout all of existence in a unified manner. Moreover, just as the [sun]light that we see is a unity, continuous and everywhere the same so that it is impossible for any part of it to be cut off from the whole, or be encircled, or be separated from its source, so too does the whole cosmos divide itself around the light of the divinities, which is itself indivisible. This light is everywhere one and the same and indivisibly present in all the powers that partake of it; from its own, perfect power it fills up everything, and in its superior causality it brings all things to accomplishment within itself.[17]

By accepting the premise that divinity is a type of light, and by assuming that it behaves like the most familiar sort of light, sunlight, Iamblichus has resolved the conflict between transcendence and interaction. He simultaneously has resolved another knotty issue of the time: the conflict between belief in a single divine principle and an apparent multiplicity of divine forces that are spread throughout the world. He argues that, because it ultimately emerged from a single source of illumination (the Father), divine light remained unified even as it seemed to be dispersed infinitely throughout the cosmos; similarly, all the light cast by the sun remains part of the same whole even as it shines, for example, through a window into a room and illuminates different objects within it. Moreover, just as sunlight is always essentially the same whether it falls upon a tree or a house, Iamblichus argues that divine light is always the same even when it seems to take on the characteristics of lower divinities through which it works to specific ends. He returns to this premise again later in his treatise, when he discusses the ways in which the divine principle manifests itself in visible "symbols" that have been planted in the material world, and stresses that the multitude of appearances presented by symbols suggests not that the divine principle itself varies in nature from time to time or place to place, but rather that the materials from which the symbols are made, or the times and places in which they exist, vary.[18] In sum, Iamblichus's belief that divinity was light, combined with his observation of the ways that light behaved in the visible world, enabled him to defend a metaphysics in which divinity was simultaneously transcendent and yet omnipresent, remotely pure and yet intimately involved with the material world.

PREPARING FOR DIVINATION AND ASCENT

Within this schema of descending light lay the seeds of practical mysticism. The theurgist's first goal was to achieve *sustasis*, an encounter with the divine (the word literally means "standing together" and in normal usage could refer to the introduction of one person to another). During such *sustaseis*, the theurgist could receive information from the gods (a process called *manteia*, cognate with the Latin root *-mancy* and usually translated as "divination") and eventually experience *anagōgē*, the temporary ascent of his soul into realms above the earthly world, where, like the charioteer of Plato's *Phaedrus*, it could gaze upon the beauty of the divine and further improve itself. In a passage that follows soon after the one given just before note 17 above, Iamblichus continues the thought that he introduced there, in order to defend the accomplishment of *sustasis* and *anagōgē* through the ritualized invocation of a divinity: "The illumination that occurs when [theurgists] invoke [divinities] is spontaneously visible and self-perfect; [the illumination] is utterly immune to being pulled down [by earthly forces] and instead shines forth due to divine energy and perfection. . . . The divinities, being benevolent and propitious, shine their light upon theurgists in generous abundance, calling their souls upwards to themselves, procurring for them a union with themselves."[19] According to this passage, illumination (literally *ellampsis,* or "shining") automatically occurs whenever a divinity appears in answer to a theurgist's invocation; this makes sense, given that divinities consist of fiery light that has descended to them from the Father. Therefore, the *sustaseis* that invocations produce are by definition also "illuminations." We further learn from the passage that during the process of *anagōgē,* divinities direct their light (*phōs*) so that it shines upon (*epilampousin*) the theurgist, which causes his soul to ascend. Elsewhere, Iamblichus tells us that divination, too, requires that divinities direct their light upon the theurgist.

We learn a little more about the mechanics of all of this elsewhere. Two principles are important. The first is a favorite of Iamblichus and of Neoplatonists in general: "like attracts like." In other words, *sustasis,* divination, and *anagōgē* will most easily occur when a mortal has made himself as much like divinity as possible. The second principle follows from the first: if divinity is composed of fiery light, the theurgist must somehow assimilate himself to fiery light.

More particularly, the theurgist had to assimilate his "vehicle" to fiery light. This English word is used by scholars to represent two separate Greek words that, although originally associated with different concepts in ancient philosophy, came together in Neoplatonism to represent a single phenomenon. The first of the Greek words is *pneuma,* a word that in everyday usage meant "breath" or "vapor"; the second is *ochēma,* a word that literally meant "vehicle" in the sense of a wheeled object that carries other objects. The Neoplatonic use of *pneuma* looks back to Aristotle's use of the word to refer to the entity that, he proposed, mediated between bodily sensations and the soul; their use of *ochēma* looks back to Plato's theory that the celestial stars had vehicles (*ochēmata*) in which they rode through the material world. Neoplatonic authors refer to the phenomenon that scholars translate as "vehicle" by either of these words, although some authors preferred one to the other.[20] When I wish to refer to the vehicle by its Greek name in this chapter, I will always use *pneuma,* because this was the term that the *Oracles* and Iamblichus generally used.

The most important functions of the Neoplatonic vehicle were to carry the human soul as it rose out of its body and ascended to the gods (*anagōgē*) and to enable the theurgist to participate in divination. One of the ways that it did this was by becoming *augoeidēs.*[21] Literally, this word means "having the appearance of light." In the context of Neoplatonic thought, in accordance with the principle of "like attracts like," a more accurate translation might be "like light." Hence, I will use as a translation here the word "luminous," which approximates this idea. Our information as to how the theurgists made their vehicles luminous is sketchy; one of our few specific statements comes from Psellus, who mentions that it required purificatory rituals involving sacred stones, plants, and incantations. It is likely that *sustasis* itself helped to make the vehicle luminous as well, for the gods' light was known to drive away demonic forces that, among other things, were blamed for arousing corporeal passions that "darkened" or corrupted the theurgist's vehicle. In a passage where he explains why demons cannot participate in theurgic divination and thus deceive mortals, Iamblichus says: "When [the gods] impart their light, that which is evil and demonic vanishes from the presence of these more excellent entities in the same manner as darkness vanishes when light is present, and [the demons] become unable to disturb theurgists at all because the gods' light bestows on the theurgists every virtue, causes them to become more orderly and well mannered in their behavior, liberates them from passions and disordered movements, and purifies them from atheistic and unholy conduct. . . . They suffer no impediment from the evil demons, nor can [the demons] obstruct the improvement of their souls."[22] The theurgist had to do his own part on a daily basis, as well. Fragment 104 of the *Oracles* admonishes him not to "defile the *pneuma* or deepen its surface." By combining remarks made by the fragment's exegete, Psellus, and similar statements found elsewhere in Neoplatonic authors, we can conclude that the fragment is warning the theurgist against becoming involved with the material world in a manner that would arouse the sorts of passions that were deleterious to the vehicle.[23]

Further ways of making both the vehicle and the soul itself luminous are described during discussions of ascent and divination. Although it is likely that there was considerable overlap between the ways in which light was used in these two procedures, I will discuss them separately in the sections that follow. For now, let us note only that once again the observable properties of light implicitly lend authority to Iamblichus's analysis: his reader will be predisposed to believe that the vehicle becomes brighter when light shines upon it because everything else in the world reacts in that way. In an era when astronomers had not yet discovered black holes, it would have been impossible to imagine otherwise.

ASCENT

In fragment 2 of the *Chaldean Oracles,* a god says to the theurgist who wishes to ascend:

> Clothing yourself in the full-armored force of the resounding[24] light,
> And equipping the soul and the intellect with the three-barbed strength,
> You must cast into your mind the complete password of the Triad[25] and wander
> Among the fiery channels not in a haphazard manner but with concentration.[26]

The theurgist must prepare himself for ascent by donning divine light. More specifically, it is probably the vehicle that surrounds or "clothes" the soul that must take on this light, as this would align with the necessity, discussed above, of making the vehicle luminous before ascent was attempted.[27] After preparing his soul and intellect as well, the theurgist "casts into his mind" (i.e., silently pronounces) magical words that enable him to enter into fiery "channels." These are light-filled channels that descend from the Father through all the strata of the cosmos, through which his invigorating light descends and back through which again, we learn from fragment 2, the properly prepared soul may travel.[28] Once the soul has entered these channels, it will continue to ascend as high as the encosmic realm,[29] provided that the theurgist concentrates on his task—here, at least, theurgy seems to align with Plotinus's ideals.[30]

Other fragments of the *Oracles* specifically describe what happens to the soul itself (as opposed to its vehicle) during *anagōgē*. As we already inferred from Iamblichus's remarks, divine help was necessary. One fragment says that the order of the *angeloi* cause the soul of the theurgist to ascend by illuminating (*phengousa*) it with fire—Julian tells us more specifically that it was *angeloi* who fell under the control of Helios who were in charge of both directing souls downward into generation and upward again during *anagōgē*.[31] Another fragment says that the order of the *angeloi* causes the soul to separate from the material world by making it lighter (i.e., less heavy or dense [*kouphizousa*])[32] with its warm breath (*pneumati thermōi*).[33] Iamblichus expresses a closely similar idea when he describes what happens to a theurgist who becomes possessed by a divinity for prophetic purposes: although the goal of the ritual is different, it is likely that the methodology was the same as that used in ascent, since both pursuits required illumination of the individual: "The greatest sign that the theurgist sees [when possession is about to take place] is a *pneuma* descending and entering the initiate [who will prophesy]; [the theurgist] is able to discern how big it is and of what type it is. He persuades it and guides it in a way that is appropriate to the mystery.[34] The recipient also sees the form of the fire before it enters him. And sometimes it is also visible to everyone who is watching, when the divinity is either ascending or descending." Finamore convincingly has suggested that the descending *pneuma* described here is divine light; thus, quite literally, "like attracts like" insofar as the divine, *pneumatic* light enters into the luminous *pneuma* of the individual.[35]

But again, although divine help was vital, the theurgist had to act as well. The *Oracles* advise that "those who drive out the soul by inhaling are set free," and that the souls who "find rest in the divine" have done so by

> . . . drawing in the flowering flames that
> Descend from the Father; from these flames, as they
> Descend, the soul plucks the soul-nourishing flower of fiery fruits.[36]

The picture is similar to that described in the so-called Mithras Liturgy, an ascent text from approximately the same time and much the same background as the *Oracles:* in the Mithras Liturgy, the human who wishes to ascend to the divine realm inhales light that descends from the heavens as deeply as he can.[37] The instructions read: "Draw in breath from the rays, drawing up as much as you can three times, and you will perceive that you have been lifted up and are ascending to the height." Similarly, it seems that by inhaling light, the theurgist rises because he literally incorporates divinity into himself.

We have already noted how much the observable properties of light, especially sunlight, underlay the theurgists' metaphysical doctrines: the sun can send forth light and yet retain its own brilliance undiminished; sunlight can illuminate material objects without sullying its own purity; sunlight brightens everything on which it falls. Similarly, the observable properties of sunlight underlay the pragmatics of ascent: sunlight can penetrate and alter seemingly solid bodies. One of the most common effects of this penetration is the production of warmth, which potentially changes the quality of the body it penetrates: bread dough becomes less dense, for example, when it becomes warm, and therefore it is able to "rise." Similarly, divine light, transmitted by the *angeloi,* passes into the theurgist's soul as warmth and, by making it less dense or heavy, enables it to rise. Another common effect of sunlight's penetration is vertical growth—plants orient themselves toward the sun. Similarly, the theurgist's soul will travel upward directly along the fiery paths of light that the Father sends down to it. The emperor Julian explicitly makes this latter comparison in his *Hymn to the Sun,* where he says: "Consider this clearly: Helios, by his life-kindling and wondrous heat, draws up from the earth all things, and calls them forth and makes them grow, separating, I suppose, corporeal things to their greatest degree of tenuity; and he makes things light [*kouphizei*] that otherwise would sink. These things ought to be understood as evidence of his unseen powers. For if among corporeal things he can make this happen through his corporeal heat, how could he not draw and lead upwards the souls of the fortunate by means of the invisible, completely incorporeal, and divine and pure essence that dwells in his rays?"[38]

DIVINATION

The biographer Eunapius reported that Iamblichus had once uncovered deception at a séance. An entity had appeared, claiming to be the god Apollo, but Iamblichus revealed it to be the ghost of a dead gladiator.

The anecdote illustrates one of the main reasons that people worried about whether information obtained during divinatory sessions was reliable—nonhuman entities could be just as deceptive as humans. The theurgists were not exempt from such concerns, and Iamblichus (who apparently had a reputation for being good at these things) undertook to explain how different sorts of entities could be distinguished from one another when they appeared to mortals.[39] Although none of the entities who would appear during a properly conducted theurgic ritual would deceive their listeners on purpose, it was nonetheless important to know with whom one was dealing for two reasons: first, as Iamblichus concedes, even theurgists might make mistakes in their rituals, thus giving inferior entities the opportunity to appear and pretend to be more important ones; second, knowing which of the many sorts of *benign* entities had appeared during a properly conducted ritual enabled the theurgist to gauge how far he had advanced and what sorts of help or information he might expect the entity to bestow.[40]

When he describes the characteristics of each sort of divinity, Iamblichus implicitly begins from a premise that is stated in a fragment of the *Chaldean Oracles:* because it consists of light, divinity has no permanent shape but only adopts shapes temporarily when appearing to mortals. "It is for your sakes," a divinity says to the theurgists in fragment 142 of the *Oracles,* "that bodies are attached to our self-revealed manifestations." The divinities had to do this because truly pure light, after all, would be impossible to see. In another fragment, divinities admonish a theurgist to "consider the shape [*morphē*] of the light that has been put forth." According to the fragment's exegete, Proclus, this refers to the fact that "although light has no shape when it is on high, it assumes a shape when it enters into procession"—that is, when it is sent downward into the material world.[41] A third fragment tells us that "the unformed [*atypōta*] become formed [*typousthai*]"; the fragment's exegete, Simplicius, explains that this refers to divinities' taking on forms in preparation for their epiphanies.[42] Here again, the observable properties of light seem to lie behind the theurgists' ruminations about epiphanies: light may be visible in the material world, but only because it is conjoined to (that is, falls upon) a physical shape; it is only then that the eye can discern the presence of light.

One of Iamblichus's guidelines for telling the difference between divinities was that the ontologically higher the divinity (that is, the further it existed from the world of objects on which divine light eventually fell), the purer its light would be and the less would its epiphany resemble anything familiar within that world. The highest divinities manifested themselves in a "uniform" (*monoeidēs*) manner, assumedly because, being closer to pure light, the epiphanies did not mimic anything we encounter in daily life—like light itself, these epiphanies were immutable. *Daemones,* who were lower on the ontological ladder, had shapes that were more complex and changeable (*poikila*), and *angeloi,* who were on a rung somewhere in between, had shapes that were simpler than those of the *daemones* but not as simple as those of the highest divinities. Pure human souls, which were on the lowest rung yet but which, at least, were now separated from their bodies, were able to take on a variety of shapes (*pantodapa*). In other words, their light, being closer to the material world, could assume the shape of various material objects or creatures.[43]

The epiphanies also varied in terms of sheer brightness: the higher the divinity, the more it shone.[44] As Iamblichus says: "The epiphanies of the gods are full of brilliant light. Those of *archangeloi* are full of light beyond that of the natural world. The *angeloi* are luminous, but *daemones* have only a cloudy light. . . . the light of souls is mixed together with many things that arise from the forces of generation." Two fragments of the *Chaldean Oracles* seem to reflect the variations in brightness and complexity of form that Iamblichus discusses. In them, the goddess Hecate tells the theurgist what to expect after he has pronounced certain invocations: "Having spoken these things, you will see either a fire leaping skittishly like a child over the aery waves, or a shapeless fire from which a voice emerges, or a rich light that whirs around the field in a spiral. But it is also possible that you will see a horse flashing more brightly than light, either also a fiery child mounted on the swift back of the horse, armored in gold or without armor, or even a child shooting arrows upright upon the back of the horse. . . . But when you see the very sacred, formless fire shining skittishly throughout the depths of the whole cosmos, listen to its voice."[45] The goddess covers all the possibilities, apparently having provided the theurgist with a variety of invocations to choose from and thereby a variety of divinities to invoke.

As in the case of *anagōgē,* the vehicle of the theurgist's soul had to be luminous before he could see the gods; this follows from the fact that seeing a god constitutes *sustasis,* which in itself requires a luminous vehicle.[46] But Iamblichus takes the doctrine of the luminous vehicle further in the course of defending divination in general. He says that, in spite of apparent differences, many of the acceptable forms of divination work in the same way and may be subsumed under a single term: *photagōgia,* or "the leading on of light." The diviner may gaze at a variety of material objects—a wall on which sacred signs have been inscribed, a bowl of specially prepared water, or "any solid place"—and thereby prophesy,[47] but it is not the material itself that contains divinity or fills the gazer with prophetic power. Rather, divine light bounces off an object that has been ritually prepared in the proper way and then passes into the prophet, further illuminating his luminous vehicle, which has also been carefully prepared. While thus illuminated, the vehicle's "imaginative ability" (*phantaskitē dunamis,* literally "the ability of the vehicle to receive or process images") is able to perceive the divine manifestations that the theurgist's bodily eyes cannot; these manifestations are emitted by the gods themselves.[48] Iamblichus extends this theory with respect to the Delphic Pythia and other "inspired" prophets, explaining that divine light pervades their luminous vehicles directly (without first bouncing off an object) and thus causes their prophetic *mania.* In some cases, an inspired prophet further prepares her vehicle immediately before a divinatory session by, for example, drinking water from a special spring, but Iamblichus insists that, contrary to popular opinion, such actions only purify the vehicle so that the divine light may better illuminate it; they are not the cause of divination itself.[49]

One form of prophecy that Iamblichus rejected as deceptive was divination in which the practitioner looked at a mirror or a bowl of liquid into which lamplight was directed, called gods or *daemones* into the liquid (where they appeared in anthropomorphic or theriomorphic forms) and then questioned them. We read a lot about this practice in magical spells that are roughly contemporary with Iamblichus and the *Chaldean Oracles.*[50] Iamblichus insists that real divinities would not stoop to either entering into bowls of water that are illuminated by means of secondary, inferior sources of light such as lamps or projecting artificial images into them; it must be wicked demons who appear in the water and mislead the prophet.[51] The significant difference for Iamblichus, then, lay not in the method used, but in the origin of the light: man-made light was bound to foster deception. Divine light, such as that emerging from the sun, was not.

Observable properties of light underlay several aspects of Iamblichus's theory of divination just as they underlay theurgic metaphysics and the theurgic theory of ascent. Two points are important. First, just as there must be light before a corporeal eye can see an object in the material world, so did the presence of divine light enable the "imaginative eye"—the "perceptive organ" within the vehicle of the soul—to see objects that existed in the divine world. The second and more specific point takes us into ancient theories of optics, with which the more philosophically trained of the theurgists, such as Iamblichus and his interlocutor, Porphyry, are almost certain to have been familiar; optics had long been part of the philosophical curriculum for both the Platonists and the Stoics, another philosophical school that influenced the development of theurgic doctrines. The Stoic theory of vision, which dominated academic discourse at the time Iamblichus was writing, offers a particularly close analogy to Iamblichus's theory of divination.[52]

According to the Stoics,[53] vision occurred when an individual's *pneuma* (which the Stoics imagined to be a mixture of fire and air that pervaded the entire physical body) flowed out of the part of the soul associated with consciousness (the "leader," or *hegemonikon*) into the corporeal eye; once in the eye, the *pneuma* introduced tension (*sunentasis*) into the outside air that lay just beyond the eye, causing the affected air to take on the shape of a cone. When this entensioned cone of air simultaneously was illuminated by sunlight (thus bringing the "outside" air into harmony with the fiery *pneuma* that had emerged from "inside"), the cone became capable of receiving the forms of objects at which the individual gazed; this constituted sight. (It is not completely clear how the cone received the forms, although the forms were sometimes described as "making an impression" [*typōsis*] on the cone of air in the way that a signet ring makes an impression in wax.)[54]

Implicit in the Stoic theory of vision is the assumption that neither external sunlight nor the individual *pneuma* was alone sufficient for sight to occur; the two had to cooperate before the physical eye could see an object. In the same way, the theurgist's luminous *pneuma* and divine light had to combine before the eye within the theurgist's soul could see the gods. It seems likely that the theurgic theory of divination was an extension of a theory of optics that was popular at the time. In other words, if Stoic theories of vision described corporeal sight as a function mediated by both the influx of *sun*light and a properly functioning optical *pneuma*, then it would have been a logical step for Iamblichus to posit that divinatory sight was a function mediated by both the influx of *divine* light and a properly functioning (that is, an *augoeidēs*) *pneuma*. Notably, the *pneuma* that must emerge from the eye before sight takes place according to the Stoic theory could also be described as *augoeidēs,* which further suggests its influence on the theurgic theory,[55] as does the fact that both divinatory sight (in the theurgic system) and corporeal sight (in the Stoic system) are processes in which objects become visible by "taking on shape" or "making impressions" (both phrases are translations of words formed on the Greek *typ-* root) within a composite created from external light and an *augoeidēs pneuma.* In explaining divination, Iamblichus has gone beyond the strictly observable properties of light into the optical theory of his day, but only as far as he would reasonably expect his readers to be able to follow. Like his other arguments, this one was based on the way that light in the material world was understood to function.

SUMMARY

Iamblichus used current knowledge of how light behaved in the material world to develop theories that explained how divinity interacted with mortals and yet preserved divinity's transcendence. By doing so, he was able to demonstrate that rituals performed in the material world could affect the individual soul—at least to his own satisfaction. We should not overlook the fact that Iamblichus's arguments implicitly begin from the premise that both divine light and the individual soul *can* be compared to material phenomena. One doubts whether Porphyry and his colleagues would have accepted this premise and, thus, whether Iamblichus's arguments could have changed any minds. As in contemporary debates between creationists and evolutionists, each side probably was preaching mostly to the converted. Not that this was pointless: *Concerning the Mysteries* sharpened the outlines of issues at stake as well as the wits of those contesting them. Iamblichus won his argument, insofar as most subsequent Platonists adopted a pro-ritual stance and also insofar as his detailed exposition influenced the course that later versions of the argument would take.[56]

In the context of this volume, one more concluding remark on Iamblichus's treatment of light may be relevant. In contrast to some other religious and mystical systems, theurgy not only allowed what might be called a "scientific" approach to understanding the divine and its effects on the world, but positively throve on it. We might not only compare aspects of the systems discussed by Ziai and Kapstein in this volume, in which light mediates between "scientific" understandings of reality and "religious" ritual and practice, but also remember how the modern master of scientific approaches to light, Albert Einstein, exasperated Niels Bohr by refusing to leave God out of their conversations on quantum physics:[57] there are those who like to keep the pursuit of worldly knowledge quite separate from matters of the spirit, and those for whom the two are inextricably bound together.

NOTES

1. I am grateful for the helpful critiques I received from John Finamore, David Hahm, and David Ulansey in preparing this article. The following are works to which I often refer herein: F. W. Cremer, *Die chaldäischen Orakel und Jamblich de Mysteriis,* Beiträge zur Klassischen Philologie, no. 26 (Meisenheim am Glan: Anton Hain, 1969); E. Des Places, ed., trans., and commentary, *Oracles Chaldaïques, avec un choix de commentaires anciens* (Paris: Société d'Édition "Les Belles Lettres," 1971); J. Finamore, "Plotinus and Iamblichus on Magic and Theurgy," *Dionysius* 17 (1999): 83–94; O. Geudtner, *Die Seelenlehre der chaldäischen Orakel,* Beiträge zur Klassischen Philologie, no. 35 (Meisenheim am Glan: Anton Hain, 1971); S. I. Johnston, *Hekate Soteira,* American Classical Studies, no. 21 (Atlanta: Scholars Press, 1990); H. Lewy, *Chaldaean Oracles and Theurgy* (1956), rev. ed., ed. M. Tardieu (Paris: Études Augustiniennes, 1978); R. Majercik, trans. and commentary, *The Chaldean Oracles: Text, Translation and Commentary,* Studies in Greek and Roman Religion, no. 5 (Leiden: Brill, 1989); G. Shaw, *Theurgy and the Soul: The Neoplatonism of Iamblichus* (University Park, PA: Penn State University Press, 1995). In general, I will not cite Majercik and Des Places's commentaries for each fragment that I discuss below unless I develop or disagree with specific points they make, but the reader is well advised to consult them. Iamblichus's treatise *Concerning the Mysteries* (*De Mysteriis*) will be cited in notes by the standard scholarly abbreviation, *Myst.,* and fragments of the *Chaldean Oracles* will be cited in notes by *Ch. Or.* fr. followed by the relevant fragment number. All other abbreviations for ancient works are the standard ones that can be found in the list at the front of Henry Liddell, Robert Scott, and Henry Jones, *A Greek-English Lexicon* (Oxford: Oxford University Press; any of the recent editions will suffice).

2. Alfred, Lord Tennyson, "The Two Voices." The passage is quoted in W. James's *The Varieties of Religious Experience,* lecture 16, where many further examples of the inexpressibility of mystical experience are given (1902; repr., New York and London: Penguin, 1982), pp. 379–429.

3. See Finamore, "Plotinus and Iamblichus"; Shaw, *Theurgy and the Soul,* pp. 1–27, esp. pp. 4–5, 11–12, and 23–26.

4. The influence of the *Chaldean Oracles* on Iamblichus is discussed by almost everyone who has studied the *Oracles* or *Concerning the Mysteries.* In particular, however, see Cremer, *Die chaldäischen Orakel;* Geudtner, *Die Seelenlehre der chaldäischen Orakel;* and comments made by Des Places, *Oracles Chaldaïques,* and Majercik, *The Chaldean Oracles,* with reference to specific fragments of the *Oracles.* See also E. Des Places, ed.,

trans. and commentary, *Jamblique: Les mystères d'Égypte* (Paris: Société d'Édition "Les Belles Lettres," 1966), pp. 14–19.

5. Discussion at Shaw, *Theurgy and the Soul,* pp. 7–8.

6. *h.Cer.* 277–78.

7. Pl. *R.* 7, 514a ff.

8. For example, Plot. *Enneades* 1.1.4.12–18, 1.7.1.19–29, 2.3.18.20–23, 3.5.2.30–33, 4.3.11.14–23 (and see A. H. Armstrong's note on this passage in the Loeb edition of the *Enneads*), 4.3.22.1–7, 4.4.35.37–43, 4.8.4.1, 5.1.2.17–23, 5.1.6.18–30, 5.3.9.7–20, 5.3.12.39–44, 5.5.7, 6.4.7.22, 6.7.16.24–32 (and see Armstrong's note), 6.9.4.10–12, 6.9.9.6–7. Generally on Plotinus's theory of emanation and his use of the metaphor of sunlight, A. H. Armstrong, *The Architecture of the Intelligible Universe in the Philosophy of Plotinus: An Analytical and Historical Study* (Cambridge: Cambridge University Press, 1940), pp. 49–64; also, W. Beierwaltes, "Die Metaphysick des Lichtes in der Philosophie Plotins," *Zeitschrift für philosophische Forschung* 15 (1961): 334–62.

9. For a brief overview of heliolatry in the Roman Empire, see H. J. Rose and J. Scheid, "Sol," in *The Oxford Classical Dictionary,* 3rd ed. (Oxford: Oxford University Press, 1996), pp. 1420–21. On Mithraism, begin with R. Beck's article "Mithras" in the same volume, 991–92; but see also R. Gordon, "Mithraism," in *Late Antiquity: A Guide to the Postclassical World,* ed. G. Bowersock, P. Brown, and O. Grabar (Cambridge, MA: Harvard University Press, 1999), pp. 582–83, who downplays the influence of Mithraism's heliolatry. On the sun in Mithraism see also D. Ulansey, "Mithras and the Hypercosmic Sun," in *Studies in Mithraism,* ed. John R. Hinnels (Rome: "L'Erma" di Brettschneider, 1994), pp. 257–64; the article is also available on Dr. Ulansey's Web site under the title "Mithras, the Hypercosmic Sun, and the Rockbirth," http://www.well.com/user/davidu/appendix2.html.

10. A good introduction to Manichaeism, with bibliography, is S. Lieu, "Manichaeism," in Bowersock, Brown, and Grabar, *Late Antiquity,* pp. 555–56. See also D. Park, *The Fire within the Eye: A Historical Essay on the Nature and Meaning of Light* (Princeton, NJ: Princeton University Press, 1997), pp. 23–27, for specific discussion of Manichaeism's treatment of light.

11. For a more detailed overview of theurgic metaphysics, see Majercik, *The Chaldean Oracles,* pp. 5–21.

12. Cf. *Ch. Or.* fr. 35, especially the two final lines.

13. Hecate was identified by the theurgists with the Cosmic Soul, an entity that dwelt at the boundary between the divine and mortal realms; see Johnston, *Hekate Soteira.* Further on Hecate's womb, see esp. chap. 4 and pp. 158–59.

14. *Ch. Or.* frs. 35 and 53; cf. also fr. 51 and see discussion in Johnston, *Hekate Soteira,* chap. 4.

15. On this "double sun" theory, see most recently Ulansey, "Mithras and the Hypercosmic Sun." Ulansey is particularly helpful in tracing the roots of this theurgic idea back through earlier Platonic authors to its origins in Plato's own dialogues. J. Finamore,

Iamblichus and the Theory of the Vehicle of the Soul, American Classical Studies, no. 14 (Chico, CA: Scholars Press, 1985), pp. 125–46, esp. pp. 134–46, is also very useful, as is Majercik, *The Chaldean Oracles,* pp. 14–15. An older but still important discussion is Lewy, *Chaldaean Oracles,* pp. 151–56.

16. Here Iamblichus uses the word *ouranos* to mean the sky that we see from earth, not "heavens" in the sense of a place where gods dwell in traditional belief.

17. *Myst.* 1.9, 31.11–18.

18. *Myst.* 7.3, 253.15–254.3. The specific example under discussion is the way in which the light of the sun (the visible expression of the divine light) changes as it enters into different zodiacal signs.

19. *Myst.* 1.12, 40.19–41.8.

20. The best treatment of the vehicle and its functions, with special attention to Iamblichus's development of the concept, is Finamore, *Iamblichus and the Theory of the Vehicle of the Soul* (above, n. 15). See also Shaw, *Theurgy and the Soul,* pp. 51–53; Majercik, *The Chaldean Oracles,* pp. 31–33; and Cremer, *Die chaldäischen Orakel,* pp. 136–39. R. C. Kissling, "The *Ochēma-Pneuma* of the Neoplatonists and the *De Insomnis* of Synesius of Cyrene," *American Journal of Philology* 43, no. 4 (1922): 318–30, is particularly useful on how the concepts of the *ochēma* and the *pneuma* were combined.

21. The term is used of the vehicle at, e.g., *Myst.* 3.14, 132.11–13, and often elsewhere.

22. Psellus *Comm.* 1132A; *Myst.* 3.31, 178.8–16.

23. See the comments ad loc. in Majercik, *The Chaldean Oracles;* and Des Places, *Oracles Chaldaïques;* and for a general discussion, Johnston, *Hekate Soteira,* chap. 4.

24. It is not completely clear why light should be described as "resounding." Lewy, *Chaldaean Oracles,* p. 193, suggests that it refers to the revolution of the heavenly spheres, which produced music.

25. The "Triad" probably refers to three divine hypostases of the Father. The reading is conjectural, however; see comments ad loc. in Des Places, *Oracles Chaldaïques;* and Majercik, *The Chaldean Oracles;* and at Lewy, *Chaldaean Oracles,* pp. 192–97.

26. *Ch. Or.* fr. 2. Further discussion at S. I. Johnston, "Rising to the Occasion: Theurgic Ascent in Its Cultural Milieu," in *Envisioning Magic: A Princeton Seminar and Symposium,* ed. P. Schäfer and H. G. Kippenberg (Leiden: Brill, 1997), pp. 165–94.

27. Cf. Lewy, *Chaldaean Oracles,* pp. 193, who also assumes it is the vehicle that must be clothed in light, although for reasons different from mine.

28. See comments at Majercik, *The Chaldean Oracles,* ad loc., with further bibliography; and Johnston, "Rising to the Occasion."

29. There was debate about just how high the soul could travel in antiquity—some argued that portions of the soul could ascend even higher than the encosmic realm. For discussion, Finamore, *Iamblichus and the Theory of the Vehicle of the Soul* (above, n. 15), pp. 145.

30. Cf. *Ch. Or.* fr. 111, which tells the theurgist to "rush to the center of the sounding light."

31. Jul. *Or.* 4.142a and 141b.

32. The verb *kouphizō* can also be used to mean "lift up" or "raise" (i.e., "make something light enough to rise"); the primary meaning of words built on the *kouph*- root, however, is lightness in the sense of airiness or buoyancy, and it was used in antiquity as an antonym for *barus,* meaning "heavy in weight."

33. *Ch. Or.* frs. 122 and 132.

34. The theurgists referred to their rites as "mysteries," indicating that they saw them as analogous to the great Greek mysteries of earlier ages, e.g., the Eleusinian and the Bacchic.

35. Finamore, "Plotinus and Iamblichus," pp. 89.

36. *Ch. Or.* frs. 124 and 130.

37. The passage from the Mithras Liturgy = *Papyri Graecae Magicae* 4.538–40. Further on these fragments and their relationship to the Mithras Liturgy, see Johnston, *Hekate Soteira,* chap. 8; and Johnston, "Rising to the Occasion" (above, n. 26).

38. Jul. *Hymn to Helios* 172b. It is interesting that Damascius, a later Neoplatonist from whom we learn a lot about theurgy, used an altogether different analogy to explain the way that divinity may fill the soul of a mortal and thus, while changing its nature, not change the essential fact that it is still a soul. Damascius compares the soul to a sponge that can absorb water and yet remain the same shape as it was before absorption (*Dubitationes et Solutiones* 2.255.7).

39. This topic is treated throughout section 2 of *Myst.*

40. *Myst.* 2.10, 91.12–15.

41. *Ch. Or.* fr. 145; with Proclus's comments from *in Cra.* 31, 12–14.

42. *Ch. Or.* fr. 144; with Simplicius's comments at *in Ph.* 613, 7–8.

43. The identification of different sorts of divinities and the nature of the light that they emit is discussed throughout 2.3, 70.9–2.9, 90.6.

44. This specific point is made at *Myst.* 2.4, 74.11–79.6. The quotation that follows is from the same section.

45. *Ch. Or.* frs. 146 and 148. Further on these fragments and the question of theurgic epiphanies, see S. I. Johnston, "Riders in the Sky: Cavalier Gods and Theurgic Salvation in the Second Century AD," *Classical Philology* 87, no. 4 (1992): 303–21; and Johnston, *Hekate Soteira,* chap. 8.

46. Iamblichus specifically mentions the need for a luminous vehicle during divination at 3.14, and Proclus similarly says "those who see the gods witness them in the luminous garments of their souls [*augoeidē tōn psuchōn periblemata*]," a phrase that brings us very close to the idea of the vehicle, which similarly was imagined to be wrapped around the soul. Cf. discussion at Shaw, *Theurgy and the Soul,* pp. 219–22; and Finamore, *Iamblichus and the Theory of the Vehicle of the Soul* (above, n. 15), pp. 145–46.

47. *Myst.* 3.14, 134.2–8.

48. Cf. the remarks of Finamore, "Plotinus and Iamblichus," pp. 90–91.

49. *Myst.* 3.11, 123.11–128.11.

50. For further discussion of this and related forms of prophecy in late antiquity, see

S. I. Johnston, "Charming Children: The Use of the Child in Mediumistic Divination," *Arethusa* 34, no. 1 (2001): 97–118.

51. *Myst.* 2.10, 90.7–95.14.

52. J. Finamore, "Iamblichus on Light and the Transparent," in *The Divine Iamblichus: Philosopher and Man of God,* ed. H. J. Blumenthal and E. G. Clark (London: Bristol Classical Press, 1993), pp. 55–64, which I encountered only in the final stages of writing this essay, similarly proposes that Iamblichus was influenced by contemporary theories of vision, although Finamore suggests that Iamblichus drew on a combination of Platonic and Aristotelian theories of vision rather than Stoic theory. Finamore uses remarks made by Julian to reconstruct Iamblichus's theory of vision in detail and particularly to explore the questions of how light travels between realms, whether it is corporeal or incorporeal (Iamblichus argues the latter, although admitting that some forms of light have a degree of corporeality), and the implications of incorporeal light for understanding light's effects on the material world.

53. The details of the Stoic theory of vision are still debated; my résumé here presents what I perceive to be generally agreed-upon points. I base it on the work of D. Lindberg, *Theories of Vision from Al-Kindi to Kepler* (Chicago: University of Chicago Press, 1976), pp. 1–18; D. E. Hahm, "Early Hellenistic Theories of Vision and the Perception of Color," in *Studies in Perception: Interrelations in the History of Philosophy and Science,* ed. P. K. Machamer and R. G. Turnbull (Columbus, OH: Ohio State University Press, 1978), pp. 60–95; and H. von Staden, "The Stoic Theory of Perception and its 'Platonic' Critics," in Machamer and Turnbull, *Studies in Perception.* Park, *The Fire within the Eye* (above, n. 10), chaps. 1–4, is also helpful insofar as he provides a general overview of how ancient theories of vision developed and their influence on later theories.

54. For the image of the stamp and the wax, see von Staden, "The Stoic Theory of Perception," p. 102. For the ancient use of *typōsis* or its cognates, *Stoic.* 2.53, 55, 56, 59. This theory bears some resemblance to the Aristotelian precept (mentioned briefly above) that sensory perceptions initiated in the material world must be mediated for the immaterial soul by a *pneuma* that surrounds it, although in this case, the *pneuma* must emerge and interact with that which lies outside before sensory perception can occur.

55. *Stoic.* 2.231.

56. On the influence of Iamblichus on subsequent Platonism, see Shaw, *Theurgy and the Soul,* pp. 6–7; and Des Places, *Jamblique* (above, n. 4), pp. 21–28.

57. B. Hoffmann and H. Dukas, *Albert Einstein, Creator and Rebel* (New York: Viking Press, 1972), pp. 193–95; J. Bronowski, *The Ascent of Man* (Boston: Little, Brown, 1973), p. 256. Generally on Einstein's personal outlook on religion (and his distrust of mysticism), R. N. Goldman, *Einstein's God: Albert Einstein's Quest as a Scientist and as a Jew to Replace a Forsaken God* (Northvale, NJ: Jason Aronson, 1997). Hoffmann and Dukas record an anecdote that underscores the difference between Einstein and Bohr: when translating Einstein's famous "Gott würfelt nicht" into English, Bohr converted "Gott" into "The Providential Authorities."

CHAPTER TWO

Suhrawardī on Knowledge and the Experience of Light

Hossein Ziai

ILLUMINATIONIST THEORY OF KNOWLEDGE

In this chapter I discuss the nature and systematic position of the "experience" of "light" in the theory of knowledge as defined in the philosophy of Illumination founded by the Persian philosopher Shihāb al-Dīn Suhrawardī (executed 1191).[1] Illuminationist philosophy is a novel reconstruction of a holistic philosophical system. We do not know in what circles or how Illuminationist works were studied immediately after Suhrawardī's execution in Aleppo, but several decades later, in the latter part of the thirteenth century, they were revived notably by the philosopher Shams al-Dīn Shahrazūrī, who wrote commentaries on selected texts, hailed Suhrawardī's philosophy of Illumination as a major achievement, and stated it to be both distinct from and more complete than Islamic Peripatetic philosophy.[2] The founder of this new system, the young, charismatic (also controversial) thinker Shihāb al-Dīn Suhrawardī, was born in the village of Suhraward in northwestern Iran during a period when some remote highland areas still had not succumbed to the Muslim rule of the Abbāsid Caliphate. Suhrawardī, who had authored nearly fifty books and treatises, was only thirty-six years old when brutally executed by the direct command of Islam's great champion against the crusaders, the Ayyūbid king Saladin. The king twice directed his son, al-Malik al-Ẓāhir, governor of Aleppo, who had befriended the philosopher and had brought him to his court and studied with him, to kill the young thinker. The young prince had at first refused the order, but finally succumbed to the command of his father. The execution in the year 1191, the same year King Richard "the Lion Hearted" had landed in Acre and was engaged in battle against Saladin, was an unusually important but also enigmatic event. I have elsewhere demonstrated that Suhrawardī's execution was due to a real and explosive political dimension artfully woven into the very core of the new scientific methodology he named "Science of Lights" (*'Ilm al-Anwār*), which I have named "Illuminationist political doctrine.[3] Suhrawardī was in effect proposing a new political order to be ruled by an enlightened philosopher-king, whose sign of authority was described in terms of a manifest, radiating divine "light" named "Farreh-ye Īzadī" that recalled the divine aura of the ancient kings and Khosrows of Iranian mythology.

Illuminationist philosophy's Science of Lights employs a constructed metalanguage named "Language of Illumination" (*lisān al-ishrāq*) where "light," as symbol, permeates every domain of the constructed Illuminationist system, including the practical and political. Thus, the term "light" (Arabic *nūr,* used also in Persian), as well as a range of attributes and related terms, such as "luminosity" (*nūriyya/istināra*), "apparentness" (*Ẓuhūr,* best signified by the German term *Evidenz*), "presence" (*ḥuḍūr,* as a manifest and thus "lit" quality of a "light"), and "intensity" (*shadda*), as well as the key technical terms "illumination" (*ishrāq*) and "vision" (*mushāhada* in the noncorporeal realm of being, and *ibṣār* in the corporeal as "sight"), are all used technically with assigned meanings determined by context. Thus all things—that is, all existent entities—are depicted as light and may be abstract, or noncorporeal, or bodily. Such entities differ in terms of their luminosity, intensity, and other attributes that may be perceived by the senses or apprehended intellectually based on rules of inference including the deductive *and* the intuitive.

The Illuminationist theory of knowledge is complex. I have discussed it in greater detail elsewhere and have indicated Suhrawardī's achievement in describing the unified theory named "knowledge by presence." This theory rests on a general proposition that is indicated by the sameness of knowing and being, generalized as the sameness of any apprehending subject and the object apprehended in any domain of apprehension, where "apprehension" (*idrāk,* in some contexts "perception") includes all its specific types: the noetic, the sensory, the inspirational, and so on. The symbolism of light is also employed in discussing epistemological processes. For example, let us take a subject, the self-conscious "I" whose degree of consciousness is stated in terms of luminous intensity. That is, the more knowing, the more intense the degree of luminosity of the subject. The measure of luminosity is determined by proximity to the Light of Lights, which is the most conscious, most intense luminous thing in the Illuminationist cosmos. Next, the knowable object is also measured in terms of its light attributes; it has to be "lit" to be "seen" and thus knowable. In this scheme the "knower" generalized (*al-mudrik*) and the "known" generalized (*al-mudrak*), when "related" by an identity-preserving operator as a one-to-one relational correspondence, signifies "knowing" generalized (*idrāk*).

For our present purposes, it is important to bear in mind that the knowing associated with any knower, whatever type of knowing it may be (the sensed, the intellected, the intuited, the dreamed, and so on), is stated in terms of the conscious "I's" knowing as determined and measured by the "experience" of light. Simply stated, a thing is known when "seen"; to know is to be illuminated; and the thing seen, thus known, must be visible. "Visibility" is also determined by the degree of light and will mean different things depending upon the context. In external reality, for example, the healthy eye will see the lit object and thus come to know what it is. In a similar manner, in the noncorporeal realm, the knowing subject, whose degree of knowing is determined by consciousness, itself a function of the experience of light, will also "see" the luminous object—but here "seeing" is extended to mean "vision." Finally and ultimately, the knowing subject, depending on the degree and nature of its experience of light, may come to have a vision of the very source of the Illuminationist cosmos, the Light of Lights.

In order to explain the new epistemology's uniform validity over the entire range of reality—the seen and the unseen, the sensed and the intellected, the phenomenal and the noumenal—Suhrawardī recognizes the need to define a different structure of the universe from that described by Avicenna in his Aristotelian theory of intellectual knowledge marked by numbered, discrete intellects. This also requires that priority be given to "essence"—the real—over existence—the derived, logical ideal. Knowledge, for the Illuminationist, is not founded on the input of sense data and the extrapolation of universal concepts. At best the universals established in logic are relative truths. Rather, knowledge rests on these foundations:

1. A knowing subject that is self-conscious and knows its "I" necessarily by means of the principle of self-consciousness. This "I" recovers, intuitively, primary notions of time-space, accepts the validity of such things as the primary intelligibles, and confirms the existence of God. Thus, knowledge is founded on innate principles, which in a somewhat Platonic manner are recovered "in" the knowing subject.
2. Knowable objects, which in accordance with Illuminationist cosmology are part of the continuum of monadlike, but continuous, luminous entities, stated to be abstract lights (*anwār mujarrada*) that are all part of the continuum whole and differ only in terms of degrees of intensity.
3. An atemporal relation between the knowing subject and the object in what is defined as "durationless time" (*ān*).

This type of knowledge is called "knowledge by illumination and presence" and is activated whenever an Illuminationist relation (*al-iḍāfa al-ishrāqiyya*) is obtained between the subject and the object.

Light symbolism is also applied to the realm of political philosophy, and this is done in a manner consistent with Illuminationist theory of knowledge. A ruler's legitimacy is seen in his manifest "luminosity," which is described by Suhrawardī using symbolism from the ancient Iranian mythos. It is "seen" in his manifest auralike "luminous" quality named Farreh, the New Persian term for the Avestan *xvarena,* meaning "radiating light." In terms of the Illuminationist political doctrine, a ruler must obtain knowledge, which determines his Farreh. In turn his Farreh may be seen and known to be his sign of legitimacy. Consider the following passage which illustrates this point: "Whoever knows philosophy, and perseveres in thanking and sanctifying the Light of Lights, will have royal Kharreh and with luminous Farreh bestowed on him, and—as we have said elsewhere—divine light will further bestow upon him the cloak of royal power and value. Such a person shall then become the natural Ruler of the Universe. He shall be given aid from the High Heavens, and whatever he commands shall be obeyed; and his dreams and inspirations will reach their uppermost, perfect pinnacle."[4]

The philosophy of Illumination begins with an attack on the Peripatetic notion of definition, which Suhrawardī modifies and expands into a more comprehensive theory of knowledge that emphasizes self-knowledge and self-consciousness as the grounds of all knowledge. This view of knowledge then serves as the foundation for a cosmology in which real essences or the true being of things is set forth in a continuous sequence of self-conscious and self-subsistent entities within a continuum, depicted as "lights," which together constitute the whole cosmos. The God of this cosmos is the Light of Lights, from whose self-radiating being emanates a light that covers all of existence, and where light is no longer is the world of privation, of nonbeing, and of the darkness wherein resides evil. According to Illuminationist epistemology, knowledge is obtained when both the subject and the object are present and manifest, that is, when there is no obstacle between them. Then and only then is the knowing subject able to grasp the essence of the object.

As stated above, the experience of light is what determines knowledge in Illuminationist epistemology. In order now to see exactly how "experiencing light" leads to knowledge, we should examine, albeit briefly, the epistemological process defined by Suhrawardī. The principles that inform the subject in the Illuminationist scheme are formed as the result of a process consisting of several stages. The first stage is marked by an activity on the part of the philosopher (the subject): he has to "abandon the world." The second stage is marked by types of experience: the philosopher attains visions of a "divine light" (*al-nūr al-ilāhī*). The third stage is marked by the acquisition of unlimited and unbound knowledge, which is Illuminationist knowledge (*al-'ilm al-ishrāqī*). The philosophy of Illumination consists of three stages which concern the question of knowledge—how to prepare for the experience of it, receiving it through illumination, and constructing a systematic view of it—plus an additional stage consisting of the process of setting down the results of the experience of illumination and of the inquiry concerning it, in written form. In sum, the first stage is an activity through which the philosopher prepares himself for Illuminationist knowledge, a certain way of life preparing for the readiness to accept "experience" and confirm its validity. The second stage is the stage of illumination. The third stage is the stage of construction. The last stage involves depicting, symbolically whenever necessary, in written form, the structure that has been constructed during the third stage.

The very beginning of the first stage is marked by such activities as going on a forty-day retreat, abstaining from eating meat, and preparing for inspiration and revelation. Such activities fall under the general category of ascetic and mystical practices, though not in strict conformity with the prescribed states and stations of the mystic path, or Ṣūfī *ṭarīqa*, as known in the mystical works of Suhrawardī's time. Through these activities, the philosopher with intuitive powers, in whom, as Suhrawardī tells us, there resides a portion of the "light of God" (*al-bāriq al-ilāhī*), is able, through "personal revelation" and "vision" (*mushāhada wa mukāshafa*), to accept the reality of his own existence and admit the truth of his own intuition. The first stage therefore consists of (1) an activity, (2) a condition (met by everyone, since we are told that every person has intuition and that in everyone there is a certain portion of the light of God), and (3) personal revelation.

The first stage leads to the second, when the divine light enters the being of the human. This light then takes the form of a series of "apocalyptic lights" (*al-anwār al-sāniḥa*), and through them the knowledge that serves as the foundation of real sciences (*al-'ulūm al-ḥaqīqiyya*) is obtained.

The third stage is that of constructing a true science (*'ilm ṣaḥīḥ*). It is during this stage that the philosopher makes use of discursive analysis. The experience is put to the test, and the system of proof used is the Aristotelian demonstration (*burhān*) of the *Posterior Analytics.* The same certitude obtained by the movement from sense data (observation and concept formation) to demonstration based on reason, which is the basis of discursive scientific knowledge, is said to obtain when visionary data upon which the philosophy of

Illumination rests are "demonstrated." This is done through a discursive analysis aimed at demonstrating the experience and constructing a system in which the experience itself can be situated and its validity readily deduced, even when the experience has ended.

The last stage consists of writing down the philosophy of Illumination. This stage, and the above-mentioned third stage, are the only components of the philosophy of Illumination to which *we* have access. The practitioner, the disciple of the Illuminationist way, would have recourse to the first two stages through experience. The disciples would have joined Suhrawardī in his retreats and would have experienced the "presence" of the experience for themselves, either individually or as part of a gestalt. Suhrawardī may have discussed his visions with the disciples (we so presume based on indications in the texts); his personal way, his "presence," would have served as the testimony for such visions, and the physical manifestations, the observed phenomenon, associated with the visionary experience, described in the *Philosophy of Illumination*, would have been witnessed by those present. What *we* have access to are the texts which are said to be symbolic portrayals of the phenomenon of the visionary experience, and we have to decide what they symbolize. Consider the following passages illustrative of the experience of light leading to knowledge and thus to apparently miraculous attributes of the subject who undergoes the experience:

(273) All of these are illuminations upon the managing light reflected upon the temple and the spirit of the soul. These are the goals of the intermediate. These lights may bear them up, allowing them to walk on water and air. They may ascend to the heavens with their bodies and associate with one of the celestial masters.

(274) The mightiest state is the state of death, by which the managing light sheds the darknesses. If it has no remnant of attachment to the body, it will emerge into the world of light and be attached to the dominating lights. There will it behold all the veils of light as though transparent in relation to the glory of the eternal, the all-encompassing Light: the Light of Lights. It will become as it were, placed within the all-encompassing Light. This is a station mighty indeed! Plato spoke from his own experience of this station, as did Hermes and the great sages.

(275) Those lights in which there is an admixture of might are of use in matters dependent upon might, and the lights in which there is an admixture of love are of use in matters dependent upon love. There are wonders among the lights! Whosoever is able to move his two faculties of might and love, his soul will hold sway over things exactly in accordance with that which corresponds to each faculty. Whoso ascends and thinks and endures will attain. Among the spiritual powers are stations, perils, terrors, and bewilderments. Each of these is known individually by those whose thought and opinion concerning divine and satanic matters is sound and whose resolve is steadfast toward

the perceptibles that strengthen each faculty: the might that strengthens dominance and the love that strengthens attraction.

(276) The visionary will understand the implication completely, learning much from a few hints. He will have patience to be resolute in all matters, the secret of this patience being entrusted to the one who holds the authority to teach the Book. He will be characterized by nearness to God most high, a spare diet and little sleep, supplication to God to ease the path for him, and a heart made refined by refined thoughts. He will ponder the clues to God's holiness enshrined in beings. He will be sincere in turning toward the Light of Lights, which is the basis of this realm, making his soul sing with the remembrance of God, the Master of the Kingdom—but worthy though this is, the sadness of the second state is more so—reciting revealed pages, in haste to return to Him in whose hand is creation and command. All these are conditions.

(277) Once the divine lights are dispersed within a man, he is clothed in a robe of might and awe, and souls bend to his command. For seekers of the waters of life, God hath a mighty spring! Who is there who will seek refuge with the light of One possessed of sovereignty and the Kingdom? Who is there who will hammer in longing upon the gate of divine glory? Who is there who will humble himself in the remembrance of God? Who is there who will go forth in search of God's guidance? No one who seeks His court will perish; neither will He disappoint the hopes of him who stands before His door.[5]

KNOWLEDGE, VISION, AND ILLUMINATION

The foundation of knowledge in Illuminationist epistemology is unqualified knowledge known with certitude (*yaqīn*).[6] There are distinctions in knowledge to be noted. Discursive philosophy, according to Suhrawardī, establishes formal validity, but knowledge based on intuition is given epistemological priority. In this way Suhrawardī does modify Aristotle's view of science portrayed in the *Posterior Analytics* by insisting that the most valid kind of knowledge is based on the "experience" of "apocalyptic lights" (*al-sawāniḥ al-nūriyya*) by the subject, which may be regarded as knowledge by means of a mode of cognition referred to as "mystical" experience.[7]

The validity of all discursive reasoning depends in principle and first upon the subject's experience. Here mystical visions, intuitions, and the experiential mode of knowledge in general are given the same epistemological certitude as the primary, self-evident (*badīhī*) premises of demonstration. Suhrawardī uses a favorite analogy to describe his view of knowledge. He compares physical observation (*irṣād jismānī*) with spiritual observation (*irṣād rūḥānī*) and states that the same kind of certitude, if not a higher level, as obtained from the world of sense data (*al-maḥsūsāt*) is obtained from observing or "seeing" all "light entities" within the continuum whole.

Illuminationist epistemological theory demands the ontological position that real existence, or the essence of the "seen" (sensed or intellectually perceived) entity, is the foundation of being and regards being in the univocal sense as purely abstract, or mental, or what may be called ideal. This ideal entity exists in the mind only and cannot serve as the foundation for the being of things "seen." The essences of these "seen" and "luminous" entities determine what they are, and in the real world what we see or experience is determined by them. Here the epistemological principle emphasized by Suhrawardī is that, to be known, a thing has to be seen (*mushāhada*) as it is (*kamā huwa*), especially if it is simple (*basīṭ*).[8] The knowledge thus gained by the person who "sees" the thing as it is will allow him to dispense with definition (*istaghnā 'an al-ta'rīf*).[9] Definition here is what Suhrawardī considers the essentialist definition, the Aristotelian *horos,* or *horismos,* which is the formula that combines genera and differentia, which in the Illuminationist scheme do not inform us of the essence in the foundations of knowledge. These arguments provide a transition from the mental approach to knowledge to the approach that emphasizes direct "vision" of the essences of real things and insists that knowledge is valid only if the objects are "sensed, seen, or experienced."[10]

Illuminationist epistemology demands that the knowing subject obtain the kind of experience, outlined above, in order to be in a position to perceive or apprehend the essence of a thing *directly.* This is said to occur in a manner that corresponds to sight as an actual encounter between the "seeing subject" and the "object seen," an encounter in which any obstacle between the two is lifted and what is obtained is a "relation" between them that determines the knowledge of essence. It is this kind of "Illuminationist relation" (*iḍāfa ishrāqiyya*) that characterizes Suhrawardī's view of the foundation of knowledge. In sum, Suhrawardī stipulates that, "should a thing be seen, then one can dispense with its definition" (man shāhadahu [al-shay'] istaghnā 'an al-ta'rīf), and that in this case, "the form of the thing in the mind is the same as its form in sense perception" (ṣūratuhu fi'l-'aql ka-ṣūratihi fi'l-ḥiss).[11] This view of knowledge is a main principle in the foundation of the philosophy of Illumination. We can therefore state that for Suhrawardī, knowledge is fundamentally obtained by means of a special mode of perception, which is called "seeing" or "vision" (*mushāhada*).[12] This special mode, said to be higher and more fundamental than predicative knowledge, emphasizes intuitive knowledge, where the subject has an immediate grasp of the object without the mediation of a predicate.[13] Thus, while for the Peripatetic, knowledge takes the form of a predicative proposition (X is Y), Suhrawardī's intuitive knowledge can be reduced to what is nowadays called an existential proposition (X is) where "is" signifies the essence, considered symbolically as a luminous light.

Suhrawardī accepts the formal Peripatetic division of knowledge into conception and assent. But for knowledge of anything to have more than purely formal validity, it must be founded on divine inspiration. The Illuminationist position stipulates that divine assistance allows the person to come to know the thing as it is.[14] The epistemological characteristic of knowledge founded on inspiration is that it is knowledge by presence and consists of the conception of a thing together with the immediate assent to it. In this way knowledge by presence distinguishes Illuminationist epistemology from the Peripatetic theory of intellectual knowledge. Further, the division of knowledge into what is self-evident (*badīhī*)—also called primary (*awwalī*)—and speculative (*naẓarī*) or acquired (*muktasab*), which is the Peripatetic division of both conception and assent, is abandoned by Suhrawardī in favor of the division of both into innate and acquired.[15] Innately knowable things, knowable because of their inherent luminosity, serve as the foundation of "sight" or "vision" (*mushāhada*), the process by which knowledge is established.[16] Certitude in knowledge is based on the recovery of innately knowable essences through visions and intuitions, which then serve as the foundation for any validity in science and thus serve as the psychological foundations of certitude in knowledge.[17]

Suhrawardī stipulates that "perception" (*idrāk*),[18] as the most general act of knowing an "absent thing" (*al-shay' al-ghā'ib*), occurs when the idea (*mithāl*) of the reality (*ḥaqīqa*)[19] of the thing is obtained by the person, that is, *in* the knowing subject.[20] Suhrawardī considers this to be a more general view of knowledge than that signified by the Peripatetics' use of the terms *ma'rifa* and *'ilm*.[21] The term *idrāk,* translated as "apprehension," or "perception," indicates various ways or levels of knowing, including sense perception (*idrāk ḥissī*) *and* intellectual perception (*idrāk 'aqlī*),[22] as well as intuition and vision. This kind of Illuminationist knowledge is validated by the experience of the "presence" (*ḥuḍūr*) of the object and is immediate; it occurs in a duration-less instant (*ān*). The examples given by Shīrāzī of such Illuminationist knowledge are the following: knowledge of God (*'ilm al-bārī*), knowledge of incorporeal separate entities (*'ilm al-mujarradāt al-mufāraqa*), and knowledge of oneself (*'ilm bi-anfusinā*).[23] Emphasizing what I mentioned above, Suhrawardī's theory of knowledge requires complete correspondence between the "idea" obtained in the subject and the object.[24] This means that to obtain knowledge, a kind of "unity," or "sameness" in contemporary language, has to be established between the subject and the object, and the subject's immediate experience of the "presence" of the object determines validity of knowledge. This view of knowledge is distinguished from Peripatetic theory of intellectual knowledge, where knowledge is established by a kind of "union" (*ittiḥād*) or "connection" (*ittiṣāl*) with the Active Intellect, after an initial separation or disjunction (*infiṣāl*). For Suhrawardī, however union and/or connection with the Active Intellect is rejected, because unity of subject and object obtained in the knowing person by an act of self-realization precludes disjunction in favor of a continuum reality, where being is a "light" determined by gradations of the manifestation of essence.

KNOWLEDGE AND KNOWLEDGE OF SELF

In the fourth "book" of the physics in his text *Intimations,* which corresponds to *De Anima,* Suhrawardī devotes an entire chapter (chap. 4) to problems such as self-knowledge, knowledge of one's essence, and self-consciousness.[25] The problem is introduced by the question "Is it not the case that you are never unconscious of your own essence [*dhātuka*] in both sleep and waking?"[26] The question is answered: If one postulates in the mind a human being who is instantaneously (*daf'atan*) created in a perfect state, not using his limbs or sense perception, this human being will not be conscious of anything except his own being (*inniyya*),[27] and this knowledge of one's essence is necessary (*wājib*).[28] Suhrawardī is here elaborating on the Avicennian doctrine that posits a kind of *cogito* that serves as the basis for the individual's knowledge of self.[29] By means of the fundamental epistemological priority given to self-knowledge, Suhrawardī establishes validity of knowledge, that is, that knowledge of essence (not possible according to the Aristotelian formula of essentialist definition) is obtained through knowledge of self by the self.

Suhrawardī's view of self-knowledge further makes a two-way identification among various "levels" of consciousness. Consciousness is identified as an essential component of the rational soul,[30] and any subject conscious of its own essence is an "abstract light" (*nūr mujarrad*).[31] Further, an "abstract light" is said to be a "self-subsisting light."[32] Therefore, the rational soul, through an "activity" of self-consciousness, is identified as, or equated with, the concept "abstract light," which links the cosmic order to the physical order via the intermediary principle of consciousness and its various levels of intensity.[33] Here self-consciousness, both as a cosmic principle and as a psychological principle, constitutes the foundation of Illuminationist knowledge and is associated with the special mode of perception referred to as "sight" or "vision" (*mushā-*

hada).[34] Again, the basic principle of Illuminationist knowledge is the relation of the "I" (*ana*, ipseity of the subject) to the essence of anything by means of the "being" (*huwa*, objectified ipseity, the that-ness) of the thing, both conscious of themselves and "in" themselves, and cognizant of what they are, necessarily.[35] From this basic Illuminationist principle of epistemology Suhrawardī draws a general conclusion, namely, that everything which is conscious of its own essence shares consciousness with all other things of the same rank; thus, consciousness becomes the principle of Illuminationist knowledge which holds true of all self-conscious beings, starting with cosmic consciousness and progressing down to individual human consciousness.[36] He concludes further that self-consciousness is equivalent to being manifest, or apparent (*Ẓāhir*), identified with "pure light" (*nūr maḥḍ*).[37] Self-consciousness is thus identified with "apparentness [or manifestation] and light-as-such" (*nafs al-Ẓuhūr wa al-nūriyya*).[38] Finally, Suhrawardī formulates the Illuminationist principle of self-knowledge and its connection to cosmic lights as follows: "Everyone who perceives his own essence is a pure light. And every pure light is manifest to, and perceives, its own essence."[39] This principle also distinguishes Suhrawardī's position from that of the Peripatetics: "A thing's perception of its own self is [the same as] its being manifest to its own essence, not its being abstracted from matter as is the Peripatetic theory."[40]

The most significant "light," in terms of knowledge and the experience of light, is the light called *Isfahbad al-Nāsūt*, which is qualified as the "managing light" (*al-nūr al-mudabbir*),[41] and is an abstract light that "controls" what is below it in rank.[42] This light is like the Holy Spirit,[43] *dator scientiae* (*wāhib al-ʿilm*) and *dator spiritus* (*ravān bakhsh*), and acts as *dator formarum* (*wāhib al-ṣuwar*),[44] which thus links the human and the cosmic realms. The light, Isfahbad al-Nāsūt, knows its self through its own self-consciousness.[45] The conclusion is that the link between the cosmic and the human is the principle of self-consciousness and self-knowledge. Multiple lights emanating from one source symbolize the light Isfahbad al-Nāsūt; these lights are called the *Isfahbadiyya* lights.[46] The multiple lights act in accordance with their "archetype" (*arbāb al-ṣanam*) at all levels, and since human self-consciousness itself is an "abstract light," there is no discontinuity between the cosmic and the human realm;[47] rather, they form a continuous whole. This theory is in marked contrast to the Peripatetic view of the Active Intellect, which is "one" and acts not in continuous, multiple manifestations (as do the Isfahbbadiyya lights in relation to their "source," the light Isfahbad al-Nāsūt), but as the *one* ultimate perfection of the intellect.[48]

Let me sum up what has been presented so far. The Illuminationist mode of perception and knowledge depends on

1. The subject: its experience of essence;
2. The object: its apparentness or manifestation (*Ẓuhūr*, similar to Husserl's *Evidenz*) and presence (*ḥuḍūr*); and
3. The Illuminationist relation (*al-iḍāfu al-ishrāqiyyu*) between the subject and the object, active when the subject and the object are "present" and "manifest" to their own essence, and thus to each other.

Knowledge is obtained when the identity preserving relational correspondence, that is to say, "sameness," relates the subject and the object, or any type of knower to its known.

Vision illumination (*mushāhada-ishrāq*) acts on all levels of reality: outwardly as sight (*ibṣār*),[49] and cosmically in that every abstract light "sees" the "lights" that are above it in rank, while the higher "lights" instantaneously, at the moment of vision, illuminate the lower in rank. The Light of Lights (*Nūr al-anwār*) illuminates everything, while the Heavenly Sun, the "Great Hūrakhsh," lights things up and so allows for vision to take place. By means of the process of illumination "light" is propagated from its highest origin to the lowest elements,[50] for example, the "controlling lights" (*al-anwār al-qāhira*) and the "managing lights" (*al-anwār al-mudabbira*).[51] Among the "managing lights" the principle lights, which directly effect the human soul, are the Isfahbad lights.[52] In general, all higher lights control and illuminate the lower ones, which, in turn, are capable of "seeing" the higher ones. The Light of Lights controls everything.[53] It is the most apparent to itself, and thus it is the most self-conscious being in the universe.[54] All "abstract lights" are illuminated directly by the Light of Lights, whose luminosity (*nūriyya*), essence (*dhāt*), and power are all one and the same.[55] The Light of Lights is self-emanating (*fayyaḍ bi-al-dhāt*), and its attributes and essence are one.[56] Human souls who have experienced the "apocalyptic lights" are called "abstract souls" (*al-nufūs al-mujarrada*), because they have freed themselves from the physical bondage of the body and are able to obtain the "creative light" (*al-nūr al-khāliq*) which bestows on them the power to know.[57] The experience of light by the Brethren of Abstraction (*ikhwān al-tajrīd*)[58] and the Masters of Vision (*aṣḥāb al-mushāhada*)[59] is described by Suhrawardī as a gradual experience of "light" in fifteen steps, starting with the experience of the "flashing pleasurable light" (*al-nūr al-bāriq al-ladhīdh*) and ending with the experience of a "light" so violent that it may tear the body apart at the joints.[60] The following passage illustrates this fully:

(272) Lights of sundry kinds shine upon the brethren of abstraction: a flash of light descending upon the beginners, shining and receding like the flash of a thunderbolt of pleasure; a stronger flashing light descending upon others, more like a terrifying thunderbolt, with which often a sound is heard like the sound of thunder or a roaring in the brain; a pleasant descending light whose descent is like warm water pouring upon the head; a light fixed for a long period, great in power, accompanied by a stupor in the brain; a light most pleasurable, not resembling a thunderbolt, but accompanied by a sweet and subtle joy moved by the power of love; a burning light moved by the motion of the power of might—when hearing drums and trumpets, it may result in things terrifying to the beginner, or in thought and imagination it may give him glory; a glittering light in a mighty blast, which in a drowning pleasure makes contemplation and vision more keen than does the sun; a flashing light, greatly pleasurable, during which one seems to be suspended by the hair of the head for a long time; a propitious light by which one seems to be seized—it seems as though the hair of the head is grasped and one is dragged roughly and tormented with a pleasurable pain; a light with a seizing that seems to be fixed in the brain; a light, extremely pleasant, shining from the soul upon the entire spirit of the soul, in which it seems as though something armors the body, and the spirit of the entire body might almost seem to have a luminous form; a light that begins as an assault, at the beginning of which a man imagines that something is being destroyed; a propitious light negating the soul, in which the soul appears to itself as something utterly suspended and wherein it beholds its own abstraction from dimensions, even if the one who experienced this had not known it beforehand; a light accompanied by the feeling of a weight almost too heavy to bear; a light accompanied by the power to move the body so great as to nearly tear asunder the joints.[61]

Finally, "light" must exist at all levels of reality for Illuminationist theory of knowledge to hold, both manifest light (*al-nūr*) necessary for sight and the abstract light (*al-nūr al-mujarrad*) necessary for the visionary experience. Stated simply, it is the Illuminationist theory of the propagation of light that determines how light comes to exist at all levels. The very origin, principle, and nexus of Illuminationist cosmology is the Light of Lights who radiates or emanates "light" because of what it is, and the propagated "rays" reach the entire cosmos.[62] The existence (self-consciousness) of the Light of Lights is not separate from its activity (illumination). Unlike the Plotinian One, from which Nous appears, from the Light of Lights another "light" is obtained which is not *essentially* different from it. In effect, that the Light of Lights *is* what it is and that it *does* what it does are one and the same. Thus, that the Light of Lights *exists* becomes a first axiom from which the whole of reality may be deduced.

Illumination and emanation, as delineated by Suhrawardī, combine two processes. The first process is the emanation of the First Light—also called the Closest Light (*al-nūr al-aqrab*)[63]—from the Light of Lights. The First Light is simply obtained (*yuḥṣal*); that is, it is not created by a willing entity.[64] The only difference between this light and the Light of Lights is in their relative degree of intensity (*shadda*), which is a measure of perfection, the Light of Lights being simply the most intense light.[65] There is no difference between these two lights regarding their modalities, and when the First Light is propagated it is not disjoint from the Light of Lights; it is *continuous* with It. This is also true of *all* the "abstract lights"; they, too, differ from one another and from the Light of Lights only in respect to intensity. The First Light (*a*) *exists* as an abstract light;[66] (*b*) has a twofold movement—it "loves" (*yuḥibbu*) and "sees" (*yushāhidu*) the Light of Lights above it and controls (*yaqharu*) and illuminates (*ashraqa*) what is below it;[67] (*c*) has a "rest," and this rest implies something like "matter," called *barzakh*, which has a "shape" (*hay'a*)—and together the "matter" and "shape" serve as a receptacle for light;[68] and (*d*), in addition, has something like a "quality" or an attribute—it is "rich" (*ghanī*) in relation to the lower lights and "poor" (*faqīr*) in relation to the Light of Lights.[69] The "richness" and "poverty" of a light corresponds to the degree of its perfection and its degree of intensity. This scheme is true of all lights. Through seeing the Light of Lights, and motivated by love and sameness, another "abstract light" is obtained from the First Light.[70] When the First Light "sees" its own poverty, its own "matter" and shape are obtained. As this process continues, the spheres and the elemental world all come to be.[71] These lights, so obtained, are the principal abstract lights, and they are multifarious.

The second process is not separate from the first, but is the result of the activity of the abstract lights. This process itself is the coupled process of illumination and vision. When the First Light is obtained, it has an immediate vision of the Light of Lights in a durationless, discrete "moment," whereupon the Light of Lights instantaneously illuminates it and thus "lights up" the "matter" and the shape associated with the First Light.[72] The light that comes to reside in the first abstract light is an "apocalyptic light" (*al-nūr al-sāniḥ*) and is the most receptive of all lights.[73] The process continues and the second light receives two lights: one light from the illumination of the Light of Lights directly, and one light from the First Light, the First Light having received it from the Light of Lights and now passing it on because of this light's transparency.[74] In the same manner, the third light receives four lights: one directly from the Light of Lights, one from the First Light, and the lights of the second light. The process continues, and the fourth light receives eight lights, the fifth sixteen lights, and so on. The result is that the number of lights (and with it the activity, intensity, and the very essence of the Light of Lights, which is self-consciousness and is symbolized as abstract light) increases according to the sequence 2^{n-1}, the Closest Light being the first member of this sequence.[75]

NOTES

1. There are several works that serve to introduce Suhrawardī's thinking; among them the following are noted: Carra de Vaux, "La philosophie illuminative d'après Suhrawerdi Meqtoul," *Journal Asiatique*, xix, vol. 19 (1902): 63–94; Max Hörten, *Die Philosophie der Erleutung nach Suhrawardī* (Halle, 1912); Muhammad Iqbāl, *The Development of Metaphysics in Persia* (London, 1908), pp. 121–50; *Anwāriyya: An 11th Century A.H. Persian Translation and Commentary on Suhrawardī's Ḥikmat al-Ishrāq*, ed. Hossein Ziai (Tehran: Amir Kabir, 1980; 2nd ed., 1984); Louis Massignon, *Receuil de textes inédits* (Paris: Paul Geuthner, 1929), pp. 111–13; Otto Spies, *Three Treatises on Mysticism by Shihabuddin Suhrawardī Maqtul* (Stuttgart: Kohlhammer, 1935); Helmut Ritter, "Philologika IX: Die vier Suhrawardī," *Der Islam* 24 (1937): 270–86, 25 (1938): 35–86; H. Corbin, *Suhrawardī d'Alep, fondateur de la doctrine illuminative* (Paris, 1939); idem, *Les Motifs zoroastriens dans la philosophie de Sohravardī* (Tehran, 1946); idem, *L'Homme de Lumière dans le soufisme iranien* (Paris: Sisteron, 1971). See especially Corbin's *Prolégomènes* to each of his following critical editions of Suhrawardī's works: *Opera Metaphysica et Mystica I* (Istambul: Maarif Matbaasi, 1945); *Opera Metaphysica et Mystica II* (Tehran: Institut Franco-Iranien, 1954); *Opera Metaphysica et Mystica III* (Tehran: Institut Franco-Iranien, 1970). See also Corbin's translations of Suhrawardī's works: *L'Archange empourpré: Quinze traités et récits mystiques traduits du persan et de l'arabe*, ed. Henry Corbin (Paris: Fayard, 1976); and *Le Livre de la Sagesse Orientale, Kitāb Ḥikmat al-Ishrāq*, trans. Henry Corbin (Paris: Verdier, 1986).

2. *al-Niẓām al-Atamm.* See Shahrazūrī, *Commentary on the Philosophy of Illumination*, ed. Hossein Ziai (Tehran, 1993), p. 5. See also Shīrāzī, *Sharḥ Ḥikmat al-Ishrāq* (Tehran, AH 1313), p. 12.

3. See my "The Source and Nature of Authority: Illuminationist Political Doctrine," in *The Political Aspects of Islamic Philosophy*, ed. Charles Butterworth (Cambridge, MA: Harvard University Press, 1991), pp. 314–84.

4. From *The Book Of Radiance*, ed. and trans. Hossein Ziai (Costa Mesa, CA: Mazda Publishers, 1998), pp. 84ff.

5. From *The Philosophy of Illumination: A new Critical Edition of the text of "Ḥikmat al-Ishrāq,"* pt. 2, "The Fifth Discourse," sec. 9, "On the State of the Wayfarers," ed. and trans. John Walbridge and Hossein Ziai (Provo: BYU Press, 2000), pp. 159ff.

6. Suhrawardī often uses the term *yaqīnī* or *mutayyaqqana* when he wants to modify knowledge with the attribute "certain." E.g., Suhrawardī, *Opera II*, p. 21. The term *yaqīnī* may be compared with ἐπιστήμη; e.g., Thābit ibn Qurra, *al-Madkhal*, pp. 4, 14, 185.

7. The distinction between discursive reasoning and intuitive knowledge had been made by Aristotle. However, he does not allow for intuition to play a principal position in philosophical construction, a point on which Suhrawardī insists. For a discussion of Aristotle's views concerning this issue see Victor Kal, *On Intuition and Discursive Reasoning in Aristotle* (Leiden: E. J. Brill, 1988), especially pp. 44–53.

8. See Shīrāzī, *Sharḥ,* p. 204: 11–14.

9. Ibid.

10. See Suhrawardī, *Opera II,* pp. 42, 134–35.

11. Suhrawardī, *Opera II,* pp. 73–74.

12. By *mushāhada,* Suhrawardī means a special mode of cognition that enables the person to have an immediate grasp of the essence of the object. Suhrawardī, *Kalimat al-Taṣawwuf* (Tehran: Majlis MS, *Majm, 'a* 3071), p. 398: "al-mushāhada hiya shurūq al-anwār 'alā al-nafs bi-ḥaythu yanqaṭi' munāza'āt al-wahm." Cf. Mullā Ṣadrā, *Ta'līqāt, Sharḥ,* p. 204 (margin).

13. I mean a kind of knowledge which is beyond ordinary knowledge. This kind of knowledge is "purely intuitive," writes Philip Merlan, "which grasps the object without the mediation of a predicate" (Merlan, *From Platonism to Neoplatonism* [The Hague: Martinus Nijhoff, 1968], p. 185). This is knowledge pertinent to things whose very nature dictates that they not have any predicates, such as God. This knowledge has to do with things "above being" and is called ἀγκίνοια by Aristotle (ibid., p. 186). It is usually translated as "intuition," or "quick wit." Cf. Aristotle, *Posterior Analytics* 2.34, 89^{b}10ff.: ἀγκίνοιά ἐστιν εὐστοχία τις ἐν ἀσκέπτῳ χρόνῳ τοῦ μέσου. Cf. idem, *Nicomachean Ethics* 6.9, 1142^{b}6ff. "The essentials of the intuitionist theory are these: I have immediate or direct acquaintance with external reality in my sense perceptions. I have immediate or direct acquaintance with internal reality, that is, with the process of mind, by introspection as the inner sense" (Joseph Alexander Leighton, *Man and the Cosmos* [New York: D. Appleton, 1922], p. 51). Plotinus is often considered the most significant Greek proponent of intuition (e.g., by Edward Caird, *The Evolution of Theology in the Greek Philosophers* [Glasgow: J. MacLehose, 1923], 1:220–21). Cf. the distinction between πειθώ and ἀνάγκη (literally, persuasion vs. logical necessity, thus the distinction between discursive and immediate knowledge), in Plotinus, *Enneads* 5.3.6.

14. Suhrawardī, *Intimations: Logic* (Berlin MS 5062), p. 2: "yua'yyid ibn al-bashar bi-rūḥ qudsī yurih al-shay' kamā huwa." "Divine assistance" is similar to the role of the Active Intellect in Peripatetic epistemology. The Holy Spirit, *rūḥ al-qudus,* and *ravān bakhsh,* which is the Persian equivalent, meaning *Dator spiritus,* as the giver of divine assistance, is identified by Suhrawardī in many instances with the the Active Intellect. It is also named the "giver of knowledge and divine aid" (wāhib al-'ilm wa'l-ta'yīd). Suhrawardī, *Opera II,* p. 201. Cf. idem, *Opera III,* p. 221: "rays emanate from the Holy Spirit." The Holy Spirit is further identified as the *Dator formarum* (*wāhib al-ṣuwar*) and with the archangel Gabriel (idem, *Opera II,* p. 265). In Illuminationist cosmology the equivalent of the Holy Spirit is an abstract (noncorporeal) light called *Isfahbad al-Nāsūt,* which, in addition to acting as the Active Intellect and the *Dator formarum,*

has a special function (which is also a kind of pure self-consciousness), because it indicates its own essence by its own self: "wa huwa al-nūr al-mudabbir al-ladhī huwa Isfahbad al-Nāsūt wa huwa al-mushīr ilā nafsihi bi'l-anā'iyya" (idem, *Opera II*, p. 201). For a detailed discussion of the role of the *Dator formarum* in Illuminationist epistemology as well as its position in physics, see Shīrāzī, *Sharḥ*, pp. 263–69. Its "highest" function is said to be to give being (*wāhib al-ṣuwar yu'tī al-wujūd*) (ibid., p. 268).

15. Suhrawardī, *Intimations: Logic*, p. 2; idem, *Paths and Havens: Logic* (Leiden MS: Or. 365), fol. 96r; idem, *Opera II*, p. 18. Cf. Baghdādī, *al-Mu'tabar* 1.7–8.

16. Suhrawardī, *Opera II*, pp. 18–19. Cf. Baghdādī, *al-Mu'tabar*, 1.4; 3.35–41.

17. This Illuminationist position in theory of knowledge may be indicative of a "Platonic" theory. Cf. F. E. Peters, *Aristotle and the Arabs* (New York: New York University Press, 1968), p. 173: "The weapon of *a priori* knowledge (*ma'rifa awwaliyya*) is used against the whole structure of Peripatetic psychology, and it is through his application of the same criterion that Abu'l-Barakāt arrives at Razian or, better, Platonic positions on absolute time and absolute space."

18. Translation of the term *idrāk* (as used by Suhrawardī) into English poses some difficulties. The term "perception" is probably an adequate equivalent, but it should be understood in the most general sense of "apprehension." For the various shades of the meaning of the term "perception" as used in philosophy, see R. J. Hirst, "Perception," in *The Encyclopedia of Philosophy*, ed. Paul Edwards (New York: Macmillan, 1967), 6:79–87. For various Greek equivalents of *idrāk* and its modifications such as *idrāk bi'l-'aql*, *idrāk bi'l-fahm*, *idrāk bi'l-ḥiss*, etc., see Soheil Muhsin Afnan, *Vazhih'namah-'i falsafi: A Philosophical Lexicon in Persian and Arabic* (Beirut: Dar El-Mashreq, 1969), pp. 98–99. Cf. F. Rahman, *Avicenna's De Anima* (London: Oxford University Press, 1959), p. 278; Avicenna, *al-Najāt*, pp. 277–79. For a history of "perception" in Greek philosophy, see D. W. Hamlyn, *Sensation and Perception* (London: Routledge and Kegan Paul, 1961), pp. 1–39.

19. Suhrawardī uses the term *ḥaqīqa* to designate *māhiyya*, i.e., *quiddity. Opera II*, pp. 16–19. Cf. Shīrāzī, *Sharḥ*, p. 45: 1–3.

20. Suhrawardī, *Opera II*, p. 15: "idrāk . . . huwa bi-ḥuṣūl mithāl ḥaqīqatihi fīka." Cf. idem, *Opera III*, pp. 2–3: "shinākht . . . ān bāshad ki ṣūratī as ān-i ū dar tu ḥāṣil shavad." The same statement is made by Suhrawardī in one of his mystical works, *Kalimat al-Taṣawwuf*, pp. 353–54.

21. Thus, the term *idrāk* as used by Suhrawardī is like a genus that covers a number of species, such as *'ilm, ma'rifa, ḥiss*, etc. Al-Ghazālī divides *idrāk* into *'ilm* and *ma'rifa* (al-Ghazālī, *Miḥak al-Naẓar*, ed. al-Na'sānī [Beirut, 1966], p. 102). In recent Iranian philosophy, *idrāk*, which is taken synonymously with *shinākht* or *shināsā'ī*, is divided into *idrāk ḥissi, idrāk dhihnī, idrāk 'aqlī*, and *shu'ūr* (both internal and external). See A. M. Mishkāt al-Dīnī, *Taḥqīq dar Ḥaqīqat-i 'Ilm* (Tehran: Tehran University Press, AH 1344), pp. 2ff.

22. See F. Rahman, *Avicenna's De Anima*, pp. 18–22, 25, 34; idem, *Avicenna's Psychology* (London: Oxford University Press, 1952), pp. 38–40.

23. Shīrāzī, *Sharḥ,* p. 38: 16–19: "al-'ilm al-ishrāqī al-ladhī yakfī fīhi mujarrad al-ḥuḍūr ka 'ilm al-bārī ta'ālā wa 'ilm al-mujarradāt al-mufāraqa wa 'ilminā bi-anfusinā." Cf. Aristotle, *Metaphysics,* 1.2, 982ᵇ28–983ᵃ11; 12.7 1178ᵇ14–16. Suhrawardī develops the details of such concepts as *al-'ilm al-ishrāqi, ḥuḍūr,* and *al-mushāhada al-ishrāqiyya* in his *Paths and Havens* (*Opera I,* pp. 480–96).

24. Suhrawardī, *Opera II,* p. 15. Cf. Shīrāzī, *Sharḥ,* pp. 40:8–41:5.

25. Suhrawardī, *Intimations: Physics,* ed. S. H. Musawi (Tehran, 2001), p. 67.

26. Ibid., p. 61: "alyasa annaka lā taghīb 'an dhātika fī ḥalatay nawmika wa yaqẓatika?"

27. Ibid. In this *Gedankenexperiment* Suhrawardī, though undoubtedly aware of Avicenna's similar idea of the "suspended" man, does not refer to him.

28. Ibid.

29. See Rahman, *Avicenna's Psychology,* p. 10; Peters, *Aristotle and the Arabs,* p. 173 n. 216.

30. E.g., Suhrawardī, *Paths and Havens: Physics* (Leiden MS: Or. 365), fol. 175r ff.

31. Suhrawardī, *Opera II,* p. 110.

32. Ibid.

33. Ibid.; cf. Shīrāzī, *Sharḥ,* p. 290: 3–17.

34. Suhrawardī, *Opera II,* p. 110.

35. Ibid., p. 112: "mā anta bihi anta . . . huwa anā'iyyatuka."

36. Cf. Suhrawardī, *Opera III,* pp. 23, 37: "dhāt-i tu dhātīst qā'im bi khud mujarrad az mādda ki az khud ghā'ib nīst." The idea of cosmic and human consciousness as a principle of metaphysics, by means of which the same principle is applied to corporeal as well as noncorporeal entities, is found in Plotinus. See Plotinus, *Enneads,* 5.3, 2–3.

37. Suhrawardī, *Opera II,* pp. 113–14.

38. Ibid., p. 114.

39. Ibid.: "kull man adraka dhātahu fa-huwa nūr maḥḍ, wa kull nūr maḥḍ ẓāhir li-dhātihi wa mudrik li dhātihi." Shīrāzī considers this to mean the union of the subject and the object. Shīrāzī, *Sharḥ,* p. 297: 2–3: "fa'l-mudrik wa'l-mudrak wa'l-idrāk hāhunā wāḥid."

40. Ibid. This section (§119) bears the title "Ḥukūma," and the description given is taken from Shīrāzī, *Sharḥ,* p. 297: 5–8.

41. Ibid., p. 201.

42. Ibid., p. 147.

43. See above, n. 14.

44. Suhrawardī, *Opera II,* p. 201.

45. Ibid.: "huwa mushīr ilā nafsihi bi'l-anā'iyya."

46. Ibid., pp. 226–28, 237.

47. In the Illuminationist cosmology, what is "emanated," or simply obtained, from the Source of light, designated Light of Lights (*Nūr al-Anwār*), is not separate from it, but is continuous *with* it; nor are the emanated lights discrete. E.g., Suhrawardī, *Opera II,* p. 128: "wujūd nūr min Nūr al-Anwār laysa bi-an yanfaṣil minhu shay' "; ibid., p. 137:

"ishrāq Nūr al-Nūr 'alā al-anwār al-mujarrada laysa bi-infiṣāl shay' minhu." Cf. ibid., p. 146: "al-nūr al-mujarrad lā yaqbal al-ittiṣāl wa'l-infiṣāl." The Light of Lights and what emanates from it form a continuum, and thus, unlike Peripatetic cosmology, Illuminationist cosmology is made up of noncorporeal, separate entities that are not discrete. The metaphor of "light" and its properties in propagating from one source describes the Illuminationist cosmology very adequately.

48. I do not wish to discuss the problem of the Active Intellect in Peripatetic philosophy in detail here. Briefly, in the common Peripatetic scheme, the Active Intellect (*al-'aql al-fa''āl*) serves both as *Dator formarum* and as "link" with the acquired intellect (*al-'aql al-mustafād*). But the significant difference between the Peripatetic Active Intellect and Suhrawardī's Isfahbad al-Nāsūt is that the latter is a continuous part of both what is below it in rank and what is above it. And unlike the Peripatetic Active Intellect, which is the tenth intellect in a "mechanical" cosmological scheme where the intellects are numbered, the Isfahbad al-Nāsūt is itself a multiplicity of abstract lights, for which it serves as *one* archetype. For a discussion of the Active Intellect, see F. Rahman, *Prophecy in Islam* (London: George Allen and Unwin, 1958), chap. 2. Cf. Aristotle, *De Anima* 3.5, 430^{a}10ff., where νοῦς ποιητικός is to be compared with *al-'aql al-fa''āl;* Avicenna, *al-Najāt,* 2.6; Alfarabi, *A¯rā' Ahl al-Madīna al-Fāḍila,* ed. M. Kurdī (Cairo, 1948), pp. 10ff; Suhrawardī, *Opera III,* pp. 53–55.

49. Suhrawardī, *Opera II,* p. 134.

50. Ibid., pp. 142–43.

51. Ibid., pp. 139–40, 166–75, 185–86. Note that the managing lights function on the human level, as *al-anwār al-insiyya* (ibid., p. 201), as well as on the cosmic level, as *al-anwār al-falakiyya* (ibid., p. 236).

52. Ibid., pp. 201, 213–15.

53. Ibid., pp. 122, 135–36, 197.

54. Ibid., p. 124.

55. Ibid., pp. 121–24.

56. Ibid., p. 150

57. This is when the knowing subject, as the self-conscious monad, becomes the creative subject.

58. Suhrawardī, *Opera II,* p. 252. These "brethren" enjoy the highest possible human rank, which is the rank of "creation," by means of which they are able to bring into being (the term used is *ījād,* which can be translated as "create") any form they wish. Cf. ibid., p. 242: "wa li-ikhwān al-tajrīd maqām khāṣṣ fīhi yaqdirūn 'alā ījād muthul qā'ima 'alā ayyi ṣūrat arādū, wa dhālika mā yusammā maqām kun."

59. Ibid., pp. 156, 162.

60. Ibid., pp. 252–54.

61. This passage is taken from "On the State of the Wayfarers," pp. 159ff.

62. The Light of Lights is self-emanating (*fayyāḍ bi al-dhāt*) and is the "active knower" (*al-darrāk al-fa''āl*) (Suhrawardī, *Opera II,* p. 117). Since any act of "knowing"

(*idrāk*) is self-manifestation, self-knowledge, and self-consciousness (ibid., pp. 110–13), the Light of Lights is pure self-consciousness and unchanging, eternal emanation (ibid., pp. 121–22, 152, 175).

63. Ibid., pp. 126–27, 132.

64. Ibid., pp. 125, 138–39. Suhrawardī does not use the more common terms *ṣudūr* or *fayḍ* to describe the emanation of light from the Light of Lights. The term used, *ḥuṣūl,* which means "to obtain," is less restricted than the other terms and conveys more of a "natural" process of propagation of light than a "desired" or "willed" emanation from the Source.

65. Ibid., pp. 119, 126–27.

66. Ibid., p. 126.

67. Ibid., pp. 135–37.

68. Ibid., pp. 132–34.

69. Ibid., pp. 133, 145–47.

70. Ibid., pp. 138–43.

71. Ibid., p. 138.

72. Ibid., pp. 139–40.

73. Ibid., pp. 138, 140.

74. Ibid., pp. 190–91, 195.

75. Ibid., pp. 138–41. The series 2^{n-1} and the series 3^{n-1} are the two series that serve as the basis of the harmony of Plato's World-Soul. See F. M. Cornford, *Plato's Cosmology* (New York: Bobbs-Merrill, n.d.), p. 49.

CHAPTER THREE

Luminous Consciousness: Light in the Tantric Mysticism of Abhinavagupta

Paul E. Muller-Ortega

Where all splendors are in the light
And all darknesses in the dark,
Brilliant light and gloomy darkness,
I praise that transcendent light.

Always new, hidden,
Yet old and apparent to all,
The Heart, the Ultimate
Shines alone with the brilliance of the Supreme.

Abhinavagupta, *Parātrīśikā-laghuvṛtti*[1]

INTRODUCTION: LOCATING THE LIGHT

The present chapter explores the notion of *prakāśa,* or the idea of consciousness as light, in the views of the preeminent exponent of the Kashmiri Hindu Tantra, Abhinavagupta (ca. 950–1014 CE). Particularly, this essay seeks to make an initial foray into uncovering the lineaments of what might be termed an "embedded Tantric argument" about light as consciousness as it is present and discernible in the Tantric works of this author. In the articulation of the mystical theories of the Hindu Tantra, Abhinavagupta employs a rich terminology of light which seemingly permeates every facet of his symbolic vocabulary (as it does that of many of his predecessors in the nondual Śaivism of Kashmir). Thus, in addition to *prakāśa,* "that which shines forth," one encounters *ullāsa,* "that which radiates brilliantly"; *sphurattā,* "the incandescent pulse"; and *sphuraṇa,* "the dazzling quintessence." Moreover, the manifestational products of such an emanation of light are termed *ābhāsa,* "splendrous appearance."

While the imagery of light is not new in Indian mysticism, it is nevertheless noteworthy that such a rich and varied semantic exploration of light should be present in this tradition. It seems reasonable to presume that in the Kashmiri mystical treatises this rich array of light terminology is rooted in and transcriptive of the meditative phenomena encountered by Tantric mystics. Indeed, Abhinavagupta employs the notion of the light in the service of at least three differentiable intellectual modalities present in his work: *prakāśa* as a philosophical construct that allows him to talk about the nonduality of Śiva; *prakāśa* as a theological notion that permits the depersonalizing and absolutizing of the deity Śiva; and *prakāśa* as a soteriological notion connected to his sophisticated Tantric mysticism. This essay thus seeks to discover what might be termed the "argument" of the light as embedded in the complexities and esotericism of Abhinavagupta's Tantric thought.

In order to pursue this line of inquiry, we must ask at the outset about the historical and textual backdrop—the sources for this concept of light as it eventually appears in the works of Abhinavagupta. However, even such a preliminary contextualizing inquiry is immediately complicated and controversial. To begin with, it must certainly be true that from one perspective the symbolisms of light are among the most ancient and elaborated in the entire Indian tradition. The contexts in which such symbolisms evolve are multiple and rich and resist even rapid depiction here. But in the broadest strokes we can mention the speculations that arise from *agni,* the illuminating and sacrificial fire of the Vedas: the Vedic *jyotir uttamam,* or supreme light (Ṛg Veda 1, 50), which makes way for the Upanishadic *ātmajyotis,* or light of the Self, and the *Bhagavad Gītā*'s conception of the *brahmatejas,* or splendor of the absolute. All of these terms imply varying religious and mystical contexts of visionary entry into the supreme light. This visionary dimension has ancient and important connections from the earliest Vedic times with the *soma,* the revelatory and ecstatic beverage, the nectar of immortality of the gods. In turn, this nexus of *agni*-fire and *soma*-liquid is connected in the Vedic canon to the brilliance of the sky and its many lights—the sun, the moon, the stars and planets, the dawn and sunset—as well as to the brilliance (*varcas*) and illumination (*śrī*) present in the natural world, including all human beings.

Thus, the sacrificial and cosmological Vedic effulgence casts its glow forward into the Upanishadic evolution with its manifold directionalities, speculations, and linkages: the fire in the sun, the fire in the stomach, the brilliant light in the smokeless fire (*Maitrī Upaniṣad* 6, 18). In the Upanishads, by more than one route, the symbolism of the light leads to the lustre of the great Self. In turn, this light of the absolute is personalized, for example, in the overwhelming theophany of Viṣṇu-Kṛṣṇa in the eleventh chapter of the *Bhagavad Gītā* in which the god's brilliance or *bhāsa* is compared to the shining brilliance of a thousand suns (*Bhagavad Gītā* 11, 12).

As well, early Indian philosophers employed numerous versions of the symbolism of the light. For example, the yoga philosopher Patañjali elaborates on the *jyotiṣmatī*—literally "that which is filled with refulgence"—as a way of talking about the yogic meditative perceptions that are filled with light (*Yogasūtra* 1, 36). In his comment on this *sūtra*, Vyāsa compares the *jyotiṣmatī* to the effulgence of the sun, the moon, a planet, or a luminous jewel. There are many other examples, of which these are just a few of the most obvious and well known. Sparks, rays, beams, ignitions, kindling: the vocabulary of light and its mystical apprehension in early India is large and varied.[2]

Nevertheless, the sources that inform Abhinavagupta's *prakāśa* flow from other less orthodox and extra-Vedic directionalities as well. If we veer slightly in the direction of early sectarian Śaivism, we find that here this rich array of light symbolisms is wedded early on to the *liṅga*, the phallic symbol for Śiva. Thus, by the time the *Śiva* and *Liṅga Purāṇas* were redacted, the *jyotir-liṅga*, the *liṅga* of light, was spoken of as an already ancient and well-established notion. The famous Śaivite myth in which the gods Brahmā and Viṣṇu encounter this great light of Śiva is but one of the manifestations of the confluence of the light symbolisms of very early India (and, it must be added, of their implied, mystical yogic environments) with that of the early sectarian experimentalists in Śaivite Yoga—as earliest exemplified by the proponents of the yoga of the *Pāśupata Sūtras*.[3]

Successive elaborations of this Śaivite yoga import many elements that are seemingly extraneous to the orderly brahminical world, not the least of which is a transgressive, heterodox sensibility fostered by skull-bearing *yogins* who long practiced in the impure cremation-ground environment. Early theological elaborations of this complex world of Śaivism appear in the anonymous scriptures of the *āgamas* and *tantras*—the Śaivite functional counterparts of Vedic *saṃhitā* revelation—and here too new dimensions are added to the symbolism of light.[4]

The notion of *prakāśa* as we encounter it in the works of Abhinavagupta both reflects and refracts all of this. For the great theologian and Śaivite master of the tenth century lives sufficiently late with regard to the evolution of Vedic and classical Indian thought that he is able both to inherit and to rework brilliantly much of what has come before. Thus, both the philosophical theology of light as consciousness that we encounter in the works of Abhinavagupta and its accompanying yogic and Tantric soteriologies are richly colored by these many precedents in the Indian tradition.

Moreover, it is this reworked and enriched notion of the *prakāśa* as the light of consciousness which is one of Abhinavagupta's most enduring conceptual contributions to later forms of the Hindu Tantra. It survives in those later, less philosophically oriented texts as a definitive moment of conceptual crystallization in the Hindu Tantra.

ABHINAVAGUPTA AND THE NONDUAL ŚAIVISM OF KASHMIR

Abhinavagupta is perhaps the greatest among the teachers of a small but rather distinguished and important series of interrelated lineages of medieval Śaivas—followers of the Hindu deity Śiva—that existed in Kashmir from about the sixth through the thirteenth century CE. This small band of Hindu intellectuals, authors, mystics, and practitioners of one of the most complex forms of the Hindu Tantra was all but forgotten in the centuries since its apparent demise as a vital tradition. In about the thirteenth century, Kashmir, like a large part of India even before this time, became part of the Islamic world, and the social supports for these lineages—they existed mostly because of royal patronage—disappeared.[5] Though the particular lineage I discuss here continues to be popularly called by the fairly confusing and even distortive appellation Kashmir Śaivism, there are a number of reasons why this term is not so appropriate and I have adopted the slightly more precise if unwieldy formulation "the nondual Śaivism of Kashmir."[6] Its most inspired exponent was the tenth-century Śaivācārya or teacher of Śaivism, Abhinavagupta, by origin a Kashmiri brahmin.[7]

Abhinavagupta was until very recently probably best known for his contributions to the development of Indian aesthetic theory. However, as a result of work done in the last four decades by a small but growing group of scholars the extent of his contributions to the development of the Hindu Tantra are finally emerging. Abhinavagupta's exegetical synthesis of Śaiva philosophical theology may generally (though also not unproblematically) be termed the Trika-Kaula because it skillfully and selectively melds together doctrinal and ritual elements drawn from these two preceptorial lineages. The term "Trika" refers to the triadic nature of the central deity, Śiva, as well as to the triad of female deities considered central in this branch of the tradition. The term "Kaula" means something like the transgressive, initiatory in-group. Abhinavagupta's Trika-Kaula synthesis is so compellingly and powerfully accomplished that, for all practical purposes, it subsequently becomes the definitive and normatively accepted formulation of what much later comes to be referred to as Kashmir Śaivism.[8] His writings give voice to one of the most sophisticated, elegant, and enduringly definitive expressions of the then emerging Hindu Tantra.[9]

Abhinavagupta lived and worked in Kashmir, traditionally a somewhat isolated geographical region of India.[10] Moreover, Abhinavagupta lived during a relatively "late" historical period in which many of the Indian religious and philosophical traditions had reached a certain established maturity. Because of this, and also because of his immense erudition and training, Abhinavagupta wrote from the perspective of one who surveys and incorporates into his writings much of the richness of the intellectual and religious resources that were available at this time. Certainly, this is borne out by an examination of what he has to say about the light of consciousness which he identifies with the deity Śiva, often in the horrendous or terrifying form of Śiva known as Bhairava.

From a doctrinal point of view, the nondual Śaivism of Kashmir is to be distinguished philosophically and metaphysically by its assertion that what is termed "Śiva"—the Absolute and primordial light of consciousness—is *advaya* or nondual. Moreover, this is a nondualism which differs in important ways from the Vedāntic *advaita.* For the Kashmiri nondual Śaivites, the nondualism or *advaya* of Śiva does not in any way imply that the world and all who dwell in it are illusory or unreal. On the contrary, they assert that this world is real precisely because and insofar as it is only Śiva, the light of the Absolute consciousness. It should be emphasized that this philosophical assertion of the reality of the world does not fall into the position of a "naive" realism. Rather, it seeks to articulate the enlightened and transformed point of view of the mystic, that is, the *jīvanmukta,* the one who is liberated while still alive. If the world is declared to be real it is so only and insofar as it is all Śiva, the unitary reality of the Absolute light of consciousness.[11] This particular teaching of *prakāśa,* or the supreme light, resides very close to the core of this tradition's most fundamental assertions about the nature of reality.[12]

It is not surprising, therefore, to find an articulation of the doctrine of *jīvanmukti*—living liberation—present in this and related traditions.[13] For one who is so liberated, this supreme light has become an all-encompassing and quotidian experience: the objective world has melted into the light of consciousness, and liberation is lived in this very body. It is in asserting the possibility of this religious, spiritual (and ultimately mystical) goal that this tradition focuses on the life-altering, individuality-transcending state of mystical life. Here this ultimate light of consciousness that is Śiva comes actually to awaken in a stable and enduring manner as a breathing, living human being.

At the core of this, there lies the experiential journey by which the *jīvanmukta* achieves the established and permanent vision of the light of Śiva. The practices or mystical methods (*upāya*) that compose this journey unfold in the living vision of the mystic who is able moment by moment to apprehend himself and the world with an illuminated vision and a transformed perception.

Taking these notions as a point of departure, Abhinavagupta elaborates a sophisticated Hindu Tantric mysticism which incorporates and melds many other symbolic elements into the notion of the light of consciousness. From a philosophical point of view, Abhinavagupta's works reflect a variety of epistemological strands or approaches to the notion of the light. In technical terms, we can discover in Abhinavagupta's works three connected—though differentiable—intellectual agendas which are best characterized in terms of the *pramāṇa,* the formal mode of knowledge (according to Indian philosophical thought) that predominates in each of them: inference (*anumāṇa*), revealed scripture (*āgama*), and enlightened knowledge or perception (*svasaṃvedana*). Each of these agendas articulates an aspect of this core doctrine of the nonduality of the light of Śiva.

In some of his works, Abhinavagupta is clearly writing primarily as a śāstraic philosopher engaged in formal, extramural debate with other schools of Indian philosophy. Here, the primary mode of discourse—the epistemological rule that governs the debate—centers on inferential logic (*anumāṇa*). His writings in the *Īśvara-pratyabhijñā-vimarśinī,* for example, primarily reflect this stance or approach. Elsewhere, Abhinavagupta is writing less as a philosophical polemicist, and more as an systematic interpreter and commentarial exegete of the revealed scriptures of Śaivism, the *āgamas* and *tantras.* Here, he seeks to elaborate a synthesis or a systematic theology which accounts for apparent contradictions in the revealed texts of Śaivism, and his appeal is to the authority of these revealed texts themselves. This is best exemplified by sections of his *Tantrāloka* where he interprets the Tantric metaphysics and esotericism of the *āgamas* and *tantras,* particularly the *Mālinīvijayottara Tantra.* In this aspect of his works he writes as a Śaivācārya, an authoritative religious and theological exponent of Śaivism. His appeal is to the authority of revealed scripture (*āgama*), which must be systematically interpreted in the light of reason and spiritual insight so that apparent contradictions may be rationalized. The major audiences for this aspect of his work were the varied schools of Śaivism prevalent in the Kashmir of his day. Thus, his mode of discourse is that of theology and the systematic exposition of the doctrines of Śaivism.

The third major intellectual agenda in his works might be called a practical theology or mysticism of Śaivism, and it is encountered primarily in his elaboration of Trika-Kaula mysticism both in his *Parātriṃśikā-vivaraṇa* and in sections of the *Tantrāloka.* Here, Abhinavagupta advances interpretations of the many Śaivite lineages into which he had been initiated as well as offers interpretations of the meanings of Tantric ritual and practice. The appeal is to the authority of his own enlightened experience (*svasaṃvedana*) as mediated to him and awakened within him by means of initiation and the transmissions of the preceptorial lineage. His audience seems to have been primarily his own initiated disciples, whom he was addressing in the role of *sadguru* or true teacher.

Abhinavagupta writes about the nature of the supreme light from all three of the above-mentioned religio-philosophical perspectives. Indeed, it is particularly when he engages the nature of the supreme light that he seems to mediate between and unify the tensions between the three different hermeneutical roles or epistemological perspectives that are clearly discernable in his oeuvre. His writings on the nature of the light, therefore, represent a highly intellectualized mysticism, in which we find a complex admixture of the three different *pramāṇas* at work and in support of one other: philosophical logic at work buttressing the revelations of scripture and both of these illuminating the direct, experiential realizations derived from mystical praxis.

It is important to emphasize that these three modes of discourse about the light are, therefore, not always neatly differentiable one from the other. Yet, they nevertheless represent different impulses toward knowledge present within the tradition that Abhinavagupta inherits. Part of the genius of his work rests precisely in his skillful capacity to meld and synthesize these different intellectual impulses into a coherent if still complex whole. From a scholarly vantage point, however, we must not allow Abhinavagupta's success at blending these different impulses or contexts within Śaivism to obscure their individual and rich contributions to his articulation of a "high" form of the Hindu Tantra, generally, and to his formulation of a descriptive view of the nature of the mystical light, specifically.

THE ARGUMENT OF THE LIGHT: TANTRIC PHILOSOPHICAL MYSTICISM

To begin with, within what might loosely be termed Tantric "philosophical theology" it is possible to distinguish three broad domains within which the argument of *prakāśa* or the light of consciousness evolves. (1) The first of these is the domain of the original revealed scriptures themselves, which, while largely ritual and yogic in their intent and focus, nevertheless are not altogether devoid of Śaiva theological matter. This, strictly and narrowly speaking, might be called the domain of *Tantra* itself. (2) Next, we can distinguish the domain of the exegetical and commentarial elaboration on these texts due to the authors of this tradition. This intellectualization and concretization of explicit religio-philosophical or theological views abstracted from the theologically often ambiguous, not to say apparently contradictory, matter of the revealed scriptures themselves is perhaps Abhinava's most enduring contribution in the evolution of his Trika-Kaula synthesis.[14] This might be termed the domain of the *tantra-śāstra* or, indeed (as aptly proposed by David White), the domain of *Tantrism* as a self-consciously confected theology.[15] (3) Finally, we can distinguish the domain of the philosophical or strictly "darshanic" texts, particularly but not limited to the already mentioned *Īśvara-pratyabhijñā-kārikā* of Utpaladeva as well as the several commentaries on this text by Abhinavagupta. This might properly be called Tantric philosophy or *tantra-darśana* in the more narrow use of this term.[16] It is important and curious that from a strictly chronological point of view, much of this third domain, as exemplified in the works of Utpaladeva and also Somānanda, precedes Abhinavagupta's "Tantrism" in his Trika-Kaula synthesis.[17]

In his masterful account of the Trika-Kaula mysticism, Abhinavagupta takes as an important dimension of his point of departure a complex "argument" about the nature of Śiva as the light of consciousness. Though the most complete version of this argument is to be found richly articulated and embedded in the complex detail of the first five *āhnikas* (or chapters) of the *Tantrāloka,* versions and pieces of it are also present in all of his other works. As has already been said, this argument about the light of consciousness is axiomatic and foundational to his entire religio-philosophical enterprise. However, Abhinavagupta nowhere presents the entirety of this argument in a single, readily accessible statement. Rather, it might be said that his entire oeuvre is his presentation of the argument of the light—buttressed by logic, filled with the precedents derived from the *āgamas* and *tantras,* and illuminated by his own mystical vision and insight.

In what follows, we examine what I have been calling "embedded Tantric argument" about the light of consciousness as present in the works of this great Tantric author. By the use of the term "embedded" what is implied is that this argument seems nowhere to be explicitly conveyed in its completeness. Rather, it is partially conveyed in many different places and within different intellectual modalities in the works of Abhinavagupta. My contention in this chapter is that an examination of the range of such passages yields a metainterpretive understanding and insight into what this tradition (and what this medieval interpreter of this tradition) thought about the nature of the light as consciousness.

By the word "argument," I am here specifically *not* referring to the syllogistic form of argument that appears in the Indian *darśana*, or philosophical systems. Rather, I am using the term in a looser and broader way to talk about a complex intellectual and religious construction in the defense and elaboration of the superiority and authority of Śaiva views and practices. Indeed, in what follows I seek to abstract an axiomatic and quasi-propositional rendering of my own understanding of the lineaments of this "embedded argument." However, this is not to say that Abhinavagupta did not employ the methods of traditional Indian inferential logic. Large sections of his commentary on Utpaladeva's *Verses on the Recognition of the Lord* are given over to his examination of the argument of the light using the methods of traditional Indian inferential logic.[18]

Moreover, in his articulation of the argument of the light in his *tantra-śāstra* works, while not altogether eschewing traditional Indian inferential logic, Abhinavagupta nevertheless takes recourse to the importation of elements that appeal to Tantric revealed scriptures and to direct mystical revelation (as well as to Śaiva yogic methodologies, Tantric ritual symbolisms, and Tantric mystical soteriologies) in ways that almost certainly would have been judged to be incompatible with or beyond the logical range of the methods of inferential argumentation employed in the *tantra-darśana* works. Particularly, in these *tantra-śāstra* portions of his oeuvre, Abhinavagupta makes frequent use of the appeal to the authority of the revealed scriptures of the *āgamas* and *tantras*. Such an appeal is not to be found explicitly in his philosophical, or darshanic, works, strictly speaking, because the appeal to the authority of revealed texts has binding force only for those who accept such texts as revealed. And, in his strictly darshanic works, Abhinavagupta is arguing and debating precisely with those groups outside the fold of Śaiva revelation, particularly with various strains of philosophical Buddhism, but also with other schools of Hindu philosophical thought and argument.

For these reasons, the notion of a Tantric argument concerning the light of consciousness means to point precisely to those sections of his works in which Abhinavagupta creates a rich exegetical and commentarial rationalization, justification, and synthesis of the teachings of the revealed scriptures of the *āgamas* and *tantras* of his tradition, and in doing so makes use of the idea of the light of consciousness as a foundational theological support. Thus, Abhinavagupta's elaboration and confection of an embedded Tantric argument as present in his *tantra-śāstra* works combines the precisions of syllogistic inferential logic with the complexities and obscure esotericisms of the āgamic texts. My claim is that there are nuanced aspects to the Tantric argument of the light of consciousness that can be specifically attended to and highlighted for interpretation.

At times, it appears that modern scholars and students of this tradition have overlooked any such differentiation and so hold that there is simply one argument about the light of consciousness, which is both expressed philosophically and also set into motion practically in the ritual, yogic, and soteriological domains of the tradition.[19] However, for purposes of this essay, it is asserted that there are important and nuanced differences between the way *prakāśa* is treated in these two domains and, further, that it is important to approach the Tantric formulations on their own terms and not as if they were always and everywhere derivative of some primary and prior philosophical articulation. For it seems certain that the interrelationship between these two domains of Abhinava's work is much more complex than that.

However, it is beyond the scope and intent of this essay to attempt at this juncture any outright comparison between these two domains of thought and expression in the works of this author. This important topic will have to be addressed in future research. For now, the task that this essay sets before itself is an initial exploratory foray into the Tantric argument about the light as consciousness and some consideration of its meanings.

THE ARGUMENT OF THE LIGHT CONSIDERED

We can ground these somewhat abstract introductory considerations by immediately turning to an exemplary passage in which Abhinava sets out his understanding of the light of consciousness. This passage is drawn from the first *āhnika* of his synoptic work entitled *Tantrasāra*, the "Essence of Tantra" (and equally of his longer *Tantrāloka*). Here, he articulates the teaching about the light of consciousness as follows:

> Therefore, here it is the true essential nature [*svabhāva*] which indeed is that highest that is to be attained. And the essential true nature of all existing things is indeed composed of light, for it is not logically possible that the essential nature of all existing things not be the light [of existence]. And that light is unitary, because it is impossible for that light to become other than what it essentially is. Thus, neither space nor time can sunder its essential unity, because indeed their essential nature is nothing but that light. Thus, the light is one, and that light is consciousness. And in this regard—that consciousness is the light of all existing things—all authorities are indeed in accordance. And that light of consciousness is not dependent on or subject to anything else. For dependence is precisely that state of being illuminated and it therefore implies the state of being illuminated by another light. But there is no such other light of consciousness that illu-

minates the light. And therefore, there is only a single, unitary, and independent light. And because of its freedom, that light of consciousness is devoid of limitations of space, time, and form, and is therefore all-pervasive, eternal, the form of everything and yet essentially formless. And its freedom is the power of bliss; its astonishment is the power of will; the fact that it is made of light is its power of consciousness; its capacity to reflect is its power of knowledge; and its capacity to assume all forms, its power of action. But even when it is united with these its principal powers or śaktis, in reality, the light united with the powers of will, knowledge, and action, is still unlimited, and reposes in its own bliss, identical with Śiva. It is this very light and no other which—manifesting by the force of its freedom in a contracted form—is thus termed the "atomic" or "limited" self [*aṇu*]. And again, due to its own freedom, it illuminates itself again, and there shines resplendently again as Śiva with an unlimited and undivided light.[20]

This first example of the Tantric "argument" about the light of consciousness represents Abhinavagupta's invitation, as it were, to direct, mystical, and experiential replication. We shall consider some of its specific themes in detail below, but we might begin generally by saying that it sets out the parameters to his introduction of the basic theoretical structures of the Śaivite yoga or mystical praxis. By combining the three epistemological perspectives outlined above, Abhinavagupta's argument of the light (both as he presents it above and in many other instances in his works, some of which we will examine below) is meant to bring forward a powerful rationalization and elaborate justification of the Śaivite mystical curriculum.

In the end, this argument makes its highest appeal to the immediacy of direct mystical vision—what I have elsewhere called experiential replication.[21] It is true that from a logical or inferential point of view, it seeks to articulate what are called the *sattarka*, or "good reasonings," that will remove doubt about this ultimate light from the mind of the "hearer" of the argument. Nevertheless, when examined in depth, these good reasonings go beyond that which compels the rational mind to give its assent. They appeal, finally, to a kind of mystical logic which compels a deeper form of assent born of the immediacy and undeniability of achieved mystical consciousness. Thus, it might be said that Abhinavagupta's embedded Tantric argument of the light seeks a kind of higher logic of mysticism in which logical proof and apodictic mystical realization perfectly coincide.

In what follows, I shall attempt to transcribe what I find to be the fundamental and axiomatic propositions regarding the nature of the light of consciousness in Abhinavagupta's work. These propositions provide us with an essential, bird's-eye view of the mystical and intellectual themes and purposes of Abhinavagupta's Śaivite Tantra.

What is displayed below is an artificially constructed interpretation of what I take to be a *krama*, a sequence implicitly present in the Tantric writings of Abhinava on the nature of the light of consciousness. We can now attempt to abstract and summarize in propositional or synoptic form the main outlines of the Tantric argument of the light as follows:

0. The light of consciousness is:	*prakāśa*
1. The light is one and its nature is freedom:	*eka, svātantrya*
2. The light is self-illuminating:	*svaprakāśa*
3. The light pulsates with power:	*vimarśa-śakti*
4. The light is self-concealing:	*svapracchādana*
5. Objective reality arises as the congealing of the light:	*visarga, sṛṣṭi, śyānatā*
6. The light is triadic: fire, sun, and moon:	*agni, sūrya, soma*
7. The Tantric mystic inwardly enfolds his individuated consciousness into the light and perceives it as being nothing but the light:	*samāveśa*
8. The Tantric mystic outwardly melts the objective outer reality into the light and perceives that it too is nothing but the light:	*vilāpita, nigālita*
9. Only the light is:	*iti eka eva prakāśaḥ*

I will now attempt to say a few commenting words about each of these summary statements, here and there returning to hear the words of Abhinavagupta himself.

0. The Light of Consciousness Is

The point of departure of the Śaivite Tantric mystic is the description of the light of consciousness called Śiva or Bhairava. The descriptions of this light are spoken with the voice of enlightenment which articulates the argument of that supreme light itself. Here the light streams forth as the vision in which the all-encompassing light of consciousness has been recognized as the unitary and nondual principle.

A *siddha*, or perfected master, such as Abhinavagupta, claims to speak from the stance of what the tradition calls the *khecarīmudrā:* the spiritual "gesture" in which consciousness moves only within its own blissful and incomparably fulfilling light. Or indeed, the *siddha* displays the spiritual gesture known as the *bhairavīmudrā,* in which—though the eyes appear to be open to the diversity and differences of the world—the only thing that is really visible to his enlightened vision is, in fact, the incandescent pulse of consciousness itself. This is the stance of the *siddha*, of the perfected master of consciousness, of the *jīvanmukta*, the one who is liberated even while still dwelling in the human body, who abides in the open-eyed *samādhi*, stabilized in the stance of the supreme.

Thus, the Śaivite tradition does not speak from the perspective of the ordinary presumptions of the world. It does not take as its point of departure the assumptions about embodiment, individual identity, and transmigratory and karmic dilemmas that constitute the *laukika* or worldly point of view. For these presumptions about reality have all been transcended in the all-encompassing mystical vision of the light. The *laukika* perspective has been experientially demonstrated to the mystic to be false. On the basis of mystical vision, the *laukika* perspective is evaluated as being based on conditions of partiality, incompleteness, and the contraction of consciousness and is thus incorrect, devoid of foundation, and ultimately unreal. The Tantric mystic's confession begins in the simplicity of the vision of the supreme light. Its first assertion is meant to be descriptive and undeniable, and it functions as a kind of axiomatic and unproven basis from which all that follows elegantly unfolds.

1. The Light Is One and Its Nature Is Freedom

From this prelogical and preconceptual space of ultimate vision, there then begin to emerge the contours of the Śaivite mystic's truth. From the unclothed and unspeakable apprehension of the light, there emerges the argument. It begins with the assertion that the light of consciousness is unitary. The meanings that are to be found in the word *prakāśa* are subtle, for while it does mean "light" in a primary sense, the tradition discovers in this word an essential, additional meaning of "existence." The assertion that there is only one light, however, remains at the unproven and axiomatic level of mystical description. It is one of the foundational ideas in a system based on nonduality. Thus, there exists only one light, says the tradition, because if there were another light of consciousness—from which the first light was to draw its light—then *that* light would be the supreme and unitary light. The light discussed here is therefore termed *anuttara,* literally "than which none higher." In other words, the supreme light is beyond all other lights, because it is not illuminated by any other light. As the unitary light of consciousness, not illuminated or dependent (*paratantra*) on any other light, that supreme light of consciousness is therefore independent and free (*svatantra*). Indeed, its very nature and power, Abhinavagupta tells us, rests on its supreme and untrammeled freedom (*svātantrya*).

2. *The Light Is Self-Illuminating*

In an essential sense, Śiva is the ultimate and he is the pure, unmanifested light of consciousness. The inevitable description of this light (*prakāśa*) is that it is self-illuminating (*svaprakāśa*). For as we have just seen, if it were illuminated by another light, it would not be that one supreme light. Nor would it be free and independent; for, being the only light of consciousness, if it were not self-illuminating, it would require some other light to illuminate it. Abhinavagupta comments on this as follows:

> The true and supreme nature of the knowable object is indeed Siva, who is nothing but the light [of consciousness]. For that whose true nature is not light is neither capable of being illuminated or of being real. . . . This light of which we speak shines everywhere; because it is undeniable, what therefore can the means of knowledge have to do with it? . . . In the *Kāmikāgama*, this reality [of the supreme light of consciousness] is said to be beyond any logical discussion of it. . . . This supreme God of the Gods does not depend on anything other than itself, but rather it is all other things that depend on it, for he is totally free. Śiva is independent and the lord of all, and thus transcends all necessity of space, of time and form, even as he is ubiquitous, eternal, and the form of all. Precisely because of his omnipresence, he is all-pervasive, and because of his eternity, he is devoid of beginning and end, and because he is the form of all, he is the source and impeller of the manifestation of all the varied forms of the world, animate and inanimate.[22]

Hence, the assertions that there is only one light which is free and independent contain within them the implicit notion that that light *must* be self-illuminating. The supreme light encountered by the mystic cannot be just that which illuminates everything else but which leaves itself in the darkness. It is not like a directional beam of light shining out to illuminate all that is before it but leaving itself and all that is behind it in darkness. Rather, the light of consciousness illuminates all around, and it thus includes itself in its illuminating power. That is all the more true, because, if it were not self-illuminating, the light would in fact contain darkness, that is to say nonlight. But, further playing on the meanings of the word *prakāśa*, light and existence are the same. Nonlight is, therefore, nonexistent within the light. Hence, because the light is *all*, and contains no non-light within it, it *must* be both the supreme light, the only light, and self-illuminating, not just that which illuminates everything else.

By qualifying the light as self-illuminating, Abhinavagupta avoids the fallacy of *regressus ad infinitum* which might accompany the qualification of this supreme light as a perceived object. The ultimate light is supreme precisely because there is no *other* perceiver which perceives it. It perceives itself, it illuminates itself. The supreme light is formed of consciousness (*saṃvidrūpa*), its nature is consciousness (*cidātman*), and it is uniformly and only consciousness (*cidekarūpa*). This consciousness is always present everywhere. In it, temporal and spatial distinctions do not hold at all. From the perspective of the realized mystic, the supreme light of consciousness thus shines as a self-evident and undeniable truth. The supreme light of consciousness is self-illuminating. Thus, Abhinavagupta asks, why is there any need to prove its reality? Ultimately, the realized mystic does not feel compelled to justify his claim to this vision in any way whatsoever.

3. The Light Pulsates with Power

Consequently, the tradition emphasizes the equal importance of what it calls *vimarśa*, the self-referentiality of consciousness. Even as the light of consciousness illuminates the world of objectivity (that will appear to arise within it), the light, as it were, curves back on itself to illuminate itself. The idea of *vimarśa* precisely asserts that consciousness has this capacity of being conscious of itself. It expresses the freedom and spontaneity of the light of consciousness. Even more important, the notion of *vimarśa* indicates the essential capacity of consciousness for self-referral. It exists only in reference to itself and no other.

The light of consciousness, says Abhinavagupta, is not just a clear crystal which, mirrorlike, reflects all things that fall upon it. It has an intrinsic capacity for self-referentiality which makes it alive and powerful rather than inert and powerless. This self-referential capacity is the *śakti,* the intrinsic power of consciousness. The *śakti* is but the expression of the freedom of consciousness, and, as such, it is responsible for the process of manifestation of all finite appearances within the infinite light. This capacity to manifest emerges out of the *vimarśa-śakti,* the capacity that consciousness has of being conscious of itself. In addition, it might be noted here that the self-referential capacity of consciousness empowers the processes of yogic *sādhana,* for the techniques of Tantric meditation seek to engage this essential characteristic of consciousness.

We might, at this point, allow Abhinavagupta to articulate all of the above in his own terms. In a passage in which he asserts that the ultimate or absolute consciousness that is Śiva is of the nature of a self-illuminating light (*svaprakāśa*), he says:

With regard to this dictum: that the supreme consciousness is self-illuminating; what need is there of any reasoning? If, in effect, that were not the case, then the totality would be devoid of consciousness and thus without light.[23]

At the beginning, reality consists only of a light [*prakāśa*] which gives life to the spontaneous self-consciousness [*vimarśa*]. It is none other than the essence of Bhairava which is full of the state of the transcendent egoity, whose essence is the self-referential capacity of consciousness and the state of absolute freedom [*svātantrya*].[24]

The theological elaborations of Abhinavagupta take this supreme light as their axiomatic foundation. There is no possibility of proving that which illuminates all things. For if there were some way of proving that light, then whatever it is that is capable of proving it would in fact itself be the supreme light. But indeed, the supreme light is self-illuminating, self-validating, exists only in reference to itself, and finally cannot be proved in any rational way. It simply displays itself to the vision of the mystic, who bows before it and accepts it as the vision of ultimacy.

4. *The Light Is Self-Concealing*

The vision of the supreme light just outlined generates a curious problem for the Tantric mystic. The Śaivite visionary lauds the light as all-encompassing, as total, as all-pervading, as eternal, as unitary, unbroken, perennial, and complete in its blissfulness and fullness. While it is true that he may feel no compunction to justify the existence or reality of this ultimate light to others, it is equally true that the privacy of mystical vision does not compel others to share its vision or accept its veracity. Therefore, even in the face of the assertion of the one and nondual light, the mystic—by his very attempt to enter into discourse with another—is confronted with the patent reality of a world of diversity and difference, a world, moreover, for which this light appears to be invisible and, indeed, nonexistent. Thus, having said this much, the Śaivite *sādhaka* or practitioner (like all other mystics) arrives at a curious dilemma. For while the vision of the supreme light of consciousness may be considered to be a final accomplishment, a silencing eradication of all conceptuality, an attainment that puts an end to the dilemmas of the mind and its various dispersive inquiries, nevertheless, in actual practice, such is not the case. If he intends to speak about this light coherently to others, then the mystic's problems are actually just beginning.

Abhinavagupta must in essence provide a philosophically and ideologically satisfying answer to the perennial query that is addressed to those who report the supremacy and unitary nature of the light. How to account for the perceived reality of the objective world? How is it, the nonmystics might ask, that given this supreme light of consciousness known as Śiva, the objective world as we see it nevertheless appears? How is it that the manifestation of a universe filled with diverse planes of existence and populated by an infinite variety of sentient beings takes place? That is to say, how does this supreme light—which is eternal, free, and unchanging in its nature—give rise to the manifestation of differences, diversity, and, most important, obscuration? And perhaps even more interesting, *why* does the light obscure itself and become the contracted, limited, transmigrating being who moves through a limited world?

The beginnings of the traditional answer for such inquiries remain decisively mystical and even somewhat irrational. For the tradition asserts that it is the mysterious play or sport (*krīḍā, līlā*) of the ultimate consciousness that it should simultaneously remain what it is and yet seemingly give way to obscuration, limitation, and contraction. Abhinavagupta tells us that "Śiva skillfully plays at the sport of concealing himself" (*svātma-pracchādhana; TĀ* 4.9–10). And, he tells us, from the highest perspective the arising of the world of manifestation and diversity does *not* finally introduce differentiation into the one light. He says, "Therefore, in that supreme light all things appear not just as reflected images, but indeed, as completely undifferentiated [from that light] just as water is in water or a flame is in a flame."[25]

It is the play between the light and the self-referential aspect of consciousness that structures the particular inflection of *bhedābheda,* dual-nondual, characteristic of the tradition. The light is supremely stable in its nondual, transcendent state and yet manifestation and differentiation do occur. However, such a process of manifestation does not represent a radical break, nor is it the emergence of a new and ontologically separate reality. It is simply an expression of the unlimited potentiality of being harbored within the ultimate light of Śiva. These appearances as separate phenomena are not, in a final and absolute sense, real. The tradition never denies, however, the reality of the manifestation of appearances as phenomena that occur within the ultimate reality of Śiva. The light is real and the phenomena that it displays are real. Like water within water or a flame within a flame, both the light and the diverse phenomena it displays are real. These manifested phenomena enjoy a reflected status in reality. At the same time, there is a final sense in which they are not ultimately real because they do not enjoy, as separate phenomena, the eternal existence and freedom of Śiva. Abhinavagupta explains all of this in a rhetorical tour de force. He says,

> The light is one, and it cannot ever be divided, and for this reason there is no possible division capable of sundering the nonduality, the Lord, beautiful with light and bliss. But [someone might object] space, time, forms, knowledge, qualities, attributes, distance, and so on, are usually considered to be diversifying elements. Not so [we reply],

because that which so appears is nothing but light. If the light were not such, then non-duality would be useless. Difference then is only a word devoid of reality. But even if we admit a portion of reality to differences, then according to what we have said, it will have its basis only in non-duality. This is a pot; this is a cloth; the two are different one from the other. The two are different from other cognizing subjects; the two are different even from me. All these are nothing but the one light, which by its own intrinsic nature displays itself in this way.[26]

Of course, this problem is not one that only the Śaiva Tantric mystics faced. In some way or another, every proponent of the ultimacy of a mystical vision has this problem of accountability when s/he returns to address the blinkered or, at the very least, agnostic world of the unenlightened. Assailed by the argumentation that derives from the perspective known in the tradition as *vyāvahārika* or *laukika*—worldly or unenlightened—the mystics of India have elaborated a series of different strategies to move through this problem. I will not rehearse these here except to say that there are two favorite strategies: either holding firm to nonduality by means of a vigorous denial of any reality whatsoever to the world or caving in on the assertion of ultimate nonduality and allowing a dualistic stance in which the opposition between the ultimate light of consciousness and the world is somehow accepted.

Neither of these strategies is adopted by the mystics of Tantric Śaivism. In essence, they adopt a third position which does not—it must be admitted—avoid all philosophical controversy, but which is satisfying to the integrity of their own position. Their solution to the problem further articulates their mystical vision and allows them, so to speak, to have their enlightened cake and eat it too. This is accomplished by holding that difference, diversity, darkness, objectivity, name and form, individuality—in short, what is in India generically termed *saṃsāra*, or the world of transmigratory destinations—all of this is nothing but the supreme play of that light of consciousness. Thus, in the above passage, we see Abhinavagupta invoking this third strategy for sustaining nonduality in the face of the apparent duality wrought by the world. This strategy is invoked as well in the following important passage:

Everything that exists resides within the blessed Lord Bhairava, and thus never departs from our heart or from the point of our tongue. It resides, therefore, within Parameśvara, who is not measured by time, is of the nature of consciousness, and is united with the entirety of all the śaktis [the potencies that rule reality]. Parameśvara constitutes a unity which coexists without contradiction with the hundreds of creations and dissolutions which are manifested by his contraction and expansion. It is by means of these that he expresses his freedom. This reality of Śiva, therefore, has neither beginning nor end. It is luminous with its own light. Its essence is a complete freedom which consists of a perfect independence determined by the fullness of all things. Within himself Śiva embraces all of the principles or *tattvas* that constitute reality, and they are therefore identical with him.[27]

Abhinavagupta will thus insist that what nonduality means is precisely that the light is capable of encompassing duality within itself without in any way sundering its nonduality. Otherwise, he argues, it is not really nonduality! To assert that a world arises within Śiva is in no way to sunder the integrity of Śiva. Moreover, he insists, those who would claim that it does simply have not understood or have underestimated the nature of Śiva as the unbroken light of consciousness.

5. Objective Reality Arises as the Congealing of the Light

Having established both the nonduality of the light of consciousness and the notion that the world of objectivity arises as a form of its supreme play, Abhinavagupta then proceeds to narrate the process by means of which the manifestation of such a world takes place. According to this dimension of Abhinavagupta's discourse, which centers on the manifestation of the world out of this ultimate, unitary light, the world comes into being by a self-obscuration of the light and the introduction of contraction and limitation. The forces that bring this about are understood to be expressions of the essential freedom of the light, which in this way plays and displays its essential nature. This process of manifestation then involves the emission, projection, or ejection (*visarga, vikṣepa, visṛṣṭi*) of the world of objectivity by means of a progressive stepping down of the ultimate radiance of consciousness so that it allows itself to be congealed (*śyānatā*), literally frozen, contained, and more limited, and thus to give rise to the appearance of the world of form. This process is narrated on a macrocosmic level in terms of the emergence of thirty-six *tattvas*, or cosmic principles of being. As a result, there arises the contracted, individualized consciousness which experiences itself as limited, small, and incomplete; as caught up in diversities and differences; and as a performer of actions.

6. The Light Is Triadic: Fire, Sun, and Moon

7. The Tantric Mystic Inwardly Melts His Individuated Consciousness into the Light and Perceives It as Being Nothing but the Light

8. The Tantric Mystic Outwardly Melts the Objective Outer Reality into the Light and Perceives That It Too Is Nothing but the Light

For the Śaivite tradition, this congealing or freezing of the light of consciousness gives rise to the triadic nature of everyday awareness. This awareness is symbolized by the triad of fire, sun, and moon. Here, the knower (*pramātṛ*) is designated as the "fire" (*agni, vahni*); the process of knowing (*pramāṇa*) is designated as the sun (*sūrya, arka*); and that which is known (*prameya*), that is to say, the objective world that is perceived by the mind and senses, is designated as the "moon" (*soma*). Says Abhinavagupta,

> If one refers to the light alone in its most manifest or evident expression, then this is what is called the sun. The moon, on the other hand, is called that light which showers down the essential blissful portion of the objects which are to be illuminated. Thus, the sun is said to be the various means of knowledge, and the moon the objects that are to be known. . . . The true and supreme nature of the fire is that of the knower, and because that form of consciousness flames forth it is celebrated as the many-rayed fire of consciousness. The knowing subject is none other than the very consciousness, which, by means of its supreme freedom, enters into a state of complete identity with the known object and thus exists completely independently. Such a knowing subject is thus of various kinds, which are determined by the varieties of known objects. That is the reason why the fire, which is fueled by the various appearing images of objective reality—that is to say, the portion of the moon—has been named by the Lord the many-rayed fire of consciousness.[28]

Thus, the ordinary consciousness of the transmigrating individual displays this triadic division into knower, knowing, and known. The light of consciousness—which is unitary in its nature—appears to take on three different and highly delimited roles. As the limited knower, it illuminates, by means of limited forms of knowledge, the experience of limited objects of perception.

It is this divided and limited reality of ordinary human awareness, then, that constitutes the starting point for the Śaivite ascensional journey of return to the nonduality of the supreme light. Such a journey will be accomplished—in the complex curriculum of Śaivite mystical practice—by means of two very different forms of recognition (*pratyabhijñā*). The first of these involves the recapitulation of the classical yogic journey of interiorization into the depths of the knower. Like Patañjali before him, Abhinavagupta posits the foundational beginnings of true *yoga* in the meditative states of introversive absorption. This first stage of the Śaivite mystical journey leads ultimately to the interior merger with the supreme light of consciousness as the intrinsic reality of the knower in the *nirvikalpa* or nonconceptual meditative absorption.

The entire domain of yogic *sādhana* that Abhinavagupta inherits from the earlier Śaivite traditions into which he was initiated essentially presupposes such as the sine qua non of the higher mystical attainments. In the terminology of Śaivism, this is the entry into *samāveśa,* or skillful, meditative absorption into the light of Śiva within the Self. It is as the culmination of these interiorizing and ascensional meditative practices that the inner recognition of Śiva as the true reality of the Self comes to be achieved.

However, the Śaivite mystical curriculum involves a second phase, as it were, of a descending or extroversive sort. Here, the awakened fire of consciousness enflamed by such states of inner recognition emerges from its transcendent isolation in the nonconceptual states of introversive mystical absorption and begins now to burn away the "fuel" of the outer objective world. The fire of the knower will burn the "fuel" of the objects of perception, here symbolically called the moon. By this means, the objective world is ultimately revealed as nothing but the supreme light of consciousness. There thus occurs a second, and much more encompassing, recognition. All this is Śiva, the Śaivite mystic proclaims; all this is nothing but the light of consciousness. It is in articulating this process of the melting or burning away of the frozen or congealed objective world that Abhinavagupta makes one of his most sophisticated esoteric contributions to the *sādhana* of Hindu Tantric mysticism. Says Abhinavagupta,

> This violent digestion is characterized by a taste for devouring all and by a fire that is continuously flaming. The disappearance obtained by this violent digestion, which is indeed the third kind, consumes by fire the kindling wood of differentiation and is thus a subject worthy of being taught. All existing things hurled forcibly into the fire that rages in the stomach of one's own consciousness abandon all differentiation and feed the fire with fuel of its own power. When the finite form of all things is dissolved by this violent digestion, then the All, which feeds and sustains the divinities of consciousness, becomes the ambrosia of immortality. The divinities, once satisfied, hold the Bhairava, who is totally full, the sky of consciousness, the God who reposes in the Heart and not elsewhere, this Bhairava they hold in identity with themselves.[29]

Using metaphorical imagery, Abhinavagupta here speaks of this in terms of the notion of a violent digestion (*haṭha-pāka*), a metaphor that once again emphasizes the physicality of the process of enlightenment. Just as there is a "fire" in the stomach that digests food and renders it useful and nourishing to the body, so also there is a flame at the center of the belly of all things, in the middle of the Heart, that violently consumes all differentiated objects. The result of this oblation is not destructive, but rather extractive. The cosmic, digestive flame raging in the stomach of consciousness extracts the immortal essence from all finite things. The various divinities feed on this essence and thus fulfill Bhairava and reach identity with him.

Thus, the procedures that allow the Śaivite mystic to melt the world of objectivity into the light of consciousness stand at the summit of the mystical processes described in Abhinavagupta's texts. When the objects of the senses are submitted to that fire burning at the core of consciousness, they release their essential nature, which is said to be the nectar or *amṛta* of consciousness. By this transmutative vision, the mystic melts the apparent objectivity of the world into the light which is its only reality. Thus, the Śaivite *sādhaka* or mystical practitioner seeks to liquefy the world into the waves and pulsations of the ecstatic light of consciousness. To describe this process, Abhinavagupta uses the expression *bhairavāgnivilāpitam,* literally "dissolved by the fire of Bhairava."[30] Alternatively he uses the Sanskrit word *nigālita,* which means also "melted," "dissolved," or "liquefied." He describes this as follows:

> Those who are purified by the true consciousness and are firmly stabilized in it are established in the path to the Supreme and do not employ any means to it. For such as those, the entire *maṇḍala* of existing reality appears before them as dissolved or melted in the fire of Bhairava, of consciousness. For them, the various impulses of pleasure, pain, doubt, and anxiety have vanished and all that remains is the supreme undifferentiated consciousness by which they are penetrated.[31]

Linking all of these various concepts together, Abhinavagupta gives an insight into this process of Tantric meditation, in which the light of consciousness which is the true and intrinsic reality of all apparently objective phenomena is released by the *yogin.* He says,

> Now as for the Supreme, as it is called here, there is a meditation on it. The light, the freedom, whose essential nature is consciousness contains within it all principles, realities, things. This light abides in the Heart. It has been described in this way in the *Triśiromata:*
>
> > The knower of truth sees that reality within the Heart like a flower within which are all external and internal things, a flower shaped like a plantain bloom. He should meditate with undistracted mind on the union there in the Heart of the sun, moon, and fire. From this meditation, as from the agitation caused by two fire sticks, one comes to experience the oblation fire of the great Bhairava, which expands and flames violently in the great fire pit known as the Heart. Having arrived at that effulgence of Bhairava, which is the possessor of the powers and full of the powers, one should contemplate its identity with the abode of the knowing subject, the means of knowledge, and the known object. That triad is the very same triad as the triad of

powers of fire, sun, and moon, as well as that of the always-arising powers of Parā, Parāparā, and Aparā.[32]

In this rich description, the Heart is seen as a sacrificial fire pit within which the light of consciousness continuously blazes and flames. Here, the triad of fire, sun, and moon, which is to say, the knower, the process of knowing, and the object of knowledge, are intertwined. The light of the ultimate flames in the Heart like a flower, specifically, like a plantain bloom, which is a thick, dark-red blossom. It is here in the Heart that the process of liquefaction, of melting or dissolving, of reducing all objective phenomena to their essential constituent, takes place. Once this is accomplished, there is released the immortal residue of the "moon" of objectivity, which is the very nectar, or *soma*, of immortality. It is this blissful nectar which the Śaivite mystic seeks continually to drink. It is in this way that the intrinsic nature of the world is revealed as the immortal light of consciousness. This same idea is taught by Abhinavagupta in another long passage:

This supreme wheel of the Absolute flows out from the Heart through the spaces of the eyes, and so forth, and ranges over the various objects of the senses. The rays of this wheel of light, systematically create the Fire [of the knowing subject], the Moon [of the known object], and the Sun [of the process of knowing], in [each moment] of the manifestation, maintenance, and reabsorption [of the external world]. In this way, as this wheel falls on the various objects of the senses [such as sound] by way of the sense-capacity openings, one should recognize that sensory object as identical with the wheel. Thus, wherever the universal wheel falls, by this methodical practice it falls in its entirety like the universal monarch. In this way, the whole multitude of paths is effortlessly dissolved in the great wheel of Bhairava, which is contained in consciousness. Then—even when all this has come to an end and all that is left are latent impressions—one should meditate on the great wheel which revolves as the overflowing of the true Self. Then, when all the fuel of the objective world has been dissolved and when even its latent residual impressions have been destroyed, the practitioner should meditate on that wheel as becoming calm, then as pacified, then as tranquil quietude itself. By this method of meditation, the entire universe is dissolved in the wheel, in that consciousness. Consciousness then shines alone, free of objects. Then, because of the essential nature of consciousness, manifestation occurs once again. That consciousness is the great Goddess. Continually causing the universe to become absorbed in his own consciousness, and continually emitting it again, the practitioner eternally becomes Bhairava.[33]

In these intricate passages, we find Abhinavagupta again playing upon old Vedic notions of sacrificial imagery: the fire of consciousness as the fire of the Vedic oblation into which offerings are made and transformed as food and sustenance for the gods. Here, the offerings are the very impulses of the activities of the senses, the objects of the senses, which are fed into the flames of consciousness. As with the earlier Vedic sacrifice, there is here as well an important digestive symbology: the fire or light of consciousness is such that in the accomplished *sādhaka* it operates to melt, digest, or dissolve the objects of the senses, the experiences of the so-called objective world, and thus to release their intrinsic and deepest reality. This is the *amṛta,* the nectar of the immortality of consciousness, which is to say, the immortal consciousness of the supreme light itself. Thus, the "moon" of the objective world melts into nectar. Abhinavagupta tells us that to achieve a state of consciousness in which the *yogin's* awareness functions continuously in this way is, in effect, to become indeed Bhairava himself. For such a state or condition emulates and, indeed, embodies the nature of the light of consciousness, which is always engaged in the creative manifestation and reabsorption of the world out of and back into its own effervescent pulsations. Thus, the Śaivite *yogin* seeks to live as that supreme and dazzling pulsation itself and to experience that it is out of his or her very own fiery consciousness that the entire complex affair of the objective universe and its diversity emerges and is ultimately reabsorbed. The moon is thus illuminated by the sun.

These elaborate images attempt to describe the experience of the realized Śaivite mystic whose every moment is sacrificial, and whose awareness is so powerfully inflamed by the light that it is able to reveal the intrinsic nature of consciousness as the essence or deepest core of every experience in life. Releasing this core to be tasted, the enlightened consciousness of the mystic continuously digests, melts, or transmutes the experience of objectivity. This releases the hidden light and core of consciousness and reveals that such an apparently "solid" objectivity "contains" only the immortal light. By these images, the Hindu Tantric tradition speaks of the world revealed as light, the daily assemblage of existence melted to release what it terms the *śivānandarasa,* the nectar of the bliss of Śiva.

9. Only The Light Is

The primacy of an immediate intuition of the light of Śiva thus remains all that is left at the end of the mystic's long journey through obscuration and contraction, and then release and enlightenment. Bhairava is the name that is given in this tradition to the native condition of consciousness, shorn of all secondary accoutrements and accompaniments and impediments: the light of consciousness as its own sheer immediacy. For the *yogis* of this Śaivite tradition, there was an inherent primacy that was given to this immediate intuition of consciousness as light. The preliminary prerequisites included the reception of the esoteric initiations proffered by this elite tradition by means of which the novice practitioner was thought to have experienced the impact of the revelatory grace (*anugraha*) of Śiva. Once these were received, the *yoga* or mystical praxis of Tantric Śaivism centered on the process of subsiding into this light of consciousness.

In fact, however, because the light of consciousness is ever present as the true and intrinsic reality of every moment of experience, such a process of subsiding into the light can be accomplished in a great many different ways. Because, for the Śaivite mystic, the light of consciousness is the inescapable fact, it can be approached from any direction. Though each moment of relative experience is thought to obscure the gleam of this great light, superimposing on it various kinds of shadowed, congealed, and limited forms of awareness, it remains nevertheless intrinsically present and aware. Thus, *any* sensory experience properly cultivated can open this dimensionality of light. Any route of entry when properly penetrated and then released reveals the light of consciousness at its core. Any thought can open this astonishing dimensionality of the Bhairavic light. Thus, for this esoteric lineage of Śaivite Tantric masters, the light of consciousness is the core phenomenon, the primary theological teaching, the primary instrument of *yoga,* and the ultimate goal of such *yoga.* Nevertheless, this apparently simple prescription masks, as I have tried briefly to illustrate, a complex worldview that resists simplification. Abhinavagupta first states the matter at length in his massive and encyclopedic text on Tantra, the *Tantrāloka.* At the outset, he says in unequivocal terms that the nature of Śiva as the light of consciousness is the primary teaching he has to convey. And then, despite the fact that he goes on to elaborate this teaching at great length in that text, he feels it necessary to restate it again in his shorter synoptic text, the *Tantrasāra* (as has been quoted above, at n. 20), and, indeed, to allude to this notion of the light of consciousness repeatedly and in many different contexts, as we have seen.

It is important to reiterate that this "argument" of the light as elaborated in these and other texts by Abhinavagupta is the philosophical, theological, and soteriological elaboration of achieved mystical insight. It seems apparent from what Abhinavagupta tells us that what he is describing is, for him, not just received scriptural wisdom, nor is it an intellectual construct that he has inherited and is then elaborating on the basis of tradition. At the core, his "argument" revolves around a fundamental and inescapable confrontation within the consciousness of the mystic, with that innermost and deepest reality, the abyss of the great Heart of Śiva.

Thus, much of Abhinavagupta's work on the mysticism of light might be termed a theological transcription of a living, experiential mysticism. And, given Abhinavagupta's intellectual predilections and character, and also given the tradition of *āgamas* and *tantras* that he inherits from his masters, it is clear that this lively and living transcription of the mystical experience of the light does not take place in a cultural vacuum. A text such as the *Tantrāloka* seeks to accommodate, in a delicate and painstaking way, the primacy of this mystical intuition of the light of Śiva to modes of philosophical and logical discourse, as well as to theological teachings and doctrines inherited from the revealed scriptures. The result is a highly intellectualized mysticism, conscious of its own activity of elaboration, clarification, and explication.

Present in these works is an attempt to confect out of a theological and philosophical vocabulary the complex ideology of a sophisticated Śaivite vision. In this way, Abhinavagupta seeks to accommodate the illuminative and metaconceptual immediacy of the unitary light that is awakened in yogic states to the words of the revealed āgamic and Tantric corpus inherited from tradition, as well as to the verbal instruction (*guruvāda*) that he had acquired from his many teachers. In this enterprise, the words of the revealed scriptures come to be understood—in a complex theology of verbal revelation—as the congealed and stepped-down impulses of the pulsation of this very light of supreme consciousness itself. Therefore, the task of philosophical and theological confrontation and accommodation, as Abhinavagupta carries it out in his works, is really understood as the juxtaposition of these two "versions," if they can be called that, of the same light of Śiva: on the one hand, that light as directly experienced in the radical intuitions of the yogic states of mystical attainment; and on the other hand, the light of consciousness as mediated to the mind through inferential logic and as transcribed into the impulses of the revealed scriptures.

To accommodate these two versions of the light is the task of the intellectual mystic. Abhinavagupta at once seeks to melt the frozen light of the scriptures such that they reveal their hidden nectar of mystical meanings. And at the same time, he seeks to allow the fluid and pulsating light of living mystical vision to congeal into the complex and diverse "worldview" of Śaivite theological thought that constitutes his intellectual production.

In accord with this program, Abhinavagupta transposes the yogic processes for the digestion and melting of the objective world to the theological and philosophical tasks of digesting and melting the multiplicity of the revealed scriptures into an orderly synthesis of the teaching. In the writings of Abhinavagupta we encounter a complex admixture of the ecstatic, mystical, visionary description—often highly poetic and charged with a kind of white heat of mystical immediacy and intensity—with the more reflective and intellectually constructed transcriptions of this visionary state as confronted in and rationally accommodated to the revealed light of Śiva as filtered through the language of the *āgamas*. These slightly cooler elaborations and arguments of a more intellectual nature are not understood, however, as ultimately foreign or extraneous to that supreme light of consciousness. They are, in effect, the reflections and illuminations that it itself has created of itself. They are its own self-condensations, in which the light is simultaneously self-concealing and self-revealing. There is much more to say on these topics. But for now, we might allow Abhinavagupta to have the last word:

The undivided light which shines in the abodes of the moon, sun, and fire—this is the supreme *bindu*. As is said by the Lord in the *Tattva-rakṣā-vidhāna*, the point or dot [*vindu*] which stands within the circle of the lotus of the Heart is to be known by means of a special absorption as characterized by the triad of man, power, and Śiva. The point is a stainless liberator. This point is a sound whose nature is a vibrating hum [*nāda*], and it is to be found in all living beings.[34]

That light exists completely independently, in itself, from the varieties of gladness and pain, of white or red, and so on. As is said by the master, there is a supreme plane of the splendor of consciousness which neither the sun nor the moon nor the fire is able to illuminate, indeed, without whose light their own capacity to illuminate would not exist. Further, that light which thus illuminates itself is consciousness.[35]

SANSKRIT TEXTS AND TRANSLATIONS

ĪPv — *Īśvara-pratyabhijñā-vimarśinī* of Abhinavagupta. Edited by Mukunda Rāma. Kashmir Series of Texts and Studies, nos. 22, 33. Srinagar: Research Department, Jammu and Kashmir Government, 1918 and 1921.

ĪPvP — *Bhāskarī: The Īśvara Pratyabhijñā Vimarśinī*. Translated by Kanti Chandra Pandey. Princess of Wales Saraswati Bhavana Texts, no. 84. Lucknow: Superintendent, Printing and Stationery, 1954.

MVv — *Mālinīvijaya-vārtika* of Abhinavagupta. Edited by Madhusūdan Kaul. Kashmir Series of Texts and Studies, no. 31. Srinagar: Research Department, Jammu and Kashmir Government, 1921.

PHṛ — *Pratyabhijñāhṛdayam* of Kṣemarāja. Edited by Mukunda Rāma. Kashmir Series of Texts and Studies, no. 3. Srinagar: Research Department, Jammu and Kashmir Government, 1918.

PHṛS — *The Doctrine of Recognition*. Edited and translated by Jaideva Singh. Albany: State University of New York Press, 1990.

PTlv *Parātrīśikā-laghuvṛtti* of Abhinavagupta. Edited by Jagaddhara Zādoo. Kashmir Series of Texts and Studies, no. 68. Srinagar: Research Department, Jammu and Kashmir Government, 1947.

PTlvG *La Trentina della Suprema.* Translated by Raniero Gnoli. Turin: Boringhieri, 1978.

PTlvP *La "Parātrīśikālaghuvṛitti" de Abhinavagupta.* Translated by Andre Padoux. Publications de l'Institut de Civilisation Indienne, fasc. 38. Paris: Editions E. de Boccard, 1975.

PTv *Parātriṃśikā-vivaraṇa* of Abhinavagupta. Edited by Mukunda Rāma. Kashmir Series of Texts and Studies, no. 18. Srinagar: Research Department, Jammu and Kashmir Government, 1918.

PTvS *A Trident of Wisdom.* Translated by Jaideva Singh. Albany: State University of New York Press, 1989.

PTvG *Il Commento di Abhinavagupta alla Parātriṃśikā.* Translated by Raniero Gnoli. Roma: Instituto Italiano per il Medio ed Estremo Oriente, 1985.

SpK *The Spanda Kārikā.* With the *Vivṛti* of Rāmakanta. Kashmir Series of Texts and Studies, no. 6. Srinagar: Research Department, Jammu and Kashmir Government, 1913.

SpKS *The Yoga of Vibration and Divine Pulsation: A Translation of the Spanda Kārikās with Kṣemarāja's Commentary, the Spanda Nirṇaya.* Edited and translated by Jaideva Singh. Albany: State University of New York Press, 1992.

SpKD *The Stanzas on Vibration.* Edited and translated by Mark Dyczkowski. Albany: State University of New York Press, 1992.

ŚS *Śiva Sūtras, The Yoga of Supreme Identity.* Edited and translated by Jaideva Singh. Delhi: Motilal Banarsidass, 1979.

ŚSD *The Aphorisms of Śiva: The Śivasūtra with Bhāṣkara's Commentary, the Vārttika.* Edited and translated by Mark Dyczkowski. Albany: State University of New York Press, 1992.

STTS *The Shath Trimshat Tattva Sandoha.* With the commentary by Ānanda. Edited by Mukunda Rāma. Kashmir Series of Texts and Studies, no. 3. Srinagar: Research Department, Jammu and Kashmir Government, 1918.

TĀ *Tantrāloka* of Abhinavagupta. Edited by Mukunda Rāma and Madhusūdan Kaul. Kashmir Series of Texts and Studies, nos. 23, 28, 30, 35, 36, 29, 41, 47, 59, 52, 57, 58. Srinagar: Research Department, Jammu and Kashmir Government, 1918–1938.

TĀG *Luce Delle Sacre Scritture.* Translated by Raniero Gnoli. Turin: Unione Tipografico-Editrice Torinese, 1972.

TS *Tantrasāra* of Abhinavagupta. Edited by Mukunda Rāma. Kashmir Series of Texts and Studies, no. 17. Srinagar: Research Department, Jammu and Kashmir Government, 1918.

TSG *Essenza dei Tantra.* Translated by Raniero Gnoli. Turin: Boringhieri, 1960.

VBhT *The Vijñāna-Bhairava.* With commentaries by Kṣemarāja and Shivopadhyāya. Edited by Mukunda Rāma. Kashmir Series of Texts and Studies, no. 8. Srinagar: Research Department, Jammu and Kashmir Government, 1918.

VBhTS *The Yoga of Delight, Wonder, and Astonishment: A Translation of the Vijñānabhairava.* Edited and translated by Jaideva Singh. Albany: State University of New York Press, 1991.

NOTES

1. *PTlv*, introductory verses 1, 3:

> yatra tejasi tejāṃsi tamāṃsi ca tamasyalam
> tejāṃsi ca tamāṃsy etad vande jyotir anuttaram
> sadābhinavaguptaṃ yat purāṇaṃ ca prasiddhimat
> hṛdayaṃ tat parollāsaiḥ svayaṃ sphūrjaty anuttaram

2. See the excellent article by Pierre-Sylvain Filliozat, "Jyotis/Tejas/Prakāśa," in *Kalātattvakośa: A Lexicon of Fundamental Concepts of the Indian Arts* (New Delhi: Indira Gandhi National Centre for the Arts and Motilal Banarsidass Publishers, 1988–96), pp. 249–99.

3. Consider the retelling of this myth in Stella Kramrisch, *The Presence of Śiva* (Princeton, NJ: Princeton University Press, 1981), p. 159:

> The fallen phallus of Rudra, transfigured as cosmic phallic pillar flaming upward from the netherworld into heaven, was the counter player of the light from beyond. The pillar rose in the cosmic night in terrible splendor from immeasurable depths. In the darkness of the flood, it was seen by Brahmā and Viṣṇu. In the total homogeneity of the dissolved universe, Viṣṇu and Brahmā were arguing over their relative supremacy when they were interrupted suddenly by the superluminous glow of a strange pillar of fire. Joined by Brahmā, Viṣṇu sped toward the indescribable light, which grew before their eyes into infinity, rending heaven and earth. Overwhelmed and terrified by their unfathomable vision, the two gods sought the beginning and end of its burning immensity. Brahmā, flying upward with the wings of his bird shape—the wild gander—could not see its top, nor could Viṣṇu, diving down for a thousand years in his shape of a boar, see the bottom of that fire *liṅga*, of him who is the light and destruction of the universe. Both of the bewildered gods returned exhausted to the level they had started from, and within the flaming *liṅga* they behold Śiva in golden glory. He illumined the dark flood, and the two gods, Viṣṇu and Brahmā, bowed before him. Thunderous laughter, or the sound *AUṂ*, issued from the pillar, filled the sky, and Śiva dispelled their fear.

4. See *ŚSD*, p. 6, for the comments of Mark Dyczkowski about the emphasis on the notion of light in Bhāskara's *Vārttika* on the *Śiva-sūtras*, as one instance of the exegeti-

cal and commentarial "discovery" of the notion of light in the early, revealed scriptures of the nondual Śaivism of Kashmir.

5. For more details, see Alexis Sanderson, "Śaivism and the Tantric Traditions," in *The World's Religions,* ed. Stewart Sutherland, Leslie Houlden, Peter Clarke, and Friedhelm Hardy (London: Routledge, 1988), pp. 692ff.

6. First of all, the term Kashmir Śaivism seems to imply that there was a single tradition of Śaivism in Kashmir, whereas it is now well known that there were several varieties, which were deeply divided both doctrinally and ritually. There were various forms of nondualistic Tantric Śaivism represented by a series of related preceptorial lineages: the Trika, Pratyabhijñā, Kaula, Krama, and Mata, which were by no means identical in practice or doctrine. In addition, there were also powerful lineages of a conservative, dualistic Śaiva Siddhānta in Kashmir, as well as the more centrally located cult of the worship of the deity Svacchanda-bhairava, a form of Śiva. Of these, it is the first, by no means homogeneous, group that seems to have been generally and imprecisely referred to as Kashmir Śaivism. Moreover, it is by no means clear that the teaching of Śaivism as propounded in any of these groups originated wholly or exclusively in Kashmir.

7. Abhinavagupta is usually counted as the most illustrious representative of the tradition which includes Vasugupta (ca. ninth century), transmitter of the foundational text known as the *Śiva Sūtras* (The Concise Aphorisms of Śiva) (*ŚS*); his disciple Kallaṭa, to whom are usually attributed the important *Spanda Kārikās* (The Aphorisms on Vibration) (*SpK*) ; Somānanda (also ninth century), author of the influential text known as the *Śiva-dṛṣṭi* (The Viewpoint of Śiva); and his disciple Utpalācārya, author of what has come to be recognized as the foundational text for the philosophical explication of the tradition, the *Īśvara-pratyabhijñā-kārikā*-s (Aphorisms on the Recognition of the Lord).

In addition to these important intellectual forebears, the tradition which Abhinavagupta inherits, and comes eventually to synthesize, includes powerful influences from a number of celebrated āgamic texts. Of these, the *Mālinī-vijayottara-tantra* is usually considered the most authoritative. Abhinavagupta studied these āgamic texts with his Kaula master, Śambhunātha, and he dedicates a large portion of his writings to an explication of the then developing Śaivite Hindu Tantra, including the lineage of the Kaulas.

Abhinavagupta was a prolific writer, and some forty-four works are attributed to him. In his *Parātrīśikā-laghuvṛtti* (*PTlv*) (roughly, The Short Gloss on the Supreme, the Queen of the Three) he presents his most concise statement on the nature of the Tantric *sādhanā,* or path. This important text may be grouped with four other texts in which Abhinavagupta explores and elaborates this Tantric environment. These are his encyclopedia of the Tantra entitled *Tantrāloka* (Light on the Tantras) (*TĀ*); a short summary of the *Tantrāloka,* known as the *Tantrasāra* (The Essence of the Tantra); a long text, the *Parātriṃśikā-vivaraṇa* (The Long Commentary on the Supreme, the Queen of the Three) (*PTv*), which comments on the same āgamic verses commented on in the *PTlv;* and the *Mālinī-vijaya-vārtika* (*MVv*), his surviving and partial expository comment on the *Mālinī-vijayottara-tantra.*

8. Nevertheless, it should be emphasized that the wider, historical placement of the nondual Śaivism of Kashmir is no easy matter to accomplish. It remains a tradition whose historical lineaments are complex and still ambiguous. What is known is that the Trika-Kaula of Abhinavagupta inherits and reshapes the teachings of a series of multiply intersecting, initiatory lineages.

9. For an overall consideration of the Hindu Tantra good sources include Teun Goudriaan and Sanjukta Gupta, *Hindu Tantric and Śākta Literature,* vol. 2, fasc. 2, of *A History of Indian Literature,* ed. Jan Gonda (Wiesbaden: Otto Harrassowitz, 1981); and Sanjukta Gupta, Dirk Jan Hoens, and Teun Goudriaan, *Hindu Tantrism* (Leiden: E. J. Brill, 1979).

10. See the list of Sanskrit texts and translations given above for full publication details of most of the important texts herein considered. See Paul Eduardo Muller-Ortega, *The Triadic Heart of Śiva* (Albany: State University of New York Press, 1989), for a longer exposition of the nature of this body of writings as well as references to the various scholars who have contributed to the "excavation" of this tradition. A dated but still useful early study is Kanti Chandra Pandey, *Abhinavagupta: An Historical and Philosophical Study,* Chowkhamba Sanskrit Studies, vol. 1 (Varanasi: Chowkhamba Sanskrit Series Office, 1963). An important and definitive study is André Padoux, *Recherches sur la Symbolique et l'Energie de la Parole,* 2nd ed., Publications de l'Institut de Civilisation Indienne, fasc. 21 (Paris: Editions E. de Boccard, 1975). One of the most prolific scholars in this field was Lilian Silburn. See, for example, her translation and study of the *Śivasūtra et Vimarśinī de Kṣemarāja,* Institut de Civilisation Indienne, fasc. 47 (Paris: Diffusion E. de Boccard, 1980), or her important study entitled *Kuṇḍalinī, the Energy of the Depths* (Albany: State University of New York Press, 1988).

11. See, for example, the discussion in *ĪPv* 4, 1, 1–5.

12. Historically, this posture is interesting because, as my colleague Douglas Brooks has insightfully demonstrated, it is precisely in the lineages of the Śāktas that versions of the elegant and complex ideology confected by the Kashmiri nondual Śaivites have survived to this day. See Douglas Renfrew Brooks, *The Secret of the Three Cities: An Introduction to Hindu Śākta Tantrism* (Chicago: University of Chicago Press, 1990).

13. In terms of "placement" of this tradition, there remain manifold interesting but vexing historical and philosophical questions about the relationship of the nondual Śaivism of Kashmir to other philosophical and religious traditions in India. For example, it is clear that the nondual Śaivism of Kashmir is aware of forms of Vedānta and has some disagreements and critiques of them. As well, there are important problems to be studied with regard to the forms of Buddhism which were powerfully operative in Kashmir at this time. Nevertheless—and without underestimating the intricacy and importance of these and other historical relationships in the formation of the contours of the nondual Śaivism of Kashmir—the autonomy and even self-sufficient creativity of the nondual Śaivism of Kashmir must also be emphasized.

14. See, on this, Alexis Sanderson, "The Doctrines of the Mālinīvijayottaratantra," in *Ritual and Speculation in Early Tantrism: Studies in Honor of Andre Padoux,* ed. Teun Goudriaan (Albany: State University of New York Press, 1992).

15. I am grateful to the brilliant insights of David Gordon White, particularly in his recent *Kiss of the Yogini: Tantric Sex in Its South Asian Contexts* (Chicago: University of Chicago Press, 2003), for this particular perspective on the use of the terms "Tantra" and "Tantrism." Of course, in a broader sense, all of Abhinava's writing falls within what might be called the "high" Hindu Tantra.

16. I would hasten to comment that these quite obviously etic adaptations of emic categories greatly transgress against the usually accepted ways these categories might emically be employed by the various Tantric traditions themselves. Thus, the notion of *tantra-darśana* might simply be viewed emically as a general name for Tantra or, indeed, Tantrism.

17. It is important to add that these three domains are here deployed strictly for the purpose of locating the context for Abhinavagupta's Tantric argument about the light within the confines of what we are calling the nondual Śaivism of Kashmir. There is clearly much more to this tradition and to the wider ambit of the Hindu Tantra than is encompassed within these three domains of Tantric philosophy and theology.

18. Thus, large sections of his *ĪPv* 1.5.1–18 are given over to an analysis of the meanings of *prakāśa*.

19. If I read him correctly, such appears to be the view of David Lawrence in his splendid book *Rediscovering God with Transcendental Argument* (Albany: State University of New York Press, 2000).

20. *TS*, chap. 1:

tatra iha svabhāva eva paramopādeyaḥ, sa ca sarvabhāvānāṃ prakāśarūpa eva aprakāśasya svabhāvatānupapatteḥ, sa ca nānekaḥ prakāśasya taditarasvabhāvānupraveśāyoge svabhāvabhedābhāvāt; deśakālāv api ca asya na bhedakau, tayor api tatprakāśasvabhāvatvāt, iti eka eva prakāśaḥ, sa eva ca saṃvit, arthaprakāśarūpā hi saṃvit iti sarveṣām atra avivāda eva | sa ca prakāśo na paratantraḥ, prakāśyataiva hi pāratantryam, prakāśyatā ca prakāśāntarāpekṣitaiva, na ca prakāśāntaraṃ kiṃcit asti iti svatantra ekaḥ prakāśaḥ, svātantryād eva ca deśakālākārāvacchedavirahāt vyāpako nityaḥ sarvākāranirākārasvabhāvaḥ, tasya ca svātantryam ānandaśaktiḥ, taccamatkāra icchāsaktiḥ, prakāśārūpatā cicchaktiḥ, āmarśātmakatā jñānaśāktiḥ, sarvākārayogitvaṃ kriyāśaktiḥ ityevaṃ mukhyābhiḥ śaktibhiḥ yukto 'pi vastuta icchājñānakriyāśaktiyuktaḥ anavacchinnaḥ prakāśo nijānandaviśrāntaḥ śivarūpaḥ, sa eva svātantryāt ātmānaṃ saṃkucitam avabhāsayan aṇuriti ucyate | punarapi ca svātmānaṃ svatantratayā prakāśayati, yena anavacchinnaprakāśaśivarūpatayaiva prakāśate |

21. See Muller-Ortega, *The Triadic Heart of Śiva,* chap. 9.

22. *TĀ* 1.52–61a (selectively):

1.52: jñeyasya hi paraṃ tattvaṃ yaḥ prakāśātmakaḥ śivaḥ
na hy aprakāśarūpasya prākāśyaṃ vastutāpi vā
1.54: prakāśo nāma yaś cāyaṃ sarvatraiva prakāśate

anapahnavanīyatvāt kiṃ tasmin mānakalpanaiḥ
1.59: kāmike tata evoktaṃ hetuvādavivarjitam
tasya devātidevasya parāpekṣā na vidyate
1.60: parasya tadapekṣatvāt svatantro 'yamataḥ sthitaḥ
anapekṣasya vaśino deṣakālākṛtikramāḥ
1.61: niyatā neti sa vibhur nityo viśvākṛtiḥ śivaḥ
vibhutvāt sarvago nityabhāvād ādyantavarjitaḥ
1.62: viśvākṛtitvāc cidacittadvaicitryāvabhāsakaḥ

23. *TĀ* 2.10:

saṃvittattvaṃ svaprakāśam ity asmin kiṃ nu yuktibhiḥ
tadabhāve bhaved viśvaṃ jaḍatvād aprakāśakam

24. *PTv*, p. 90:

prathamata eva tathā vimarśajīvitaprakāśamayatvam eva sattvaṃ, tat ca svātantryavimarśasārāhaṃbhāvabharitam iti bhairavarūpam eva.

25. *PTv*, p. 133:

tena—jala iva jalaṃ jvālāyām iva jvālā sarvathā abhedamayā eva bhāvā bhāsante, na tu pratibimbakalpenāpi kevalaṃ.

26. *MVv* 1, 620b-626a:

prakāśa eka evāyaṃ yaś cirān na vibhidyate
ata eva hi bhedo 'sti na kaścid yo maheśvaram
advayaṃ saṃprabhindīta prakāśānandasundaram
deśakālākṛtijñānadharmopādhyantarādayaḥ
sāṃmatā bhedakatvena bhānti cet sā vibhā tathā
na ced vibhaiva sā tādṛk tad advaitam idaṃ sphuṭaṃ
bheda ity eṣa śabdas tu kevalam pratibhojjhitaḥ
astu vā bhedakalanā pratibhāsaṃprarohiṇī
uktanītyā tu tatraiva sapratiṣṭhā bhaviṣyati
ayaṃ ghaṭaḥ paṭaś cāyaṃ tāv anyonyavibhedinau
pramātrantarabhinnau ca tau matto 'pi vibhedinau
iti prakāśa eko 'yaṃ tathāmarśasvarūpakaḥ

27. *PTv*, pp. 142–43, comment on verses 5–8:

akālakalite saṃvidātmani satataviśvaśaktyaviyukte svātantryavaśasaṃkocavikāsāvabhāsitasaṃhṛtisṛṣṭiśatāviruddhaikarūpatadātmakavapuṣi parameśvare 'smajjihvāgrahṛdayānapāyini bhairavabhaṭṭārake sarvamasti. . . . tasmāt śivatattvamidam anādyantaṃ svayam prathamānaṃ pūrṇatātmakanirapekṣatāmātrasatattvasvātantryasāram antaḥkroḍīkṛtyātmataikaparamārthaṃ

28. *TĀ* 3.120–25a:

prakāśamātraṃ suvyaktaṃ sūrya ityucyate sphuṭam
prakāśyavastusārāṃśavarṣi tat soma ucyate
sūryaṃ pramāṇam ity āhuḥ somaṃ meyaṃ pracakṣate
anyonyam aviyuktau tau svatantryāvapy ubhau sthitau
bhoktṛbhogyobhayātmaitad anyonyonmukhatāṃ gatam
tato jvalanacidrūpaṃ citrabhānuḥ prakīrtitaḥ
yo 'yaṃ vahneḥ paraṃ tattvaṃ pramātur idam eva tat
saṃvid eva tu vijñeya tādātmyād anapekṣiṇī
svatantratvāt pramātoktā vicitro jñeyabhedataḥ
somāṃśadāhyavastūtthavaicitryābhāsabṛṃhitaḥ
tata evāgnir ūditaś citrabhānur maheśinā
jñeyādyupāyasaṃghātanirapekṣaiva saṃvidaḥ

29. *TĀ* 3.261–64:

alaṃgrāsarasākhyena satataṃ jvalanātmanā
haṭhapākapraśamanaṃ yat tṛtīyam tad eva ca
upadeśāya yujyeta bhedendhanavidāhakam
nijabodhajaṭharahutabhuji bhāvāḥ sarve samarpitā haṭhataḥ
vijahati bhedavibhāgaṃ nijaśaktyā taṃ samindhānāḥ
haṭhapākena bhāvānāṃ rūpe bhinne vilāpite
aśnantyamṛtasādbhūtaṃ viśvaṃ saṃvittidevatāḥ
tās tṛptāḥ svātmanaḥ pūrṇaṃ hṛdayaikāntaśayinam
cidvyomabhairavaṃ devam abhedenādhiśerate

30. *TĀ* 2.35.
31. *TĀ* 2.34–36:

iti ye rūḍhasaṃvittiparamārthapavitritāḥ
anuttarapathe rūḍhās te 'bhyupāyāniyantritāḥ
teṣām idaṃ samābhāti sarvato bhāvamaṇḍalam
puraḥstham eva saṃvittibhairavāgnivilāpitam
eteṣāṃ sukhaduḥkhāṃśaśaṃkātaṃkavikalpanāḥ
nirvikalpaparāveśamātraśeṣatvam āgatāḥ

32. *TĀ* 5.19b–25a:

tatra dhyānam ayaṃ tāvad anuttaram ihocyate
yaḥ prakāśaḥ svatantro 'yam cittasvabhāvo hṛdi sthitaḥ
sarvatattvamayaḥ proktam etac ca triśiromate
kadaṃlīsaṃpuṭākāraṃ saṃbāhyābhyantarāntaram
īkṣate hṛdayāntaḥsthaṃ tatpuṣpam iva tattvavit
somasūryāgnisaṃghaṭṭaṃ tatra dhyāyed ananyadhīḥ

taddhyānāraṇisaṃkṣobhān mahābhairavahavyabhuk
hṛdayākhye mahākuṇḍe jājvalan sphītatāṃ vrajet
tasya śaktimataḥ sphītaśakter bhairavatejasaḥ
mātṛmānaprameyākhyaṃ dhāmābhedena bhāvayet
vahnyarkasomaśaktīnāṃ tad eva tritiyaṃ bhavet
parā parāparā ceyam aparā ca sadoditā

33. *TĀ* 5.27b–36:

etad anuttaram cakraṃ hṛdayāc cakṣurādibhiḥ
vyomabhir niḥsaraty eva tattadviṣayagocare
taccakrabhābhis tatrārthe sṛṣṭisthitilayakramāt
somasūryāgnibhāsātma rūpaṃ samavatiṣṭhate
evaṃ śabdādiviṣaye śrotrādivyomavartmanā
cakreṇānena patatā tādātmyaṃ paribhāvayet
anena kramayogena yatra yatra pataty adaḥ
cakraṃ sarvātmakaṃ tat tat sārvabhaumamahīśavat
itthaṃ viśvādhvapaṭalam ayatnenaiva līyate
bhairavīyamahācakre saṃvittiparivārite
tataḥ saṃskāramātreṇa viśvasyāpi parikṣaye
svātmocchalattayā bhrāmyac cakraṃ saṃcintayen mahat
tatas tad dāhyavilayāt tat saṃskāraparikṣayāt
praśāmyad bhāvayec cakraṃ tataḥ śāntaṃ tataḥ śamam
anena dhyānayogena viśvaṃ cakre vilīyate
tatsaṃvidi tataḥ saṃvid vilīnārthaiva bhāsate
citsvabhāvyāt tato bhūyaḥ sṛṣṭir yac cinmaheśvarī
evaṃ pratikṣaṇam viśvaṃ svasaṃvidi vilāpayat
visṛjaṃś ca tato bhūyaḥ śaśvad bhairavatām vrajet

34. *TĀ* 3.111b–113a:

avibhāgaḥ prakāśo yaḥ sa binduḥ paramo hi naḥ
tattvarakṣāvidhāne ca taduktaṃ parameśinā
hṛtpadmamaṇḍalāntaḥstho naraśaktiśivātmakaḥ
boddhavyo layabhedena vindur vimalatārakaḥ
yo sau nādātmakaḥ śabdaḥ sarvaprāṇiṣv avasthitaḥ

35. *TĀ* 3.114b–116:

hlādataikṣyādi vaicitryaṃ sitaraktādikaṃ ca yat
svayaṃ tannirapekṣo 'sau prakāśo gurur āha ca
yan na sūryo na vā somo nāgnir bhāsayate 'pi ca
na cārkasomavahnīnāṃ tatprakāśād vinā mahaḥ
kim apy asti nijaṃ kiṃ tu saṃvid itthaṃ prakāśate

PART TWO

Transformative Visions and Their Vicissitudes

The existence of mystical states absolutely overthrows the pretension of nonmystical states to be the sole and ultimate dictators of what we may believe.

William James, *The Varieties of Religious Experience*

The contributions in part 1 emphasized some of the ways in which light has been conceived as instantiating and disclosing the presence of the divine but were not solely concerned with matters of religious ontology; they referred, too, to the ascent and divinization of the adept upon whom the vision of the divine light is bestowed. It is this theme, the role of light in the mystic's progression to the culmination of his or her path, that now becomes our prime point of focus. For the encounter with the divine through the medium of light is seldom a chance occurrence passively received. Regardless of its precise form, it most often takes place in the context of active spiritual (i.e., ritual or contemplative) practice within established traditions, which contribute to the formation of (some would say constitute) the experience and its interpretation. The experience, moreover, may be thought to catalyze or to provide evidence of a remarkable transformation in the very being of the practitioner.

Assumptions such as these were very widely diffused in late antique and medieval Orthodox Christianity. As Andrew Louth tells us in "Light, Vision, and Religious Experience in Byzantium,"

Through[out] the tradition of Byzantine monastic spirituality, there is to be found the idea that a significant stage is reached in the progress of the intellect (*nous* in Greek) to knowledge of God and union with him, when the intellect becomes aware of its own light. This experience, if it is genuine and not a hallucination, is a sign that the intellect has attained the state that Evagrios calls *apatheia*, a state of transcendence over disturbing thoughts and feelings. . . . But beyond this awareness of its own light . . . there lies the encounter with God himself, which much of the tradition of Byzantine monasticism, and especially that of Byzantine hesychasm, regards as an experience of the uncreated light of the Godhead.

The apparently straightforward picture sketched out here, however, became deeply problematic for Byzantine theology, and Louth's investigations turn not so much on the manner in which experiences of light were characterized by Orthodox theologians as on the ways in which they came to be theologically contested: were such experiences authentic or were they deceptive? if authentic, just what then did they reveal of "the reality of encounter and communion between the uncreated God and created humanity"? As Louth underscores for us, although mystical experiences of one kind or another may constitute an important category for some religious traditions, this is not a category that floats apart from, or is privileged above, the constructive intellectual and devotional practices that inform those same traditions. Thus, for Theophanes of Nicaea, "What at first sight seems to be an exceptional experience—beholding the light of Tabor in prayer—is *identified* with the most normal liturgical action of the life of any Orthodox Christian, the reception of Holy Communion."

In "Hermeneutics of Light in Medieval Kabbalah," Elliot Wolfson examines the transformation of the mystic in relation to the phenomenology of light as disclosed in two of the masterworks of medieval kabbalah, the *Book of Illumination* (*Sefer ha-Bahir*), and the *Book of Splendor* (*Sefer ha-Zohar*). Like Andrew Louth, Wolfson insists that we must recognize the impossibility of disentangling experience from interpretation in the framework of the textual traditions he is considering:

Behind the multifaceted symbols and interpretations of biblical verses found in the *Zohar* is a fraternity of mystics ecstatically transformed by contemplation of the divine light refracted in nature, the soul, and the Torah. There is indeed genuine ecstatic experience underlying the hermeneutical posture of the *Zohar*. For the zoharic authorship, therefore, there is a basic convergence of the interpretative and revelatory modes; the act of scriptural interpretation is itself an occasion for contemplative study and mystical meditation.

We may hold, then, that for the traditions of medieval kabbalah, the study of the Torah was in itself a modality of engagement in the divine light. As we have seen in the case of Orthodox Christianity, the distinction between exceptional experience and the "most normal" expression of one's religious life is undone, or, as we may perhaps put it here, it dissolves in the light.

In the concluding chapter of part 2, "The Strange Death of Pema the Demon Tamer," the present writer investigates Tibetan Buddhist traditions concerning the attainment of the "rainbow body" (*'ja'-lus*) at death, whereby the adept physically melts into light, merging matter with spirit and in this way demonstrating his or her ascent to the zenith of realization. Nevertheless, though Tibetan religious writers almost universally acknowledged the truth of the reports of at least some such events, they were by no means unanimous in their assessment of the religious significance of them. Contestation over such matters within traditions requires that we carefully qualify our assumptions regarding cultural context:

> We have become accustomed in recent years to speaking of experiences as culturally constructed or, better, as mediated by the constructions of language and culture. Nothing that I have presented here would refute that view. But we should be wary, lest we come to speak of cultural constructions themselves as the rigid repetitions of culturally specific paradigms. What is constructed can at best be described as a malleable field, in which received tradition and the lived experiences of individuals enter into dialogue and through their dialogue form and reform one another. Thus, to interpret references to particular types of religious experiences, in this case experiences relating to light and saintly death, even within a well-specified tradition, in this case Tibetan esoteric Buddhism, we must remain context sensitive, just as we must when comparing entirely different traditions.

As the experience of light became a contested category in the Byzantine sources studied by Andrew Louth, so too the achievement of the rainbow body in Tibetan Buddhist thought. Thus, despite the transformative properties attributed to the experience of divine light, experience alone is not presumed by these traditions to be self-validating; it must be subject to sustained scrutiny and ongoing debate.

CHAPTER FOUR

Light, Vision, and Religious Experience in Byzantium

Andrew Louth

This chapter is principally concerned with the experience of the divine, uncreated light in monastic writers belonging to the hesychast tradition (a term I shall explain in a moment); this is, I think, natural, for it is this tradition that dominates our perception of the Christian Byzantine tradition, whether one is looking at the historical era of the Byzantine world, brought to an abrupt conclusion in 1453 with the sack of Constantinople by the Ottomans, or is concerned with the increasingly significant presence of the Byzantine Orthodox tradition (including the Slav Orthodox tradition, but in distinction from the Oriental Orthodox tradition, of the Syrians and Copts, for instance) in today's world, a result of both the fall of the iron curtain and emigration from traditionally Orthodox countries over the past two centuries. But the question of light and religious experience is a wider one than what we might call the "light mysticism" of the hesychasts, and I want to start by indicating something of that.

We can begin with quite ordinary light, whether the light of the sun or that created by candles and (traditionally) oil lamps, and their place in the quite ordinary experience of Byzantine worship. Perhaps the oldest hymn in Christian Greek, which can be traced back to the third century and is possibly even older, is addressed to the "joyful light" of the glory of the Trinity, symbolized by the lighting of the evening lamp at sunset. It is sung to this day at the evening service of vespers, celebrated at sunset (and in monasteries still, clocks are set by the setting of the sun): as the sun sets, and with it the light of the world, the evening lamps symbolize the eternal light of the Godhead (the "light that knows no evening," as it is sometimes put), which is celebrated in the hymns and psalms of vespers. This use of light, both artificial and natural, was highly developed in the Byzantine world (and is still maintained in the Orthodox Church today). Churches are orientated, that is, they face east, which is the direction Orthodox Christians face when they pray (even privately). It is from the east that the sun rises, and churches are orientated not to some geographical east, but to the point on the horizon at which the sun rises on the feast day of the dedication of the church (this was also the case in the West until the end of the Middle Ages, save in cases where local geography made it impossible). It is therefore north of east if the feast day of dedication (of a saint, or of a mystery such as the Trinity or the Nativity of Christ) is in high summer, south of east if it is in the depths of winter. It has recently been shown by I. Potamianos with what care the orientation of the church was calibrated in medieval times, and further, how in the domed churches characteristic of the Middle and Late Byzantine periods, the sills of the windows around the base of the dome were polished and fixed at such an angle that the horizontal rays of the rising sun were directed up on to the icon of Christ Pantocrator that looked down from the top of the dome, with the result that in the darkness of the church the icon of Christ would seem to hover in the reflected light of the rising sun.[1] At vespers on the preceding evening, the light from the west would shine through the open door of the church directly on to the door of the icon screen, or iconostasis (which separates the sanctuary from the nave), so that at the "little entrance" at vespers, just before the singing of "Joyful Light," the Gospel Book, carried in the procession, would enter the shaft of light as the priest turned to enter the sanctuary through the holy doors of the iconostasis. Such care in the use of natural light demonstrates the importance attached to the symbolic significance of light in Byzantine worship: light, symbolic of God, and more precisely of Christ as the "Sun of righteousness" (Mal. 4:2), coming into the world in his Nativity and rising over the world in his Resurrection.

But light also features in Byzantine religious experience as characterizing the illumination of God's revelation. Claims about the reality of such an encounter with the uncreated light of the Godhead lie at the heart of hesychast spirituality. But there is another encounter with light in religious experience that needs to be mentioned before we come to the question of the encounter with the divine light of God himself. Beginning with Evagrios, the fourth-century theorist of the monasticism of the Egyptian desert, and continuing constantly through the tradition of Byzantine monastic spirituality, there is to be found the idea that a significant stage is reached in the progress of the intellect (*nous* in Greek) to knowledge of God and union with him when the intellect becomes aware of its own light. This experience, if it is genuine and not a hallucination, is a sign that the intellect has attained the state that Evagrios calls *apatheia*, a state of transcendence over disturbing thoughts and feelings: "This

FIGURE 4.1. Morning light in Hagia Sophia, Constantinople. (Dumbarton Oaks, Byzantine Fieldwork Archives, Washington, DC.)

is a proof of *apatheia*, when the intellect begins to see its own light, and remains calm during the visions of sleep, and can look at things with serenity."[2] But beyond this awareness of its own light, which I think means something like an awareness of its own powers of contemplation, there lies the encounter with God himself, which much of the tradition of Byzantine monasticism, and especially that of Byzantine hesychasm, regards as an experience of the uncreated light of the Godhead himself, to which we shall now turn.

BYZANTINE HESYCHASM

Claims to such an experience on behalf of the monks of Mount Athos, the peninsula in Northern Greece that since the tenth century has been the greatest centre of Orthodox monasticism, became a matter of controversy in the fourteenth century, and the echoes of that controversy are still palpable in Orthodox theological circles. Synods in Constantinople upheld the hesychast claim to be able to see the uncreated light of the Godhead and endorsed the theological rationale for this, presented by Saint Gregory Palamas, with his distinction between the essence and energies of God, according to which God is unknowable in his essence but genuinely knowable in his energies, in which God is himself known and not merely something about God. Preeminent among these divine energies is the uncreated light of the Godhead, the light in which Christ was transfigured before his disciples on Mount Tabor, for which reason the uncreated light came to be called the light of Tabor, or the "Taboric light." This hesychast understanding of the whole Byzantine tradition was reasserted in the modern period in influential form in the *Philokalia*, compiled by Saint Nikodimos of Hagiorite and Saint Makarios of Corinth and published in Venice in 1782. The *Philokalia*, soon translated into Slavonic and then into Russian, has had an enormous impact on modern Orthodoxy: virtually all the great names of twentieth-century Orthodox theology—Lossky, Florovsky, Meyendorff, Greeks such as Nellas and Mantzaridis and even Yannaras, the Romanian Stăniloae, and such representatives of monastic theology as Archimandrite Sophrony of Essex and Bishop Hierotheos Vlachos—can be regarded as standing in a "Philokalic" or "Neo-Palamite" tradition. This tradition of "Byzantine mysticism" is then a living tradition, which only makes it the more difficult to approach it in a critical, scholarly way. Most scholarly work on Byzantine mysticism that has been done in the past hundred years, including the edition of texts, has been done from within this tradition, with the result that the perspective represented by the *Philokalia* has been taken for granted. The few attempts to stand outside this tradition—from the work of the learned Jesuit orientalist Irénée Hausherr to most recently the work on Symeon the New Theologian by the Orthodox priest John McGuckin—have been interpreted as being "hostile" to the tradition by those standing inside it.[3]

The *Philokalia* itself can be regarded as signposting the hesychast (or Byzantine) mystical tradition, a tradition starting with Saint Antony the Great (though the text attributed to Saint Antony is spurious), continuing through fourth- and fifth-century monastic authors such as Evagrios, Mark the Hermit, and Diadochos (Makarios of the "Makarian Homilies," but only in the emasculated epitome of Symeon Metaphrastes), later monastic authors associated with Sinai, such as Hesychios and Philotheos, Saint Maximos the Confessor (to whom the largest section is devoted), the mysterious Peter of Damascus (author of a long epitome of monastic teaching), Symeon the New Theologian and his disciple Nicetas Stethatos (Nicetas heavily represented, Symeon surprisingly slightly), and then Saint Gregory Palamas (to whom the next largest section after Saint Maximos is dedicated) and others associated with the hesychast controversy, such as Theoliptos of Philadelphia, Gregory of Sinai, and Kallistos and Ignatios Xanthopouloi. I say "signposting," for the list of authors included in the *Philokalia* is not to be, and has not been, regarded as definitive: both the Russian and the Romanian versions of the *Philokalia* have supplemented Nikodimos and Makarios's original selection with monastic authors such as the Gaza monks Barsanouphios, John, and Dorotheos, John Climacus of Sinai, and Isaac the Syrian. What the *Philokalia* does is to canonize a tradition of hesychast spirituality stretching right back from the hesychast controversy to the fourth century; quite what lies behind this creation of a canon is not clear, though it is very likely that the selection derives from many years, probably centuries, of monastic formation: these are the kinds of works monks were recommended to read by their spiritual fathers, especially in the Athonite tradition (I am not suggesting for a moment that the creation of a hesychast tradition by the *Philokalia* is in any way parallel to the more or less contemporary deliberate confection of the Scottish clans and tartans, as described by Hugh Trevor-Roper).[4] But once seen as part of a tradition, works are read with presuppositions that may be foreign to the spirit in which they were originally written.

If one asks what it is that characterizes this hesychast tradition, one might sum it up by saying that it is a tradition of (originally monastic) prayer based on repetition of the Jesus prayer ("Lord Jesus Christ, Son of God, have mercy on me, a sinner"), under the direction of a spiritual father, which leads to a conscious experience of the presence of God, often in the form of a vision of light. When one reads the *Philokalia* in this tradition, all of this is presupposed. But one element of this, perhaps the most striking and distinctive element, seems to be quite a latecomer to the tradition, save for the odd exception, and that is the use of the Jesus prayer. The nineteenth-century saint Ignaty Brianchaninov, in his book *On the Prayer of Jesus,* takes for granted the antiquity and universality of the practice of the Jesus prayer.[5] The same is true of Father Lev Gillet (writing under the pseudonym "a monk of the Eastern Church") in his book *On the Invocation of the Name of Jesus.*[6] This "tradition" was rather brutally handled by Irénée Hausherr in his *Noms du Christ et voies d'oraison,*[7] and a much more historically sensitive account can be found in the frequently reprinted work by Bishop Kallistos (Ware) of Diokleia, *The Power of the Name: The Jesus Prayer in Orthodox Spirituality.*[8] In contrast, the importance of praying under the guidance of a spiritual father is ancient and continuous (though not always explicit in the works included in the *Philokalia*).

What, however, about the stress on experience, especially the experience of seeing the divine light? In the developed tradition, as we see it in the hesychast controversy, the Transfiguration of Christ is regarded as a kind of archetype of the experience of the hesychast: the uncreated light of the Godhead is called the light of Tabor, the "Taboric light." The question I want to pursue is not the obvious one about the authenticity of such experience, and its antiquity and continuity within the Byzantine tradition, largely because it seems to me that such a question begs so many other questions that I am not sure how one would set about answering it. I am more interested in what is being claimed by appeal to such experience, and also in what I shall call the "construction" of such an experience, for I take it for granted that there are no experiences that are uninterpreted, that experience and interpretation are inextricably bound up with each other. It is clearly not possible to deal with the whole of the Philokalic tradition, and I shall simplify my task by limiting my presentation to three figures: Saint Maximos, Saint Symeon the New Theologian, and Theophanes of Nicaea. But first a word about the inclusion of Symeon. It seems that, so far as the Greek tradition is concerned, he is a comparative newcomer to the tradition.[9] Saint Gregory Palamas knows of him, and appeals to him, but shows scarcely any awareness of any of his writings (he seems more familiar with Nicetas's *vita* of the saint). Even in the *Philokalia* of Saint Nikodimos and Saint Makarios, his presence is slight: of the three works attributed to him, one is inauthentic (a work on the Jesus prayer, of which the authentic Symeon seems unaware), and in the original version, one is present only in a translation into modern Greek (included in an appendix). But in this century, largely as a result of the critical edition of his works begun by Archbishop Basil Krivocheine, and brought to fruition by Jean Darrouzès and Johannes Koder, Symeon has become one of the most popular hesychast authors, and a major resource for what I have called above Neo-Palamism. My three authors each offer something rather different: with Saint Maximos I shall be concerned with his interpretation of the Transfiguration, as it seems likely that he contributes much of the interpretative framework of hesychasm; with Saint Symeon I shall be concerned with his experiences of the divine light, for, with whatever real knowledge of his work, the hesychasts appealed to Symeon as a precursor;[10] with Theophanes of Nicaea we shall look at his "Five Discourses on the Taboric Light," recently edited by Ch. Sotiropoulos.[11]

SAINT MAXIMOS THE CONFESSOR

Saint Maximos discusses the Transfiguration in three places, all in relatively early works of his belonging to the period when he was a monk, first in Asia Minor in the vicinity of Constantinople and then in North Africa—that is, the decade 625–35, before he intervened in the Monothelite controversy and brought upon himself the wrath of the emperor and his arrest, exile and death. Despite some differences, and even apparent contradictions, in these interpretations, there is an impressive consistency, and I shall present a synthetic account, though concentrating mostly on the longest account, that found in the tenth of his "Difficulties," or *Ambigua*. Much of the common ground in Maximos's several interpretations is due to antecedent tradition in interpreting the Transfiguration, a tradition that so far as the Greek East was concerned was largely established by Origen.

The different aspects of the account of the Transfiguration are interpreted as shedding light on the progress of the Christian toward knowledge of God and union with him, something made possible by the Incarnation. He follows Origen in seeing the limitation of the Transfiguration to the "inner three" among the disciples as indicating that God appears in different forms to different people, in accordance with their spiritual aptitude (a principle that informed the Incarnation itself, in which God's self-manifestation in Christ was tailored to the different people he encountered). Only Peter, James, and John, who were closest to Jesus among the disciples, were permitted to see Jesus transfigured. So in his *Centuries on Theology and the Incarnation*, Maximos presents the Mount of the Transfiguration as a symbol of the spiritual life: at its foot the Lord appears in the form of a servant, at its summit in the form of God, "the form in which he existed before the world came to be" (*Centuries* 2.13).[12] In the *Ambigua*, the Transfiguration is also related to the spiritual progress of the disciples: the disciples are presented as having "passed over" from seeing Christ as "without form or beauty" (Isa. 53:2) to seeing him as "fair with beauty beyond the sons of men" (Ps. 44:3). Maximos interprets this as a passing over from understanding Christ primarily as the "Word made flesh" to understanding him as the "One in the beginning, with God, and God"—a passage from the end of the Johannine prologue to its beginning, so to speak. He calls this "passing over" from the "Word made flesh" to the "Word, in the beginning, with God" a movement of *apophasis,* negation or denial, and this *apophasis,* he says, the disciples have learned from—or perhaps better: experienced in beholding—the blinding radiance of the face of the Transfigured Lord.

Here we encounter something quite original in Maximos's interpretation of the Transfiguration. According to the Gospel accounts, Christ's face shone like the sun (so Matthew; "was altered" is how Luke puts it), and his garments became radiantly white. In his first interpretation of the Transfiguration, in his *Quaestiones et Dubia,* Maximos had commented on the radiant face of Christ, playing on the ambiguity in the Greek word for face, *prosopon,* which can also mean "person": "the face of the Word, that shone like the sun, is," Maximos says, "the characteristic hiddenness of his being."[13] What Maximos means is that the radiant face of Christ reveals the divine person that he is. The Council of Chalcedon in 451 had endorsed a definition according to which, in the Incarnate Christ, there are two natures—the divine and the human—united in a single person. The fifth Ecumenical Council (of Constantinople, in 553) clarified this by affirming that that one person is divine, "one of the Trinity." In a way typical of Maximos, the precise words he uses allude to the exact distinctions of the Christology of the Councils. But there is more; for if on the Mount of the Transfiguration the blinding radiance of the face/person of the Word reveals the "characteristic hiddenness" of the being of God, then apophatic theology—the theology of denial—is our acknowledgment of the divinity of Christ, for God is beyond any conception or image that we could have of him, so to acknowledge the divine is to pass beyond cataphatic, or affirmative, language, to the silence of denial. This language of apophatic and cataphatic theology was introduced into Byzantine theology by Dionysios the Areopagite, but the use to which it is put is Maximos's own. For Dionysios, apophatic and cataphatic theologies spelled out the dialectic involved in our predicating attributes or names of God: the dialectic of affirmation and denial steered a way between the twin errors of anthropomorphism and agnosticism in our attempt to say something about God. But for Maximos the terminology of apophatic and cataphatic theology seems to be bound up with our confession of the union of divine and human natures in the single divine person of the Incarnate Word: acknowledgment of the divine radiance of the face of Christ draws us into apophatic theology, for the dazzling radiance of the face of Christ is beyond affirmation and can only be regarded in silent—apophatic—wonder. Every time Maximos interprets the Transfiguration, he employs in this Christological way Dionysios's distinction between apophatic and cataphatic theology.

FIGURE 4.2. *The Transfiguration,* icon by Theophanes the Greek, Tretyakov Gallery, Moscow. Originally in the Cathedral of the Transfiguration, Pereslav.

The face became radiant, but Christ's clothes, too, became white. Developing Origen's interpretation, Maximos takes the whitened garment of Christ as referring to the words of Scripture or indeed to Creation itself and is led into a long digression in which he expounds the parallelism of Scripture and cosmos. The cosmos is like a book, and the Bible is like the cosmos: both consist of words, *logoi,* which, though diverse, when read with understanding form a single harmonious whole, the meaning of which is the mind of God himself.

Maximos then proceeds to explore further the two sides of the Transfiguration, symbolized by the two figures who appeared with Jesus, Moses and Elijah.[14] This is done at length, in seventeen meditations. Some of it is traditional—Moses and Elijah symbolizing the law and the prophets, for instance; much of it is arcane and fascinating. Toward the end, we encounter again the contrast between apophatic and cataphatic theology. First, Maximos seems to be following Dionysios. But this is followed by a meditation in which the distinction between apophatic and cataphatic theology is focused on the person of Christ, as we have already seen, the silent wonder of *apophasis* being a response to the dazzling radiance of Christ's face. Here Maximos says that, through accepting a human form, the Word has become a "symbol of himself," in order "through this manifestation of himself to lead to himself in his complete and secret hiddenness the whole creation, and while he remains quite unknown in his hidden, secret place beyond all things, unable to be known or understood by any being in any way whatever, out of his love for humankind he grants to human beings intimations of himself in the manifest divine works performed in the flesh."[15] The next meditation affirms the primacy of apophatic theology in Christological terms: "the light from the face of the Lord, therefore, conquers the human blessedness of the apostles by a hidden apophatic theology."[16] Three meditations then explicitly expound cataphatic theology in terms of the cosmic dimension of the Word made flesh.

What we find in Maximos is an approach to the Transfiguration which discovers there a thoroughly Christocentric theology—a theology that leads to and from the person of Christ and finds in everything illumined by the uncreated light of his radiance the revelation of Christ in nature and in Scripture.

The Transfiguration, as understood by Maximos, is a kind of matrix for the whole of Christian theology. It is also presented as something to be experienced: apophatic theology is a face-to-face encounter with Christ, the Mount of the Transfiguration is where the ascent of the Christian to communion with God takes place. It could be said that in his interpretation of the Transfiguration, Maximos assimilates Mount Tabor to Mount Sinai, which for Dionysios and Gregory of Nyssa, and behind them for Clement of Alexandria and

Philo, as the mountain that Moses ascended, is a figure of the ascent to God to be made by every earnest Christian. But note what kind of experience is envisaged. Maximos is not writing an experiential account; he has nothing to say about what kind of experience is involved in encountering Christ; there is not the slightest hint of anything autobiographical, or even of any account of personal experience at second hand (save for a few rare instances, but even then it is what is revealed by the experience that is the point, not the experience itself).[17]

SAINT SYMEON THE NEW THEOLOGIAN

Symeon the New Theologian (949–1022) is very different from Maximos (of whom Symeon shows no conscious unawareness, to judge from his writings), not least so far as the matter of appeal to personal experience is concerned. But in this respect, as John McGuckin has pointed out, Symeon is exceptional in the whole Byzantine tradition.[18] Assimilating Symeon to the "hesychast tradition," as most scholars who have written on Symeon have tended to do, is, at first sight, odd. He is the great exception, not the traditionalist, and it is not unlikely that it was for this reason that he was so controversial in his own day. The vita by his disciple, Nicetas Stethatos, was clearly an attempt to rehabilitate Symeon when the tide of opinion had turned and his relics were returned to Constantinople thirty years after his death, but to judge by the manuscript tradition this attempt had no lasting success.[19] As an attempt at rehabilitation, Nicetas's vita obscures or even distorts the events of Symeon's life that led to his encountering so much opposition. Most modern scholarship has, however, been inclined to follow Nicetas in its admiration for Symeon and indeed goes beyond Nicetas, in a way that was not open to Nicetas himself, by enrolling Symeon in the ranks of hesychasts. This has led, as McGuckin has demonstrated in the article I have already referred to, to a persistent attempt to interpret Symeon in hesychast terms, and in particular to interpret his visions of light by taking the Transfiguration as the paradigm of such visions. McGuckin has no difficulty in showing that this involves willful misinterpretation of what Symeon says. But, as he points out, the way in which Symeon is misinterpreted is also due to the fact that most scholars who have concerned themselves with Symeon have adopted a crudely "realist" approach to his visions, indeed both to his visions and to the account of the Transfiguration itself. A properly critical approach needs to treat Symeon's visions not simply as straightforward records, but as literary texts composed for a purpose by someone who was certainly not ignorant of the skills of rhetoric. In his article, McGuckin sets out a taxonomy of Symeon's visions, distinguishing first between analogical uses of vision (where the language of vision is used metaphorically, without there necessarily being any reference to an actual visual experience) and "epiphanic" visions, in which Symeon gives accounts of experiences of vision (usually by himself, though following the Apostle Paul in 2 Cor. 12 [sometimes by explicit allusion], this is usually expressed indirectly). In his account of "epiphanic" visions, McGuckin outlines a typology of three biblical paradigms of vision: first, what he calls the "Sinai" paradigm, divine epiphany on a mountain, to which paradigm the Transfiguration belongs; second, the "Pauline" paradigm, to which belong the conversion experience on the Damascus road and the rapture to the third heaven of 2 Cor. 12; third, the "open heaven" paradigm of Stephen's vision in Acts 7. 55. I am not sure that this typology is altogether satisfactory—the second example of the Pauline paradigm and the "open heaven" paradigm, both of which have an apocalyptic context, as McGuckin remarks,[20] perhaps belong together—but let us pass over that for the present. The importance of McGuckin's article is in offering such a typology at all, and using it to analyze Symeon's visions. He shows that for Symeon's visions the *least* appropriate paradigm is that of the Transfiguration; indeed, only once does he find this paradigm at all explicit.[21] It is, in fact, he claims, the Pauline paradigm that is most important for Symeon, and the point of his appeal to visions is to authenticate his claim to authority, an authority derived from his spiritual father, Symeon "Eulabes."[22]

McGuckin concentrates on biblical paradigms partly because he maintains that Symeon's grasp of the theological tradition was in fact rather thin.[23] I am not sure that Symeon was as theologically ignorant as McGuckin makes out; indeed, it seems to me that it is unlikely that he was uninformed about the Byzantine monastic tradition. *Catechesis* 22 contains accounts of both the vision Symeon received when he was a devout layman, under the direction of Symeon, his spiritual father, and the later vision he experienced as a young monk. Here the first vision is described thus:

One day he was standing in this fashion and was saying out loud: "O God be merciful to me a sinner" (more in the spirit than using his mouth), when suddenly there shone on him in great profusion a divine illumination from on high which entirely filled that place. Thereupon the young man was no longer aware of himself. He could not remember whether he was in a house or even under a roof at all. For all around he could only see the light. Even if his feet were on the ground he was not aware of it; he had no fear of falling, no care in this world. Nothing of what touches a man, or beings endowed with a body, could then touch his thought for he forgot the entire world and was altogether present in that immaterial light, and was even himself, or so it seemed to him, become light. He was flooded with tears of an inexpressible lightness and joy. Then his mind rose up to heaven and perceived another light, even brighter than that which was close to him. And what a marvelous sight! For near to the light was standing the saint of whom we have talked, the old man, equal to the angels, who had given him his instructions and the book.[24]

In *Catechesis* 16, Symeon gives account of the effects of the divine vision (according to his biographer, Nicetas, the same vision as that just recounted from *Catechesis* 22): "It caused rejoicing, when it appeared, and wounded me when it hid itself. It made itself so close to me, transported me to the heavens. It is a pearl; it is the light which clothes me, which appeared to me like a star, which remains incomprehensible for all. It shines like the sun, and there I discerned all the creation enclosed. It showed me all that it contained and bade me to respect my proper limits. I was closed in under a roof and between walls, yet it opened the heavens for me. I lifted my eyes, sensibly, to contemplate heavenly realities, and then all appeared to me as it was at first."[25]

Among the several points one might comment on, I want to draw attention to the experience of light flooding Symeon and eliding his consciousness of his earthly situation, so that he feels transported beyond earthly dimensions to heaven. There is another, much earlier account of such an experience, in Dionysios's eighth letter. This is the letter to an abbot, not himself a priest, who had driven from the sanctuary a priest who was accepting the repentance of someone who was, in the abbot's opinion, beyond reprieve. Toward the end of the letter, he tells a story about a holy man of Crete, called Carpos. During his prayer, in which he was incensed by someone who had brought about the apostasy of someone newly baptized, he suddenly had a vision. The account of the vision begins thus: "As he described it, the place where he was seemed to be shaken completely and then split into two halves in the middle from the roof down. A shining flame appeared coming down to him from heaven (for the place now seemed to be in open air). The sky itself seemed to be unfolding, and in the vault of heaven Jesus appeared in human form amid an endless throng of angels."[26]

It is the same kind of experience as those just quoted from Symeon, conforming to McGuckin's third apocalyptic "open heaven" type. Dionysios's account, as has often been remarked, is modeled on an even earlier account found in the works of the monk Neilos.[27] Attention has been drawn recently to parallels between monastic "mysticism" and the visions found in apocalyptic literature by Alexander Golitzin:[28] he speaks of monastic mysticism as "interiorized apocalyptic." The visions just described by Symeon and Carpos would fit such a category. But there is another parallel between Carpos and Symeon. When he introduces Carpos, Dionysios mentions that Carpos never celebrated the "holy rites of the mysteries" unless there appeared to him, during the preparatory prayers, "a sacred and auspicious vision."[29] Symeon made a similar requirement for the exercise of the priesthood. For instance, in his nineteenth hymn, he asserts: "even if someone has received all the grace of the Spirit and is free of sin from his mother's womb, it does not seem to me proper that he celebrate the divine rites, or touch the untouchable and dread mysteries, unless God, by his command and election, give him assurance by divinely enlightening his soul and kindling him with the desire of divine love."[30] Symeon made a similar demand for the authentic reception of the Eucharist: "forgiveness of sin and participation in divine life are bestowed on us not only in the bread and wine of communion, but in the divinity that attends them and without confusion mysteriously mingles with them. I say 'mysteriously' [*mystikos*], for the divinity is not revealed to everyone, but to those who are worthy of eternal life. It makes those who see it sons of light and of the day; for the ones who do not see the light despite its great clarity are those who sit in darkness."[31] But such an emphasis on felt experience of the presence and communication of the divine in connection with the sacraments is, in fact, a commonplace in Byzantine monasticism. For instance, in John Moschos's *Spiritual Meadow*, there is story of a monk who, when celebrating, "did not perceive the coming of the Holy Spirit in the accustomed manner."[32] He is distressed and returns to the sanctuary in tears. It transpires that the Holy Spirit did not descend because the oblation was already consecrated—by a lay monk who had recited the anaphora over the oblations while he was bringing them to the monastery! But for our purposes the key expression is "in the accustomed manner": his perception of the descent of the Spirit was what he normally experienced when celebrating the Eucharist. There are stories of other monks who were accustomed to behold the descent of the Holy Spirit:[33] it was a mark of great holiness in the celebrating priest. Perhaps Symeon is not so exceptional after all; rather, he represents an enduring tradition in Byzantine monasticism that laid stress on conscious experience of divine things, and especially of God's sacramental activity. Maybe it was Symeon's reassertion of this tradition in the face of the more confident assertion of hierarchical authority by the patriarch and the clergy of the Great Church at the turn of the millennium that made Symeon so controversial in Constantinople. Such an analysis only fills out McGuckin's main claim, that in these "epiphanic" experiences we see a claim to authority by Symeon the monk. But this claim is not so exceptional: it was a long-standing monastic claim in Byzantium. Such experience, such acquisition of the Holy

Spirit, was the goal of monasticism—something that Symeon makes clear at the end of *Catechesis* 16, when he begs his monks to create in themselves a contrite heart and a humble soul so that, thanks to their tears and their repentance, they may be found worthy one day of the "vision and the enjoyment here below of the ineffable benefits of the divine light."[34]

THEOPHANES OF NICAEA

We come to Theophanes, the third bishop of Nicaea bearing that name, who around 1380 wrote five discourses on the "Taboric light." There is no doubt that the appeal to the vision of the light of Mount Tabor was an appeal to experience, an appeal dismissed by the Calabrian monk Barlaam as an hallucination. For Barlaam no experience, and certainly no experience mediated by the senses, as a vision of light must be, could be an experience of the ineffable God. To experience light not emanating from normal created sources, such as the sun, was to have a hallucination. As is well known, Barlaam's attack on such claims, which had been made by monks of the Holy Mountain of Athos, provoked a bitter controversy in the already failing Byzantine Empire. The most famous defender of the monks was Saint Gregory Palamas, who had been an Athonite monk himself and became archbishop of Thessaloniki in 1347. Saint Gregory's defense invoked the distinction in God between his essence, which is unknowable, and his energies, by which he makes himself known: it is a distinction *within* God; the divine energies are God; they are not some kind of lesser intermediary. The claim of the hesychast monks to see the uncreated light of the Godhead was therefore a claim to see God in his energies, not in his essence, which remains unknowable. This defense of the hesychast vision of the divine light was endorsed by synods held at Constantinople in 1341, 1347, and 1351 and given formal expression both in the *Hagioretic Tome,* issued by the monks of the Holy Mountain (1340–41) and also in additions to the formal proclamation of Orthodox belief, reaffirmed each year on the first Sunday of Lent, called the *Synodikon of Orthodoxy.* Controversy, however, continued and was perhaps only finally extinguished by the collapse of Byzantium itself in 1453.

Theophanes' discourses belong to later stages of the controversy. From their title, "On the Taboric Light" ("Peri thaboriou photou"), one might expect that there would be a defense, analysis, and even account of such experiences of beholding the light of Tabor. What in fact we find is a sophisticated philosophical discussion (in which, incidentally, Theophanes shows himself to be well versed in Aristotelian conceptual analysis) of the nature of our participation in God. So far as the light of Mount Tabor itself is concerned, these homilies address two issues. First, in the first two discourses, Theophanes argues that the light of Tabor is identical with the "life-giving and deified body of God the Word" (1.94f.)—identical, that is, neither less than nor greater than, nor even equal to, but identical with. A consequence of this, which Theophanes draws out, is that to deny the reality of the the vision of the Taboric light is equivalent to denying the reality of divine communion in the body and blood of Christ in the Eucharist. What at first sight seems to be an exceptional experience—beholding the light of Tabor in prayer—is *identified* with the most normal liturgical action of the life of any Orthodox Christian, the reception of Holy Communion. The argument between the hesychasts and their opponents is not, then, about the reality or otherwise of rare "mystical" experiences, but rather about the reality of participation in God at all. Doubts about the possibility of communion with God through the visible light of Tabor cannot be doubts that stop there; such doubts will dissolve the reality of communion with God through the bread and wine of the Eucharist in Holy Communion. The controversy is not about mysterious, or "mystical," experiences at all, but about the reality of communion between the uncreated God and created human kind. The second issue, which is first raised in the third homily, concerns the appeal made by the opponents of hesychasm (the Akindynites, Theophanes calls them) to the passage in Maximos's tenth *Ambiguum*, which we have already discussed, where he expounds the mystery of the Transfiguration. There Maximos says that the light of the Transfiguration was a "symbol" of the transcendent Godhead. Therefore, the Akindynites argue the Taboric light was not itself divine, but only a symbol of the divine. Theophanes' response to this is twofold: on the one hand, a symbol is not necessarily distinct from the reality it symbolizes; on the other hand, what Maximos means is not that the light was a symbol of the Godhead, but rather that it was a symbol of the incomprehensibility of the Godhead. I mention this mainly because it shows something that is not always evident in the extant texts, how important Maximos's exposition of the Transfiguration was in the hesychast controversy: it was Maximos's long pondering on this mystery that provided the matrix for interpretation of the hesychast vision of the divine light. And that brings us full circle, for when we started with Maximos, we noted that though his theology was concerned with a face-to-face encounter with Christ, no kind of prominence was given to psychological analysis of experiences of light: light was a way of saying something about the reality of the encounter, rather than a way of describing its psychological modalities. So with Theophanes: although he is defending experiences related by holy monks, the focus of his defense is on the reality of encounter and communion between the uncreated God and created humanity.

CONCLUSION

By way of conclusion, I would like to make a few points about the place of visions of light in the Byzantine tradition. First of all, behind it lies the rich language of vision in the Bible, in which we can discern several paradigms, and these paradigms serve different purposes, of which our writers are well aware. We need to be clear that we are speaking of visions of light, in the plural: there are different kinds, different matrices of interpretation. Secondly, following on from this, we need to be cautious of the prominence given to the Transfiguration as a paradigm of experience of light in the fourteenth-century hesychast controversy, given the importance this controversy has assumed in modern Orthodoxy, and therefore for scholars interested in the Byzantine tradition, many of whom, if they are interested in religious matters at all, belong to, or are sympathetic to, Orthodoxy as it currently understands itself. Thirdly, the perception of the Transfiguration as a paradigm of experiences of light owes a very great deal to Maximos and has more to do with stressing the reality of communion between the uncreated and the created than with the modalities of psychological experience. Fourthly, the link between Symeon and the hesychasts is not that Symeon is a precursor of hesychasm in the matter of visions of light, though in other respects he shares much with them—his stress on personal experience, for instance, and on the importance of spiritual fatherhood. Rather, it seems to me that Symeon is a kind of virtuoso of experiences of light, drawing on all the biblical paradigms to express a multifaceted understanding of the nature of Christian experience (something that the article cited by John McGuckin has made clear, though even he tends to oversimplify the different ways in which appeal to experiences of light can function). But Symeon is not simply exceptional: he shares with the earlier (and later?) Byzantine monastic tradition a kind of "open heaven" mysticism of what Alexander Golitzin has called "interiorized apocalyptic," which is closely related to sacramental experience. Further research is needed before we can know how deep and extensive such monastic experiences of light are within Byzantine monasticism.

NOTES

1. See Iakovos Potamianos, *To Fos sti Byzantini Ekklisia* [Light in the Byzantine Church] (Thessaloniki: University Studio Press, 2000).

2. Evagrios, *Praktikos* 64, in *Traité pratique*, ed. A. Guillaumont and C. Guillaumont, Sources Chrétiennes, no. 171 (Paris, 1971), p. 648.

3. See n. 22 in John A. McGuckin, "The Luminous Vision in Eleventh-Century

Byzantium: Interpreting the Biblical and Theological Paradigms of St. Symeon the New Theologian," in *Work and Worship at Theotokos Evergetis,* ed. Margaret Mullet and Anthony Kirby, Belfast Byzantine Texts and Translations, vol. 6, no. 2 (Belfast, 1997), pp. 90-123.

4. See Hugh Trevor-Roper, "The Invention of Tradition: The Highland Tradition of Scotland," in *The Invention of Tradition,* ed. Eric Hobsbawm and Terence Ranger (Cambridge: Cambridge University Press, 1983), pp. 15-41.

5. Saint Ignaty Brianchaninov, *On the Prayer of Jesus,* trans. J. M. Watkins, 2nd ed. (London, 1965).

6. Father Lev Gillet, *On the Invocation of the Name of Jesus* (London: Fellowship of St. Alban and St. Sergius; repr., Oxford: SLG Press, 1970).

7. Irénée Hausherr, *Noms du Christ et voies d'oraison,* Orientalia Christiana Analecta, no. 157 (Rome: Pontificale Institutum Orientalium Studiorum, 1960).

8. Bishop Kallistos (Ware) of Diokleia, *The Power of the Name: The Jesus Prayer in Orthodox Spirituality,* Fairacres Publication 43, rev. ed. (Oxford: SLG Press, 1977).

9. He was always more popular in the Russian tradition; see Hilarios Alfeyev, *St. Symeon the New Theologian and Orthodox Tradition* (Oxford: Clarendon Press, 2000).

10. See Gregory Palamas, *Triads in Defence of the Holy Hesychasts* 1.2.12, in *Grégoire Palamas, Défense des saints hésychastes,* ed. J. Meyendorff, Spicilegium Sacrum Lovaniense, Études et Documents, no. 30, 2nd ed. (Louvain, 1973), p. 98.

11. Ch. G. Sotiropoulos, *Niptikoi kai Pateres ton Meson Chronon* (Athens, 1996) (the homilies are to be found on pp. 175-302).

12. Maximos the Confessor, *Capita theologica et oeconomica* 2.13 (PG 90.1130D-1132A).

13. Maximos the Confessor, *Quaestiones et Dubia,* ed. J. H. Declerck, Corpus Christianorum Series Graeca, no. 10 (Turnhout: Brepols; Leuven: University Press, 1982), 191 (p. 134).

14. Maximos the Confessor, *Ambigua* 10.31: PG 91.1160B-1169B; English translation, *Maximos the Confessor,* trans. A. Louth (London: Routledge, 1996), pp. 128-34.

15. *Ambigua* 10.31b: PG 91.1165D-1168A.

16. *Ambigua* 10.31a: PG 91.1168A.

17. See, for instance, *Ambigua* 10.3: PG 91.1113D.

18. McGuckin, "The Luminous Vision," p. 95 n. 3.

19. See Saint Symeon the New Theologian, *Ethical Discourses,* ed. A. Golitzin, vol. 3, (Crestwood, NY: St. Vladimir's Seminary Press, 1997), p. 22. (This "vol. 3" is in fact a monograph on Symeon by Golitzin).

20. McGuckin, "The Luminous Vision," p. 101.

21. In the account of what McGuckin calls an assimilation of Vision II (the vision toward the beginning of his monastic life) to Vision I (the "conversion" vision before he became a monk) in *Catechesis* 35.6, see "The Luminous Vision," p. 118. The text used here and elsewhere for Symeon's writings is that edited by J. Darrouzès, B. Krivochéine, and others in Sources Chrétiennes, no. 51 (*Chapîtres théologiques, gnostiques et pratiques*

[Theological, Gnostic and Practical Chapters]), nos. 96, 104, and 113 (*Catéchèses* [Catecheses]), nos. 122 and 129 (*Traités théologiques et éthiques* [Theological and Ethical Treatises]), and nos. 156, 174, and 196 (*Hymnes* [Hymns]) (Paris: Le Cerf, 1957-73).

22. It seems to me that McGuckin spoils his case by arguing that in all the paradigms the central concerns are the same, viz., authentication of authority, and the establishment of the basis for a program of reform: see "The Luminous Vision," pp. 101f.

23. This is the burden of his article "St. Symeon the New Theologian (949-1022): Byzantine Spiritual Authority in Search of a Precedent," in *The Church Retrospective*, ed. R. N. Swanson, Studies in Church History, no. 33, (Woodbridge: Boydell Press, 1997), pp. 75-90.

24. *Catechesis* 22.88-104.

25. *Catechesis* 16.127-36.

26. Dionysios, *Epistula* 8, ed. A. M. Ritter, Patristische Texte und Studien, no. 36 (Berlin: Walter de Gruyter, 1991), p. 190.

27. See Neilos, *Epistula* 2: PG 79.297D-300C.

28. In unpublished papers he has shown me, and also in his contribution to the XIII International Conference on Patristic Studies, Oxford, 1999.

29. *Ep.* 8 (Ritter, p. 188).

30. *Hymn* 19.159-65.

31. *Ethical Treatise* 10.189-97.

32. *Pratum spirituale* 25.

33. Ibid., 27, 150.

34. *Catechesis* 16.159-64.

CHAPTER FIVE

Hermeneutics of Light in Medieval Kabbalah

Elliot R. Wolfson

In consideration of the possibility of cross-cultural, universalistic tendencies in the history of mysticism, a phenomenon such as light naturally presents itself as a plausible candidate. Indeed, the central role occupied by light and the process of illumination in the range of experiences studied under the rubric of mysticism has been well established. The acknowledgment of the ubiquity of this phenomenon does not necessarily mean that the specificity of each religio-cultural setting in which it appears should be ignored. In line with several contemporary scholars, I am of the opinion that in the analysis of mysticism (as is the case with respect to other aspects of the history of religions) one can avoid the extremes of a universalism that does not allow for the diversity inherent in each tradition and a contextualism that categorically denies the possibility of transcultural unity. The meaningful classification of the term "mysticism" necessitates an awareness of both the uniqueness of the different traditions and the shared elements.

A balanced view with regard to this matter was articulated by Clifford Geertz in language that can still be useful in the current debate over this issue: "If, however, we use a concept like 'mysticism'—or 'mystic' or 'mystical'—not to formulate an underlying uniformity behind superficially diverse phenomena, but to analyze the nature of diversity as we find it, then pursuing the different meanings the concept takes in different contexts does not dissolve its value as an ordering idea but enriches it. . . . In this area of study, at least, the interest of facts lies in their variety, and the power of ideas rests not on the degree to which they can dissolve that variety but the degree to which they can order it."[1] Reflecting on the words of Geertz, Peter Awn astutely remarked: "The fact that historians of religion, in their attempts to describe the univocal character of the concept mysticism, have, in spite of themselves, attested to the diversity inherent in each tradition's experience of the mystical, is not a sign of failure but one of hope."[2]

I assume that the particular example of light confirms this general theoretical position. Light cannot be characterized meaningfully in terms of one religion to the exclusion of another. It is patently absurd to speak of light as distinctively Jewish, Christian, Muslim, Hindu, Taoist, or Buddhist. Light is light—a tautological utterance that conveys at once utter simplicity and infinite complexity. To be sure, the experience of light in different cultural settings will vary in accordance with beliefs, symbols, and myths that shape that culture. The pious Jew will experience Torah as light and light as Torah, the devout Christian will experience Jesus as light and light as Jesus, and so on. On this point I acknowledge a critical element of the constructivist argument: I do not think there is justification on epistemological grounds for distinguishing too sharply between experience and description.[3] The incongruities between mystics from various religions are not due simply to the attempt to lend expression to the experience; they are part and parcel of the experience itself, the contours of which are shaped by the particular setting whence it arises. This recognition, however, does not preclude the possibility of demarcating a universal element to the experience.[4] Quite to the contrary, it is precisely by attending and appropriating the contextual that one can take hold of the transcontextual.[5] To recognize that the Jewish mystic experiences light differently from the Christian mystic rests on the discernment that light cannot be meaningfully described as distinctively Jewish or Christian. This paradox is the inexplicable light that illumines our way, breaking open the ground, but in so doing providing the platform on which we will stand.

Turning my focus particularly to Jewish mysticism, it is no exaggeration to say that light is one of the most important symbols that has informed the texture of the experience of the divine related from multiple perspectives in works of a mystical orientation. This tendency runs from the ancient chariot speculation of Hekhalot literature to modern Hasidism and beyond to contemporary attempts of Jewish renewal. For the purposes of this chapter I will focus on the trend of medieval Jewish mysticism known in scholarly literature as theosophic-theurgic kabbalah, which has been contrasted with the other major trend, known as ecstatic-prophetic kabbalah.[6] In the past, I availed myself of this typological distinction, but of late I have begun to express doubt about the viability and usefulness of this classification, for I believe it leaves a misimpression both with respect to the ecstatic elements of theosophy and to the theosophic underpinnings of ecstasy.[7] Lest one consider this simply a pedantic issue in philology, let me note that the terminological concern goes right to the heart of the subject of this study, for by appreciating the complex weave of theosophic and ecstatic strands of medieval Jewish mystical traditions, one can better comprehend the ontological and phenomenological assumptions related to light and the experience of illumination.

The centrality of light in medieval kabbalah is evident from a mere glance at the titles of some of the major texts of the tradition. To mention one obvious and striking illustration: The formative period of kabbalistic literary activity, which extends roughly from the middle of the twelfth century to the beginning of the fourteenth, is bound, as it were, by two pseudepigraphic works, *Sefer ha-Bahir,* the *Book of Illumination* attributed to Nehuniah ben ha-Qanah, and *Sefer ha-Zohar,* the *Book of Splendor* attributed to Simeon ben Yohai. The choice of these titles is not coincidental or trivial. On the contrary, the medieval kabbalists behind the composition and/or redaction of these works were cognizant of the centrality of the symbol of light in the constitution of the mystical enterprise. Indeed, as I have elaborated elsewhere, the ontology of light provides the hermeneutical framework for the experience as well as for the theosophic presumptions regarding the divine.[8]

In both the *Bahir* and *Zohar,* moreover, there is an exegetical framing that imparts information to the reader regarding the nature of mystical illumination. I would go further and say the scriptural citations provide the parameters within which the experience can be relived. From that vantage point there is no reason to distinguish in a hard-and-fast manner between interpretation and experience when assessing the nature of the contemplative visualization that lies at the heart of the kabbalistic worldview.[9] The process of interpreting the relevant biblical passage occasions the experience that the passage is itself describing. Reading is thus a double mirroring, the mirror of the reader reflecting the mirror of the text and the mirror of the text reflecting the mirror of the reader. But in a mirror that reflects a mirror all that can be seen is reflection, indeed, a reflection of a reflection, the splintering of images that is the very essence of light. The splendor of God that illumines the soul of the enlightened kabbalist is refracted through the prism of Scripture insofar as the latter is itself considered the incarnate form of the imaginal body of the divine.

Let us turn our attention in a more focused way to the phenomenon of light and illumination in the two kabbalistic anthologies that I mentioned. The bahiric text thus begins: "R. Nehuniah ben ha-Qanah said: In one verse it is written, 'Now the resplendent light (*'or bahir*) cannot be seen, though it is in the heavens' (Job 37:21), and another verse says, 'He made darkness his screen' (Ps. 18:12), and it says, 'Dense clouds are around him' (ibid., 97:2). There is a conflict. The third verse comes and tips the balance, as it written, 'Darkness is not dark for you; night is as light as day; darkness and light are the same' (ibid., 139:12)."[10] The title of the collection, *Sefer ha-Bahir,* is obviously derived from the expression *'or bahir* used in the verse from Job. The expression is interpreted by the redactor of the bahiric text as a reference to the divine nature, which is portrayed as a radiant light. But this verse is set against two other verses from Psalms wherein God is depicted as concealed by darkness. The ostensible clash between these verses is resolved by yet another verse from Psalms wherein the opposites are identified: darkness and light with respect to God are the same. The bahiric text begins, therefore, with a destabilization of the very categories of light and darkness as they apply to God. In the divine nature, opposites are identical and there is thus no antinomy between light and darkness. Radiant light (*'or bahir*) is itself the mystery of darkness (*ḥoshekh*).

From a historical and textual point of view it seems that the opening comment of *Sefer ha-Bahir* reflects the orientation cultivated by kabbalistic fraternities in twelfth-century Provence who were influenced by the intellectual mysticism of Neoplatonic writings and perhaps some of the other speculative currents of Islamic esotericism, which were probably transmitted through Hebrew translations. In this study, I will mention some important passages in the corpus of material known as *sifrut ḥug ha-'iyyun,* the literature that was composed by Jewish mystics referred to by scholars by the name "circle of contemplation," a name that is derived from what is considered to be the foundational text of the circle, *Sefer ha-'Iyyun.* The influence of these small and highly complex treatises on the subsequent development of theosophic speculation, including the *Zohar* in its disparate parts, has been well noted by scholars. It is probable that this circle originated in Provence in the late twelfth century,[11] although it has also been suggested that they evolved in Castile in the second half of the thirteenth century.[12] For my purposes the precise date and location of this material are not that essential. What is of primary interest is the paradoxical depiction of light as darkness that one finds consistently in these texts.

In what is apparently the earliest recension of *Sefer ha-'Iyyun,* the powers of the divine are said to emanate from the "supernal mystery," *seter 'elyon,* in the manner of scent from scent, or that of flame from flame. The first of these powers is identified as primordial wisdom (*ḥokhmah qedumah*) in which is manifest the radiance of God's glory hidden from the eye (*kavod ha-nistar min ha-'ayin*). Pushing language to its limit, the mystic responsible for this text writes of this divine potency in a way that clearly reflects that his speculation streams from the inner depth of contemplative experience: "The substance that we can comprehend from his truth, may he be blessed, is the matter of the pure light of life, the unalloyed gold that is written and sealed in the splendor of the beautiful canopy, which is composed of the radiance of the luminous splendor, in the image of the soul of which there is no comprehension at all, an effulgence that is entirely incomprehensible, and he is unified in the primordial wisdom."[13]

The continuation of the emanative process is described in more light images. Based on the technical term employed in rabbinic literature to depict the prophetic vision of Moses,[14] the remaining potencies of the Godhead are collectively identified as the "luminous mirrors" (*'aspaqlari'ot ha-me'irot*),[15] which are said to glow with the light of Venus. Without getting further enmeshed in the description of the unfolding of these lights from the mysterious darkness, what is critical for us to note is that in the account of the primordial wisdom the essential paradox of mystical vision, already implicit in the opening passage of the *Bahir,* is reaffirmed: divine wisdom is the radiant splendor that discloses the essential hiddenness of the supernal mystery, but even so it remains incomprehensible to human beings. The mystic engaged in contemplation of the divine attributes is illumined by the resplendent darkness that forever exceeds the visionary parameters of human experience. Not only is it is the case that the light that is seen is seen within the primordial darkness—for where else would light be seen but in darkness?—but the light that is seen is the darkness that is invisible.

There is, however, another critical element implied in the description of the primordial wisdom, which involves the linguistic nature of this radiance. This is alluded to in the passing remark regarding the "unalloyed gold that is written and sealed in the splendor of the beautiful canopy." Although the matter is not discussed in detail, it is evident from this comment that there is a convergence between the symbolism of light and the symbolism of language, a theme that is well attested in kabbalistic literature through the generations.[16] In a second work from this literary circle, *Ma'ayan ha-Hokhmah,* the *Fountain of Wisdom,* the convergence of the two symbolic fields is dealt with more extensively. According to this text, the primary divine potencies, which are identified as thirteen types of permutation related to the Tetragrammaton, are said to come about through a fivefold process that involves various linguistic and numerical activities on the part of God. In the final analysis, since the letters serve as semiotic and arithmetic markers, it is easy to imagine how these two activities were combined. For my purposes what is significant is the description of the five stages of this process that occurs toward the beginning of the text: "How is the affixing [of letters] [*tiqqun*][17] [accomplished]? To bring forth the word [*davar*] in the utterance [*ma'amar*] and the utterance in the word, the affixing in the permutation [*ṣeruf*], the permutation in the affixing, the combination [*mikhlal*] in the computation [*ḥeshbon*] and the computation in the combination, until all the words are placed in the font of the flame [*ma'ayan ha-shalhevet*], and the flame is in the font until the point that there is no comprehension and no measure to the light that is concealed in the surplus of the hidden darkness [*'orah ha-mit'alemet be-tosefet ha-ḥoshekh*]."[18] In a subsequent passage from this composition, the primal ether (*'awir ha-qadmon*), identified as the holy spirit through which the letters of the name are articulated, is said to produce an incomprehensible light, which is also referred to as the primordial darkness (*ḥosekh ha-qadmon*).[19] Let me cite the text verbatim: "And a number of springs emerged rapidly like sparks that issue forth as one, and they spread out to several parts as when the blacksmith strikes his hammer. Afterward there emanates one fountain whence flows the darkness, and the darkness is mixed from three colors."[20] Concerning this darkness one may not investigate, for even Moses was denied the opportunity to inquire of this darkness, which is identified exegetically as the invisible face of God.[21] In another passage, the paradoxical situation of the light that is concealed in darkness is expressed in even more dazzling and darkening terms. "From the primordial darkness . . . comes forth the existence of everything, and from it issues the spring . . . and it is called the light that is darkened from light [*'or haneḥshakh me-'or*],[22] for it is concealed, and it is impossible for the essence of the being of this darkness to be known. Therefore, it is called the darkness that darkens . . . for no creature can gaze upon it, even the angels that sit first in the kingdom of heaven. . . . The marvelous light [*ha-'or ha-mufla'*] receives the exchange from the light that is darkened from illuminating, and it is the principle of all the colors but there is no fixed color within it; it is like the violet [*tekhelet*],[23] and everything is equal within it, for the darkness that emanates from the light is the *'alef*, as we have said, and this is the voice as it is articulated, which is called movement [*tenu'ah*]."[24]

One can sense how in these passages the mystical articulation is pushing beyond the limits of language to speak of the ineffable: The light that is seen in the concealment of darkness is the word that is written by being erased. But it is precisely this hidden light or eclipsed word that is the image (*demut*) of the invisible God. Alternatively, one can view the light as the garment in which the darkness of the divine is disclosed in its concealment even as it is concealed in its disclosure. In a somewhat later recension of *Sefer ha-'Iyyun*, the paradox of the concealed disclosure is expressed in terms of the image of God wrapping himself in a garment, which is based in part on an earlier midrashic reading of the relevant biblical verses:[25]

In the beginning the blessed holy One created the marvelous light, and at the time that it was created there emanated together with it several types of splendor from the powers of unity. They grew strong and vibrated, and the marvelous light was conjoined to the side of wisdom that is called mystery. Permission was not given for it to shine until the blessed holy One created all the lights that emanate on account of the strength of the powers, and from them the marvelous light grew strong in effulgence and shined forth. . . . The mystery, which is the primordial wisdom, produces a light, and at the time that the blessed holy One created it, he extended it like a canopy. . . . this is the light that sparkles from the marvelous light, which is extended by the power of unity like a garment. Its brilliance grows strong and shines upon the hidden unity through the wondrous power. Therefore it is verily the marvelous light, for on account of the abundance of its splendor with which it shines and radiates, it is darkened from illuminating in terms of visual perception, just as with respect to the sun it is too strong for a person to gaze upon its actual brilliance. If a person looks upon it, the pupils of his eyes are darkened, and he cannot open them on account of the abundance of the effulgence that increases and shines forth. Thus the blessed holy One darkens the marvelous light from the comprehension of every created being, and he did not give permission to any created being to comprehend its truth at it is. . . . When it arose in the mind of the blessed holy One to bring forth the emanated beings from his power, he wrapped himself in the marvelous light, as it says, "wrapped in a robe of light," and then immediately afterward "You spread the heavens like a tent cloth" (Ps. 104:2). All of this was in order to reveal his equanimity, for he is balanced on every side, above and below, before and behind, for they are hidden and revealed. He made known everything that what was hidden and that was revealed, and he thus instructs about his unity.[26]

The garment through which the concealment of God is revealed is the mysterious light that darkens from the brightness of its own luster. But this garment is at the same time understood to be the word of God by which the silence is articulated. In yet another recension of *Sefer ha-'Iyyun,* the divine is described as the "light of life, pure and refined, which is composed of the splendid radiance of the resplendent light that is incomprehensible."[27] This invisible, radiant light is compared to a soul that makes for itself an image that is like the body. What is essential for my purposes is that the word used for image, *dumiyyah,* connotes both the sense of likeness and that of silence. The former conveys the idea that the light must be disclosed through an image in the manner that the soul is manifest through the body, but the latter relates to the fact that of this image nothing can be properly said. We see, again, how the ocular and the verbal converge in the mystical insight.

As I have already noted above, the convergence of the symbolism of light and the symbolism of language is one of the most important themes that has shaped the ecstatic element of theosophic kabbalah. The most important term employed by medieval kabbalists to refer to the divine emanations, *sefirot,* is itself sufficient to convey this dual sense: The word derives from the root *sfr,* which can be vocalized as *sefer,* "book," but it is associated as well with the word *sappir,* "sapphire." Additionally, the root *sfr* can be vocalized as *safar,* "to count." No single English word can adequately account for the richness of the range of semantic meaning linked to the term *sefirot,* which denotes concurrently the sense of luminosity (*sappir*), speech (*sefer*), and enumeration (*sefar*). At the heart of the mystical experience that informs the worldview of the kabbalists is the concurrence of these three fields of discourse: The potencies of the divine are experienced as the translucent letters that are enumerated within the book written by God. But just as the letters by means of which the book is inscribed are made visible only in the absence of any word proper, so the light can be seen over and only against the background of darkness.

In a similar manner, in the *Zohar* the key text that informs the approach to the ecstatic vision is the eschatological promise related in the words of Daniel, "and the enlightened will shine like the splendor of the sky" (Dan. 12:3). The very title of the zoharic anthology is derived from this verse; hence, to appreciate the experiential dimension implied in the name of the book, one must properly grasp the intent of the use of the word *zohar* in this verse as it is read by the kabbalist exegete. As I have argued at length elsewhere, this verse concurrently relates to the ontological assumption regarding the nature of the divine light and to the phenomenological condition underlying the mystical experience of that light.[28] The enlightened, *maskilim,* is an encoded reference to the kabbalists, a terminological usage that is attested in some of the earliest kabbalistic sources. That the enlightened will shine like the splendor of the sky means that the mystic visionaries are illumined by and transformed into the gradation of the divine to which the word *zohar* refers. To cite one of various relevant passages from the zoharic material: "'And the enlightened will shine like the splendor of the sky'—the enlightened are they who contemplate the mystery of wisdom; they 'will shine,' for they sparkle in the splendor of the supernal wisdom; 'like the splendor,' the radiant, effulgent light that comes out from Eden."

Any attempt to understand the religious texture of the *Zohar* must take into account the fact that the theosophical ruminations are not merely speculative devices for expressing the knowable aspect of God, but are practical means for achieving a state of ecstasy through which the mystic is assimilated into the splendor of the Godhead. The texts themselves—at the compositional level—reflect the mystic's experiences of the divine pleroma and the reintegration of his soul with its ontological source. Behind the multifaceted symbols and interpretations of biblical verses found in the *Zohar* is a fraternity of mystics ecstatically transformed by contemplation of the divine light refracted in nature, the soul, and the Torah. There is indeed genuine ecstatic experience underlying the hermeneutical posture of the *Zohar.* For the zoharic authorship, therefore, there is a basic convergence of the interpretative and revelatory modes; the act of scriptural interpretation is itself an occasion for contemplative study and mystical meditation. The midrashic condition of the *Zohar* is thus inscribed within the circle of experience and interpretation: the vision that generated the text may be re/visioned through interpretive study. This has important ramifications for understanding the textual and phenomenological parameters of visionary experience in Jewish mystical sources. Study itself was viewed as a mode of "visual meditation"—a technique known in medieval Christian mysticism as well—in which there is an imaginative recreation of the prophetic vision within the mystic's own consciousness. In the zoharic corpus, the two modes, revelation and interpretation, are identified and blended together. This convergence is due to the fact that the underlying theosophic structure provides a shared phenomenological basis. In the hermeneutic relation that the mystic has to the text he is once again seeing God as God was seen in the historic event of revelation. In short, from the vantage point of the *Zohar,* visionary experience is a vehicle for hermeneutics as hermeneutics is a vehicle for visionary experience.

From the perspective of the zoharic symbolism, the process of visual contemplation is decidedly textual in nature. The intertwining of the two modalities reinforces the merging of the imagery of light and the linguistic symbolism, which I discussed above in conjunction with the Iyyun material. For the zoharic authorship the primary task of the pious individual is to contemplate the divine form, but the way to achieve that end is by visualizing God's shape as it is embodied in the text of Scripture whose mystical essence is that of the name. The paradox articulated at the beginning of the *Bahir* and further developed in the Iyyun compositions regarding the coincidence of the opposites of light and darkness when applied to God is affirmed as well in the *Zohar.* To cite one dictum that makes this point succinctly: "R. Isaac said: When the holy one, blessed be he, created the world and wanted to reveal the depth out of the hiddenness and the light from within the darkness, they were contained within one another. . . . And all things were contained one within the other, the good inclination and the evil inclination, right and left, Israel and the nations, white and black. All things were dependent on one another."[29] The normal dichotomies that regulate one's behavior, the moral distinction between the good inclination and the evil inclination, the spatial distinction between right and left, the ethnoreligious distinction between Israel and the nations, and the perceptual distinction between white and black, all dissolve in the oneness of the Infinite. What is most important for our immediate discussion is the overcoming of any distinction between light and dark; in the depths of the infinite Godhead they are one. The ultimate experience of mystical illumination is such that the kabbalist perceives the light that is darkness and in so doing is transformed into the very darkness that is light.

The point is underscored in several passages in the zoharic literature according to which the key verse from Daniel 12:3, "and the enlightened will shine with the splendor of the sky," is applied to the entity that is called the *boṣina de-qardinuta'*, to which is attributed the task of giving measure and boundary to the luminous emanations that make up the shape of the divine. Mystical gnosis is portrayed in certain zoharic texts specifically in terms of the praxis of measuring the configuration of the divine in accord with this entity, a mystery that is even related to the proclamation of the principle of monotheism in Judaism. In my previous work, I have translated *boṣina de-qardinuta'* as the "hardened spark," which I have identified further as the aspect of the divine mind that corresponds to the phallus. In some kabbalistic texts, however, this expression is rendered as the "black flame." It is possible that both readings are correct and that the upper phallic aspect is precisely the light that is dark. Support for this interpretation is found in the fact that in several zoharic passages the phallic potency is described in terms of the symbol of light, especially the image of radiant or sparkling flashes of light, which would appropriately characterize the *boṣina de-qardinuta'*. In any event, it is telling that the zoharic kabbalists have understood the primary experience of contemplative illumination in terms of this image. For the mystic visionary the object is to visualize the darkened light in order to be illuminated by its luminous darkness. In the ecstatic vision, the mystic approximates the ontological state of the divine in which the opposites coincide. In this state, there is no darkness set in opposition to light, for the most brilliant light is the most impenetrable darkness. In this moment, there is no difference between lucidity and obscurity, translucence and opaqueness. Not only is there an overcoming of these logical antinomies, but language itself breaks down, for what can we call the darkness that is light but the light that is darkness? The posing of the question in this way indicates that we are on the wrong track, for we are still laboring under the weight of the Aristotelian law of noncontradiction. The mystical vision of light wells up from the spring of insight, that is, inner sight, wherein opposites are not set against one another. The mystic sees by not seeing; the God that he visually contemplates is the invisible God; the light that is darkness is seen through the light darkly, the dark light perceived by the eye that is closed.[30] The mystic is transformed thereby into the luminous darkness that is God. Of this brilliance one can say nothing, but in saying nothing the ineffable is pronounced.

NOTES

1. Clifford Geertz, *Islam Observed* (Chicago: University of Chicago Press, 1971), pp. 23–24.

2. Peter J. Awn, *Satan's Tragedy and Redemption: Iblis in Sufi Psychology* (Leiden: E. J. Brill, 1983), p. 6.

3. Elliot R. Wolfson, *Through a Speculum That Shines: Vision and Imagination in Medieval Jewish Mysticism* (Princeton, NJ: Princeton University Press, 1994), pp. 119–24, 326–32. The two most important essays in which Steven Katz sets out his theoretical agenda are "Language, Epistemology, and Mysticism," in *Mysticism and Philosophical Analysis,* ed. Steven T. Katz (New York: Oxford University Press, 1978), pp. 22–74, and "The 'Conservative' Character of Mystical Experience," in *Mysticism and Religious Traditions,* ed. Steven T. Katz (Oxford: Oxford University Press, 1983), pp. 3–60. Katz's impact on the field has been substantial, occasioning a number of significant responses. For example, see the essays collected in *The Problem of Pure Consciousness: Mysticism and Philosophy,* ed. Robert K. C. Forman (Oxford: Oxford University Press, 1990); and *The Innate Capacity: Mysticism, Psychology, and Philosophy,* ed. Robert K. C. Forman (Oxford: Oxford University Press, 1998). Forman's introductions are helpful in articulating the essentialist claim in terms that respond philosophically to the constructivist argument. For a useful survey of the debate, see Robert S. Ellwood, *Mysticism and Religion,* 2nd ed. (New York: Seven Bridges Press, 1999), pp. 15–23.

4. The position I have staked, the middle way that collapses the antinomy between extremes, is consonant with a view expressed by other scholars. For example, Denise Lardner Carmody and John Tully Carmody, *Mysticism: Holiness East and West* (New York: Oxford University Press, 1997), p. 12, define mysticism as the "direct experience of ultimate reality." Aware of the contextualist criticism of unmediated experience, they explain their definition: "Therefore, in putting 'direct experience' into our working description of mysticism, we are not necessarily denying either mediation by the mystic's cultural tradition or a meditational use of sights, sounds, bodily postures, or other aids. Rather, we are saying that the core of the experience, what the mystic stresses when describing the moment, is a vivid presence of ultimate reality (however named) that makes any intermediary transparent and secondary. One could say, in fact, that in mystical consummation the mediator (tradition or icon) has done its job so well that it becomes a translucent lens; or, in some cases, one could say that the mystic feels as though everything intermediary has fallen away so that darkness or a wraparound presence renders ideas, words, images—everything particular or partial—inoperative, beside the point."

5. Jess Byron Hollenback, *Mysticism: Experience, Response, and Empowerment* (University Park, PA: Pennsylvania State University Press, 1996), pp. 75–76, speaks of the "intrinsic contextuality or historicity" of the mystical state of consciousness; that is, "its perceptual and existential content exhibits a high degree of sensitivity to the mystic's cultural context and historical situation. . . . When I say that the mystical experience is amorphous, I am observing that its content (and its effects) differ from one religious tradition to the next. . . . It should now be clear that when one says that mystical experience is amorphous this is simply another way of stating that, in the vast majority of cases, one can never isolate either its content or its effects from the mystic's historical context. Indeed, the content of almost every mystical experience seems to be structured in such a manner as to empirically validate or otherwise legitimize many elements of that description of reality that are either expressly or implicitly present in the mythologies, dogmas, or rituals that form the core of that religious tradition to which the mystic adheres. Not only do mystics empirically confirm the existence of a domain of experience that remains inaccessible to the five senses but also the structure of what they perceive to be ultimate reality is consistent with the descriptions given or implied of it by the revelation(s) or rituals that found their particular religious traditions." What is shared by different traditions is the amorphous quality that the experience has no shape out of context; ironically, precisely the specificity of context proves to be transcontextual. A similar view is at work in Gershom Scholem's understanding of mystical experience as formless and thus potentially iconoclastic. The "conservative" character of religious institutions helps rein in the "revolutionary" element of mysticism and thereby prevent the formlessness of the "original experience" leading to the dissolution of all form. See Gershom Scholem, *On the Kabbalah and Its Symbolism,* trans. Ralph Manheim (New York: Schocken Books, 1969), pp. 7–11.

6. The intellectual roots for this typological classification of two schools of kabbalistic orientation are found in nineteenth-century scholarship, particularly the work of Adolf Jellinek, *Auswahl kabbalistischer Mystik* (Leipzig, 1853), pp. 24–26; and idem, *Philosophie und Kabbala* (Leipzig, 1854), erstes Heft, p. xi. The typology figured prominently in the schema adopted by Gershom Scholem, *Major Trends in Jewish Mysticism* (New York, 1956), p. 124, but it has been developed most fully in the work of Moshe Idel, *Kabbalah: New Perspectives* (New Haven, CT, 1988), pp. xi–xx. Needless to say, Idel has utilized this typological grid in other studies too numerous to delineate in this note. For a review of the history of scholarship on Abulafia, see Ronald Kiener, "From Ba'al ha-Zohar to Prophet to Ecstatic: The Vicissitudes of Abulafia in Contemporary Scholarship," in Gershom Scholem's *Major Trends in Jewish Mysticism 50 Years After,* ed. Joseph Dan and Peter Schäfer (Tübingen: J. C. B. Mohr, 1993), pp. 145–59.

7. To date, the most sustained challenge on my part to the typological distinction between theosophic and ecstatic kabbalah can be found in Elliot R. Wolfson, *Abraham Abulafia—Kabbalist and Prophet: Hermeneutics, Theosophy, and Theurgy* (Los Angeles: Cherub Press, 2000). Other scholars of medieval Jewish mysticism have begun to question the legitimacy of the typological taxonomy. For instance, see Haviva Pedaya, "'Pos-

sessed by Speech': Towards an Understanding of the Prophetic-Ecstatic Patterns among Early Kabbalists" [in Hebrew], *Tarbiz* 65 (1996): 565–636; and Melila Hellner-Eshed, "The Language of Mystical Experience in the Zohar: The Zohar through Its Own Eyes" [in Hebrew] (Ph.D. diss., Hebrew University, 2001). A section from this dissertation was published in Melila Hellner-Eshed, "'A River Issues Forth from Eden': The Language of Mystical Invocation in the Zohar" [in Hebrew], *Kabbalah: Journal for the Study of Jewish Mystical Texts* 2 (1997): 287–310.

8. Wolfson, *Through a Speculum That Shines,* pp. 270–88.

9. An excellent study of the convergence of the experiential and interpretative modes in medieval Christian mysticism is found in Amy Hollywood, *The Soul as Virgin Wife: Mechthild of Madgeburg, Marguerite Porete, and Meister Eckhart* (Notre Dame, IN: University of Notre Dame Press, 1995).

10. *The Book Bahir: An Edition Based on the Earliest Manuscripts* [in Hebrew] (Los Angeles, 1994), § 1, p. 119.

11. The fullest treatment remains Gershom Scholem, *Origins of the Kabbalah,* trans. Allan Arkush, ed. R. J. Zwi Werblowsky (Princeton, NJ: Princeton University Press, 1987), pp. 309–64.

12. Mark Verman, *The Books of Contemplation: Medieval Jewish Mystical Sources* (Albany: State University of New York Press, 1992), pp. 1–30.

13. I have translated the text as it appears in Verman, *Books of Contemplation,* p. 34. For an alternative rendering, see ibid., p. 42.

14. Babylonian Talmud, *Yevamot* 49b.

15. Scholem, *Origins,* p. 330.

16. The point is well captured by Gershom Scholem, "The Name of God and the Linguistic Theory of the Kabbala," *Diogenes* 80 (1972): 165: "For the Kabbalists, however, the Sefiroth and the letters . . . were simply two different methods in which the same reality might be represented in a symbolic manner. In other words: whether the process of the manifestation of God, his stepping outside under the symbol of light, and his diffusion of knowledge and reflection is what is represented, or whether it is to be understood to be the activeness of the divine language, of the self-differentiating word of the creation or even the self-explanatory name of god. In the last analysis, this, for the Kabbalists, is no more than a question of the choice between symbolic structures which are in themselves equally arranged—the symbolism of light and the symbolism of language." On the relationship of light mysticism and language-mysticism in the Iyyun material, see Scholem, *Origins,* pp. 325–26, 333–34.

17. On the technical use of the term *tiqqun* in conjunction with the activity of scribal writing, see E. R. Wolfson, *Circle in the Square: Studies in the Use of Gender in Kabbalistic Symbolism* (Albany: State University of New York Press, 1995), pp. 171–72 n. 68.

18. MS Vatican, *Biblioteca Apostolica ebr.* 236, fols. 24a–b.

19. See Scholem, *Origins,* pp. 331–33.

20. MS Vatican, *Biblioteca Apostolica ebr.* 236, fol. 26b.

21. Ibid., fols. 26b–27a.

22. This is the reading in MSS Vatican, *Biblioteca Apostolica ebr.* 236, fol. 27b, and Cambridge University Library, Add. 643, fol. 21a. MS New York, Jewish Theological Seminary of America 1822, fol. 4a, reads "'or haneḥshakh meha'ir," which should be translated as the "light that is darkened from illuminating." MS Munich, Bayerische Staatsbibliothek 56, fol. 133a, reads "'or haneḥshakh," the "light that is darkened."

23. The reference is to the color of the fringe garment, which, according to rabbinic interpretation (attributed to R. Meir), is comparable to the bluish purple of the sea, which is compared to the sky, which is in turn compared to the throne of glory. See Babylonian Talmud, *Menahot* 43b; *Hullin* 89a.

24. MS Vatican, *Biblioteca Apostolica ebr.* 236, fols. 27b–28a.

25. See A. Altmann, *Studies in Religious Philosophy and Mysticism* (Ithaca, NY: Cornell University Press, 1969), pp. 128–39.

26. I have translated the text established in Verman, *Books of Contemplation*, pp. 66–68.

27. Ibid., p. 92.

28. Wolfson, *Through a Speculum That Shines*, pp. 383–92.

29. *Zohar* 3:80b.

30. Wolfson, *Through a Speculum That Shines*, pp. 380–83.

CHAPTER SIX

The Strange Death of Pema the Demon Tamer

Matthew T. Kapstein

[A]t Manikengo . . . we had been told the story of a very saintly man who had died there the previous year. We went to the house where he had lived, and met his son and his wife who recounted the miracle that had occurred at the old man's death.

In his lifetime he had erected a group of "*Mani* stones" on which he had carved a great number of *mantras* and *sutras* and he had also set up a *chöten* (*stupa*) among them.

In his youth he had been a servant with a wealthy family, but in middle age he left his employment to receive meditational instruction in a monastery. Though he had to work for his living by day, he spent most of his nights in contemplation only allowing himself two to three hours' sleep. His compassion was so great that he always helped every one in need, and opened his house at all times to pilgrims and the very poor. While carrying out his daily work he used to practise meditation in his own way, though his son who was a monk told him that he should carry out more formal spiritual exercises, but this he could not accept. Though he had hitherto always been in good health, three years before his death he fell ill and his family began to be very worried, yet he himself appeared to become increasingly happy. He composed and sang his own songs of praise instead of traditional Buddhist chants. As his illness became more and more serious, lamas and doctors were called in, with his son telling him that he must now remember all the teaching that he had received, at which he smiled, saying, "I have forgotten it all, and anyway there is nothing to remember; everything is illusion, yet I am confident that all is well." Just before his death the old man said "When I die you must not move my body for a week; this is all that I desire."

They wrapped his dead body in old clothes and called in lamas and monks to recite and chant. The body was carried into a small room, little bigger than a cupboard and it was noted that though the old man had been tall the body appeared to have become smaller; at the same time a rainbow was seen over the house. On the sixth day on looking into the room the family saw that it had grown still smaller. A funeral service was arranged for the morning of the eighth day and men came to take the body to the cemetery; when they undid the coverings there was nothing inside except nails and hair. The villagers were astounded, for it would have been impossible for anyone to have come into the room, the door was always kept locked and the window of the little resting place was much too small.

The family reported the event to the authorities and also went to ask Chentze Rinpoche about the meaning of it. He told them that such a happening had been reported several times in the past and that the body of the saintly man had been absorbed into the Light. They showed me the nails and the hair and the small room where they had kept the body. We had heard of such things happening, but never at first hand, so we went round the village to ask for further information. Everyone had seen the rainbow and knew that the body had disappeared. This village was on the main route from China to Lhasa and the people told me that the previous year when the Chinese heard about it they were furious and said the story must not be talked about.[1]

Among the special doctrines of the Great Perfection (*rdzogs-chen*) tradition of meditation, an esoteric system shared by the Nyingmapa order of Tibetan Buddhism and the Bön religion, is the teaching that some adepts who achieve the highest realization attain a "rainbow body" (*'ja'-lus*) at death. When this takes place, the adept's physical remains dissolve into light and so make manifest the thoroughgoing transformation of the person that has been catalyzed by prior spiritual discipline. In the passage reproduced here, the late Chögyam Trungpa, Rinpoche, describes an occurrence that took place in eastern Tibet during the early 1950s.

It was not long after I first read his words that I began to consider the rainbow body as a significant question for Tibetan religious culture, and not just an anecdotal oddity emphasized, before Trungpa, primarily in Western occultist literature. My own teacher, Serlo Khenpo Sanggye Tenzin (1924–1990), had been among those who had visited the family described above, shortly after the old man's passing in 1952/53, and his account closely resembled Chögyam Trungpa's. I first discussed it with him in 1974, and soon afterward I also met the son mentioned above, the one who had recommended "more formal spiritual exercises" to his father and who then lived near Darjeeling. Under the impact of his father's dissolution at death, it seems that (as one might expect under the circumstances) his world had been quite overturned, and he had long ago abandoned a mainstream monastic vocation in favor of the more eccentric lifestyle of a yogin and adept of the Great Perfection system of yoga and meditation. Through these and other encounters, I became familiar with Tibetans who had some knowledge of traditions concerning the rainbow body and their views of the matter and so gained a dawning recognition of their complexity. In particular, I was intrigued by a short text by the famous adept and scholar Mipham (1846–1912), to which my teacher had introduced me. In it, Mipham responds to the consternation expressed by a number of his associates concerning the recent death of a famous meditation master of the Nyingmapa (Rnying-ma-pa) order, Pema Düdül (Nyag-bla Padma-bdud-'dul, d. 1872),[2] Pema the Demon Tamer. Mipham's comments open as follows:

> In my own dwelling, on the eighteenth day of the month of Pūrvabhādra, during the wood boar year of the fifteen cycle [= 1875], some of the brethren who were staying with me strongly encouraged me with a request that they had made repeatedly in the past, saying, "We've conversed with some who are critical and wise, who say, 'Listen! It's a lie that this one called Pema Düdül has passed away in the rainbow body, the body of reality. In general, there can't be rainbow bodies in such bad times as these. And even if one attributes [the attainment of the rainbow body] to the specific path of the Great Perfection, it's said that the four visions [which characterize the highest realization of the Great Perfection] must be gradually perfected [before this can happen], and that, in the end, speech becomes no more than an echo, just repeating [what others say to the individual concerned]. But on the day preceding his death he was loquacious! Moreover, though one must abandon outer and inner activities in nine ways, he was maintaining a retinue and disciples!' For these and other similar reasons, nowadays there are disputants of our own and other [sects] who have come to be doubtful about this. So what's all this about? Please tell us something!"[3]

Mipham's text aroused my interest above all owing to the clarity with which it demonstrated that Tibetans themselves had sometimes expressed puzzlement and doubt about the rainbow body, and that it was thus seen by some as a problem, as much as for others it may have been a matter of faith. Mipham, in responding to his inquirers, did not so much attempt to prove that the event in question actually happened as he did to establish its plausibility. And this provides an appropriate agenda for our investigation, that is, to examine the framework of Tibetan Buddhist belief and thought in virtue of which the rainbow body is, for some at least, a matter of plausibility. Of course, in our present context it will not be sufficient just to repeat Mipham's response to his interlocutors,[4] who, despite their doubts, were participants in the Tibetan Buddhist belief system; what is required, certainly, is a broader reflection upon the category of "light" in Buddhist and Tibetan religious thought, particularly in its relation to death and to sanctity.

In attempting to consider the background in virtue of which some Tibetan Buddhists regarded the decease of persons in a rainbow body as a possible occurrence, we must distinguish carefully between physical plausibility and what we might term moral, or spiritual, plausibility. In the context of our own culture, for instance, in science fiction and philosophical puzzle cases, we readily admit in theory the physical possibility that persons may be reduced to light and then even reconstituted, as anyone familiar with the phrase, "Beam me up, Scotty!" well knows. Still, we should be surprised should some future technology actually achieve transport by beaming. More to the point, however, is that, for our culture of the imagination, there is absolutely no moral dimension to this sort of reduction of persons to light: intergalactic mass murderers may be just as well beamed as Captain Kirk. For Tibetan religious culture, however, the attainment of the rainbow body was in most cases thought to signify an extreme degree of spiritual perfection, or at the least a quasi-divine status, and to plausibly occur only when such perfection was realized. It was, moreover, the precise relationship between the rainbow body and spiritual excellence that was often considered problematic. Thus, in the passage cited above, Mipham's inquirers do not express any doubt regarding Pema the Demon Tamer's reputation as a religious master; what they question is whether his particular mode of religious life was consonant with the extremity of ascetic and visionary perfection in virtue of which the rainbow body was thought to be a possible attainment; indeed, they question whether any religious life in these "bad times" could achieve that. Here is the description given in Pema Düdül's own biography, summarizing the account that was the source of their puzzlement:

> In the water ape year, called *Aṅgira* [1872], on the new moon of the peaceful month of Vaiśākha, the venerable lama [Pema Düdül] set up a meditation tent and dwelt there. He instructed his disciples to come and had them all settle into meditation, the receptacle [of faith, i.e., the guru, visualized] upon the crowns of their heads. And he then recited [prayers] such as:
>
> In all lifetimes, inseparable from the genuine guru,
> May you enjoy the glory of the Dharma,
> And, perfecting the virtues of the stages and paths,
> May you attain to the level of [the primordial buddha] Vajradhara!
>
> He then said, "Now, go back to your own places. After sewing shut my tent flap, no one is to come here for seven days."
>
> The spiritual sons and disciples did what the lama had told them and returned to their own places feeling mentally ill at ease. At dawn on the seventh day, they performed prostrations before the meditation tent which was the lama's dwelling, and they opened it up. The lord's robes and meditation seat, his hair, and the nails of his fingers and toes were there on his bed, but the maṇḍala of his body had disappeared. At that, the spiritual sons and disciples lamented very much in sorrow, whereupon the sky was all filled by rainbow lights and such. At that time, some intelligent and supremely religious persons and some who were certainly his closest spiritual sons met him in contemplative experiences, visions, and dreams, in which he granted them his approval in speech, comforted them with the highest teachings, and so forth.[5]

Once again, however, we must underscore that our subject matter here in the first instance has little to do with particle physics.

INDIAN BUDDHIST DISCOURSES OF LIGHT AND THEIR TIBETAN LEGACY

Listen! The great resentment of the unholy toward the holy
Resembles weeds drifting atop pure water.
There are two reasons for it: jealousy's sting
And ignorance due to lack of learning or discernment.
If it be owing to the sting of envy,
As when our Lord [Buddha] was crudely disparaged
By extremists and by Devadatta,
Then that only [reflects] the magnificence of ultimate reality.
"When he approached the point of enlightenment
The earth came to quake six times,
Whereupon Māra grew discontent"—
It is just as is thus said.
If it be owing to sectarian partisanship,
So that one [sect's proponents] chastise others
On account of attainments they themselves do not possess,
That would be shameful beyond all shame!
In the varied Tantra collections of the new and ancient schools,
The dissolution of the coarse body
Into a body of light is established;
And many scholars and saints of India and Tibet
have been thus transformed.
To say that all of that is nothing at all
And thus to debase the magnificence of the Tantras—
Does this not cut down virtue's tree
With a blunt hatchet of words?

In fact, early Indian Buddhism was in some respects ambivalent about light imagery. Though the Buddha's awakening was often compared in early suttas to radiant light, strong currents in the early traditions resisted such positive imagery and preferred to understand the highest attainments in negative terms. Images of light and so forth were to be understood metaphorically, or as symptoms of penultimate realization. Though the miracles attributed to the Buddha are often described in terms of manifestations of light, these represent the Buddha's remarkable impact upon his disciples and others and are not thought to describe the highest enlightenment itself; they are merely a by-product thereof. Though later Buddhism would always retain a tendency to favor the way of negation, nevertheless, it is equally true that imagery of light continues to develop, and indeed proliferates, in the sūtras of the Mahāyāna. In scriptures such as the *Laṅkāvatāra*, the *Gaṇḍavyūha*, and the *Daśabhūmika*, the relations between buddhas and bodhisattvas, and between the latter and the mundane realms in which they are active, are often described in terms of exchanges of light (plate 1), and the transmission of enlightenment and lesser blessings occurs via pathways of rays and luminous energies. Indeed, not a few of the buddhas of the Mahāyāna pantheon have names that accentuate their affinities with light: Amitābha ("Limitless Light") and Vairocana ("Radiant Splendor") are just the two best known examples. That the Buddha's teaching, the Dharma, is itself regarded metaphorically as light is demonstrated by the explicit occurrence of similes to this effect and by the titles of several important sūtras, most famously the *Suvarṇaprabhāsottama* (*Supreme Golden Light*).

Despite the effulgent imagery with which the discourses of the Mahāyāna are suffused, we must be very cautious about the interpretation of philosophical and mystical references to light and radiance even here. While it is clear that the authors of the Mahāyāna do wish to assert that the encounter of aspirants with buddhas and other exalted beings may be marked by intensive visions of light, it is much less clear that they wish to impart any sense of metaphysical ultimacy to these discourses of luminosity. An excellent, short example of this reticence may be found in connection with the interpretation of a very widely cited sentence near the beginning of the *Aṣṭasāhasrikā Prajñāpāramitā* (*The Perfection of Wisdom in Eight Thousand Lines*): "Mind is not mind. The nature of mind is clear light" (tac cittam acittam. prakṛtiś cittasya prabhāsvarā). Though some later Tibetan authors do suggest that this lends support to the concept of a sort of luminous spiritual substance underlying the mind, the most influential of the Indian commentators on this text, Haribhadra, by contrast says: "Wherefore it is far removed from the nature of the one and the many, the *nature*, or essence, *of mind*, being unoriginated, *is clear light;* for the darkness of all conceptions of being is destroyed."[6] Thus, Haribhadra will commit himself to no more than a metaphorical interpretation of the light of the mind. In this, his perspective seems entirely continuous with the dominant scholastic trends of early Buddhism.

Tantric Buddhism, with its strong emphasis on techniques of visualization and yoga in which phenomena of light are intensely experienced, did reinforce the tendency to adopt pronouncedly cataphatic ways of speaking in later Indian Buddhism. Tibetan traditions inherited both this and, above all through the

Madhyamaka school of philosophy, a continuing scholastic emphasis on the *via negativa.* This is well exemplified by some of the ways in which light figures as a category in Indian and Tibetan yoga and Tantrism, particularly in the systems that came to be transmitted by the Kagyüpa (Bka'-brgyud-pa) order and those streams of Tibetan Tantrism most closely allied with it.

The Kagyüpa were founded in the eleventh century on the basis of the teachings of the Indian mahāsiddhas ("great adepts"), especially Tilopa, Nāropa, and Maitripa, and emphasized a system of Tantric yoga in which the experience of luminosity, or "clear light" (*'od-gsal*) was of central importance, for this was identified in some contexts with the fundamental ground of being.[7] The propensities that give rise to the diversity of mundane experience are sometimes described in Kagyüpa Tantric commentaries as originating in a primordial movement within the original ground, a movement thematized as "dark energy" (*mun-rlung*) that becomes ramified throughout the network of subtle energy channels constituting the esoteric reality (*guhyārtha, sbas-don*) of the body. The dialectic of light and dark (or pure and impure) energies within the body becomes a focal point of yogic practice, and, though the precise terminology varies to a great degree and often gives way to purely symbolic expression, it is a notable theme in much of Kagyüpa Tantric literature.

Nevertheless, Kagyüpa thought on this point is not in fact so manichaean as this may seem. That it is not is due primarily, I think, to the force of two important doctrinal tendencies. One, as we have already seen, is the extreme resistance, inherited from certain of the earlier Buddhist philosophical traditions, to an affirmative discourse concerning ultimate reality. Thus, even within Kagyüpa writings on yoga and meditation, luminosity is often treated as a description given by analogy to an experience or state that is in fact not capable of being described in ordinary language at all. A good example of this occurs in an influential manual on the Mahāmudrā, the "Great Seal," which is the pinnacle of Kagyüpa meditation instruction. The author, Götsangpa (Rgod-tshang-pa Mgon-po-rdo-rje, 1189–1258) is among the most admired of the early masters of the tradition, and here he says:

> The intention of all buddhas throughout the three times, naturally present in all sentient beings, and manifest in the appearance of the six aggregates [of the five physical senses and the intellect], is called "natural luminosity." But, however one designates it, it refers to the appearance of the six aggregates without contrivance. . . . Though one may assert it to be the clear light experienced, for instance, at death, nevertheless, in the absence of the realization of the dharmakāya [the "body of reality"], the luminosity [of which I am speaking here] remains ungrasped. That [experience of clear light at death]

is just mundane conceptual activity. Mundane conceptual activity is ignorance. And ignorance is the opposite of what we mean by "luminosity."[8]

The qualification "in the absence of the realization of the dharmakāya" is of course the crucial point here: it is not the experience of light per se that is enlightening, but rather the manner in which that, or for that matter any other experience, is itself understood. I shall return to the question of the experience of clear light at death shortly; obviously, this theme is most pertinent to our present subject matter.

A second doctrinal theme that militates against the tendency to attribute ultimacy to the phenomenal dichotomy of light and dark, at least in the context of yoga and meditation, is the general antidualism of the Mahāyāna. The opposition between the light of gnosis and dark energy must therefore be resolved in a realization that reaches the ground prior to their differentiation. We would expect that one result would be that on some occasions the phenomenon of darkness, or obscuration, itself comes to be revalued as an intimation of illuminating experience. As we shall see below, this is indeed what we do sometimes find in the literature.

With this in mind, then, let us turn to aspects of the literature itself and begin by considering a short verse treatise, *The Garland of Gems* (*Ratnamālā*) and the commentary on it.[9] The basic text is perhaps an Indian work, but the commentary, though attributed to the Indian master Abhayadatta, is certainly a Tibetan composition that may have originated as a Tibetan disciple's record of Abhayadatta's oral expositions of the verse text. The work is presented as an epitome of instructions on Tantrism and yogic practice stemming from the Indian Buddhist mahāsiddhas; in its content it is strongly allied with early Kagyüpa material though it is not clear to what extent the text as we have it was known within the early Kagyüpa tradition.[10]

The commentary treats the verses of *The Garland of Gems* as teachings delivered by several different mahāsiddhas to a maimed and tormented demoness in response to her quest for an antidote to her suffering. At the outset, the demoness requests the instruction of Lūipa, who says to her, "Your fault is not knowing your own nature. If you know that, you'll be freed from appearances, not to speak just of bodily appearances." When she then asks, "What's it to know your own nature?" he responds, "It is a luminous gnosis, in which the continuum of mundane reality comes to an end."

"Luminous gnosis" (*'od-gsal ye-shes, prabhāsvarajñāna*) is in fact the core soteriological concept in *The Garland of Gems,* and all of the instructions that follow are intended to amplify or clarify this concept, usually in response to the demoness's protest, following each teaching, that she doesn't quite get what the siddhas are trying to teach her. We may share her puzzlement. Just what is the "luminous gnosis" of which Lūipa speaks? The commentary explains it as follows:

When the entire continuum of the attributions of existence, appearance, emptiness, idea, mind, and thought comes to an end, we speak of "luminous gnosis." Like the radiance of a precious gem, it is "incessant," and for this reason is characterized as "without boundary or center, and thus pervasive." Like uncompounded space, it embraces everything, from the highest heavens to the depths of hell. . . . It is "like the fire of Malaya Mountain" that incinerates all it encounters.

This passage well illustrates the ambivalence of light imagery in many Buddhist contexts, and the manner in which that ambivalence continued to inform Buddhist Tantrism and yoga. On the one hand, the luminosity of luminous gnosis seems clearly to be analogical, just as it had been in Haribhadra's definition, cited above: it refers to the "clearing" that is realized when all mundane conceptual activity comes to an end. On the other, the description is so reinforced by reference to the radiance of gems and of fire that it is difficult to conclude that there is no phenomenological content intended here whatsoever. This apparent ambivalence, however, does not at all characterize those later portions of the text that focus upon Tantric visualization techniques and exercises involving the subtle energies of the body. In these contexts, it seems certain that the phenomenological component of the light imagery is literally intended. Thus, for example, the verse that the siddha Mīnapa sings to the demoness:

The bodily vessel becomes elemental light,
A melting stream of divine ambrosia above.
In the mass of reality's light,
Conceptions of the six aggregates are exhausted.

The commentary explains:

This refers to the creative visualization of the deity . . . the bodily mansion becomes like a vase, filled with the light of the elements . . .

Atop that mansion of elemental light, you must contemplate a white HŪṂ which is in its nature a divinity embodying the essence of mind, radiating light, and from which there is a melting stream of ambrosia. It dissolves into the elements, intermingling thus with the bodily vase. Mind itself, in essence a divinity, of the nature of the elements, now dissolves into light. . . . The sign of contemplative success is an experience of outer warmth, and in this way one is clothed by the elements, while inner awareness is nourished by this contemplation, so that one is thus fed.

It is quite clear that in this case, whether we are referring to visualized or to visionary experience, "light" is being used to characterize those experiences phenomenologically. The analogical conception of luminous gnosis, however, has not been entirely forgotten. When the demoness is unable to make much progress in the visualization exercise just described, Nāgārjuna offers encouragement by explaining that her tormented condition would be "changed to bliss if she had the power to realize the *nature of mind* to be a mass of light, a solar orb." Given the diction of the text, the reference here to the "nature of mind," which also of course echoes Haribhadra's usage, points directly back to Lūipa's teaching of "luminous gnosis"—the phenomenal light of visionary experience is thus in the final analysis a token, a sign whose intention is that which transcends all experience that can be characterized in phenomenal terms.

I have argued so far that in *The Garland of Gems* light imagery is employed primarily in two ways: first, it refers analogically to transcendent gnosis, and in this usage remains ambivalent about the phenomenal features of luminosity as that is ordinarily understood; and, second, it refers phenomenologically to experiences of light that occur in connection with specific types of yoga and meditation practice. That these are indeed two distinct usages, but are nevertheless closely tied to one another in this tradition, is further emphasized in the concluding sections of the work, which discuss a system of yoga attributed to Tilopa, the Kagyüpa's major Indian patriarch. As elsewhere in the Kagyüpa traditions, Tilopa's teaching is broadly divided into two complementary aspects: there is the teaching of the abstract contemplation of the absolute, which is elsewhere called Mahāmudrā; and there are a series of methods of Tantric yoga which focus upon our ephemeral states of being. The first is summarized in the commentary as follows:

> Natural, luminous gnosis is the final significance of the view [of the Mahāmudrā]. It is the skylike body of reality, which is not engendered by any cause and is therefore without any result. . . . [I]n its essential nature, the skylike radiant light of mind can neither be exemplified nor designated.
>
> So, then, can no experience be cultivated of it?
>
> There is an experienceless cultivation of experience, meditationless meditation, incessant absorption, a result that is never to be attained, but from which one is never separated.

The text thus remains determined to avoid fixing in phenomenal terms its conception of the final significance of luminous gnosis.

If the foregoing represents Tilopa's teaching of the ultimate view of luminous gnosis, his description of its cultivation through meditation and yoga returns, as we have seen before, to emphasize experienced content. Here, he stresses that mind is to be understood as radiant light, and body as apparition, and that their connection is to be realized in the "liminal states" (*bar-do, antarābhava*) of waking experience, dream, and the passage from death to rebirth. Here the experiences of light, bliss, and embodiment are closely interrelated, providing the conditions whereby mundane embodiment becomes itself a vehicle of enlightenment. Referring to the waking state during our present lifetime, for example, the text tells us:

> The liminal passage from birth to death is the period during which all sorts of conceptions become concretely manifest, so that one is embodied in the "body of karmic maturation." But conceptual activity may be disclosed as luminous in nature, and this luminousness in turn may be intermingled with the emotions and passions, purifying them. How so? On the path of transformation one holds the conceptions to be gods and goddesses, while on the path of desire one engenders bliss while relying upon the subtle channels and fluids, and on the path of liberation one engenders bliss relying upon the Inner Heat of the body. Finally, on the path of great liberation, one does not hanker after those sorts of bliss at all, but realizes them to be of the nature of radiant light and so intermingles radiant light with passion.

The text later expands upon this notion of radiant light, in its relation to the psychophysical regime of Tantric yoga and meditation upon the absolute, in these words:

> When proficiency in the Inner Heat is achieved by day, radiant light comes to be grasped by night in four ways: there is the natural radiant light, which is the purity of all phenomena; the radiant light of concentration, arising in the contemplative experience of the yogin in union with his consort; the radiant light of sleep, when coarse mental activity comes to a halt in deep sleep; and the radiant light of death, arising when, during the liminal passage between death and rebirth, the bodily elements are deceased.

Radiant light, then, though in the final analysis free from phenomenal qualifications, is nevertheless disclosed in phenomenal modalities that differ in relation to the experienced framework: as the bliss of the Inner Heat, arising most forcefully in the yoga of sexual union; as the subdued and pervading clarity that accompanies the cessation of mental activity in trance and deep sleep; or as the light refracted into bewildering multiplicity of experiences characterizing both the dream state and the dreamlike state of consciousness migrating from death to rebirth.

Earlier, I mentioned that there is a sense in which, because the ultimate transcends the dichotomy of light and darkness, it must embrace darkness too. This is not an explicit theme in our present text, but it is suggested in one passage in connection with the teaching attributed to the weaver Tantipa, whose cryptic verse reads:

Free from both renunciation and possession,
If you come to know, you'll not enter bewilderment's city.
But like Nanda and the gemstone light,
You'll find the city itelf to be supreme bliss.

The commentary explains that as Nanda, the king of the nāgas, perceives the light of the wish-granting gem that is invisible to all others, in the same way the adept perceives that the "city" of obscuration and bewilderment *is* the domain of luminous gnosis, of the highest bliss. Elsewhere, Kagyüpa writers may treat darkness itself as an expression of luminosity—the clarity of night seems to converge with the clarity of day. A fine example of this is found in the writings of the sixteenth-century Karmapa hierarch Mikyö Dorje (Karma-pa VIII Mi-bskyod-rdo-rje, 1507–54), who recounts that in the midst of a vision of the poet-sage Milarepa, he becomes absorbed by the blackness of Milarepa's hair: it is the blackest black he has ever seen, blacker than anything, and yet it is of the nature of light.[11]

If darkness can, in a sense, point to the light, the reverse is sometimes also the case: the yogin's experiences of light, in and of themselves, may in fact be expressions of ignorance. This is a well-formed theme in Kagyüpa meditation manuals, and we have seen an example earlier, in the words of Götsangpa. Starting with the simple dichotomy of light and dark, therefore, we find that these opposites pervade one another, that in some sense light and dark are no different. Their interpretation, both in texts and in contemplative practice, is subtle and not always evident. And this is without regard to the many differing modalities of light—dim, radiant, or effulgent; diffused, refracted or sparkling, monotonal or multicolored; internal or external; holographic or unidimensional; and so on—that pervade the texts of Tibetan religious traditions.[12] The color codes of Tibetan Tantric iconography also merit consideration in this context, but about this I limit myself to one observation that is particularly appropriate here: the blue color of the primordial buddha Vajradhara, the embodment of the ultimate reality that is the dharmakāya according to the Kagyüpa tradition, may be described and depicted as either the light blue of a clear and bright daytime sky or the near black of a moonless night (plate 2).

THE CLEAR LIGHT OF DEATH

If you say that in this degenerate age,
The [body of light] has never been observed to occur,
That would amount to rejection of doctrine . . .
Do you wish to affirm that nowadays,
In this land of snow mountains,
The teaching of the Vajrayāna is no more?

In the teaching of the Kagyüpa master Götsangpa, we have seen that he was at pains to distinguish the luminosity of the mind, as realized by the adept in meditation, from the phenomenal experience of clear light at death. This, he said, if not involving the realization of the dharmakāya, the "body of reality" that is the ultimate nature of things, the metaphysical ground of the Buddha's awakening, is merely an expression of nescience. In the Kagyüpa and other Tibetan Tantric traditions, instructions relating to death are in fact among the primary topics in relation to which the theme of mind's luminous nature is developed. This may be illustrated by the *Instructions Concerning the Liminal State* (*Bar-do'i gdams-pa*) composed by the eleventh- to twelfth-century adept Khyungpo Neljor.[13]

The widespread promulgation of Indian Tantrism in Tibet from the eleventh century onward encouraged the treatment of death, in some contexts, as the occasion for the application of specific techniques of Tantric yoga and meditation which, ideally at least, would have been practiced by the adept in the course of his or her earlier training. Significantly, knowledge of such techniques was also assimilated to what appears to have been an autochthonous Tibetan custom of calling the dead, so that a body of literature arose in which funerary rituals and Tantric instructions were to some extent integrated with one another. The culmination of this process occurred with the appearance, probably in the fourteenth century, of the so-called "Tibetan Book of the Dead."[14]

Khyungpo Neljor, in relation to these developments, appears as a bridge figure. Originally trained within the traditions of the Bön religion and the old Nyingmapa order of Tibetan Buddhism, he turned from these to participate in the new influx of Indian Tantrism into Tibet that occurred during the eleventh century. Nevertheless, it is not always clear in his works just where we are to draw the line between indigenous Tibetan and Indian themes and motifs. For example—and this is an example pertinent to our theme of the body of light—when in the course of his travels in India he encounters the enigmatic woman adept, Niguma, who will become his main teacher, his hagiography offers this description:

I wandered throughout India, and asked, "Who, among the accomplished masters, seems to have come face to face with the Buddha himself?" The paṇḍitas and siddhas concurred, "That would be the Paṇḍita Nāropa's lady, the ḍākinī of enlightened awareness called 'Niguma.' She abides in the three pure stations [i.e., the eighth through tenth bodhisattva stations, from which there is no falling back], and she has really requested instruction in the dharma from the great Vajradhara himself." When I asked where she was residing just then, I was told that those of pure vision might meet her anywhere, but that one of impure vision could search everywhere for her without success; for she dwelt upon the pure stations, and her embodied form had become the stuff of rainbows.[15]

Often, Indian traditions concerning the great Buddhist Tantric adepts speak of them passing from this world into the realm of the "sky-farers" (*khecara*). The allusion to a rainbow embodiment in this case may, however, reflect a Tibetan trope. A similar caution must apply to our reading of Khyungpo Neljor's *Instructions Concerning the Liminal State.* In the opening sections of this text, the author establishes a general framework based on the states of waking consciousness, dream, and death that broadly accords with what we know of Tilopa's teachings as summarized in the *Garland of Gems,* and about which Khyungpo writes:

Now, the ground to be purified by the yogin consists of the three bodies of the liminal states, and they are purified [respectively] by these three: [the practices of Tantric yoga known as] creation-and-perfection, dream, and luminosity. . . . The three bodies of the liminal states are those of the liminal state of birth-and-death, the liminal state of the dream, and the liminal state of possible being.

The first, the liminal state of birth-and-death, is the duration from birth until death, and is the body of maturation. . . . Having amassed many virtues and sins, which mature as the varied pleasures and pains one experiences, this [physical body] is the body of maturation.

Second: having gone to sleep, until one awakens, there is the liminal state of the dream, which is the body of latent dispositions. . . . It is the body of latent dispositions because the mass of the latent dispositions of this lifetime comes forth in dreams.

Third: from death until one takes birth there is the liminal state of possible being, the body of mind. . . . .

The body of maturation is purified by [the visualization of] the body of the deity. . . . The body of latent dispositions is purified by the emanation and transformation of the dream. . . . The body of mind is purified by luminosity.

The framework for Khyungpo Neljor's teaching, therefore, is precisely similar to that which we have examined above, in connection with the *Garland of Gems.* Khyungpo Neljor's primary concern, however, is with last of the three liminal states, that of the body of mind that is purified by luminosity during the passage intervening between death and rebirth. The liminal state itself unfolds in three stages corresponding to the dissolution of consciousness into luminosity at death, the visionary experiences of the period that follows, and the subsequent entry into a realm of rebirth. The first of these is characterized by the clear light experienced at death that had been mentioned by Götsangpa. In Khyungpo Neljor's text, this is described in some detail. Here Khyungpo directs the adept to realize that the luminosity identified with the ultimate nature of the mind and the experience of clear light at death are really no different. In other words, the adept is to overcome the failure to grasp the underlying reality without which the experience of clear light alone is merely "mundane conceptual activity":

One should evidently realize that both the luminosity that has been meditatively cultivated [during one's lifetime] . . . and the spontaneously arisen, natural luminosity [occurring at death] are no different. . . . Because form first dissolves into sound, forms become indistinct. When sound dissolves into odor, the ear no longer hears. After odors dissolve into taste, the nose does not smell them. Because taste dissolves into the tactile, the tongue does not experience taste. After tactile sensation dissolves into abstract phenomena and the complexion of the body goes bad, bodily sensations are then no longer felt. Such is the dissolution of objects. After that there is the dissolution of the elements. As is said . . .

> First earth dissolves into water.
> Then water dissolves into fire.
> After fire has dissolved into wind,
> Wind, too, dissolves into consciousness.
> Consciousness, the apprehending subject,
> Proceeds [to dissolve] even as far as luminosity.

Thus, as noted earlier, "luminosity" is what remains when all else has been stripped away, whether in the yogin's cultivation of an intense concentration in which all objectivizations are systematically eliminated or through the process of dissolution at death. Training in Tantric methods of contemplation is intended to render it possible to recognize this luminosity of death, without being overcome by it, in which case, as Götsangpa had warned, it "remains ungrasped." For the yogin who does comprehend the process of dissolution, however, it is essential to attend to the precise modalities of luminosity that now unfold. Khyungpo Neljor continues:

After consciousness has dissolved into luminosity, four cognitions arise: [they are called] appearance, diffuse appearance, appropriation, and possession. With respect to them these five marks arise . . . :

First, it is like a mirage,
Second, like the moon,
Third, like the sun,
Fourth, like darkness,
And fifth, like a cloudless sky,
In which the nonconceptual,
without limit or center, will arise.

The four cognitions are each described in some detail, so that Khyungpo supplies a nuanced phenomenology of the dissolution of consciousness in the experience of light. The first cognition, called "appearance," is characterized as follows:

[W]hen consciousness dissolves into luminosity, the outer mark is like the moonrise, while the inner mark is like the occurrence of a mirage, with light rays of five colors. At that time, abiding with sparkling clarity in the nonconceptual cognition called "appearance," the first instant occurs. . . . At that time, because aversion is not borne even towards a murderous enemy, it is called "empty."

The precise significance of the distinction between the "outer mark" and "inner mark" is not made explicit, but it is nevertheless elucidated to some degree in the passages that follow. In essence, these suggest that the concern here is the distinction between the field of consciousness and the contents thereof. All has in any case now dissolved into luminosity, but that luminosity is not experienced as an invariant ether; it is a sphere of experience in which certain characteristic phenomena, whose natures are equally luminous, are disclosed. Khyungpo adheres to a fixed mode of exposition, specifying the outer and inner mark, in treating the moments that follow:

Second, when "appearance" dissolves into "diffusion," the outer mark is like sunrise, while the inner mark is like the occurrence of fireflies. At that time, abiding in startling clarity in the nonconceptual gnosis called "diffusion," which is exceedingly clear and free from the conception of the apprehending subject, the second instant occurs. . . . At that time, no desire arises even for divine boys or girls, so that it is called "great emptiness."

In the next phase, a theme we have encountered earlier, that of the convergence of luminosity and darkness, is elaborated:

Third, the dissolution of "diffusion" into "appropriation": the outer sign is thick blackness, like dark nightfall. The inner sign arises that is like a lamp unmoved by the wind. At that time, there is "appropriation," a nonconceptual gnosis that is clear and without any subjective apprehension. . . . That phase, when there arises pristine clarity, of the nature of light, is called "extremely empty."

The light that dawns within that darkness is marked by the subsiding of all remaining tendencies to conceptual activity and objectification. The subtle duality that originates at the moment of conception is here at last resolved. Though thoroughly free from conceptual activity, it is a state that is nevertheless described in affective terms as "blissful":

Fourth, when "appropriation" dissolves into "possession," the outer sign is like the rising of the morning star at dawn, while the inner sign is like the clear autumn sky suffused by the brilliance of the sun. After that, the white and red aspects of father and mother [= semen and blood], as the pair A-HAṂ [= e-go], meet at the heart, whereupon there arises the experience of bliss and emptiness. At that time there is "possession," called "natural luminosity." Free from all the taints of conceptual craving, one abides in the fourth instant in that nonconceptual bliss and clarity, unobjectified and surpassing the intellect. . . . Because that cognition causes [all affective and dualistic] conceptions . . . , subtle and coarse, . . . to dissolve in luminosity and cease, it is called the pristine cogntion wherein all is naturally empty. It is said . . . ,

> Just as various clouds,
> Having different colors and shapes,
> Arise from the expanse of the sky
> And return, indeed, to that,
> So all natures,
> Entities characterized by three [modes of] appearance,
> Which, without exception, involve objectifications,
> Will dissolve in luminosity.

That this is precisely what is meant by the "luminosity of death" in this context is made explicit in a concluding recapitulation:

"Appearance" is the luminosity that is cultivated [in contemplative practice], "diffusion" is the luminosity of absorption [in deep meditation], "appropriation" is the unsoiled, uncorrupted luminosity, and "possession" is the natural luminosity that is an inherent principle. . . . And that, moreover, is called the "body of reality at death." For, as Āryadeva says:

> Death is absolute truth, while birth is the relative.

Thus, it may be called the "luminosity of death," or the "natural luminosity." One who has previously become accustomed to luminosity [in contemplative practice], and abides in that, [merging] with natural luminosity, like the meeting of mother and son, will not see the cities of the six families [of rebirth] in the liminal state thereafter. Rather, from that unborn luminosity the [buddhas'] two bodies of form incessantly, naturally arise, emerging in spontaneous presence. The one [who realizes this] matures and liberates all sentient beings, each one in accord with his or her needs, until saṃsāra is emptied. As it says in the *Play of Pristine Gnosis* and other Tantras:

> The individual who has grasped luminosity
> Does not see the cities of the liminal state,
> But arises for the sake of others in the body of form,
> Like the gem that grants all wishes.

Such is the one of highest acumen, who, by attaining the Great Seal in a single lifetime, is awakened as a buddha.

By contrast, those of us who fail to realize the nature of this light of the dharmakāya will reemerge from an ephemeral absorption in it, to continue to migrate in the liminal state until driven by the force of karma to an appropriate realm of rebirth:

> [W]hen one who is not much accustomed to luminosity cannot remain in the luminosity of that first liminal state [which includes all the phases discussed so far], then for three and a half days of the first week visions of the body of one's former life will emerge, including one's country, house, wealth, possessions, and relations, and when the sensory faculties are all complete, one will then have a mental body. . . . At that time, one does not know oneself to be in the liminal state.

Owing to this unknowing, luminosity now drifts confusedly into dreamlike visions that finally become concrete as one meanders into circumstances fit for rebirth.

Khyungpo Neljor's *Instructions Concerning the Liminal State* very well exemplifies the manner in which the process of death, and its relation to the contemplative experience of light as engendered through methods of Tantric yoga, came to be conceived in Tibetan religious culture generally; but specifically it represents the perspective of those traditions that were most influenced by the Indian Buddhist Tantrism of the early second millenium. Clearly, "light" does not describe univocally a particular type of religious experience, but instead characterizes a broad experiential sphere requiring a fuller phenomenology to disclose its varied modalities. Significantly, too, it demonstrates that, for Tibetan Buddhist Tantric thought, there is a sense in which everyone dissolves into light at death. What is conspicuously absent is the notion that this dissolution may sometimes become physically manifest, through the adept's attainment of a rainbow body. Indian Tantrism and yoga had attributed such powers as celestial flight and physical disappearance to certain adepts, regarding these as significant but not ultimate attainments. Nevertheless, it appears that the Indian background of many aspects of Tibetan Buddhism supplies only part of what we need in order to understand the conception of the reduction of the body to light in Tibetan religious culture.[16]

EARLY TIBETAN ILLUMINATIONS

Because mere invisibility
May be due to obscurations caused by daemons of the eight classes,
Something more than that alone
Is needed as a proof of faith.

The texts we have surveyed above—the commentary on the *Garland of Gems* of the mahāsiddha tradition and Khyungpo Neljor's *Instructions Concerning the Liminal State*—are Tibetan works dating to about 1100 and strongly reflect the ascendancy of Indian Buddhist Tantrism in Tibet during the period in which they were composed. While they illustrate the prominence of light imagery in that context, they do not yet hint at the actual dissolution of the physical person into light, with perhaps the exception of Khyungpo's description of his teacher Niguma as embodied in the "stuff of rainbows" (though, as we have seen, this perhaps reflects a Tibetan rather than an Indian trope). Of course, there is a sense in which the person may be said to dissolve into light at death, but it is the mind, not the body that so dissolves; no claim is advanced that this dissolution into luminosity occurs in the shared domain of common sensory experience. Apparently, then, the Indianized dimensions of Tibetan religion do not by themselves explain the remarkable conception of the rainbow body. We must turn now, therefore, to examine some of the other sources of Tibetan Buddhist thought on this matter.

The ancient kings of Tibet, from whose line the monarchs of the seventh- to ninth-century Tibetan empire arose, were held to be divine in origin. The first seven kings, known collectively as the "seven heavenly thrones" (*gnam-la khri-bdun*), demonstrated their divinity at death by leaving no earthly remains at all. A twelfth-century work offers this description:

With reference to those seven [kings known as the "seven heavenly thrones"], they possessed, on their crowns, the so-called divine daemon cord [*lha'i smu-thag*]. This was a ray of white light. When those seven passed from suffering [in Buddhist usage this would mean "attained nirvāṇa"] and journeyed to the realm of the gods, they dissolved into light from their feet upwards, and after the light faded into the sky, they left no corpses behind. So it is said that the mausoleums of the seven thrones were planted in space.[17]

As we shall see below, some Tibetan Buddhist writers were inclined to associate reports of the rainbow body primarily with beliefs such as these, and not at all with the properly Buddhist light imagery we have examined earlier. However that may be, it is clear that the equation among divinity, kingship, light, and elevation in space is an ancient and compelling dimension of the autochthonous Tibetan religious system. Moreover, it is equally clear that these associations in some respects lent themselves to an assimilation with the Indian Buddhist imagery of light. If, for example, Khyungpo Neljor's description of Niguma as an embodiment of rainbows reflects a Tibetan trope, it should now be apparent that the Indian image of "sky-faring" would have readily been interpreted in relation to indigenous Tibetan conceptions of the close association among divinity, light, and sky.

In addition to the Tibetan cultural background and the influx of Indian Buddhism that began in the eighth century, there were several other important sources of the developing Tibetan religious culture of the late first millennium which, in one way or another, accentuated the religious significance of light. We know, for instance, that the Iranian world played a role here, and that Manichaeism in particular became to some extent known during the age of the Tibetan empire, as did Nestorian Christianity. Nevertheless, we cannot now trace the precise impact of Iranian and Middle Eastern religions upon the Tibetan world in any detail.[18]

Chinese religious traditions also assumed considerable importance in early medieval Tibet, and here the evidence is clearer. A ninth-century Tibetan Chan text found at Dunhuang, for example, provides brief hagiographical accounts of a lineage of teachers, and peculiar light phenomena are regularly mentioned in the accounts of their deaths. A good example is found in the hagiography of the final member of the lineage, the Tibetan adept Namkei Nyingpo:

> The preceptor Namkei Nyingpo, having worshipped the emanation [*sprul-pa*] of Trhiga Shingyong (Khri-ga-shing-yong), gave forth light from his body. Again, when he entered the place of retreat at Yam-yog, wonders appeared such as his being accompanied by a five-colored cloud. Meditatively cultivating the path of the doctrine in a single lifetime, he reached the culmination of his commitment to abide in the ascetic virtues. Thereafter, in his seventy-first year, on the twenty-ninth day of the spring month *ra-ba*, during a dog year, he adopted the unwavering vajra-posture in the retreat place of Zhong-pong and passed beyond time without change of complexion. That night, in the middle of the night, two great lights continuously arose in the sky between Srin-po Peak and the ridge of Zhong-pong Mountain, below the hermitage, and the whole district was illuminated until they set in the west. Many countrymen saw it in common, including Pelgi Gyeltsen (Dpal-gyi-rgyal-mtshan), master of the *saṃgha* of

the Ten Directions, 'Byi-lig, and Gwan Lodrö ('Gwan Blo-gros). At the conclusion of the sevenfold rites, there was a religious feast for five hundred gods and men. After prayers were recited, during the third watch in the middle of the night, at the base of the cliff behind the hermitage, a great light arose and passed away in the western direction.[19]

It is quite clear that aspects of this narrative resemble reports of adepts' deaths that we find in the later literature of the Great Perfection traditions. One may no doubt also detect here some affinity with Chinese accounts of the *Lives of Eminent Monks,* whose death narratives have been studied by Jacques Gernet.[20] (Compare, too, the visions of light described in Raoul Birnbaum's chapter below.) As Gernet notes, the Chinese Buddhist hagiographies may be in some respects related to those of Taoist adepts and immortals. On referring to a collection of the lives of the immortals, the *Liexian zhuan,* which has been studied and translated by Max Kaltenmark, one in fact finds many interesting points of comparison. Thus, for example, the hagiography of Ningfengzi tells us that he was "capable of producing smoke tinted with five colors,"[21] which recalls Namkei Nyingpo's five-colored cloud. As will be seen below, the resemblances between certain of the death narratives in Taoist and Tibetan hagiographies are far more suggestive than just this alone.

THE WAY OF THE GREAT PERFECTION

On the day [of Pema Düdül's death] the inner and outer conjunctions
Obscured the suns of a billion worlds,
And for seven days rainbows and rays and masses of light
Were directly perceived surging through space,
Causing ordinary appearance to disappear—
Wouldn't it be mad to disavow this?
At that time, among the persons who assembled there—
The Kathok Dzarka incarnation [Kaḥ-thog 'Dzar-ka sprul-sku] and many others
Endowed with peerless learning and discernment,
As well as many hundreds of ordinary folk,
Who, having first heard of [Pema Düdül's] passing, gathered together—
What they actually, inerrantly saw
In direct perception common to all
Was like a risen sun that they could not obscure
Even when they attempted to shield [their eyes] with their hands.

In its origins, the Tibetan contemplative tradition of the Great Perfection (*rdzogs-chen*) remains mysterious. Samten Karmay, in his monograph *The Great Perfection,* has presented several of the most important Dunhuang documents relating to the Great Perfection systems, so we need not duplicate his efforts here.[22] The texts he has studied date to about the ninth century, and the Great Perfection as presented within them is an extremely spare, often markedly apophatic approach to Buddhist meditation. This is illustrated by the short *Rig-pa'i khu-byug* (*The Cuckoo of Awareness*), a famous work for the later tradition whose earliest version has been identified by Karmay among the Dunhuang texts:

Svāsti! Homage to the glory of glories, the transcendent lord Samantabhadra, who is the vajra of body, speech, and mind, and great bliss spontaneously perfected!

> As varied nature is nondual,
> Even in diffusion it is without elaboration.
> Though there is no conception of just-what-is,
> It is effulgent (Vairocana) and omnibeneficent (Samantabhadra).
> Renouncing the disease of grasping effort,
> One becomes settled, abiding spontaneously.[23]

The Great Perfection teaching, as revealed in such materials, appears to be in most respects closely related to other Mahāyāna systems of nonconceptual contemplation, but it nevertheless involves a distinctively Tantric frame of reference, marked here, for instance, in the prologue introducing the verses by its invocation of the "three secrets," the "vajra of body, speech, and mind." Its reference, in the fourth verse line, to the esoteric buddha Vairocana-Samantabhadra[24] probably is intended, as reflected in my translation, as a double-entendre: it identifies the nondual nature of things with buddhahood, while using the buddha's name and epithet as descriptive expressions as well. If this is correct, then the mention of Vairocana here perhaps previsions the important role of light imagery in the later, developed Great Perfection traditions. In the course of their development, on the basis of the humble beginnings represented in such short texts as *The Cuckoo of Awareness,* those traditions expanded to become an enormously elaborated family of esoteric systems within the Bön religion and the Buddhist Nyingmapa order, and this occurred during the ninth through twelfth centuries. This is not the place to review these properly historical questions, but it is significant that the first narratives of adepts passing into the body of light seem also to date from this time. These include the legendary accounts of the Indian patriarchs of the Great Perfection traditions, accounts that were almost certainly not derived from India.[25] Here, I shall focus upon the stories of a line of Tibetan adepts that perhaps do refer to historical persons, even though the tales as we now know them are largely legendary in character.

In question are the hagiographies of the lineage of the Great Perfection teachings known as the Great Perfection in the Area of Mind (*rdzogs-chen sems-phyogs*) and the Vajra Bridge (*rdo-rje zam-pa*).[26] In these tales, curiously recapitulating the history of the ancient Tibetan kings, we find a line of seven successive figures, beginning with the celebrated translator Vairocana, who disappear at death, until finally the masters of this teaching begin to die leaving their bodies behind. The figures concerned are said to have lived during the late eighth through early eleventh centuries. The theme of the rainbow body is clearly in evidence in the lives of three hermits—Vairocana's disciple Pang Mipham Gönpo (Spang Mi-pham-mgon-po) and his disciples—who shared the same retreat cave in far eastern Tibet and in great old age all vanished in the same year:

> In this way, the bodies of the three masters and disciples vanished in the Wa Senge [Fox Lion] Cavern during the same year of the snake, one after the other, like mists, or rainbows, fading away.

It is, however, in the hagiographies of their three successors—Nyang Cangcup-tra, Nyang Sherap Jungne, and Bagom—that a fuller narrative begins to emerge. The accounts of the first two are initially presented in extremely spare terms.

> Nyang Cangcup-tra . . . vanished without a trace, like a cloud disintegrating on a mountainside. . . .
>
> Nyang Sherap Jungne . . . experienced the naturally manifest, unbiased intention of the Great Perfection, and, after hanging his robe, rosary, and skull-cup on a juniper tree on the summit of Lhari in Phukpoche, his body vanished in the sky, just like a brilliant rainbow.

The life of their successor Bagom, however, adds to these brief notes a report of the specific signs of contemplative mastery they demonstrated that presaged their attainment of the rainbow body. Here is what takes place when Nyang Cangcup-tra comes to visit his disciple and grand-disciple:

> As master Sherap Jungne and Bagom looked on from the left and the right, the master, who was between them, became invisible. As their astonishment grew, he changed into a whirlwind one cubit high, which, after spinning to and fro, turned into a fire. The fire then turned into a bronze bowl for water-offerings, filled to the point of overflowing. Then, in a fury, it turned abruptly into the master himself. When he had thus revealed his power over the activity field in which the four elements are overcome, he said, "From the time when the impurities of the elements are removed, and until their pure essences vanish, this may occur. . . . [I]t is most important to remain undistracted."

And later Nyang Sherap Jungne repeats his master's wonderful trick:

Once when Bagom went to gather wood in the forest of Pelbu, he saw the red glow of a fire around their thatched cottage; but the master had not lit a fire. Thinking the house was ablaze, Bagom went to investigate, but the thatched cottage appeared as before without a sign of fire. When he asked him what had happened, the master replied, "I became absorbed in the contemplation of fire. Do you not remember my guru, Nyang Cangcup-tra?"

Finally, in the narration of Bagom's own death, though tradition does hold him to have attained the body of light, it is released only in the course of his cremation. The account interestingly resembles in part that of the death of the eastern Tibetan Chan master Namkei Nyingpo, which we have seen above. Moreover, in its report of the concealment of the corpse in a family shrine and the perception of uncanny lights by persons outside, it is also similar to the recent account of the rainbow body with which this chapter began:

In his ninety-eighth year he passed away without sickness. His wife, Como Kangmo, did not show the body to outsiders, but she cremated it in the household shrine. All of the people outside saw a pot-sized ball of light go off into the sky. No remains at all were left behind.

Despite the variations in the rainbow body narrations we find here, it is clear that the attainment of the rainbow body has now begun to be regarded as a sign of spiritual perfection within the Great Perfection traditions. As a result, the failure of recognized masters to pass away in a body of light itself comes to be seen as an aberrant phenomenon requiring some explanation. This emerges already in the hagiography of Bagom's successor, Dzeng Dharmabodhi (ca. late eleventh to early twelfth centuries):

During his cremation the sky was filled with rainbows. Many relics and stūpas were discovered [among his ashes]. Because he continued to protect his disciples, his impure body did not dissolve into the rainbow body; but, in fact, he fulfilled all the signs of having passed into nirvāṇa on the primordially pure level which is beyond all phenomena.

The notion that an active involvement with disciples is an obstacle to the attainment of the rainbow body emerges as a distinct theme in a number of other works concerning personages of approximately the same time period, as it does here, in the hagiography of one of Dzeng Dharmabodhi's most renowned contemporaries, Zurcung Sherap-tra (1014–74):

Lama Zurcungpa resolved to remain absorbed in practice for twenty-four continuous years on Mount Trak Gyawo, and so to pass away in the rainbow body. . . . At one point he spent a long period without even his attendant coming to serve him. Eventually, when no trace of smoke or noise emerged from his hermitage, the attendant, fearing that some illness had befallen the master, went to investigate. He found the guru with his mouth and nose covered with cobwebs. Thinking that he had passed away, he cried out loud. The master's concentration was disturbed and he said, "If I had remained in that state I would have become free from this burdensome skull! Now I shall have to take rebirth once more." . . . It appears that [this account refers to] the indication of success on the path, whereby the body becomes many particles of the pure essence [i.e., light] alone, [which takes place] when [clinging to] reality is exhausted all at once.[27]

It is, of course, in relation to accounts such as these that we must understand the puzzlement expressed by Mipham's companions in reaction to the reports of the death of Pema the Demon Tamer, which motivated them to exclaim in disbelief that "he was maintaining a retinue and disciples!"

In the preceding section, based upon the evidence of a Tibetan Chan text from Dunhuang, I suggested that Chinese hagiographical traditions may be among the sources of inspiration for the materials we are considering. And it will not be difficult to discern many points of contact with Raoul Birnbaum's investigations later in this book. (It is perhaps significant, in this regard, that Mount Wutai was an important site of Tibetan-Chinese religious interaction.) Interestingly, however, it turns out to be in the Taoist accounts of the immortals that we find some of the most striking similarities. Marcel Granet, for instance, discusses the hagiographical use of the logograph *yin*, "le terme caractéristique de la *retraite-évanouissement* des sages dits taoïstes," which refers especially to sages dissolving into mountains. In Granet's view, the mysterious disappearance of the sage at death may be related to his refusal of kingship, which recalls for us that in Tibet the conception of the dissolution into light at death first appears to have concerned royal death in particular.[28]

The *Liexian zhuan*, mentioned earlier, affords further points of comparison. Throughout this work, as Max Kaltenmark remarks, "le dieu ou le chamane devient lui-même fumée, nuage et pluie."[29] This is precisely what we have seen in the accounts of Nyang Cangcup-tra and Nyang Sherap Jungne above. Another prominent theme is *shi jie*, translated by Kaltenmark as "délivrance par une mort apparente."[30] In the biography of Huangdi, for instance, we read:

Quand arriva le jour de sa mort, on le ramena au mont K'iao pour l'enterrer. (Plus tard) la montagne s'écroula: le cercueil était vide et le corps avait disparu; seules son épée et ses sandales étaient encore présentes.[31]

And in the biography of Lu Zhang:

Il se nourrissait de nénufars, de mousses et de moelle de roches. Au bout de deux cents ans, il annonça sa propre mort. Des troubles empêchèrent qu'on ne procédât à l'enterrement définitif. Plus tard, lorsque son fils (Lu) Ki voulut l'inhumer, il ne trouva pas le cadavre, seul un ouvrage intitulé le *Sceau de Jade* en six chapitres se trouvait dans le cercueil.[32]

Such accounts immediately recall Tibetan hagiographical accounts like that of Nyang Sherap Jungne, whose body vanished after he had left "his robe, rosary, and skull-cup on a juniper tree on the summit of Lhari in Phukpoche," as well as the more recent testimony of Pema Düdül's biography: "The lord's robes and meditation seat, his hair and the nails of his fingers and toes were there on his bed, but the maṇḍala of his body had disappeared."

Before leaving this brief excercise in Tibeto-Taoist comparison it will be worthwhile to note as well the elaboration of remarkably similar typologies of saintly death within the two traditions. The *Neipian,* a fourth-century Chinese treatise, states:

According to scriptures on transcendence, superior practitioners who rise up in their bodies and ascend into the void are termed celestial transcendents (*tianxian*). Middle-level practitioners who wander among noted mountains are termed earth-bound transcendents (*dixian*). Lesser practitioners who first "die" and then slough off (*xiansi houtuo*) are termed "escape-by-means-of-a-corpse-simulacrum transcendents" (*shijie xian*).[33]

A millennium later, in one of the masterworks of the Tibetan Great Perfection, the *Treasury of the Supreme Vehicle,* the renowned Longchen Rabjampa (Klong-chen Rab-'byams-pa, 1308–63) offers this much elaborated scheme:

Concerning the ways of death among the highest [adepts,] there are four, namely, ways of death resembling sky-farers, knowledge holders, conflagrations, and the sky. When the yogin of highest perseverance passes away directly without remains, it is as when a sky-farer dies, her corpse perceived by no one at all. This is a sign of awakening in buddhahood, without any intervening liminal state. A supreme yogin, in order to establish others in the teaching, may vanish in the sight of the public in the midst of a mass of light and accompanied by sounds and lights. This resembles the knowledge holders who, when they ascend to ever higher planes, do so bodily, going into the sky with sounds and lights that are visible to all. It is a sign that one will act on behalf of beings by means of inconceivable emanations throughout inconceivable realms. This occurred, for example, in the case of the great lord among yogins, Cetsün Senge Wangcuk.[34] As for the manner of death for a yogin who has reached the ends of experiential cultivation, it is a death that resembles the spontaneous extinction of great conflagrations that have consumed the fuel that was their material cause. It is a sign that the afflictions are liberated at the very site of their origination, that the elements, which are their material cause, are exhausted, and that one has arrived at a deconcretion of corporeal conditions. Examples are the mother and brother of Dampa Gyer, who both emerged from a cave in Tsari, blazing in a mass of light, and then vanished in space. In the way of death that is like the sky, when the atomically constituted body of the yogin, who is established on the plane of primordial purity, breaks like a pot, there is an intermingling as one, free from the sequence of before and after. So long as bodily appearance remains, it is like the space from which substance has been removed, while realization, or primordial purity, abides in the luminosity of the heart within the body. As when a pot breaks, so that the space within and the space without become so intermingled that one cannot tell them apart, here one is awakened in buddhahood, not distinguishing the body that has been reduced to its atomic constituents from the awareness within. This is a sign of liberation that has penetrated the plane of primordial purity.

In those cases, both the ways of death of the sky and sky-farers are ways of death due to Cutting Through Resistance, which establishes primordial purity, in which the body is reduced to its atomic constituents. The ways of death of both the conflagration and the knowledge holders are those of liberation in the spontaneous presence of All-Surpassing Realization.[35]

If one asks, wherefore such ways of death? they may emerge when there breaks open an expanse in which as a sign of conviction in the natural Great Perfection, one's mind will not tend toward common religious systems; as a sign that its significance has been mastered, one who directly perceives its significance is unpreoccupied with verbal analysis; because one has mastered the realization of primordial purity, one has recognized one's future destination; because death is no longer fearsome, one performs no longevity sādhanas or death avoidance rites whatsoever; because one acquires effortless confidence regarding the abiding nature of reality, one abandons all activities of the three gates [of body, speech, and mind]; and, because one has realized everything to be the great primordial emptiness, without ground, and so is, with respect to anything, free from apprehensions of substance and attribute, one departs from the fundamental disposition of reality for not even an instant.

For such yogins there is no need for prognostications of the signs of death, rites to avoid it, or spiritual exercises [specifically relating to death]. Having transcended view and meditation, religious practices neither help nor harm. What is intrinsically apparent arises in primordial purity and spontaneous presence, so that the locus of freedom has arisen as naturally present. For when one dissolves in the expanse of primordial purity and spontaneous presence, one is free.[36]

It is by no means clear how we are to understand the apparently close similarities between conceptions of the physical disappearance of adepts at death, as found in the Chinese Taoist and Tibetan Great Perfection traditions. At present, an actual historical connection between them can neither be firmly established nor decisively ruled out.[37] Be that as it may, it is clear that in the view of both traditions the alchemical transformation of the person through ascetical practice must ultimately issue in a physical transformation, in which the subtlest nature of the body, its affinity with ether and light, is manifestly disclosed (see plate 3).

APOLOGETICS AND POLEMICS

In the special texts of the Great Perfection,
It is said there are two ways the four visions are perfected:
Sequentially and all at once.
This is also explained in the [seventeen] Tantras and in *The Treasury of the Supreme Vehicle.*
Though it is generally the case that, without perfecting what is lower,
What is higher cannot be attained,
Who would say that it was inwardly impossible
For him to attain those [four visions]?
The point is that, when the agitations of the three gates are exhausted,
There is an abandonment of all the dispositions
Engendering the impure active energies;
But it would be indeed foolish to hold one-sidedly
That one just becomes like a mute.
Because he was an empowered individual
And because he was possessed by aspiration for others' sake,
Why should it not be that speech and so forth emerged
Effortlessly in others' perceptions?
This venerable master throughout his whole life
Let go of mundane activity and strove for the heart of spiritual attainment.
Above all, this one renounced
All outer and inner actions, and with one-pointed intent
At the so-called White Rock in Shang
For more than ten years of his life in all
Survived on the alchemy of water and leaves,
And continuously, day and night,
Contemplated the profound path; so that, by traversing that path,
The ten powers were disclosed.
Thereafter this holy man, according to the needs
Of place, time, and person,
So as to indicate the magnificence of the teaching,
And to generate faith among those of good fortune,
Proclaimed his own nirvāṇa
With the lion's roar of truth,
For he was empowered in whatever he did.
This he proclaimed in all quarters,
Like the Lord of Sages in ages past.
At that time, upon his own bed,
The coarse body became a rainbow mass.

By stages just his hair and his nails remained,
But even that was owing to the need [of ordinary persons for relics].
If there had been no such need,
Even the hair and nails would have disappeared.
So it was that for the fortunate shrines of the faithful,
So that confident faith would be aroused in all,
His bodily remains were refined into rainbow clarity,
Except for just that much.

It is perhaps noteworthy that no evidence has so far come to my attention of traditional Tibetan Buddhist thinkers' expressing doubts regarding the belief that some persons do vanish in light at death. There appears to have been a cultural consensus that such events do sometimes take place. What was subject to dispute, rather, was the assessment of the religious value and meaning of these occurrences. For the apologists of the Bön religion and the Buddhist Nyingmapa order, the attainment of the rainbow body was regarded as confirming the realization of the highest spiritual goal, the attainment of buddhahood. Thus, Dudjom Rinpoche, head of the Nyingmapa order until his death in 1987, summarizes the entire history of reports of the rainbow body as part of a polemical defense of his tradition:

As for how the supreme and common accomplishments were visibly disclosed, without fail, by those who experientially cultivated the tantras of the Ancient Translation School and the esoteric instructions composed by those who dwelt on the great level of the awareness-holders: there were seven successive generations of disciples beginning with Pang Mipham Gönpo, who did so by means of the instructions of Spatial Class of the Great Perfection. There were seven generations in the lineage which passed from Nyang Tingdzin Zangpo to Dangma, and so on, whose physical bodies dissolved in to the rainbow body . . . by means of the path of the esoteric instructions on inner radiance . . .

It is impossible, too, to enumerate all those who passed into the rainbow body by the paths of the profound treasures. . . . Even during this late age, this may still be illustrated. For example, in 1883/4 . . . the lord among accomplished masters, Rikdzin Pema Düdül, vanished in a body of light. Afterwards, when his personal disciple, the treasure-finder Rangrik Dorje, passed away at Mindröling, his remains vanished into light. . . . During that same period, there were thirteen disciples of the great treasure-finder Düjom Lingpa who attained the rainbow body. Furthermore, very close to the present day, there have been many whom I remember, who were manifestly perceived to have dissolved into the rainbow body without leaving even a trace of their bodies behind: Lingtsang Dzapa Trashi Özer of Dokam in 1935/6 . . . , followed by his regent, Lodrö Gyeltsen, in 1937/8 . . . , followed by Derge Yilungpa Sonam Namgyel in 1952/3. . . .

In addition, one cannot number those [recent figures, including two of the authors' own teachers, whose] physical bodies mostly vanished into light, accompanied by sound, light, earthquakes and various other miracles.[38]

The disappearance into the body of light, therefore, has become an important aspect of Nyingmapa apologetics.

However, others were less sure that this line of argument was valid, even if one accepted that some adepts did pass away in this fashion. Welmang Könchok Gyeltshen (Dbal-mang Dkon-mchog-rgyal-mtshan, 1764–1853), a well-known polemicist of the Gelukpa order, the "official" school of Tibetan Buddhism since the seventeenth century, writes as follows:

Again, it is repeatedly explained that in the so-called *Vajra Bridge*, if one realizes the significance of instantaneousness, one will attain buddhahood in a single lifetime and the bodily mass will pass away without remainder, and that if one experientially cultivates the *Innermost Spirituality*, having purified one's mind, the bodily mass will be freed from corruption, and that if one experientially cultivates the precepts of the Nyingmapa, one will pass away without remainder.

[To these claims we respond:] It is said that during the age when Bön was widespread, the kings of Tibet, relying upon a divine daemon cord, left no corpses. These [tales] appear to resemble the accounts of "decease in the rainbow body," "fading away in the body of light," and the bodily mass's "passing away without remainder." Nevertheless, though some of those in the [early Indian Buddhist] *śrāvaka* orders hold that, when [nirvāṇa] without remainder [is attained] the continuum of matter and consciousness comes to an end, they do not maintain that the former bodily mass vanishes. And some of the proponents of Mind Only, except for [affirming that] when [nirvāṇa] without remainder [is attained] obscuration and the continuum of obscuration come to an end so that the "genuine limit" is disclosed after one is born in a body of mind within a lotus-enclosure in a pure paradise, similarly do not maintain that one fades away like a rainbow. . . . Although the thousand buddhas of the Auspicious Aeon are arhats without remainder, it is explained that besides being embodied they leave relics behind. For the aspiration to attain supreme enlightenment requires action by means of the two form bodies [the buddhas' emanational body and body of rapture] on behalf of beings until sentient beings are exhausted; so how could this be if the body fades away like a rainbow? If you hold the so-called pure rainbow body to be the "pure illusory body" or the "body of subtle vital energy and mind" [as taught in the "new" Tantras accepted by the Gelukpa order to which the author belonged], there would seem to be no special profundity besides what [is found in the teachings of] the new Tantric schools—rest content with that![39]

In short, Welmang maintains that buddhahood requires bodily existence precisely in order to fulfill the Buddha's spiritual purpose, to instruct others and guide them to liberation. It follows from his perspective, therefore, that, whatever else may be said concerning the rainbow body, it is no sign of buddhahood. On the contrary, it represents the adept's withdrawal from the commitment of the Mahāyāna path.

Returning now to the hagiography of Pema the Demon Tamer, it is clear that these issues were very much on the author's mind, for following the account of the master's death, given above, we find these apologetical remarks:

These events are an amazing report, which accords with the manner in which the master of the teaching of the supreme vehicle, Garap Dorje (Dga'-rab-rdo-rje), and many other knowledge holders who achieved perfection instructed fortunate disciples by means of the body of gnosis. As a supplement to what we have already explained, [we add that] having arrived at the culmination of the primordially pure view that cuts through all resistance, the concrete physical body is either naturally purified or reduced to atomic particles, as when Pang Mipham Gönpo and others passed away—but this is a topic that is nectar for the hearts of those who are fortunate. Oh yes!

In brief, this holy man, beginning from the time when formerly he undertook fierce austerities, liberated his intention from all objectifying orientations, surpassed the accounting of virtue and sin, refined compassion boundlessly, intermingled appearance and mind in a single taste, freed himself from care for food and clothing, and maintained his physical frame with just water and a cotton robe. In lamplight and sunlight his body cast no shadow. His feces and urine had neither impurity nor odor. His body was as light as cotton wool. He passed unimpeded through torrents and cliffs. He was endowed with clairvoyance and more. Thus, it may be proved through both scripture and reason that [his attainments] in no way contradicted the measures and marks of the Great Perfection's path of primordial purity that cuts through all resistance and [its path] of the four spontaneous visions.[40]

Events such as those we have been considering have continued to be reported sporadically throughout the past century. Trungpa Rinpoche's record of the passing of Yilungpa Sonam Namgyel in 1952 was given above, and the 1935 death of the renowned Bönpo master Trashi Gyeltsen (Lingtsang Dzapa Trashi Özer in the citation from Düdjom Rinpoche above) is another widely known instance.[41] The most recent example dates to 1998, with the death of Khenpo Achö (Mkhan-po A-chos, 1918–1998) in the same region, now part of western Sichuan, in which Pema the Demon Tamer once lived. In this case, the event was reported even by the mainland Chinese press:

A Demised Lama Shrinks

According to *Garze Daily*, an 80-year-old Abbot Ngaqiong with the Longmo Monastery in Xinlong County passed away on September 13. His remains, laid open in a hall for seven days according to Buddhist rituals, shrank to the size of an ink bottle on the afternoon of the sixth day, to the size of a bean on the eighth day and disappeared on the 10th day. What remain are hair and nails.[42]

The following year saw the publication of a biography of Khenpo Achö, which in its description of his death, and in its apologetical comments, adheres to much the same pattern found in the earlier writings we have surveyed above.[43]

IN SEARCH OF A CONCLUSION

Hey, hey! The fruit of meditation on the path
Is the realization of enlightenment when affliction is exhausted,
But nowadays there are those learned about the path
Whose afflictions of anger and lust ever increase.
With reference to this holy man, throughout his whole life,
Those who tried hard to scrutinize him for just a sign
Of anger or lust never found it!
All knowledgeable persons speak with one voice on this.
So if your reasoning takes as its premise
The austerities he practiced
And his freedom from affliction,
In contrast to those who practice the Dharma at leisure,
Wrapped up in the afflictions of anger and lust,
[You will conclude that] his was the liberated life of a superior man—
The infallibility of causality is certain!
There can be no contradiction
Between the path of attainment and the fruit attained.
For those of faithful confidence,
Logical confutation about this has no place.
Therefore, those with the good fortune to have entered the path
Respectfully sing this melodious praise song:
"Hey! hey! this Vajrayāna
Is a miraculous wonder!"
Its fame, like the sky,
Expands without any limit at all.
If you deny it through fear,
You merely reduce yourself.

We have become accustomed in recent years to speaking of experiences as culturally constructed or, better, as mediated by the constructions of language and culture. Nothing that I have presented here would refute that view. But we should be wary, lest we come to speak of cultural constructions themselves as the rigid repetitions of culturally specific paradigms. What culture constructs can at best be described as a malleable field in which received tradition and the lived experiences of individuals enter into dialogue and through their dialogue form and reform one another. Thus, to interpret references to particular types of religious experiences, in this case experiences relating to light and saintly death, even within a well-specified tradition, in this case Tibetan esoteric Buddhism, we must remain context sensitive, just as we must when comparing entirely different traditions. We have seen, for example, that even if we hold that the entire phenomenon of the rainbow body to be a Tibetan cultural construction, it was nevertheless one that could be in important respects contested in Tibet itself. Cultural constructions of this degree of complexity can by no means be defined monolithically.

But let us note that to define this phenomenon as a "cultural construction" at all is itself deeply problematic, for in this case that requires some rather strong assumptions on our part about physical possibility. The problem that we confront here, of course, is that, unlike many types of claimed religious experience, such as visions and most mystical experiences, that can be interpreted as events occurring within the subject's consciousness alone, the rainbow body purports to describe a physical event. It belongs to the class of miracles. Who are we to say that it never occurs? Again, let us note that we *are* willing to countenance the idea of persons dissolving into light in our universe of science fiction; why not, then, in Tibet?

Several aspects of the phenomenon can perhaps be explained naturalistically: in the high altitude environment of Tibet, for instance, and particularly in Eastern Tibet, which is more moist than the thoroughly desiccated western parts of the Tibetan plateau, strange light phenomena are very common. Interestingly, most of our reports of the rainbow body emanate from these regions. (In one valley I visited in 1990, I was stunned by what seemed to be a light show every evening, and when I asked a local acquaintance whether or not this sort of thing was common, he responded bemusedly, "Not very. Probably some yogi has gone off in a rainbow somewhere near here!")

Perhaps, too, we should recall it is normal for the human body to shrink somewhat at death owing to desiccation; this is why the hair and beard frequently seem to grow for a period following death. In some cases, this shrinkage apparently can be quite extreme. Of course, I am not saying that this would account for circumstances under which only hair and nails would remain, but I think that it is plausible to suggest that the rainbow body, even if we treat it as a Tibetan cultural construction, is one that may be in some respects supervenient upon physical facts.

A purely physical explanation, however, even if it could be achieved, would remain inadequate. What surely must complement it is another type of story altogether, a story about the religious, and not the physical, nature of light. That I have attempted to supply in outline throughout this chapter. Here let me emphasize only that, for the Tibetan Buddhist tradition generally, intensive visions and experiences of light are regularly associated with some types of yogic and contemplative practice and may sometimes be induced by contact with persons, places, and objects thought to be imbued with great spiritual power. It is, I think, in the convergence of all of the factors I have been reviewing that Tibetan belief in its own terms becomes plausible. If, in a phrase well known to Western religious tradition, "the spirit was made flesh," the Tibetan religious world with equal seriousness believed that there have been numerous occasions on which the flesh returned to the spirit.

NOTES

1. Chögyam Trungpa, Rinpoche, *Born in Tibet* (London: George Allen and Unwin, 1966), pp. 95–96.

2. Some sources, including Dudjom Rinpoche, Jikdrel Yeshe Dorje, *The Nyingma School of Tibetan Buddhism: Its Fundamentals and History,* trans. Gyurme Dorje and Matthew Kapstein (Boston: Wisdom Publications, 1991), give 1883 as the year of Nyag-bla Padma-bdud-'dul's death, but the earlier date of 1872 is certainly correct. This is confirmed by the passage given at n. 5 below, as well as by the dating of Mi-pham's text, cited in n. 3, to 1875.

3. 'Jam-mgon 'Ju Mi-pham-rnam-rgyal, *Gzhan stong mkhas lan seng ge'i nga ro* (Ser-lo dgon-pa, Nepal, xylographic edition), fols. 18b3–21a4.

4. Nevertheless, as a matter of interest I do give large parts of Mipham's verse response at the beginning of each section throughout the present chapter.

5. *Nyag bla padma bdud 'dul gyi rnam thar dang mgur 'bum* (Chengdu: Si-khron mi-rigs dpe-skrun-khang, 1998), p. 130.

6. *Abhisamayālaṃkārāloka,* ed. P. L. Vaidya, Buddhist Sanskrit Texts Series, no. 4 (Darbhanga: Mithila Institute, 1960), p. 292. For an example of the interpretation of the sūtra's affirmation that "the nature of mind is clear light," in the context of a Tibetan contemplative tradition, see Dudjom Rinpoche, *The Nyingma School of Tibetan Buddhism,* 1:334.

7. For an introduction to the Buddhist mahāsiddha traditions, with references to earlier research, see my "King Kuñji's Banquet," in *Tantric Religions in Practice,* ed. David White (Princeton, NJ: Princeton University Press, 2000), pp. 52–71.

8. *Ro snyoms phyag rgya chen por sgang dril ba rgyal ba rgod tshang pa'i gsung* (Rtsib-ri xylographic edition).

9. The present summary and all citations of the *Garland of Gems* are based upon my

translation of the text given in "King Kuñji's Banquet." The Tibetan text is found in 'Jam mgon Kong sprul Blo gros mtha' yas, *Gdams ṅag mdzod: A Treasury of Instructions and Techniques for Spiritual Realization* (Delhi: N. Lungtok and N. Gyaltsan, 1971), 11:92–143.

10. The transmission lineage of the traditions of the eighty-four *siddhas* is given in 'Jam mgon Kong sprul Blo gros mtha' yas, *Gdams ṅag mdzod*, 12:770.

11. *Bka'-brgyud mgur-mtsho* (Mtshur-phu xylographic edition). See also *Rain of Wisdom*, trans. Nalanda Translation Committee (Boulder, CO: Shambhala, 1980), p. 20.

12. Thus, for example, one of the common clichés of both meditation manuals and accounts of visionary experience is the set phrase *'od-zer-snang-gsum*, the "trio of [intense] lights, rays, and [diffuse] illumination."

13. Khyung-po Rnal-'byor, *Bar-do'i gdams-pa*, in *Encyclopedia Tibetica* (New Delhi: Tibet House, 1972), 93:150–67. On Khyung-po Rnal-'byor and his tradition, see my articles "The Shangs-pa bKa'-brgyud: An Unknown School of Tibetan Buddhism," in *Studies in Honor of Hugh Richardson*, ed. M. Aris and Aung San Suu Kyi (Warminster: Aris and Phillips, 1980), pp. 138–44, "The Illusion of Spiritual Progress," in *Paths to Liberation*, ed. Robert Buswell and Robert Gimello (Honolulu: University of Hawai'i Press, 1992), pp. 193–224, and "The Journey to the Golden Mountain," in *Tibetan Religions in Practice*, ed. Donald Lopez, Jr. (Princeton, NJ: Princeton University Press, 1997), pp. 178–87.

14. See my *Tibetan Assimilation of Buddhism: Conversion, Contestation and Memory* (Oxford University Press, 2000), chap. 1, pp. 5–10, for a brief review of these developments. Bryan Cuevas, *The Hidden History of the Tibetan Book of the Dead* (Oxford: Oxford University Press, 2003) provides now a thorough account.

15. Kapstein, "The Illusion of Spiritual Progress," p. 195.

16. To be sure, later Tibetan Buddhist writers do often attribute the body of light to some of the Indian Buddhist masters (as, in a sense, Khyung-po had done with reference to Niguma), but they are nevertheless careful to distinguish this from the more "mundane" achievements of Tantric yoga. Dudjom Rinpoche, *The Nyingma School of Tibetan Buddhism*, 1:489, for instance, remarks: "Though one can make one's body invisible by mundane methods, such as alchemy, seminal retention, and the energies which circulate the lamp-like vital energy . . . the aforementioned masters [of the Buddhist anuyoga lineage] transformed their physical bodies . . . into radiant light by relying on . . . the non-discursive pristine cognition of the path of insight. We must recognize there to be a great difference between these methods."

17. *Bka'-chems ka-khol-ma* (Lanzhou: Kan-su'u mi-rigs dpe-skrun-khang, 1989), pp. 84–85.

18. For some valuable suggestions, see Per Kværne, "Dualism in Tibetan Cosmogonic Myths and the Question of Iranian Influence," in C. I. Beckwith, ed., *Silver on Lapis: Tibetan Literary Culture and History* (Bloomington, IN: Tibet Society, 1987) , pp. 163–74. Earlier research on Manichaean and Nestorian contacts with Tibet is reviewed in my *The Tibetan Assimilation of Buddhism*, p. 31.

19. Bibliothèque Nationale, Pelliot tibétain 996. The manuscript was first studied in

Marcelle Lalou, "Document tibétain sur l'expansion du dhyāna chinois," *Journal Asiatique* 231 (1939): 505–23.

20. Jacques Gernet, "Les suicides par le feu chez les bouddhistes chinois du Ve au Xe siècle," in *L'Intelligence de la Chine: Le social et le mental* (Paris: Gallimard, 1994), pp. 168–206, and "Moines thaumaturges," in *Le Vase de béryl: Études sur le Japon et la Chine en hommage à Bernard Frank,* ed. Jacqueline Pigeot and Hartmut O. Rotermund (Paris: Philippe Picquier, 1999), pp. 13–25. See also James Benn, "Where Text Meets Flesh: Burning the Body as an Apocryphal Practice in Chinese Buddhism," *History of Religions* 37 (1998): 295–322. Though it goes beyond the concerns of the present chapter, a related theme that is similarly common to both Chinese and Tibetan Buddhist hagiographical traditions is that of the spontaneous combustion of the adept, often on the funeral pyre. See, for instance, the hagiography of Dorje Lingpa (Rdo-rje-gling-pa, 1346–1405), in Dudjom Rinpoche, *The Nyingma School of Tibetan Buddhism,* 1:789–92.

21. Max Kaltenmark, *Le Lie-sien tchouan: Biographies légendaires des Immortels taoïstes de l'antiquité,* (1953; repr., Paris: Institut des Hautes Études Chinoises, 1987), p. 43 (biography of Ning Fong tseu): "il était capable de produire des fumées teintées des cinq couleurs." I thank Christine Mollier (CNRS, Paris) for her suggestions regarding this and other sources on Chinese religions.

22. Samten Gyaltsen Karmay, *The Great Perfection: A Philosophical and Meditative Teaching of Tibetan Buddhism* (Leiden: E. J. Brill. 1988).

23. This text was first studied in Samten Gyaltsen Karmay, "The Rdzogs-chen in Its Earliest Text: A Manuscript from Tun-huang," in *Sounding in Tibetan Civilization,* ed. Barbara Nimri Aziz and Matthew Kapstein (New Delhi: Manohar, 1985), pp. 272–82. The translation given here, however, is my own.

24. In the later Great Perfection tradition Vairocana and Samantabhadra are often treated as two distinct buddhas. But in this early work, given especially the force of the fourth verse line, it seems best not to interpret this as referring to two separate figures. "Samantabhadra" is a common epithet of the Buddha, and in Indian Buddhist Tantric works frequently refers to the guru, divinized as Vajradhara.

25. Dudjom Rinpoche, *The Nyingma School of Tibetan Buddhism,* 1:490–501, provides the traditional narrative.

26. They are discussed in ibid., 1:542–50, from which the quotations in this section, unless otherwise noted, are drawn.

27. Ibid., p. 642.

28. Marcel Granet, *Danses et légendes de la Chine ancienne,* réédition (Paris: PUF, 1959), 1:81–82 (esp. n. 4 on *yin* [= Mathews character no. 7448]); pp. 295: "On le voit: le thème *taoïste* des sages cachés qui se suicident ou s'évanouissent mystérieusement, et qui deviennent Dieux en refusant d'être Rois, se raccorde au thème des ministres qu'on exécute ou qui s'enfuient après un excès de fortune. L'un et l'autre thèmes s'apparentent aux thèmes des Rois fictifs et des Morts divinisantes." (Emphasis original.) See also Isabelle Robinet, "Metamorphosis and Deliverance from the Corpse in Taoism," *History of Religions* 19 (1979): 37–70.

29. Kaltenmark, *Le Lie-sien tchouan*, p. 38.

30. Ibid., pp. 38, 45, 52, 74, 92. Kaltenmark, *Lao tseu et le taoïsme* (Paris: Seuil, 1965), p. 146, offers this summary: " «Monter au ciel en plein jour», telle sera désormais la formule consacrée pour désigner l'apothéose finale du Taoïste qui a réussi la transsubstantiation de sa personne. Certains, il est vrai, s'en vont plus discrètement: il paraissent mourir comme de simples mortels, mais leur mort n'est qu'apparente, car si l'on ouvre le cercueil après un délai, le corps a disparu et est remplacé par le bâton, l'épée ou les sandales du défunt." Cf. also Henri Maspero, *Le Taoïsme et les Religions chinoises* (Paris: Gallimard, 1971), pp. 218–19, 353–54, 482; and Isabelle Robinet, *Méditation taoïste* (Paris: Dervy Livres, 1979), pp. 254–57, "La mutation libératrice, la dissolution bienheureuse."

31. Kaltenmark, *Le Lie-sien tchouan*, p. 51.

32. Ibid., p. 72. The peculiar diet of the adept is significant. See, e.g., Jean Lévi, "L'abstinence des céréales chez les Taoïstes," in *Études chinoises* 1 (1983): 3–47, esp. pp. 20–21: "l'adepte avant de se dépouiller de son enveloppe corporelle et d'accomplir sa transmutation est saisi d'un feu intérieur qui le dévore comme un brasier."

33. Robert Ford Campany, *To Live as Long as Heaven and Earth: A Translation and Study of Ge Hong's Tradition of Divine Transcendentals* (Berkeley: University of California Press, 2002), p. 75. In the quaintly outdated translation of James R. Ware, *Alchemy, Medicine and Religion in the China of A.D. 320: The Nei P'ien of Ko Hung* (Cambridge, MA: MIT Press, 1966), p. 47, this reads: "The genii classics say that processors of the highest class raise their bodies into the void and are then designated Heavenly Genii. Those of the second class resort to the famous mountains and are designated Earth Genii. The third class sloughs off the body after death and is designated Corpse-freed Genii."

34. On Lce-btsun Seng-ge-dbang-phyug (eleventh century), one of the important Tibetan patriarchs of the Great Perfection traditions, see Dudjom Rinpoche, *The Nyingma School of Tibetan Buddhism*, 1:557–59.

35. Dudjom Rinpoche, *The Nyingma School of Tibetan Buddhism*, 1:337–45, summarizes this topic. All-Surpassing Realization (*thod-rgal*) represents the highest division of the Great Perfection teaching.

36. Klong-chen Rab-'byams-pa Dri-med-'od-zer, *Theg-pa'i mchog rin-po-che'i mdzod* (Gangtok: Dodrup Chen Rinpoche, n.d.), vol. Waṃ, plates 444–46.

37. Evidence for early knowledge of Taoism in Tibet is rather thin, but nevertheless clear. The *Sba-bzhed*, an eleventh-century (?) history of the eighth-century adoption of Buddhism as the Tibetan state religion, for instance, mentions the transmission of the teachings of *Le'u-tshe*, i.e., Laozi (*Sba-bzhed ces-bya-ba-las Sba Gsal-gnang-gi bzhed-pa bzhugs* [Beijing: Mi-rigs dpe-skrun-khang, 1980], p. 14). It is uncertain whether this refers to the *Daodejing* or to later traditions of Laozi, e.g., the notorious *Huahujing*.

38. Dudjom Rinpoche, *The Nyingma School of Tibetan Buddhism*, 1:918–19. As noted earlier, the date given here for the death of Padma-bdud-'dul should be corrected to 1872.

39. Dbal-mang, in Se-ra rje-btsun Chos-kyi-rgyal-mtshan et al., *Dgag lan phyogs bsgrigs* (Chengdu: Si khron mi rigs dpe skrun khang, 1997), pp. 699–700.

40. *Nyag bla padma bdud 'dul gyi rnam thar dang mgur 'bum,* pp. 132–33.

41. "Among *Bon-pos* . . . there was *bKra-shis rGyal-mtshan* of *Khams,* who produced fifteen volumes of works, including a history of *Bon.* He lived the life of a hermit, and when he died some forty years ago, he is supposed to have disappeared leaving no mortal remains behind. Such lamas are known as 'rainbow bodies' (*'ja'-lus-pa*). Only the *Bon-pos* and the older orders make such claims, for the *dGe-lugs-pas* are more prosaic in their religious practice"(David Snellgrove and Hugh Richardson, *A Cultural History of Tibet* [New York: Frederick A. Praeger, 1968], p. 246). In the Tibetan biography of this figure—Bskal-bzang bstan-pa'i rgyal-mtshan, *Shar rdza ba bkra shis rgyal mtshan gyi rnam thar* (Chengdu: Si khron mi rigs dpe skrun khang, 1988)—the master's final dissolution is recounted on pages 99–101. A more detailed account is given in Dbra-ston Bskal-bzang bstan-pa'i rgyal-mtshan, *Shar rdza ba bkra shis rgyal mtshan gyi rnam thar* (Beijing: Krung go'i bod kyi shes rig dpe skrun khang, 1992), pp. 416–28.

42. From the magazine *China's Tibet,* vol. 10, no. 3. I would like to thank Daniel Winkler for first sending a copy of this article to me.

43. I am grateful to Dan Martin for sharing with me a copy of this work, by the well-known (in Sichuan) Rnying-ma-pa lama Mtsho-po Rdor-blo. Unfortunately, Dr. Martin's example is missing both title page and publication information. It seems to have been printed in Chengdu in 1999 and, like several of the author's earlier publications, was distributed privately.

PART THREE

In the Sight of the Eye

The words "disinterested aesthetic contemplation" are a contradiction in terms and a pure non-sense.

Ananda K. Coomaraswamy, "A Figure of Speech or a Figure of Thought?"

In part 1, we emphasized the presence of the divine as light—whether conceived physically or otherwise—and in part 2 our focus was light as a goal and source of spiritual transformation, considering, too, some of the conflicts of interpretation that light mysticism has entailed. In part 3 we return to reflect upon physical light in its relation to the divine, and in underscoring this relationship it is fitting that all three chapters in this section are concerned with important aspects of visual culture. In this context, involving the production of art and architecture designed so as to express and to evoke religiously valued manifestations of light, the notion of *constructing* religious experience may sometimes be understood quite literally.

Catherine Asher's contribution, "A Ray from the Sun: Mughal Ideology and the Visual Construction of the Divine," demonstrates both the ideological commitment to light imagery that surrounded Mughal notions of the ruler's divinity and the determination with which this commitment informed imperial artistic projects. Consider, in this connection, the use of white marble in the tomb of the saint Mu'in al-Din Chishti:

In 1579, Shaikh Hussain . . . rebuilt the dome of Mu'in al-Din's tomb. Exactly what changes he made are not clear, but he must have been responsible for its current marble facing, probably added to match the white marble walls. On the dome's interior he provided a long Persian inscription which, when read in conjunction with the tomb's appearance, gives us clues to the meaning of the iconography of white marble. Addressed to "Lord of Lords, Mu'in al-Din," the saint is called the "Sun of the sphere of the universe," recalling the dome's prominent shape. The poem then goes on to liken praise of the saint, who is enshrined in this tomb, to a "precious pearl," alluding to the luster of the marble surface as well as referring to the saint's luminous qualities and his abilities to bestow *baraka.* The tomb is more resplendent than "the sun and the moon [who] rub their forehead at your threshold," a reference to this act of devotion and respect performed when entering a saint's shrine. It ends, "As long as the sun and moon endure, may the lamp of the Chishtis possess light." White marble, then, a fabric which absorbs and reflects light, a metaphor for God, in the Mughal context is a reference to the divine, in this case, the divine as manifested by light.

The construction of the architectural edifice thus contributes to the experiential construction, in the life of the devotee, of a sense of communion with the divine that is provoked by the saturation of white light in a setting of established sanctity.

The cultural construction of religiously valued sites of experience may be itself inspired by spiritually charged attention to natural phenomena, or by visionary experiences. In "Light in the Wutai Mountains," Raoul Birnbaum considers textual and visual representations of three distinctly different types of light phenomena traditionally observed in the Wutai Mountains of northern China. These include unusual lights that appear at dusk or in the night sky, radiance that emanates from certain objects of power (for instance, sculptures, relics, and scriptures), and the dazzling, light-filled visionary experiences of individual Wutai residents and pilgrims. Among them we find

textual narratives of monks who saw fully realized architectural assemblages as light-filled visions. Sometimes they entered these structures, according to the accounts, and sometimes they sketched out these buildings based on memories of the vision. At least four of the major Tang period monasteries at Wutai shan are said to have been built under such circumstances, and pavilions or other structures have been raised at preexisting monasteries based on reports, such as that of the monk Niuyun. The intent was to replicate with earthly materials the buildings made of light. These structures then were not only places for inhabitation and religious activity, but also solid testimony to the immanence and power of Wenshu, testimony that he is present at Wutai shan, that one stands within his buildings under his protection, that he could appear at any moment.

Echoing Catherine Asher's description of architectural programs designed to induce religious experiences of light, Birnbaum's discussion introduces us to religious architecture whose very conception was said to have been derived from visionary illuminations. Human constructive activity and revelatory vision here merge and determine one another.

The evocation of light through artistic construction is explored, too, in Mimi Hall Yiengpruksawan's contribution, "The Eyes of Michinaga in the Light of Pure Land Buddhism." Art cooperates here with a highly specific regime of spiritual practice, above all, the visualization of the buddha Amitāyus in the Pure Land, Sukhāvatī:

> Visual cultures around Pure Land texts and themes have been well developed in Central and East Asia since at least the sixth century CE, with some of the most elaborate examples seen in Japan of the eleventh and twelfth centuries. Such art forms range in iconography from paintings of Amitāyus in his palace in Sukhāvatī to architectural programs that seek to replicate on earth the very structures and luxury of that pure land. The representations generally involve extensive use of precious materials such as gold, silver, mother of pearl, and crystal or glass. In tandem with the texts these corporeal embodiments of the Pure Land teaching achieve, in very concrete terms, the type of visionary encounter promoted in the sūtras. The need to see Amitāyus in his purified realm is met through art in concrete ways that lend support to the mental evocations that are at the crux of the process. It becomes possible to render visible to the somatic eye that which is not so easily seen.

In Yiengpruksawan's fascinating study, however, both visualization and artistic commission assume emphatic significance in connection with the blindness of Michinaga, the nobleman who commissioned the particular temples and shrines she studies. In his devotion to a religious vision of light, it appears, Michinaga sought to compensate for, and perhaps also to regain, the worldly sight he had lost.

CHAPTER SEVEN

A Ray from the Sun: Mughal Ideology and the Visual Construction of the Divine

Catherine B. Asher

The Taj Mahal, India's most famous monument, was officially known as the Rauza-i Munawwar, that is, the Illumined Tomb. Its name suggests a more than passing interest in light imagery. Built by the Mughal ruler Shah Jahan in the mid-seventeenth century, the tomb epitomizes the Mughal concern for adapting religious symbolism, especially elements associated with light and auspicious sight, to an iconography of royalty. There were three major forces that inspired these artistic developments. One was the Mughals' devotion to the Chishtiyya *silsila* (order) of Sufi saints; the second was the draw to Hindu, Jain, and Zoroastrian concepts of worship, particularly those associated with *darshan,* auspicious sight, and fire veneration. The third was the presence of scholars at court who were intimate with the concepts of divine illumination as set forth by the Iranian philosopher and mystic Shihab al-Din Yaya Suhrawardi in the twelfth century. By combining these elements and giving them new meaning the Mughals thus translated religious experience into material form for a royal ceremonial. The adaptation of these iconographies is directly related to an increasing desire to portray the ruler as extraordinary, at times even taking on the status of a saint or god.

The Mughals, Chaghtai Turks from Central Asia descended from the Timurids as well as from Chinghiz Khan, came to power in India in 1526. Until the mid-sixteenth century the Mughals were engrossed in establishing and maintaining power; thus, relatively little effort was spent establishing a sustained dynastic ideology. That changed under the third Mughal emperor, Akbar (r. 1556–1605). Over the course of time he came to be presented as a semidivine ruler who, like a father to his people, was directly concerned with his subjects' welfare. How this happened is worth reviewing, for often Mughal art and architecture are discussed as if these features were full blown in even Akbar's earliest works, for example, the tomb he built for his father, Humayun; only by reading these works in a historical context, however, can their meaning be grasped. Akbar inherited the throne at the age of twelve; for a few years he remained under the influence of powerful nobles and women of the court but by 1560 was able to emerge as an independent agent and creative thinker. For about the next two decades, Akbar was engaged in enlarging and consolidating his domain, transforming the precarious state he inherited into a major empire of considerable wealth and stability. Several developments during this period are key to understanding subsequent transformations in Mughal ideology as well as art and architecture. As early as 1562 Akbar manifested an interest in Sufism, particularly in the Chishtiyya *silsila.* By the 1570s Shaikh Mubarak and his sons, Faizi, a brilliant poet, and Abu al-Fazl, the future mastermind of Mughal state ideology, all steeped in the Suhrawardi tradition of illumination thought, had entered the court, and by the mid-1570s they were producing a potent effect with their liberal influence over the young king.[1] Concurrent with Abu al-Fazl's influence, Akbar became interested in a variety of religious traditions as a way of finding truth, including Hinduism, Jainism, Christianity, and Zoroastrianism.

AKBAR AND THE CHISHTIYYA

Akbar's interest in Sufism and the Chishti saint Khwaja Mu'in al-Din commenced when he was twenty years old. At this time, in early 1562, during a hunt, the young Akbar heard the devout singing *qawwali,* that is, ecstatic devotional songs, about the virtues and greatness of the Muslim Sufi saint Khwaja Mu'in al-Din of Ajmer.[2] He was so smitten by the rapture of the songs and their singers that he wished to visit the shrine himself, in order that he might benefit from the deceased saint's *baraka,* that is, his spiritual essence. Shortly afterward he made his first pilgrimage to Khwaja Mu'in al-Din's *dargah* (shrine). Again in 1568 he made another pilgrimage, this one traveling on foot for 365 kilometers. Then, until 1579, Akbar paid homage at the Ajmer shrine for the annual celebration of Khwaja Mu'in ud-Din's *'urs,* that is, the commemoration of the saint's death or literally, his marriage with God. Before he abandoned this rite, Akbar had visited the shrine fourteen times. These visits were true spiritual ones, and he would spend considerable time there praying and in religious discussion. But there was a political element as well. In 1570 Akbar, believing the *dargah* was mismanaged, banished the tomb's chief attendant and assumed the right to make this appointment himself, thus achieving political control over, not only spiritual involvement with, the Chishtiyya.[3] By linking himself with the Chishtiyya, revered by Muslims and Hindus alike, Akbar bolstered his own popularity.

Khwaja Mu'in al-Din Chishti's status among Sufi saints in general, but also in Indian society, was tremendous. Some historical background of the saint and the development of his shrine is helpful in understanding his impact. A follower of the newly established Chishti Sufi order, Khwaja Mu'in al-Din Chishti came to India sometime in the late twelfth century. Although our knowledge of Mu'in al-Din is from hagiographical sources, erasing the boundaries between myth and fact, it appears that he advocated what was to become the ideal doctrine, at least for the pre-Mughal Chishtiyya: an intense love of God that Mu'in al-Din likened to a burning desire; a general eschewing of contact with kings; a life of poverty; the practice of *sama'*, that is, dance and especially music, as a way of finding mystical union with God.[4]

Sufi saints including Mu'in al-Din had achieved *fana'* (annihilation), experiencing visions of God's brilliant light. Even Akbar upon hearing "two heart-ravishing stanzas" of *qawwali* in 1578 saw flashes of divine lights; in the same year he had another mystic experience which Abu al-Fazl was to call the "ecstasy of vision."[5] The authority for perceiving God as light commences with the famous Sura al-Nur of the Qur'an, that is, the chapter entitled Light, which commences: "God is the Light of the Heavens and the Earth. The parable of His Light, as if there were a Niche . . ."[6] Playing on this passage as well as one of God's ninety-nine names, al-Nur, that is, The Light, Sufic poetic imagery describing God as the sun, the full moon, or the stars was well established.[7] Amir Khusrau, a fourteenth-century Indian Persian poet, had special veneration for the Chishti saints and composed verses employing similar light imagery.[8] Akbar's son and successor, Jahangir, refers to hearing verses by Amir Khusrau sung.[9] Even today many of Amir Khusrau's compositions are performed by *qawwals* (singers of devotional songs) during the weekly *sama'* sessions;[10] it is possible that these are similar to if not the same songs Akbar first heard in 1562.

The Chishtiyya became the most popular Sufi order in north India and numerous Chishti *khanqahs* (Sufi hospices) were established throughout the subcontinent. In pre-Mughal India these orders were essentially brotherhoods whose success hinged on the total obedience of the disciple (*murid*) to his master (*pir*). Sufis lived together in a *khanqah*, which had simple structures for religious discussion and sleeping (*jama'at khana*), small cubicles used by senior Sufis for residence and meditation (*hujras*), and other simple buildings, often more pillared verandas than enclosed structures, for meeting devotees in search of guidance. Another significant unit was the kitchen, where food was cooked not only for the resident Sufis, but, more important, for distribution to the poor and needy.[11] If adequate food was not available for the Sufis and the poor, the poor had priority. Each of these highly organized *khanqahs* was headed by a shaikh whose authority paralleled in many ways that of temporal rulers. After the death of founding or lead shaikhs, these simple *khanqahs* were slowly being transformed into *dargahs*. *Dargah* in Persian literally means "palace," but in the Indian context the transformation of a saint's *khanqah* came to mean the structural tomb built over the grave of a major saint and its surrounding complex. Khwaja Mu'in al-Din's grave was the preeminent Sufi site in the Indian subcontinent. It appears than until the fourteenth century little attempt was made to embellish the site. In the fifteenth century Ghiyas al-Din Khalji, ruler of Mandu, a Tughluq successor state in western India, and a Chishti admirer, built the enormous Buland Darwaza as an entrance to the Ajmer tomb complex of Khwaja Mu'in al-Din.[12] However, to the best of our knowledge the rest of the complex, including the saint's grave, remained rudimentary at best.

The question of when Mu'in al-Din's tomb took on its present form is significant for our understanding of subsequent Mughal architecture and its associations with light imagery. No historical account indicates when the square-plan tomb, faced with pure white marble, was erected (fig. 7.1) However, an inscription on the tomb's inside walls indicate it was embellished, if not initially constructed, in 1532.[13] There are several reasons to assume that the pristine, white marble exterior walls were already in existence when Akbar first visited the tomb in 1562. For one, he provided a mosque at the shrine, but surely had the tomb been in need of refurbishment, he would have attended to that first, given his devotion to the saint. A painting from an illustrated manuscript of the history of his reign, the *Akbar Nama,* showing him in homage before the tomb, indicates that it was at least white in color, although it is impossible to judge the material (fig. 7.2).[14] Finally, white as an appropriate color for saints' shrines had been established earlier, for example, at the tomb of Shaikh Ahmad Khattu at Sarkhej in Gujarat, a province in western India. This *dargah* was an important model for the palace located at the site of a Chishti *khanqah* that Akbar was building at Fatehpur Sikri between 1570 and 1585.[15]

In 1579, Shaikh Hussain, a hereditary attendant of the *dargah,* rebuilt the dome of Mu'in al-Din's tomb.[16] Exactly what changes he made are not clear, but he must have been responsible for its current marble facing, probably added to match the white marble walls. On the dome's interior he provided a long Persian inscription which, when read in conjunction with the tomb's appearance, gives us clues to the meaning of the iconography of white marble. Addressed to "Lord of Lords, Mu'in al-Din," the inscription calls the saint the "Sun of the sphere of the universe," recalling the dome's prominent shape. The poem then

FIGURE 7.1. Tomb of Mu'in al-Din Chishti, *dargah* of Mu'in al-Din Chishti, Ajmer.

FIGURE 7.2. Akbar paying homage at the *dargah* of Mu'in al-Din Chishti, from the *Akbar Nama*. (Reproduced with permission of the V&A Picture Library.)

goes on to liken praise of the saint, who is enshrined in this tomb, to a "precious pearl," alluding to the luster of the marble surface as well as referring to the saint's luminous qualities and his abilities to bestow *baraka*. The tomb is more resplendent than "the sun and the moon [who] rub their forehead at your threshold," a reference to this act of devotion and respect performed when entering a saint's shrine. It ends, "As long as the sun and moon endure, may the lamp of the Chishtis possess light."[17] White marble, then, a fabric which absorbs and reflects light, a metaphor for God, in the Mughal context is a reference to the divine, in this case, the divine as manifested by light.

At this time white marble structures are limited exclusively to the tombs enshrining important saints. A case in point is the palace complex Akbar built at Fatehpur Sikri in thanksgiving for the accurate prediction by another Chishti saint, Shaikh Salim, for the birth of his son and heir. The large palace complex has two focal points, the palace itself consisting of administrative and living units and a great *khanqah,* the focus of which was a huge mosque, built for Shaikh Salim Chishti. All these buildings are composed of red sandstone. The mosque bears some white marble trim, but it is only a minor part of the overall fabric. When in 1572 Shaikh Salim died, a stunning tomb (fig. 7.3) was provided for him in the courtyard of his *khanqah,* thus transforming the complex into a *dargah*. This tomb, although not completed until 1580–81, is pure white marble, like that at the more famous Chishti *dargah* in Ajmer and that of Nizam al-Din Chishti in Delhi, which had been renewed in white marble some twenty years earlier. At Shaikh Salim Chishti's tomb, however, the references to light are made more explicit, for the tomb's exterior walls are composed of exquisitely carved screens (*jalis*), thus allowing for the entrance of diffused light. Ironically it was not completed until Akbar began to break with the Chishti, in fact, with saint veneration in general. It was about this time that Akbar began to cast himself in the guise of a saint; he perceived himself as a *pir,* or guide, and his closest nobles as *murids,* or students. In spite of Akbar's increasing lack of interest in saints, even today the tomb is a major pilgrimage site, especially for those desiring the birth of a son.

Tombs of Sufis, rendered in white marble symbolizing God's light, are a clear reflection of Akbar's interests in mysticism, but I believe this can be seen in the mausoleum he built for his father, the previous Mughal emperor, Humayun, as well.[18] This tomb, in Delhi, was commenced in 1562, the same year Akbar first went on pilgrimage to Ajmer, and it was completed in 1571. The tomb's appearance—its high, bulbous marble dome and large, high plinth, its garden setting and elaborate interior plan known as an eight-paradise type—draws heavily on Iranian models.[19] This is not surprising since the architects

FIGURE 7.3. Tomb of Shaikh Salim Chishti, Fatehpur Sikri.

were from Bukhara. It is the tomb's mihrab, the interior prayer niche, that appears to reflect Akbar's interest in Sufism. Rather than being solid, as is usual, its arched-shaped frame is composed of carved stone screens allowing for the entrance of light. Any Muslim would immediately recognize this as a visual reference to the famous chapter, Nur, or Light, in the Qur'an where God's presence is likened to a light in a niche. It would seem that Akbar's interests in light symbolism, even early in his reign, were not limited to Sufis, but extended to the imperial Mughals themselves.

ABU AL-FAZL AND HIS IMPACT ON MUGHAL IDEOLOGY

The impact of Abu al-Fazl (1551–1602), a scholar and theologian, on Akbar and the evolving ideology of Mughal statecraft can not be overemphasized. A brilliant scholar, Abu al-Fazl was trained in illumination philosophy by his father, Shaikh Mubarak, whose own reputation and scholarly credentials were impeccable. Although both his father and his brother, the well-known poet Faizi, entered service in the Mughal court before Abu al-Fazl, he far exceeded them in stature and rank. Akbar had heard of Abu al-Fazl's genius before they met in 1575, about the same time when the emperor first felt he had time to systematically consider religious matters in the court.[20] In this same year Abu al-Fazl joined the Mughal service at the low rank of 20; by the time he was killed in 1602 he had attained a rank of 5,000, one of the highest possible.[21] His impact on Akbar's thought appears to have been immediate, not surprising since the emperor was already sympathetic to many of the ideas that Abu al-Fazl would refine over the next fifteen years or more. All the same, until 1579 Abu al-Fazl was under constant attack from the traditional court *'ulama* (scholars and jurists of Islam having authority over legal matters).[22] Then Akbar, in a move masterminded by Abu al-Fazl, was able to assume unprecedented power in matters of Islamic religious doctrine; to further minimize the influence of the *'ulama,* he sent many of the most strident among them on the hajj.[23] From then until Abu al-Fazl's assassination in 1602—which was arranged by Akbar's heir apparent, the future Jahangir—his influence, heavily tinged with illumination thought, colored every aspect of the court, including artistic production, and subsequent Mughal attitudes toward kingship.

Before understanding how Abu al-Fazl applied illumination philosophy to the daily workings of empire, it might be useful to review the most basic outline of this thought, since these ideas have a bearing on subsequent developments in Mughal art and architecture. Abu al-Fazl was deeply influenced by Shihab al-Din Suhrawardi's theory of *ishraq* (illumination), which, as S. H. Nasr, A. Schimmel, and M. A. Razavi indicate, ingeniously combined classical Greek and Roman thought with pre-Islamic Zoroastrian concepts as well as Sufi mystical treatises, for example, those of al-Hallaj and al-Ghazzali, especially his *Mishat al-Anwar* (*The Niche for Lights*).[24] The importance of light imagery for Suhrawardi, who argues that all existence is a reflection of God's brilliant blinding light, is paramount. He claimed that the ontological status of any being or object depends on the degree of its illumination, which is transmitted by dazzling angels. However, only those beings fully imbued with divine light can be true masters of the age, and those possessing this light will gain power and wisdom, including the ability to rule justly and benevolently.[25]

Abu al-Fazl's personal commitment to *ishraqi* philosophy was profound; al-Nur, one of God's ninety-nine names, was among his favorites for recitation. So, too, this is seen in one of his verses that commences, "Oh God! In whatever direction I turn, I find Thee manifested; at whatever particle I look, I find Thy Light. The Kaba of clay points in one direction but the qibla of the heart in all directions."[26] Here we gain a sense of Abu al-Fazl's open-mindedness, explaining in part why traditional jurists so resented his hand in state affairs. But how did he apply illumination philosophy to create a new order in the Mughal state?

Abu al-Fazl applied Suhrawardi's complex notion of an illumined being, the master of an age, to Akbar himself, perceiving and presenting him as a divinely imbued monarch.[27] Textually this is revealed in the opening pages of Abu al-Fazl's history of Akbar, the *Akbar Nama,* the first volume of which he commenced about 1590 and presented to the emperor in 1597–98.[28] Written in the language of Suhrawardi's *ishraqi* thought, where divinely revealed light is handed down from one divinely inspired philosopher to another,[29] Abu al-Fazl's work traces Akbar's lineage from Adam, the first man, through the prophets common to the Qur'an and Old Testament, reaching a Mughal princess, Alanquwa, who is, like Mary, miraculously impregnated. Specifically Alanquwa was impregnated with a ray of divine light. Also like Mary, Alanquwa is pure and virtuous, giving birth to not one, but three sons. The one whose name is Nairun, that is, Light Produced, becomes the progenitor for the Mughal house. A lengthy portion of this text provides the entire lineage of these rulers sired by Nairun including such illustrious figures as Chinghiz Khan and Timur, who pass on this concealed light to each new generation until this light is revealed when Akbar accedes to the Mughal throne in 1556.[30]

Abu al-Fazl presents Akbar as a Perfect Man, an ideal ruler who, according to Islamic theology, is imbued with God's light. At one point Abu al-Fazl even claims the emperor was superior to all beings of the recent past, including even Khwaja Mu'in al-Din Chishti of Ajmer.[31] In his remarkable *A'in-i Akbari*, essentially a comprehensive manual of the Mughal state, Abu al-Fazl opens the text: "[Akbar] is a man of high understanding and noble aspirations who, without the help of others, recognizes a ray of Divine power in the smallest things in the world. . . . True greatness in spiritual and worldly matters, [he] does not shrink from the minutiae of business, but regards their performance as an act of Divine worship. . . . No dignity is higher in the eyes of God than royalty, [for] a king is the origin of stability."[32] Here we learn that Akbar, imbued with divine light, is able to deal with all issues, large and small, and at the same time realizes God is everywhere. He is, in essence, a Perfect Man. Akbar, in accordance with long-standing Islamic tradition, is responsible for maintaining stability, that is, executing justice.[33] Abu al-Fazl, echoing Suhrawardi, goes on to say: "Royalty is a light emanating from God, a ray from the sun, the illuminator of the universe. . . . Modern language calls this light *farr-i izidi* (the divine light) and the tongue of antiquity calls this light *kiyan khura* (the sublime halo). It is communicated by God to kings without the intermediate assistance of any one, and men, in the presence of it, bend the forehead of praise towards the ground of submission. . . . Many excellent qualities flow from this light. [One is] a paternal love towards his subjects. Thousands find rest in the love of the King; and sectarian differences do not raise the dust of strife."[34] In short, Akbar's divinely bestowed office has several important implications: first is his ability to receive extraordinary divine revelation, which he shared with men such as Plato and many of the pre-Islamic Iranian kings who were designated by Suhrawardi as possessing divine light; second, he is like a father to his subjects, borrowing from ancient Indian concepts of kingship; third, Akbar is dedicated to communal harmony, corresponding to Suhrawardi's belief that the divinely enlightened ruler will rule benevolently; his state will be an enlightened one. As a Perfect Man with profound inner qualities, Akbar is symbolically larger than life. Together these three qualities generate perhaps the most important concept of Akbar's fifty-year reign, a policy of *sulh-i kul*, that is, peace toward all. Although many examples could be given, suffice it to say that Akbar, already predisposed to non-Muslims before Abu al-Fazl's presence at court, began to take even more measures assuring that all subjects, regardless of religious belief, had equal rights. Examples include the abolition of a tax formerly imposed on Hindus when gathering for religious events, grants given for the support of non-Muslim religious institutions, and the inclusion of non-Muslims in the Mughal administration. After Abu al-Fazl's entrance into the court, Akbar began to celebrate non-Muslim festivals at court, abolished another special tax on non-Muslims, and instituted regular discussions in court at which representatives from a number of religious traditions participated.[35]

VISUAL LIGHT SYMBOLISM UNDER AKBAR

Painting

So far we have seen that Akbar's interest in light imagery, already apparent with his devotion to the Chishtiyya, escalated under the influence of Abu al-Fazl and his promotion of illumination philosophy. The question now is, how did this fascination manifest itself in visual form? The most obvious example is Akbar's public and private veneration, borrowed from Zoroastrian rite, of light in the form of sun and fire. Abu al-Fazl writes in his *A'in-i Akbari*, "His Majesty maintains that it is a religious duty and divine praise to worship fire and light; surely, ignorant men consider this forgetfulness of the Almighty, and fire worship. But the deep-sighted know better. . . . How beautifully Shaikh Sharf al-Din [a fourteenth-century Indian Sufi] said: 'What can be done with a man who is not satisfied with the lamp when the sun is down?' Every flame is derived from that fountain of divine light, and bears the impression of its holy essence . . . The fire of the sun is the torch of God's sovereignty."[36] Abu al-Fazl then proceeds to explain how Akbar worships the sun in a ceremony, lighting extraordinary candles at twilight. This private act is then mirrored publicly by the lighting of a glowing lantern, known as an *akas-diya*, that is a Light of the Sky, hoisted on a pole about 120 feet high, which can be seen for a considerable distance. Abu al-Fazl states, "before the lamp was erected, men had to suffer hardships from not being able to find the road."[37] While this statement can be taken literally, doubtless the words have a deeper meaning referring to divinely illumined Akbar as the guiding light of the empire.

One of the conservative court scholars and jurists, al-Badauni, who lost Akbar's favor with the ascendancy of Abu al-Fazl, wrote a secret history that was highly critical of the emperor's reign. His accounts, albeit negative, are most useful for details on Akbar's mode of worship. Introduced under the influence of Zoroastrian priests, whose presence had been felt at court since 1578, a constant fire was kept burning in the palace, for "it is one of the signs of God, and one light from His Lights."[38] Al-Badauni was all the more revolted when Akbar began to worship the sun publicly and the entire court had to stand in respect as the candles and lamps were lighted.[39] In this ceremonial we see actual light and fire being used to evoke God's presence while at the same time confirming Akbar's status as an emanation of divine light. Can we see similar imagery on the painted page or in permanent architecture?

Akbar's painting workshop was prolific, producing multiple sumptuous illustrated manuscripts, many of them concerning history, especially histories of Akbar's immediate predecessors and his Timurid and Mongolian ancestors. Among the most interesting of these is Abu al-Fazl's *Akbar Nama,* that is, the *History of Akbar.* Two illustrated copies, contemporary with Akbar's reign, are extant, but the text of neither is complete. Which of these copies was the one Abu al-Fazl presented to Akbar upon completion of the first volume of the text is a point debated among scholars; many favor the copy today in the Victoria and Albert Museum in London.[40] Some believe that its 116 illustrations were executed for a history of Akbar's reign written before Abu al-Fazl was ordered to author his own version.[41] John Seyller has argued that an older text has been altered and pasted over some of the original words, while in other cases entire new pages of Abu al-Fazl's prose have been added.[42] Susan Stronge has recently shown that the text that Abu al-Fazl revised was his own text and argues that its illustrations were all executed sometime between about 1590 and 1595,[43] a period when Abu al-Fazl exercised profound influence over Akbar.

Nearly fifty artists worked on this manuscript, and generally at least two worked on each illustration, one responsible for the composition and outline (*tarh*) and the other for the color painting (*'amal*); a third artist at times worked on portraiture (*chehra nami*).[44] With so many artists working on a single text, it is not surprising that there is a wide range of styles and compositions among its folios. Of the intact 116 illustrated pages, over fifty of them contain portraits of Akbar. In spite of the stylistic diversity of the pages overall, the emperor is easily and immediately recognizable for several reasons.[45] One is that each painting of him is definitely a true portrait; Abu al-Fazl notes that Akbar sat so his portrait could be drawn.[46] Consistently Akbar is shown with a round, flattish face, small eyes, and straight brows; in illustrations where he is mature, he sports a distinctive mustache with down-turned ends. He is easily distinguishable from others surrounding him.

In most of these pages from the *Akbar Nama* there is considerable activity with a large number of people present. All the same the viewer's eye is quickly drawn to the emperor. In a double-page composition depicting Akbar watching a battle between two rival groups of holy men, the composition is filled with frenzied ascetics who attack one another with swords and arrows.[47] The most intense action is on the right page below Akbar, who is seated on a horse just above the violent fighting. Behind him are courtiers, landscape, and a town of stone-built structures. In spite of all this commotion and detail Akbar stands out, in part, because the artist who designed the composition, Basawan, has left an area around him where there are no other people. He is separated from ordinary men, just as Abu al-Fazl claims that Akbar is superior to other mortals. Also underscoring his role as emperor here, as in most of his other portraits in this *Akbar Nama,* are an imperial standard and fly whisk, an ancient Indian symbol of kingship, just near his head. Often the patterns of these standards are floral with a central medallion known as a *shamsa,* that is, sun motif, a reminder that Akbar is imbued with God's light.

In these manuscript pages the emperor is depicted proportionately larger than the other figures, thus again visually affirming his superior larger-than-life status. In the face of adversity, Akbar is always depicted as tranquil. This is evident in the composition where Akbar watches enraged ascetics fight; here the point is to show Akbar as rational, when others in matters of religion are not. Another double-page composition, depicting Akbar riding a enraged elephant, may seem to deny his rational nature, but in fact shows him favored by God. The young emperor, Akbar, mounted a mad elephant, who tore across an unstable pontoon bridge across a raging river (fig. 7.4).[48] This is an event of Akbar's twentieth year, in which he claims he rode the elephant to test God's faith in him.[49] This event occurred just before Akbar first decided to visit the shrine of Khwaja Mu'in al-Din, as if one event led to another, indicating the young king's divinely inspired status. The illustration shows the youthful emperor riding calmly atop the charging elephant while those around him are frantic with terror. Even in the face of adversity Akbar is illumined with God's divine grace.

In this painting and most others from this manuscript Akbar wears extremely simple clothing, usually white, while most others wear either more elaborate or brightly colored garb. White is a color associated with purity, often used to denote the spiritual purity of saints and ascetics,[50] and also is the

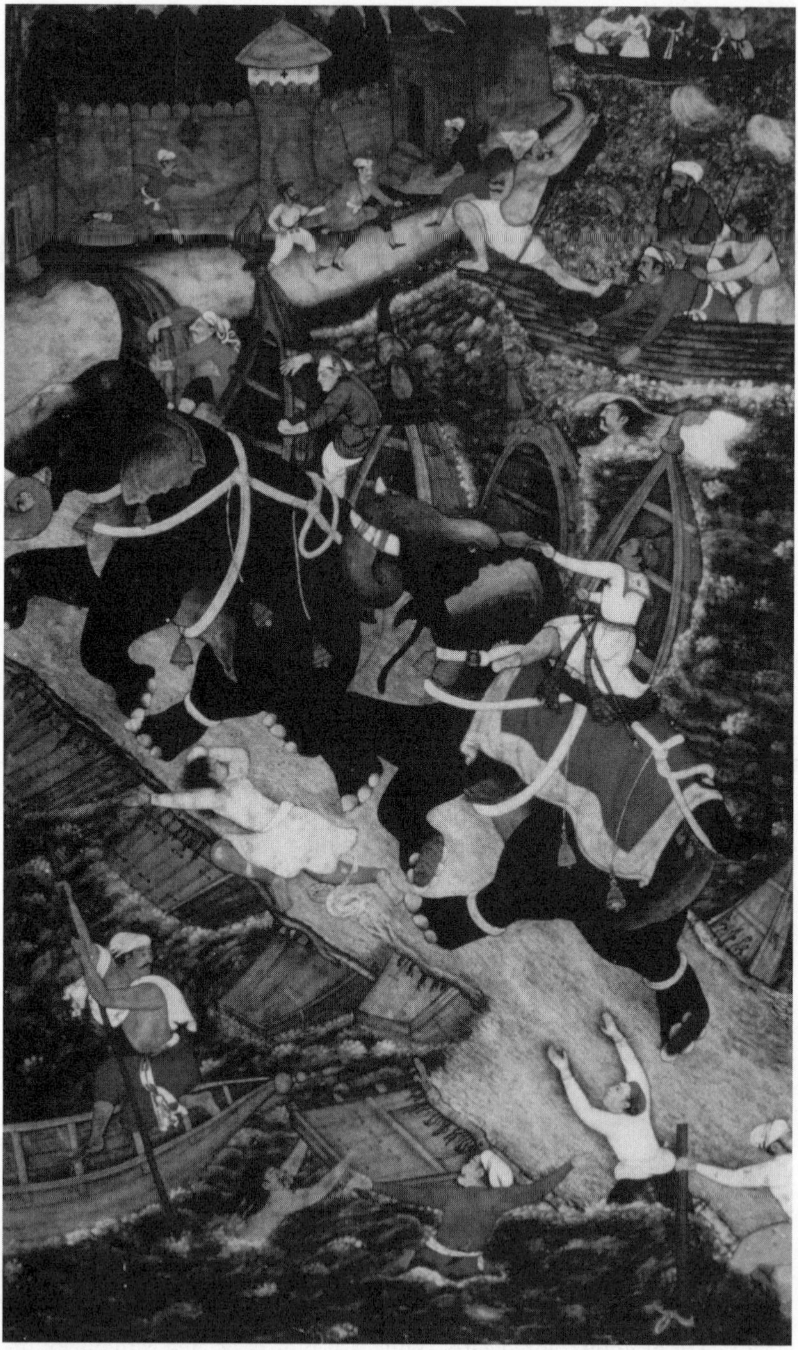

FIGURE 7.4. Akbar riding a mad elephant, from the *Akbar Nama*. (Reproduced with permission of the V&A Picture Library.)

color of the main Chishti tombs. The choice to depict him almost always wearing white seems a conscious one. This is especially so in illustrations associated with the Chishtiyya—for example, one of Akbar walking on foot to the shrine at Ajmer, a distance of some 365 kilometers, to give thanks for the birth of his son, and another at the shrine itself.[51] The color of his clothing links him with the shrine of Mu'in al-Din Chishti, casting him as the saint. It was during this visit on which he walked on foot to the shrine that Akbar claimed the authority to decide who would be the *dargah*'s caretaker. Two years earlier, in 1568, when it was learned that Akbar intended to visit the Ajmer shrine, the *dargah*'s attendant had a vision of Khwaja Mu'in al-Din proclaiming that Akbar's spirituality was even greater of that of the famous saint. In the attendant's vision the Khwaja said, "if [Akbar] knew the amount of his own spirituality he would not bestow a glance on me the sitter-in-the-dust of the path of studentship."[52] In an illustration, from the slightly later *Akbar Nama,* the emperor is shown praying, possibly at the Chishti shrine of Farid Shakar-i Ganj at Pakpattan.[53] Here he is shown wearing orange garb, which is the color of the clothing worn by those belonging to India's highest saintly lineage, a legacy that Akbar has assumed.[54]

Mughal artists thus used pictorial devices of color, scale, and appropriate placement to suggest Akbar's light-filled status. Moreover, by depicting Akbar as tranquil or positively engaged in contrast to the mood of others, he appears endowed with God's grace.

Having examined characteristics of some of these pages, it is necessary to discuss the nature and audience for whom these illustrated works were intended, as well as the role Akbar played in their execution. Here, too. scholarship is divided in two camps: one consists of those who believe that Akbar was personally involved in approving the paintings for his illustrated histories and that they had propagandistic value, as I have suggested here; the other consists of those who believe such texts were simply precious objects with value only to an extremely limited audience and little if any legitimizing value.[55] That these two views, with some revision, are compatible is not as far fetched as it might sound. Akbar clearly was interested in the minute workings of his court, for Abu al-Fazl states, as I cited earlier, "[Akbar] does not shrink from the minutiae of business."[56] He goes on to say, "If [Akbar] can not perform everything himself, he ought to select one or two men of sagacity and understanding, of liberal views . . . and be guided by their advice."[57] In discussing the importance of painting, he indicated that the supervisors laid out new paintings weekly before Akbar, and the emperor rewarded the best artists.[58] This suggests that the planning of paintings was not left to the whim of artists, but rather that some level of imperial control was exerted. True, these were small objects, books to be held and read containing paintings to be admired. Equally true is that the audience would be small and intimate. Contrary to some scholarly belief, a small but select audience does not mean the images would lack a didactic or even symbolic meaning.

The Mughal court system was pyramidal, with Akbar, the peak, surrounded by a small group of elites, who in turn would have their own following. This increasingly large body of followers ultimately all owed alliance to the divinely illumined Akbar. This is not unlike the Sufi system where the *pir* and his many *murids*, who in turn become *pirs*, all owe allegiance to a common deceased saint. Akbar even institutionalized this system at the upper echelons by creating a disciple-like relationship between himself and his most trusted nobles. Known as the Din-i Ilahi, it was believed by many to be a new faith, but it was in fact a means of insuring absolute loyalty to Akbar the king.[59] It would seem likely that the illustrated imagery in the *Akbar Nama*, to be shown only to those of the inner circle, would play the same role. Finally, we must remember that the *Akbar Nama* was a history written about and for a house which had a keen sense of its own place in the larger world, so the *Akbar Nama* and its potent visual images were a record for posterity, not just for contemporaries.

Architecture

Akbar, we know, initiated ceremonial associated with the veneration of light in the Mughal court. While al-Badauni, Akbar's critic, states that some of this was performed publicly, we must imagine that the notion of public here was limited to those who had access to the inner chambers of the palace. The Mughal emperor was considerably more accessible when he showed himself to his public from a projecting window, known as a *jharoka-i darshan* (public viewing window). This window opened from an exterior wall in the palace to a public spot which anyone could enter. This presentation ceremony would assure his subjects the emperor was well, thus insuring stability; at this venue subjects could approach the king with their grievances.[60] But the implications of this practice are more complex and combine Akbar's three superior characteristics stressed by Abu al-Fazl at the opening of his Mughal manual of state, the *A'in-i Akbari:* Akbar, imbued with divine light, is a Perfect Man who, like a father to his people, is responsible for assuring justice for all, that is, for upholding the policy of *sulh-i kul,* universal toleration.[61]

Abu al-Fazl charged Akbar with the execution of justice, a concept based on well-established Perso-Islamic traditions, and added to this the Indian concept of kingship identifying the ruler as a father to all his subjects, not just his Muslim or even Sunni Muslim ones, thus encouraging *sulh-i kul.*[62] He has conflated the Islamic notion that kings should be accessible to their subjects with the Hindu practice of *darshan,* that is, beholding.[63] The practice of *darshan* in the royal context derives from a religious concept in which beholding a deity's image bestows an auspicious blessing on the beholder. Hindu kingship extended *darshan* to the monarch. Since the Mughals believed themselves semidivine, the adaptation of *darshan* in their own court ceremony with all its connotations—secular and sacred—was intentional.

We know little about *darshan* as enacted by Hindu rulers before Akbar's time. We do not know where it was performed, nor do we have details of the ceremony surrounding it, although we know a great deal about *darshan* of a deity as represented by an image in the sanctum of a temple (*garbhagriha*).[64] There the image is installed in a chamber deep within a temple. The devotee has *darshan,* that is, s/he sees the auspicious image of the god by entering the temple and reaching its inner threshold. The imperial Mughal practice of *darshan* is documented by chroniclers—both Mughal writers and foreign travelers—and by material remains at the palace sites. It appears that this ceremony became more elaborate over time and its implications more overt. For now, let us understand this practice under Akbar.

It is not possible to reconstruct when the practice of presenting Akbar to his people as if he were a god, in a public venue, first occurred. The practice is not mentioned in the *Akbar Nama,* although this is not surprising, since this history does not focus on the routine but on the extraordinary. It is discussed in the *A'in-i Akbari,* which, as a manual of state, details practice and ceremony but gives no clue about how or when this practice came into existence. There we learn that Akbar presents himself, "after performing morning devotions . . . from outside the awning, to people of all ranks, whether they be given to worldly pursuits, or to a life of solitary contemplation. . . . this mode of showing himself is called . . . *darshan;* and it frequently happens that business is transacted at this time."[65]

The earliest surviving *jharoka-i darshan* is at Fatehpur Sikri, suggesting the practice of the emperor's public presentation commenced with Abu al-Fazl's arrival at court.[66] It consists of an overhanging balcony probably derived from the small projecting windows that abound on earlier Rajput palaces, although there they appear to be functional, not ritual, features.[67] At Fatehpur Sikri the *jharoka* is aligned with Akbar's sleeping chamber and with his private audience hall.[68] Because Akbar's personal quarters at Fatehpur Sikri—an architectural extension of himself—are centrally situated between the *jharoka* and his private audience hall, his role as the upholder—imbued with semidivine light—of justice to all is visually underscored.

The picture we have so far is one of Akbar's daily presentation of himself as if he were a deity; that is, he reveals himself so others might have *darshan*, auspicious sight. Underscoring the religious aspect of this ceremony were the presence, among others, of devotees, known as *darshaniyya* or *darshani;* they offered prayers for the emperor's health and safety, and many would fast until they had gazed upon the emperor's face.[69] But at the same time, this was not a silent ceremony, as it might be when partaking *darshan* in a temple, for Abu al-Fazl indicates that frequently business was transacted, meaning justice was maintained.[70] Interaction between two people, one considered spiritually superior to the other, is much closer to what occurs in the *dargah* between a *pir* and *murid* or a shaikh and a devotee, where the enlightened guides the novice. Akbar positioned in his *jharoka* enacts the role of an enlightened father to his children or a spiritual master to his students. With Akbar presented in this window the image of deity and saint are conflated into a single figure. He is cast as a *pir-i zinda,* a living saint, touched by God's light, for those who are able—or who choose—to interpret his presence in this manner.

Abu al-Fazl continuously developed the textual rhetoric of light imagery associated with Akbar the emperor; however, its translation into visual form and ceremonial was less overt. This may have been in part because Akbar did not actively build after his departure from Fatehpur Sikri, the period when Abu al-Fazl's influence was on the rise. The exception was the provision of a small white marble pavilion in the Agra fort, probably his *jharoka-i darshan,* given the location on the fort's outer wall.[71] Since the first one at Fatehpur Sikri was made of red sandstone, and the use of white marble suggests a visual vocabulary more explicitly associated with the divine, this *jharoka-i darshan* was probably provided when the court shifted residence to Agra after 1590.

Increasingly in visual form we see the tendency to blur the role between ruler and divine. The conservative approach in the matter of visual forms expressing that Akbar was an emanation of divine light was probably a reflection of Akbar's and Abu al-Fazl's belief that religion was a matter of inner reflection, and not one of conspicuous external display. In illustrations of the emperor the sense of his illumined status was indicated by scale, emotion, color, and composition, but not by the actual presence of elements associated with the verbal vocabulary of illumination thought as expounded by Abu al-Fazl. All that would change with the next two Mughal emperors, Jahangir and Shah Jahan.

JAHANGIR AND SHAH JAHAN

Eager to obtain the throne, Prince Muhammad Sultan Salim, the future Jahangir (r. 1605–27), revolted against Akbar in 1600, establishing his own court in a Mughal fort at Allahabad, in eastern India. The prince struck coins in his own name and assumed imperial titles. Akbar sought to consult his confidant and biographer, Abu al-Fazl, then in the Deccan. Prince Salim, however, had Abu al-Fazl assassinated in 1602, realizing that it was the older statesman, not himself, who had Akbar's ear.[72] While Salim's revolt did not shake the stability of the Mughal empire, it did sour relations between father and son. It was only as he was dying that Akbar designated Salim his successor.[73]

Upon the death of Akbar in 1605, Muhammad Sultan Salim assumed the imperial throne. He took the title Nur al-Din Muhammad Jahangir Badshah Ghazi; hence the name Jahangir, by which he is most commonly known. Salim explains in his memoirs, which he began writing at the time of his accession, that he took the name Jahangir, meaning "World Seizer," since it was the business of kings to control the world; he claimed the *laqab* (title of honor) Nur al-Din, "Light of the Faith," was appropriate since, in his own words, his accession "coincided with the rising and shining on the earth of the great light, the sun."[74] The assumption of this title indicates, amid much other visual evidence, that the importance of light and light imagery under Akbar continued under Jahangir. For example, light imagery is also apparent in painting commissioned by Jahangir, especially in his allegorical portraits, as well as in imperial funereal architecture. How ironic, then, that Jahangir, responsible for the brutal murder of Abu al-Fazl, creator of much of the light imagery associated with the emperor's semidivine status, made extensive use of light imagery in his own writing and art. This visual imagery is further refined and increasingly formalized under the next Mughal ruler, the son of Jahangir, Shah Jahan (r. 1628–58), who in portraiture and through architecture presents himself as an *ishraqi*-inspired Perfect Man.[75]

Mughal ties with the Chishtiyya, actively maintained by Akbar until 1579, were revived by Jahangir and then sustained by Shah Jahan. Jahangir's personal memoirs, known both as the *Jahangir Nama* and the *Tuzuk-i Jahangiri,* open with an account of Akbar's journey on foot to the great Chishti shrine in Ajmer and Shaikh Salim's prophecy of the birth of a son.[76] Subsequently in his memoirs, Jahangir recalls that early in his childhood the dying Shaikh Salim had placed his turban on the young prince's head, saying that he would be the saint's spiritual successor.[77] Jahangir and later his son, Shah Jahan, enact this role by endowing the Chishti shrines when on pilgrimage. Such patronage must be viewed as an attempt to link Mughal rule to a spiritual source, specifically the one that once had guided Akbar. It is also motivated by personal piety; over time the renewed Chishti-Mughal link suggests increased orthodoxy in official policy, especially once Shah Jahan comes to power.

The written image of light so powerfully developed by Abu al-Fazl to reflect Akbar's status as a semidivine ruler was adapted by both Jahangir and Shah Jahan in a much more public way. Jahangir not only entitled himself Nur al-Din (Light of the Faith), but also first gave his favorite wife the title Nur Mahal (Light of the Palace) at their marriage in 1611 and then later bestowed the title Nur Jahan (Light of the World) on his formidable queen.[78] Shah Jahan, too, adopted lofty titles that evoke an image of light, calling himself Shihab al-Din, "Meteor of the Faith" and "Lord of the Auspicious Conjunctions." This second title was borrowed from his ancestor Timur and refers to the movements of planets in the heavens.[79] *Nur,* "light," was featured in the official names of royal gardens and country estates, for example, the Chesma-i Nur (Fountain of Light), the Bagh-i Nur Afshan (Light Scattering Garden), and Bagh-i Nur Manzil (Garden of the Palace of Light).[80] Visually the impact of *nur* in the name was heightened when these gardens were used at night and lighted by lamps placed behind cascading water. In such a setting the semidivine ruler literally was surrounded by that light which Abu al-Fazl described in more metaphoric and less concrete terms.

Translating Abu al-Fazl's imagery of divine light into concrete form, artists began to depict Jahangir and Shah Jahan in portraiture with their heads surrounded by a nimbus of light. Exactly when this first occurred in Jahangir's reign is difficult to assess, since scholarly opinion varies regarding the dates of many Mughal paintings from this period. Portraits of Jahangir from the very earliest days of his reign do not feature these halos of light, but by about 1610 some of his portraits include them.[81] A notable example is an illustration showing a young prince Salim seated with his namesake, Shaikh Salim Chishti.[82] Both saint and prince are illumined by halos, stressing visually the link between the Chishtiyya and the Mughal house which Jahangir had made explicit in the opening of his memoirs.

Perhaps the most explicit reference to the Chishti-Mughal dynastic link is a double-page portrait, essentially an allegorical portrait, depicting a nimbused Khwaja Mu'in al-Din handing Jahangir, who also has a halo, a globe with a key surmounted by a Timurid crown (plates 4–5).[83] Wearing a halo indicating his semidivine status, Jahangir receives the key to the Timurid world, symbolizing his legitimate right to rule (for the Mughals were descendants of Timur), from

Mu'in al-Din, who by now has become the spiritual guardian of the Mughal house. Further underscoring the Mughal-Chishtiyya alliance are Jahangir's lustrous pearl earrings, which were a sign of his devotion to the saint whom he credits with curing him of an illness in 1614.[84] Both saint and king are bound by wearing white clothing, although Jahangir's elaborate jewelry and sash (*patka*) indicate his temporal as well as spiritual role as ruler. This portrait clearly had tremendous dynastic import, since Shah Jahan later had his father's portrait removed from the album and replaced with that of his own.[85]

A second well-known portrait of Jahangir, also an allegorical work, shows him snubbing James I of England and the Ottoman sultan while he hands a book to a holy man, who has been identified as Shaikh Husain Chishti of Ajmer.[86] Shaikh Husain had been banished by Akbar in 1570, but pardoned in 1600. Verses on the painting read: "Although kings stand before him . . . he looks inwardly towards dervishes."[87] Jahangir's head is surrounded by a brilliant gold halo consisting of the sun and moon, and it is so dazzling that even the putti (nude children with wings) in the sky have to hide their faces. Here the illumined king is shown as concerned with a contemplative life, not a mundane one; at the same time we are reminded of the dynastic Mughal-Chishtiyya legitimizing tie.

Other illustrations represent historical, not metaphoric events, for example, Jahangir's well-known durbar scene, today in the Boston Museum of Fine Arts.[88] Probably intended for inclusion in an illustrated copy of the *Jahangir Nama*, a nimbused Jahangir in the throne of his public audience hall (*jharoka-i 'amm o khass*) is enthroned before the nobility. In the upper right corner of his white marble *jharoka* is a painted image of the Virgin Mary. Such imagery was extremely popular with Jahangir, and a number of paintings intended for Mughal histories indicate their presence on Jahangir's throne.[89] Rather than a reflection of Jahangir's desire to convert to Christianity, as the Jesuits at court so firmly believed,[90] the image's presence was yet another reminder to those present, and one considerably easier to see than the artist's imagined halo, that Jahangir, the emperor, was descended from a long line of illustrious kings descended from Alanquwa, who was miraculously impregnated by a ray of light.

While most portraits of Jahangir show him with a halo of divine light, there is none of Shah Jahan without one. Understanding Shah Jahan's portraiture is closely linked to his personal concept of kingship, which was more finely honed than Jahangir's. Shah Jahan's 30-year rule was dominated by an outward sense of prosperity and stability unmatched even during Akbar's rule. At the same time, almost every aspect of courtly culture became increasingly formalized. Shah Jahan was portrayed as an aloof, ideal king in texts and on the illustrated page; the emperor personally supervised the painting workshop and approved the final version of all his histories, so concerned was he about his image.[91] Official histories present him as a just leader and staunch upholder of orthodox Islam, but they give little insight into the emperor's personal thoughts, a considerable contrast to our knowledge of both Akbar and Jahangir. The painted image of Shah Jahan parallels the literary one. The emperor is portrayed in an idealized manner—while he ages over time, his features remain flawless. For example, his skin and features are as perfectly preserved in a portrait of him in old age as they are in one of him at twenty-five.[92] His inner character is never revealed, and he is always depicted in a profile view which does not allow for distortion by introducing perspective and other illusionistic techniques.[93] Rather, his role as semidivine king of the world, a play on the meaning of his name, is the focus of each portrait. His face is always surrounded by a halo.

In court scenes where Shah Jahan is depicted dispensing justice enthroned within his public audience hall, Ebba Koch has argued that the hall in which he is seated is modeled on contemporary mosques. Shah Jahan fills the position in these scenes where in the mosque a mihrab (prayer niche) would be located.[94] Frequently mihrabs are embellished with an image of a mosque lamp, referring to the famous Light verse from the Qur'an discussed in conjunction with Humayun's tomb. Shah Jahan's position in these paintings, as well as in the actual audience hall which they depict, suggests he, like the mihrab, is filled with God's light.

In some of Shah Jahan's portraits, especially ones where he is the only dominant figure, the metaphoric nature of his semidivine and just quality is taken so far as to show small angels above his head, often crowning him, while at his feet are the lion and the lamb of peace (fig. 7.5).[95] Both these features are derived from European prints and books, such as the *Polyglot Bible,* which had made their entrance at court in the reigns of Akbar and Jahangir.[96] While the visual rendition of angels crowning the emperor from heaven is probably inspired by skyborne putti in the second illustrated title page of the *Polyglot Bible,* the idea behind this representation comes from *ishraqi* philosophy.[97]

A second and more subtle example is a Shamsa, a sun medallion, that was included in one of Shah Jahan's albums (*muraqqa'*) containing loose paintings and calligraphic compositions.[98] The presence of multiple birds in the composition suggests that the seemingly abstract work reflects *ishraqi* thought, where bird imagery is often used as a metaphor for the soul's quest for union with God.[99] Attar's mystical poem *Mantiq al-Tayr,* known in English as the *Conference of the Birds,* is a model for this notion. In the poem thousands of birds,

FIGURE 7.5. Shah Jahan standing on a globe and crowned by angels. (Courtesy of the Freer Gallery of Art, Smithsonian Institution, Washington D.C. [F1939.49].)

representing the soul, set out in quest of the perfect king. In the end, only thirty birds survive the rigorous journey and find the king, that is, God, in the form of a blinding light more brilliant than the sun and stars.[100] In the center of the Shamsa, painted almost completely in various shades of gold, suggesting the brilliance of God's light, is a calligraphic roundel giving Shah Jahan's name and title, Shihab al-Din, "Meteor of the Faith." The imagery and Persian text, subtle as it might seem, cast Shah Jahan as a semidivine ruler imbued with God's light. Thus, Abu al-Fazl's Perfect Man, inspired by illumination thought, achieves its mature form visually under Shah Jahan, who personally supervised the construction of his own image.

Both Jahangir and Shah Jahan continued Akbar's custom of presenting himself to the public at the *jharoka-i darshan,* in the role of a *Pir-i Zinda* (Living Pir) full of God's light. Jahangir showed himself during the time of the rising sun in a *jharoka* on the palace's outer wall that faced the east so he would be associated with the rising sun and in the evening in one on the west, again so he would be associated with the sun and light imagery.[101] Edward Terry, present at Jahangir's court in 1616, indicates the presence of *darshaniyya,* reporting that many were assembled, shouting for the king's and queen's long life, and music was sounded to announce the imperial presence.[102] The cries and music in the imperial presence recall a new type of worship based on *bhakti,* a form of devotion which verged on adoration, that centered on the Chaitanya sect, a religious development among Vaishnavites, worshipers of the various forms of the Hindu god Vishnu. Under this *bhakti*-influenced movement, large groups of devotees came to have *darshan* of Krishna, a form of Vishnu, when the curtain before the god was briefly lifted seven times a day. During these times for *darshan,* music would sound and the devotees would cry out the name of god. A painting intended for the *Jahangir Nama* showing Jahangir at his *jharoka* window is instructive, for among the assembled crowd are both musicians and *darshaniyya,* devotees of the emperor who, under Akbar, would not eat until they had seen the emperor's illumined face (plate 6).[103] The *darshaniyya* are clearly distinguishable from the other court members by their bare torsos. One is of particular interest, for on his forehead is the U-shaped mark, applied in yellow paste, worn by followers of Vishnu including the Chaitanya (plate 7). Around his neck he wears wooden beads associated with Hindu holy men. While his appearance as described thus far is normative for a Hindu devotee, his elaborate turban and pearl earrings are not. Shortly after Jahangir began to wear pearl earrings as a sign of his devotion to Khwaja Mu'in al-Din, many nobles followed suit; whether they did so as a sign of devotion to Jahangir or the saint or just to be in fashion is not clear. But the appearance of the pearl earrings on this ascetic as well as a turban which closely resembles that often worn by Jahangir may reflect his status as a *darshaniyya,* seeking sight of the illumined ruler.

The illustration is equally instructive regarding the appearance of Jahangir's *jharoka,* since most of his palace architecture was dismantled and rebuilt under his successor, Shah Jahan. This *jharoka,* clearly at the Agra fort as indicated by the red sandstone fortifications,[104] and its surrounding structures here are white marble, a material associated primarily with saints' tombs. Akbar, near the very end of his reign, as we saw earlier, used marble for a pavilion, probably his *jharoka-i darshan,* located in the same projecting turret depicted here, to suggest his semidivine status. Whether this is Akbar's *jharoka* or whether Jahangir renewed it, the message sent was identical. This *jharoka* is depicted having a gilt roof, a notion which Shah Jahan further embellished in his rebuilt *jharoka-i darshan* at the Agra fort, situated in the same east-facing location.[105] Here Shah Jahan presented himself to the public outside the fort on the terrain below. This pavilion was surmounted by a *bangala* roof, that is, a deeply sloping curved roof seen only on structures used by the emperor, that was gilded.[106] Shah Jahan's official chronicler, Lahauri, notes that when the emperor presented himself to his subjects under this gilt roof, it appeared as if there were two suns.[107] One was light from the morning sun reflected on the roof of this pavilion. The other, Lahauri said, was the emperor himself. Light reflected from the gold roof appeared to crown the king with a halo of the sort often depicted in contemporary paintings and described in literature.

Other features seen in Shah Jahan's Agra fort that were intended to underscore his semidivine illumined status included a throne niche whose appearance was enhanced by powerful imagery. It consists of four bulbous baluster columns supporting a curved roof that was inspired by European royal and religious prints.[108] Beside these structural baluster columns, the baldachin's carving is embellished with a relief representation of a sun medallion at the top, thus continuing the long-standing Mughal fascination with sun and light imagery. According to Lahauri, the court historian, within this pavilion was Shah Jahan's golden throne, which he likens to the highest heaven.[109]

So far we have limited our discussion of the imperial Mughal association with divine light to painting and architecture that is essentially secular in nature. There is one other aspect of artistic patronage that, while secular, could be construed as considerably more religious in nature. This is the construction of imperial tombs. In the tomb Akbar provided for his father, Humayun, the use of a pierced mihrab, allowing for the entrance of light, suggested that Sufic imagery concerning light was being applied to a royal tomb albeit in a highly subtle manner. The multistoried, tiered tomb Jahangir provided for his father, Akbar, just outside the city of Agra, pushed this notion even further.[110] The tomb, built in the early seventeenth century, is centered in a formal Mughal four-part garden. A Persian inscription on the complex's entrance gate reads: "These are the gardens of Paradise. Enter them and Live Forever," making clear that the setting is intended as an earthly replica of those eternal gardens promised to the faithful on the Day of Judgment.[111]

While most of the actual tomb is constructed of sandstone and stucco, the top floor, which contains the false sarcophagus is marble, reminiscent of the tombs of the major Chishti saints. But unlike those domed tombs, this one had an upper story that remained open to the sky. In the center is a magnificently carved white marble cenotaph; at its north end is a lamp stand (*chiraqdan*), also rendered in finely carved white marble. It was probably intended for a ceremonial fire, which Akbar venerated. Many believe that such an exquisitely rendered marble cenotaph, carved with the ninety-nine names of God and intricate floral motifs, could not have been intended to remain exposed to the elements and that once there must have been a central dome. Yet an uncovered cenotaph is the grave type that meets orthodox approval and may have been the reason for the open top story of Akbar's tomb. But that is only a partial explanation. Considering the Mughal fascination with light and light symbolism, the placement of this cenotaph directly under the sun and moon follows especially the interests of Akbar and Jahangir. Underscoring this interpretation is the final verse of the Persian inscription on the tomb's entrance gate, which reads: "May his [Akbar's] soul shine like the rays of the sun and the moon in the light of God."[112]

Increasingly we are seeing marble, formerly associated only with the Chishtiyya, being used for structures which showcased the imperial Mughals as emanations of divine light. Thus, the blurring between the lines of divinity and royalty, which had commenced earlier, is further enhanced visually. This trend peaks not surprisingly under Shah Jahan, who provides an unprecedented number of white marble buildings either associated with the imperial Mughal family and for their use or as structures at Chishti shrines, particularly the *dargah* of Mu'in al-Din.[113] Among the most famous of these buildings today is doubtless the Taj Mahal, known officially as the Rauza-i Munawwar, that is, the Illumined Tomb. It was largely built between 1632 and 1647 as a tomb for Shah Jahan's favorite wife, Mumtaz Mahal, who died in childbirth in 1631, but it is not absolutely clear whether it was intended as the emperor's own tomb as well. However, its name, Rauza-i Munawwar, an epithet shared with the site of the Prophet Muhammad's tomb in Medina,[114] suggests that Shah Jahan, who perceived himself like Muhammad as a Perfect Man, planned it to be his own tomb and not just that of his wife. In any event, he was buried there after his death in 1666. While court historians give us precise clues to the meaning of many of Shah Jahan's buildings, for example, the *jharoka-i darshan* at the Agra fort, in which the emperor's appearance is likened to that of the sun, no such textual suggestions concerning imagery exist for the tomb. Much historical information is known,[115] but scholars disagree on the symbolism of the Taj Mahal. One scholar has argued that it is a visual representation of the Throne of God as envisioned on the Day of Judgment, while others disagree strongly with this interpretation.[116] Whatever its larger meaning, this extensive use of white marble must have been intended to evoke a sense of divine presence, for light constantly changes and plays against the glistening surface.

The Taj Mahal is a structure whose significance is greater today than it was at the time of its construction. It had little impact on future Indian architecture. True, it was admired by the Mughal family, members of the nobility, and European travelers throughout the Mughal period and beyond, but it essentially marks the end of the tradition of building large-scale tombs for the Mughal monarchs.

Given the historical context of its construction, recent cultural reconstructions of the Taj Mahal arouse a sense of irony. Today thousands come to India with seeing this famed structure as their main goal; I even know one Western scholar who upon seeing the Taj Mahal for the first time, especially its white marble surface, which changes with the light, actually spoke of undergoing a mystical experience.[117] The image of the Taj Mahal, more than any other in the world, has become a symbol of excellence. Over the past twenty years advertisements featuring the Taj Mahal have been associated with fine china, expensive cars, aged whisky, top-end cameras, premier-quality life insurance, luxury hotels, and more.[118] Even the government of India features this tomb in glossy, full-page advertisements inviting tourists to experience paradise on earth. These are far cries from any Mughal-intended image of the divine.

The association of Shah Jahan's illumined mausoleum with high-quality products may be harmless—perhaps the proud emperor would have been delighted with this universal acclamation of his architectural output. But other modern associations are more pernicious, and based only on a partial understanding of history. Land for the Taj Mahal was purchased from the Hindu Raja of Amber, Mirza Raja Jai Singh, who served in the Mughal court.[119] This fact has been distorted by such authors as P. N. Oak, a member of the Institute for Rewriting Indian History, who have presented not only the Taj Mahal but also a number of other Muslim-built structures on the Indian subcontinent as products of Hindu patronage.[120] Oak's ideas, while patently insupportable, have been popularized through various media, among them books, E-mail listservs and Web sites on the Taj Mahal which claim, for example, that it was constructed as a temple.[121] Such claims manipulated by members of the Hindu right wing, whether in the subcontinent itself or in the diaspora, use artistic creation to discredit Muslims and the very basis for a secular democracy in modern India. Whatever its original meaning, the Taj Mahal was part of the legacy of Abu al-Fazl's *ishraqi* philosophy. Today it has become for some a symbol of that which Abu al-Fazl and Akbar would have most abhorred, the pitting of religious groups against one another instead of the promotion of *sulh-i kul*, universal toleration.

NOTES

1. For a summary of these events see John F. Richards, *The Mughal Empire* (Cambridge: Cambridge University Press, 1993), pp. 29–47; and Saiyid Athar Abbas Rizvi, *Religious and Intellectual History of the Muslims in Akbar's Reign* (New Delhi: Munshiram Manoharlal, 1975), pp. 76–103.

2. Abu al-Fazl 'Allami, *Akbar Nama*, trans. H. Beveridge, 3 vols. (1907–39; repr., Delhi: Rare Books, 1972–77), 2:237, hereafter cited as *Akbar Nama*.

3. *Akbar Nama*, 2:510. Al-Badauni, *Muntakhab-ut-Tawarikh*, trans. G. S. A. Ranking, W. H. Lowe, and W. Haig, 3 vols. (1884–1925; repr., Patna: Academic Press, 1973), 2:309 and 3:136–40, however, suggests it is Akbar's annoyance at an old yet humble man not accustomed to the new courtly ceremony more than a political move.

4. P. M. Currie, *The Shrine and Cult of Mu'in al-Din Chishti of Ajmer* (Delhi: Oxford University Press, 1989), pp. 20–65; Wahiduddin Begg, *The Holy Biography of Hazrat Khwaja Muinuddin Hasan Chishti* (Ajmer: W.D. Begg, 1960), p. 111.

5. *Akbar Nama*, 3:345–48. This was during a hunt where he released all the animals and afterward cut his hair short in the manner of Indian ascetics.

6. Qur'an 24:35, in *The Meaning of the Glorious Qur'an*, trans. Abdullah Yusuf Ali, 2 vols. (Beirut: Dar al-Kitab, 1938), 1:907–8.

7. Annemarie Schimmel, *Mystical Dimensions of Islam* (Chapel Hill: University of North Carolina Press, 1975), pp. 63, 96, 115, 130, 215, 259–63.

8. Asloob Ahmad Ansari, "Mystical Poetry of Ameer Khusrau," in *Life, Times and Works of Amir Khusrau of Dehlavi*, ed. Zoe Ansari (New Delhi: Seventh Centenary National Amir Khusrau Society, 1975), pp. 222–24.

9. Muhammad Nur al-Din Jahangir, *Tuzuk-i Jahangiri*, trans. A. Rogers, ed. H. Beveridge, 2 vols. (1909–14; repr., Delhi: Munshiram Manoharlal, 1968), 1:169, hereafter cited as *Tuzuk*.

10. Regula Burckhardt Quraishi, *Sufi Music of India and Pakistan: Sound, Context and Meaning in Qawwali*, 2nd ed. (Chicago: University of Chicago Press, 1995), pp. 19–27.

11. Khaliq Ahmad Nizami, *Life and Times of Shaikh Nizam-u'd-din Auliya* (Delhi: Idarah-i Adabiyat-i Delli, 1991), pp. 57–60.

12. S. A. I. Tirmizi, *Ajmer through Inscriptions* (New Delhi: Indian Institute of Islamic Studies, 1968), p. 16.

13. Ibid.

14. Michael Brand and Glenn D. Lowry, *Akbar's India: Art from the Mughal City of Victory* (New York: Asia Society Galleries, 1985), p. 73. Although there is about a thirty-year difference between the event and the painting, had the tomb's surface been changed during this period, it is difficult to believe no record of it would exist. William Finch in *Hakluytus Postumus; or, Purchas His Pilgrimes*, ed. Samuel Purchas, 20 vols. (Glasgow: James McLehose and Hons, 1905–7), 4:61, notes in 1611 that the paving around the tomb was marble.

15. Catherine B. Asher, *Architecture of Mughal India* (Cambridge: Cambridge University Press, 1992), p. 56.

16. Tirmizi, *Ajmer through Inscriptions*, pp. 30–31. He had been banished in 1570 as the tomb's custodian, since Akbar felt Husain mismanaged the shrine. This construction was possibly an attempt to regain Akbar's favor.

17. Ibid.

18. Asher, *Architecture of Mughal India*, pp. 44–47.

19. Ebba Koch, *Mughal Architecture: An Outline of Its History and Development (1526–1858)* (Munich: Prestel, 1991), pp. 43–44.

20. Rizvi, *Religious and Intellectual History of the Muslims*, pp. 99, 106, 107. While Faizi did have an official rank, Shaikh Mubarak's association with the court seems casual. M. Athar Ali, *The Apparatus of Empire: Awards of Ranks, Offices and Titles to the Mughal Nobility (1574–1658)* (Delhi: Oxford University Press, 1985), p. 15, indicates when he died but provides no rank.

21. Rizvi, *Religious and Intellectual History of the Muslims*, p. 107; Athar Ali, *Apparatus of Empire*, p. 30.

22. Rizvi, *Religious and Intellectual History of the Muslims*, pp. 128–40.

23. Richards, *Mughal Empire*, pp. 39–40; Rizvi, *Religious and Intellectual History of the Muslims*, pp. 141–74.

24. Shihab al-Din Yahya Sohravardi, *The Book of Radiance*, trans. Hossein Ziai (Costa Mesa, CA: Mazda Publishers, 1998); Mehdi Amin Razavi, *Suhrawardi and the School of Illumination* (Richmond: Curzon Press, 1997); Schimmel, *Mystical Dimensions of Islam*, pp. 259–63; Richards, *Mughal Empire*, p. 46; Seyyed Hossein Nasr, "The Relation between Sufism and Philosophy in Persian Culture," *Hamdard Islamicus* 6, no. 4 (1983): 33–47, and "The Spread of the Illuminationist School of Suhrawardi," *Islamic Quarterly* 14, no. 3 (1970): 111–21. Also see Ziai's chapter in this volume.

25. Hossein Ziai, "The Source and Nature of Authority: A Study of al-Suhrawardi's Illuminationist Political Doctrine," in *The Political Aspects of Islamic Philosophy*, ed. Charles Butterworth (Cambridge, MA: Harvard University Press, 1992), pp. 311–18, 322–29, and the same author's contribution to this volume.

26. Rizvi, *Religious and Intellectual History of the Muslims,* pp. 344–45.

27. John F. Richards, "The Formulation of Imperial Authority under Akbar and Jahangir," in *Kingship and Authority in South Asia,* ed. J. F. Richards (1978; repr., Delhi: Oxford University Press, 1998), pp. 303–4, claims Abu al-Fazl is following the commentary of Shahrazuri, who includes in his work many references to Suhrawardi.

28. Rizvi, *Religious and Intellectual History of the Muslims,* pp. 262, 266.

29. Ziai, "Source and Nature of Authority," p. 327.

30. Richards, "Formulation of Imperial Authority," pp. 297–98; *Akbar Nama,* 1:1–222 deals with this. For passages from the same text on Alanquwa see, 1:37–39, 178–83; for Chinghiz Khan, 1:191–92; for Timur, 1:204–12.

31. Richards, "Formulation of Imperial Authority," p. 293; *Akbar Nama,* 2:476–77.

32. Abu al-Fazl ʿAllami, *A'in-i Akbari,* 3 vols., vol. 1 trans. H. Blockmann, ed. S. L. Gloomer, vols. 2 and 3 trans. H. S. Jarrett (1871, 1948–49; repr., Delhi: Aadiesh Book Depot, 1965; and New Delhi: Orient Books, 1968), 1:1–2, hereafter cited as *A'in-i Akbari.*

33. See, for example, Nizam al-Mulk, *Siyasat Nama,* trans. H. Darke as *Book of Government or Rules for Kings* (London: Routledge and Kegan Paul, 1960), pp. 9–22.

34. Ziai, "Source and Nature of Authority," pp. 307–8, 311–12; *A'in-Akbari,* 1:3.

35. Richards, *Mughal Empire,* p. 39; Rizvi, *Religious and Intellectual History of the Muslims,* pp. 104–40.

36. *A'in-i Akbari,* 1:50–51.

37. Ibid., 1:52.

38. Al-Badauni, *Muntakhab-ut-Tawarikh,* 2:268–69.

39. Ibid.

40. John Seyller, "Codicological Aspects of the Victoria and Albert Museum *Akbarnama* and Their Historical Implications," *Art Journal* 49, no. 4 (1990): 370–80.

41. Ibid., p. 380. Seyller states there are 116 illustrations, but most scholars, on the basis of the Victoria and Albert's inventory number, state there are 117 paintings.

42. Ibid., pp. 379–83.

43. Susan Stronge, *Painting for the Mughal Emperor: The Art of the Book, 1560–1660* (London: V and A Publications, 2002), p. 84.

44. Geeti Sen, *Paintings from the Akbar Nama: A Visual Chronicle of Mughal India* (Varanasi: Lustre Press, 1984), pp. 53, 55.

45. See Deborah Levine Brown, "The Victoria and Albert Museum *Akbar Nama:* A Study in History, Myth and Image," 2 vols. (Ph.D. diss., University of Michigan, 1974), 1:41–67, for some of this analysis.

46. *A'in-i Akbari,* 1:115.

47. Sen, *Paintings from the Akbar Nama,* plates 42–44; Stronge, *Painting for the Mughal Emperor,* pp. 52–53.

48. Sen, *Paintings from the Akbar Nama,* plates 21, 22, 23; *Akbar Nama,* 2:223–35; Stronge, *Painting for the Mughal Emperor,* pp. 76–77.

49. *Akbar Nama,* 1:232–35.

50. See Amina Okada, *Indian Miniatures of the Mughal Court* (New York: Harry N. Abrams, 1992), pp. 5, 172, 189, 196, 234.

51. See Sen, *Paintings from the Akbar Nama,* plate 59; Brand and Lowry, *Akbar's India,* plate 32; *Akbar Nama,* 2:243, 510–11; Stronge, *Painting for the Mughal Emperor:* p. 78.

52. *Akbar Nama,* 2:476–77.

53. Linda York Leach, *Mughal and Other Paintings from the Chester Beatty Library,* 2 vols. (London: Scorpion Cavendish, 1995), 1:299–300, plate 42; it is not clear how Leach identifies the setting as Pakpattan, since the text around the image has been removed. *Akbar Nama,* 3:335.

54. Quraishi, *Sufi Music of India and Pakistan,* p. 3.

55. Those favoring a symbolic meaning include Brown, "Victoria and Albert Museum Akbar Nama," 1:41–67; Okada, *Indian Miniatures,* pp. 17–26; and Stuart Cary Welch, *India: Art and Culture 1300–1900* (New York: Metropolitan Museum of Art, 1985), p. 149; those against this view include Seyller, "Codicological Aspects," p. 387, and Daniel Ehnbom, private correspondence.

56. *A'in-i Akbari,* 1:1.

57. Ibid.

58. Ibid., 1:113.

59. Richards, "Formulation of Imperial Authority," 305–7.

60. *A'in-i Akbari,* 1:165.

61. Ibid., 1:1–4.

62. While a paternalistic aspect of kingship is found elsewhere in the Islamic world, much more public was the traditional Indian monarch who assumed a role known as *ma-bap,* i.e., mother and father to his subjects. It is this aspect that was adapted by Abu al-Fazl and distinguished Mughal concepts from other Islamic ones.

63. For a traditional Islamic view of the need for a ruler's accessibility, see Nizam al-Mulk, *Siyasat Nama,* p. 14. Hindu kingship and *darshan* are examined by Ronald Inden, "Ritual, Authority and Cyclic Time in Hindu Kingship," in Richards, *Kingship and Authority in South Asia,* pp. 74–75. *Darshan* in Akbar's court is explained in *A'in-i Akbari,* 1:165. Among the most useful European observations of *darshan* at the later Mughal court are Thomas Roe, *The Embassy of Sir Thomas Roe to India, 1615–19,* ed. W. Foster (London: Oxford University Press and Humphrey Milford, 1926), pp. 84–86, 270, 276, 282, 325; and Edward Terry, in Purchas, *Hakluytus Postumus,* 9:47–48.

64. For a description of *darshan* at a Hindu temple during the seventeenth century in Mughal India, see Jean-Baptiste Tavernier, *Travels in India,* 2 vols., trans. and ed. V. Ball (London: Humphrey Milford and Oxford University Press, 1925), 2:183–84; Diana L. Eck, *Darsan: Seeing the Divine Image in India,* 2nd ed. rev. (Chambersburg, PA: Anima Books, 1985), pp. 3–4, explains *darshan* in modern terms. Her explanation parallels Tavernier's experience.

65. *A'in-i Akbari,* 1:165.

66. Ebba Koch, "Architectural Forms," in *Fatehpur-Sikri*, ed. M. Brand and G. Lowry (Bombay: Marg Publications, 1987), pp. 125–26, 130; Asher, *Architecture of Mughal India*, pp. 62. Abu al-Fazl came to Fatehpur Sikri in 1575, although Akbar had been residing there since the early 1570s, but given that construction continued until 1585, when the court shifted to Lahore, the location of this *jharoka* on an outer wall could easily have been added after 1575. This structure and its ceremonial has all the hallmarks of Abu al-Fazl's genius.

67. For an illustration, see G. H. R. Tillotson, *The Rajput Palaces: The Development of an Architectural Style, 1450–1750* (New Haven, CT: Yale University Press, 1987), p. 49.

68. Koch, "Architectural Forms," p. 125.

69. *A'in-i Akbari*, 1:217; al-Badauni, *Muntakhab-ut-Tawarikh*, 2:405; Muhammad Hashim Khafi Khan, *Muntakhab al-Lubab*, trans. S. Moinul Haq as *Khafi Khan's History of ᶜAlamgir* (Karachi: Pakistan Historical Society, 1975), pp. 215–16; Roe, *Embassy of Sir Thomas Roe*, p. 276.

70. *A'in-i Akbari*, 1:165.

71. Nur Bakhsh, "The Agra Fort and Its Buildings," in *Annual Report of the Archaeological Survey of India for 1903–04* (Calcutta: Superintendent of Government Printing, 1906), p. 180; this pavilion is no longer extant. The marble *jharoka* in the Lahore fort's public audience hall may date to Akbar's reign, and thus would probably have been similar in appearance. Ebba Koch, *Shah Jahan and Orpheus: The Pietre Dure Decoration and the Programme of Shah Jahan's Throne in the Hall of Public Audience at the Red Fort of Delhi* (Graz: Akademische Druck- und Verlagsanstalt, 1988), plate 6.

72. *Tuzuk*, 1:24–25.

73. Kamgar Husaini, *Ma'asir-i Jahangiri*, tr. A. Alavi (Bombay: Asian Publishing House, 1978), p. 53.

74. *Tuzuk*, 1:2–3.

75. It is not the point of this chapter to provide an exhaustive discussion of the use of light imagery by these two rulers; rather I will provide salient examples giving an overall analysis of how Abu al-Fazl's ideas were translated into visual terms, at the same time determining what aspects of Abu al-Fazl's conception of the Mughal state were rejected. I have omitted any discussion of the prince Dara Shukoh's patronage, in spite of his devotion to Sufis and Sufi ideals, since he, unlike his father and grandfather, did not employ light imagery as a visual means to bolster his image.

76. *Tuzuk*, 1:1–2.

77. Ibid., 2:70–71.

78. Ibid., 1:319.

79. 'Inayat Khan, *The Shahjahan Nama of 'Inayat Khan*, trans. and ed. W. E. Begley and Z. A. Desai (Delhi: Oxford University Press, 1990), p. 17.

80. *Tuzuk*, 1:269–70, 341; 2:75–6, 197.

81. Milo Cleveland Beach, *Mughal and Rajput Painting* (Cambridge: Cambridge University Press, 1992), pp. 97, 99.

82. Okada, *Indian Miniatures*, p. 39.

83. Leach, *Mughal and Other Paintings,* 1:386–89, 398.

84. *Tuzuk,* 1:267.

85. Leach, *Mughal and Other Paintings,* 1:389; John Guy and Deborah Swallow, eds., *Arts of India: 1550–1900* (London: Victoria and Albert Museum. 1990), p. 81; Stuart C. Welch, *The Art of Mughal India* (New York: Asia Society, 1964), plate 43.

86. Okada, *Indian Miniatures,* p. 37; Richard Ettinghausen, "The Emperor's Choice," *De Artibus Opuscula* 40 (1961): 341–63.

87. Ettinghausen, "Emperor's Choice," p. 342.

88. Vishakha N. Desai, *Life at Court: Art for India's Rulers, 16th-19th Centuries* (Boston: Museum of Fine Arts, 1985), pp. 12–14.

89. Milo Cleveland Beach, Ebba Koch, and Wheeler Thackson, *King of the World: The Padshahnama, an Imperial Mughal Manuscript from the Royal Library, Windsor Castle* (London: Azimuth Editions and Sackler Gallery, 1997), pp. 95, 97.

90. Edward Maclagan, *The Jesuits and the Great Mogul* (London: Burns, Oates and Washborne, 1932), pp. 33, 54–55, 69–74.

91. Ebba Koch, "Hierarchical Principles of Shah-Jahani Painting," in *King of the World: The Padshahnama, an Imperial Mughal Manuscript from the Royal Library, Windsor Castle,* ed. M. C. Beach, E. Koch, and W. Thackson (London: Azimuth Editions and Sackler Gallery, 1997), pp. 131–32.

92. Koch, *Shah Jahan and Orpheus,* plate 55; Guy and Swallow, *Arts of India,* p. 81; Stronge, *Painting for the Mughal Emperor,* p. 128.

93. Koch, "Hierarchical Principles of Shah-Jahani Painting," p. 135.

94. Ibid.

95. For examples, see Milo Cleveland Beach, *The Imperial Image: Paintings for the Mughal Court* (Washington, DC: Freer Gallery of Art, 1981), pp. 186–88; Koch, *Shah Jahan and Orpheus,* plate 55; Leach, *Mughal and Other Paintings,* 1:393–94, 401, 404–5.

96. Koch, *Shah Jahan and Orpheus,* pp. 33–35.

97. Brand and Lowry, *Akbar's India,* p. 99; Richards, *Mughal Empire,* p. 46; Razavi, *Suhrawardi and the School of Illumination,* pp. 45–47.

98. Anthony Welch, *Calligraphy in the Arts of the Muslim World* (New York: Asia Society; Austin: University of Texas Press, 1979), pp. 9, 194.

99. Razavi, *Suhrawardi and the School of Illumination,* pp. 18–19.

100. Farid ud-Din Attar, *The Conference of the Birds,* trans. and intro. Afkham Darbandi and Dick Davis (London: Penguin Books, 1984), pp. 214–20.

101. Terry, in Purchas, *Hakluytus Postumus,* 9:47–48.

102. Ibid.

103. Okada, *Indian Miniatures,* pp. 180–82; Anthony Welch and Stuart Cary Welch, *Arts of the Islamic Book: The Collection of Prince Sadruddin Aga Khan* (London: Asia Society; Ithaca: Cornell University Press, 1982), pp. 208–12.

104. At that time only the Agra and Allahabad forts were built of red sandstone; Jahangir had no contact with the Allahabad fort after he ascended the throne. The painting dates to about 1620, and there are many reasons, including those nobles present in

the painting, that it cannot represent the period of his rebellion when he resided in the Allahabad fort.

105. Koch, *Mughal Architecture*, plate XIII.

106. Koch, *Shah Jahan and Orpheus*, pp. 14–15.

107. Nur Bakhsh, "Agra Fort," p. 181.

108. Ebba Koch, "The Baluster Column: A European Motif in Mughal Architecture and Its Meaning," *Journal of the Warburg and Courtauld Institutes* 45 (1982): 251–62.

109. Nur Bakhsh, "Agra Fort," p. 179.

110. Asher, *Architecture of Mughal India*, pp. 105–11.

111. Edmund W. Smith, *Akbar's Tomb, Sikandarah*, Archaeological Survey of India, New Imperial Series, vol. 25 (Allahabad: Superintendent Government Press, 1909), pp. 31–35.

112. Ibid., p. 35.

113. For purposes of simplicity here I am including the patronage of Shah Jahan's daughter, Jahan Ara, as well the emperor's. See Asher, *Architecture of Mughal India*, pp. 174–78, 215–16.

114. I am most grateful to Barbara D. Metcalf for this insight.

115. For art historical and historical data, see W.E. Begley and Z. A. Desai, eds., *Taj Mahal: The Illumined Tomb: An Anthology of Seventeenth-Century Mughal and European Documentary Sources* (Cambridge, MA: Aga Khan Program for Islamic Architecture; Seattle: University of Washington Press, 1989); and Elizabeth B. Moynihan, ed., *The Moonlight Garden: New Discoveries at the Taj Mahal* (Washington, DC: Arthur M. Sackler Gallery; Seattle: University of Washington Press, 2000).

116. For these views, see Koch, *Mughal Architecture*, p. 99; and Wayne E. Begley, "The Myth of the Taj Mahal and a New Theory of Its Symbolic Meaning," *Art Bulletin* 61 (1979): 7–37.

117. This well-known art historian will remain anonymous.

118. Pratapaditya Pal, "Introduction," in *Romance of the Taj Mahal*, ed. P. Pal, J. Leoshko, et al. (London: Thames and Hudson; Los Angeles: Los Angeles County Museum of Art, 1989), pp. 9–13.

119. Begley and Desai, *Taj Mahal: The Illumined Tomb*, pp. 163–67.

120. P. N. Oak, *Taj Mahal Is a Hindu Palace* (Bombay: Pearl Books, 1968); and P. N. Oak, *The Taj Mahal Is a Temple Palace* (New Delhi: Oak, 1974), are just two examples among many.

121. A particularly insidious web site is Zulfikar Khan, "The Taj Mahal: A Hindu Temple-Palace," (http://www.flex.com/~jai/satyamevajayate/tejo.html) (June 17, 1999). This author's highly inflammatory discussion of Islam and Muslims in general makes it unlikely that Zulfikar Khan is his or her real name; rather, this Muslim name appears to have been adopted to give the site a sense of legitimacy otherwise lacking.

PLATE 1. The bodhisattva Maitreya, who will be the next Buddha, enthroned in the Tuṣita heaven. The motif of the rainbow-colored, undulating light rays, surrounded by the solar aureole, is suggestive of much earlier Buddhist painting from a variety of sites along the Central Asian Silk Road. Northeastern Tibet, sixteenth or seventeenth century. (Courtesy of the Shelley and Donald Rubin Foundation.)

PLATE 2. Padmasambhava as a mahāsiddha, the primordial buddha Vajradhara in the sky above, with rays of rainbow light linking the two registers. Far eastern Tibet (Khams), eighteenth century. Note the use of color washes, a technique influenced by Chinese painting, to accentuate the quality of luminosity. (Courtesy of the Shelley and Donald Rubin Foundation.)

PLATE 3. Guru Padmasambhava radiating rainbow light. The artist's conception here powerfully evokes the image of the "rainbow body." Nineteenth century.

PLATES 4–5. Mu'in al-Din handing Jahangir a globe surmounted by a Timurid crown. (Reproduced by kind permission of the Trustees of the Chester Beatty Library, Dublin.)

PLATE 6. Jahangir at his *jharoka*, Agra fort, from the *Jahangir Nama.* (Collection of Prince and Princess Sadruddin Aga Khan.)

PLATE 7. Detail of plate 6 showing a *darshaniyya.* (Collection of Prince and Princess Sadruddin Aga Khan.)

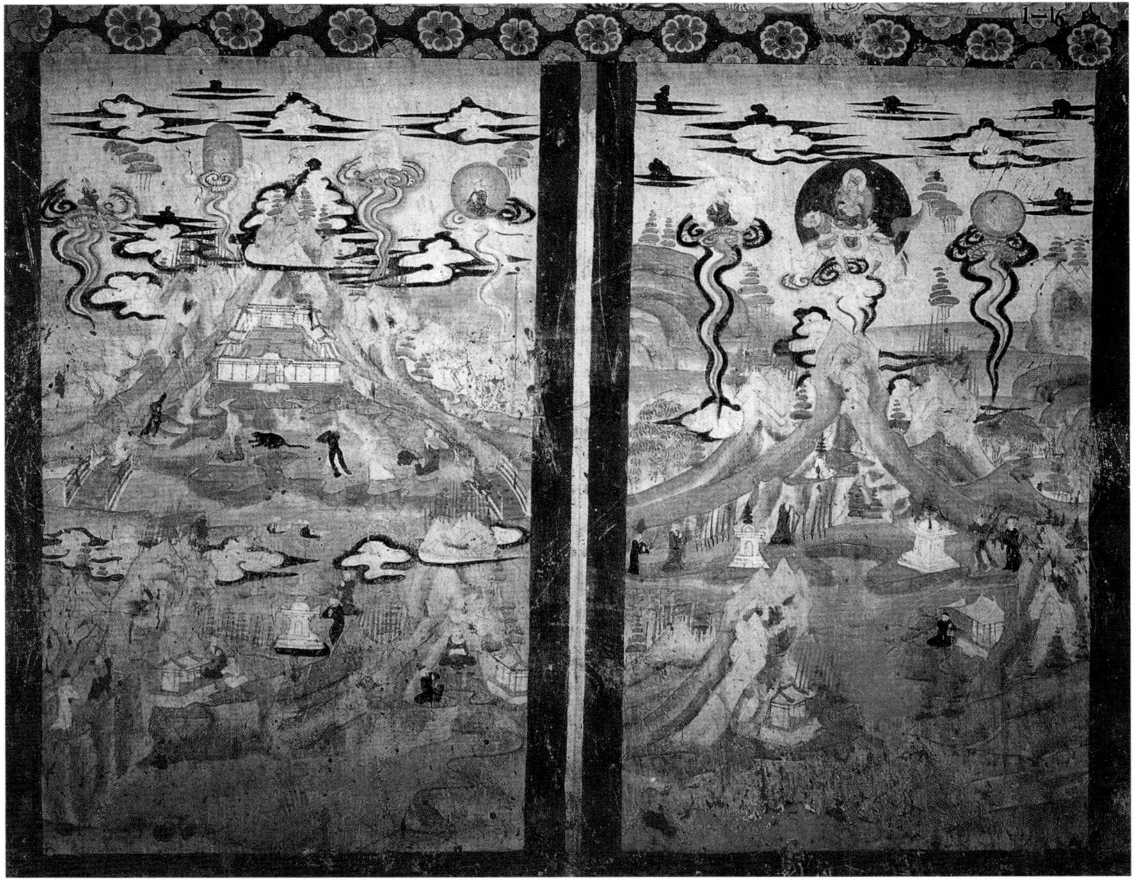

PLATE 8. Two views of the Wutai Mountains, with manifestations of light and auspicious clouds above (including Wenshu and unidentified figures), and Buddhist figures and architectural structures below. Dunhuang cave 159, west wall, lower section.

PLATE 9. Right side of the panoramic wall painting of the miraculous world of the Wutai Mountains. Refer to p. viii for detailed description.

PLATE 10. Detail from the right side of the panorama. Refer to p. viii for detailed description.

PLATE 11. Northern Terrace summit and surroundings. Refer to p. viii for detailed description.

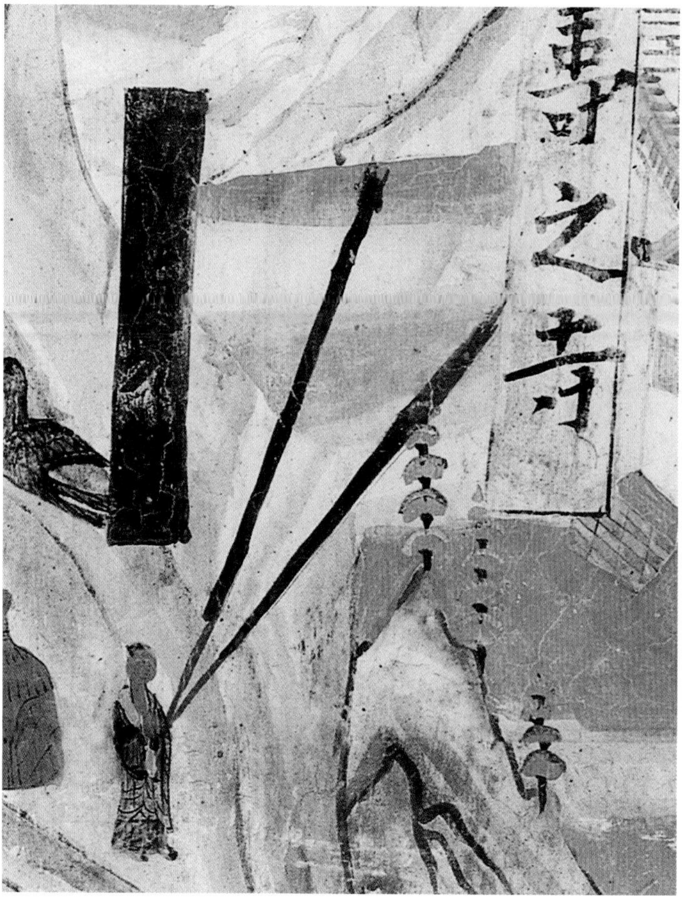

PLATE 12. A solitary meditator in monastic garb standing before his retreat as multicolored rays of light strike him (or emanate from his body?). An auspicious bird flies above. See plate 11, *lower right*—slopes of the Northern Terrace—for visual context.

CHAPTER EIGHT

Light in the Wutai Mountains

Raoul Birnbaum

The full range of Buddhist literature makes abundantly clear that spectacular manifestations of light may occur at many sites—indeed, at any site—throughout the world, in response to certain causes and conditions. But the Wutai Mountains in northern China are the preeminent site in China for such events. Reports of these appearances of light have become central to characterizations of the power of the place. By association, its inhabitants also shine brightly within this power.

Wutai shan, or the Five Terrace Mountains, is an extensive complex of mountains and valleys centered around a group of five towering, flat-topped peaks. Long known as a region where strange and uncanny events took place, since the seventh century it has been famous throughout the Buddhist world as the seat of earthly manifestation of the celestial figure Wenshu pusa (known also in Western literature by his Sanskrit name, Mañjuśrī Bodhisattva), lord of insight. Pilgrims go there to have direct experiences with this bodhisattva, whose manifestations take many forms, including that of light. This chapter focuses on tales of several types of light phenomena, including those associated with the presiding deity. These tales are preserved and transmitted in the vast body of written, oral, and visual materials associated with this pilgrimage center.

At the outset I must emphasize that investigation of religious experience—the experience of seeing this light and its indigenous interpretations—should not be separated from the wider cultural context of the narratives, since the narratives constitute the source field that provides the subject of investigation. What I study in this chapter is not experience per se, but reports of experience, representations of experience. The bulk of the materials discussed here span some nine centuries, and one aim of this chapter, beyond analytical and contextualized description, is to point out shifts and changes over this *longue durée.*

The very large body of written narratives makes clear that manifestations of light may be public (that is, a visible manifestation seen simultaneously by more than one person) or private (the individual experience of a dream, vision, or meditative trance). Of course, one can become aware of and study elements of another person's experience if it is expressed in some form of representation, such as an oral, written, or pictorial narrative. (In Buddhist China, visionary experience also has been set forth in architectural narratives, as we will see below.) These representations of private experience become public through circulation and take on a social life independent of the individual's actual experience, whatever that was.

In surveying the available narratives, I consider light in relation to special places and special persons. "Special" in this context means "powerful," and a key issue in thinking about the reports of these manifestations of light is the evidentiary function of the phenomena. Narratives of these manifestations should be read as narratives of power: assertions that the places and persons are highlighted precisely because they are powerful, however humble they otherwise might appear.

The evidentiary functions stem from the convergence of two distinct cultural traditions: indigenous Chinese discourses on natural responses to the moral power of the ruler, whose body extends to controlled physical territory and the social-political space of a state; and the luminous world of the Mahāyāna Buddhist scriptures that were introduced to China from Central Asia and India. In both of these cultural complexes the appearance of bright light signifies appropriate power, and on this matter at least, in actual practice in China, these two interpretive modes merged without great conceptual collisions.

Based on the extraordinarily wide range of light imagery in scriptural and liturgical texts, as well as in miracle tales and records of strange events, one might argue that Chinese Buddhist worlds are "vision dominated." Still, a strong case also could be made for the primacy or at least equality of some of the other senses, focusing on the significance of sound and hearing, or the importance of fragrance and smell.[1]

In the midst of this sensory overload, various counternarratives emerged. Reasonable arguments have been made for the primacy of types of experience that are characterized by the *absence* of sensory response, or for the importance of the absence of light in describing deep spiritual experience. This involves a step back from what is understood as the phenomenal world, a step back from a world of flickering appearances that have no enduring substance and thus should not be relied upon. Such approaches often are associated with the discourse of Chan practitioners. In addition, there is another element that has been important in considering Wutai shan phenomena: not only is there light that comes from the outside and sometimes can be seen by all present at its manifestation, but also there is light that comes from within. Tales about internal light form a counternarrative to concerns about the seductive allure of external phenomena, but of course concerns also arise about the seductive allure of internal phenomena.

We can find numerous tales of manifestations of light in a wide range of Chinese Buddhist works from very early times to the present day. Indeed, the legendary initial transmission of Buddhism to China occurs in a dream experienced by the Han emperor Ming (r. 58–75 CE), where he is startled and intrigued by a flash of light—the shining golden body of a flying figure—that his courtiers later identify for him as "the Buddha."[2]

Chinese Buddhists—and their institutions, creations, and social interactions—are embedded in Chinese contexts. And in that larger world light has long been a significant element of a certain kind of vocabulary of power, a vocabulary that relies on interpretation of specific natural as well as supernatural elements. Certain types of plants, birds, rocks, weather, springs, and watercourses are fundamental to analyses of the power of place.[3] In addition to concrete physical phenomena readily observable by all, supernatural phenomena also are important elements of this vocabulary of power. The sudden smell of fragrant incense, the tolling of invisible bells and chimes, radiant shining lights—all these are signs of power that testify to the presence of spirits or to the inherent power of an extraordinary individual.

There are many basic tales of strange perceptions of sound and smell that have occurred at Wutai shan. They are akin to the basic experiences of light phenomena in the same records, so I will include a few typical examples here, before proceeding to the tales of light that are the principal subject of this essay. The examples below have been drawn from the earliest extended record of life in the Wutai Mountains, the work now known as *Ancient Records of the Clear and Cool Mountains* (*Gu Qingliang zhuan*), credited to the monk Huixiang and composed in the last quarter of the seventh century:

- A Tang monk named Tanyun came to Wutai shan, attracted by tales of Wenshu's appearances there and the reputation for sanctity of the many monastic inhabitants. When he reached the base of the mountain region, he became aware of a strong fragrance. And when he came to the Great Faith Monastery (the central establishment in the heart of the region), he heard the sound of bells tolling spontaneously.[4]

- Monk Lingcha came to Wutai shan in the seventh month of 675. In the late summer of that year, he climbed to the peak of the Northern Terrace, where he stayed in a temple for two nights. During that period, he heard bells tolling at each of the six times of daily worship, and in the night he heard the sounds of a flock of several hundred flying birds. He looked all around him, but there was nothing to be seen.[5]
- The renowned master Ji (or Kuiji), principal disciple of the learned philosopher-pilgrim Xuanzang, came to Wutai in 670 with over five hundred lay disciples and clerics in order to repair and renovate temples. On the Central Terrace many among this group perceived an unusual fragrance, and they heard the sounds of bells and stone chimes.[6]

I have included these brief episodes to set a preliminary backdrop against which some of the tales of light may be viewed. No matter how spectacular the described manifestation, it should not be forgotten that light forms one element in a larger vocabulary of signs of power. And an essential characteristic of the auditory and olfactory phenomena, as described in the brief narratives, carries over to many of the descriptions of visual phenomena: they are perceived in culturally distinctive and apprehensible ways. When these Buddhist monks report intensified sensory perceptions, they hear the solemn bells and chimes of ritual music, and they smell incense, something that is offered to the deities and thus is associated with the appearance of these spirits in material realms. As we will consider below, when Chinese Buddhists see "strange" things, according to the surviving reports what they see makes sense in the context of the cultural milieus within which the observers are embedded.

PUBLIC MANIFESTATIONS OF LIGHT

Let us turn now to a long passage from the same early compendium of lore about the Wutai Mountains. Composed by Huixiang at a time when these mountains were wild and remote, this seventh-century narrative plunges us directly into a world of powerful persons and strange phenomena. Huixiang's precise recounting of the experiences reported here, rather more sharply detailed than some other tales in his work, suggests that he may well have heard these accounts from the protagonists, who were his direct contemporaries. I have included the entire passage, rather than simply abstracting the references to light phenomena, so that these phenomena can be seen within their larger contextual field, as presented by the medieval Buddhist author.

Śramaṇa [Fully Ordained Monk] Huizang, of the White Horse Monastery in Luoyang, originally was from Fen City. He was a monk of elevated purity who lived in retirement [outside of worldly spheres]. He was filial and reverent towards the emperor. He extensively restored the White Horse Monastery. Wherever he roosted, a flock of the famously virtuous gathered round; wherever he stood, a field of blessings was planted. Zang was deeply dedicated to meditative stillness. Among his group, he was known as the leader.

In the fourth month of the first year of the Tiaolu reign period [679], together with Meditation Master Hongyan of Fenzhou, Śramaṇa Huixun of Aijing Monastery also in Fenzhou, Śramaṇa Lingzhi of Hanzhou, Śramaṇa Mingyuan of Baizhou, and comrades from various directions including Śramaṇa Lingyu and others, Master Huizang went to the Sahā Monastery.[7] There they settled for the ninety-day summer retreat period, engaged in purification and repentance practices. Released from the "quiet dwelling" period of the summer, they then climbed the terraces in succession, together with about fifty clerics and laymen.

Meditation Master Zang and thirty others were about to go together to the Central Terrace when they saw a flock of white cranes, which they followed for several leagues. As they reached the terrace summit, the cranes suddenly disappeared. When the monks Mingyuan, Lingyu, and others—eighteen in all—first set out for the Eastern Terrace, they saw a five-colored auspicious cloud. When he later departed, Monk Huixun also saw it, just as those who had preceded him. Some sixty paces southeast of the buddha stupa [reliquary structure] on the Central Terrace, Mingyuan further saw a multicolored auspicious light, shaped like a buddha image. This light was about three *zhang* [roughly thirty feet] tall. When some persons moved about, the light also moved with them. They prostrated themselves more than twenty times, and after a long while the light then disappeared.

About thirty paces south of Great Flower Pool [on the Central Terrace], Monk Lingzhi saw a light like the sun. Its height was about three *zhang*, and it was composed of layers of hundreds and thousands of different colors, each layer distinct from the others. It is difficult to fully put into words the appearance of this misty light. The whole group, whose appearance and clothes [ordinarily were marked by] dignified bearing, crouched down and stretched forth, bent over and looked up [to examine the apparition]. And within the light this all could be seen, as if one drew near to a bright mirror. As for Zhi and the others—their eyes were dazzled and their spirits lost, their hearts and "souls" were greatly unsettled. They prostrated themselves with beseeching sincerity, and the light vanished in an instant. At the same time that Zhi and the others saw the light, three novices in front of the buddha stupa were engaged in burning incense on the crowns of their heads and on their arms, in this way offering their bodies in worship. These novices also saw the light on the eastern side.

Zang and his companions made a circuit through the terraces, walking for seven days, and then they set out on their return journey.[8]

This brief seventh-century account takes us into a world of mysterious phenomena—sudden appearances of auspicious birds, multihued clouds, and flashing lights—that are witnessed by famous persons. It is a world in which strange events engage the senses and are interpreted in very particular ways. Within its Chinese context, this account most certainly is "early medieval," not only in its characteristic narrative flow and linguistic structures, but also in the protagonists' particular kinds of response to the light.

The report of the experiences of Huizang's party is a narrative, of course, and like the other tales included in this essay, it follows certain guidelines particular to the time, place, and cultural circumstances of its composition and intended readership. These concise narratives may reflect memories of events, or they may create memories that suggest that events have occurred, but these descriptions set within certain socially acceptable forms should not be confused with any experience itself. And it is striking that in a cultural world in which fluent literacy may have been the preserve of perhaps a tenth of the population, these are the rare narratives that have been committed to writing and have survived over quite a few centuries.

The seventh-century account of the experiences of Huizang and his party has certain basic characteristics that mark such tales from the early Tang. It begins by identifying specific individuals (in this case, men of high religious status), and it repeatedly fixes time and place with as much clarity as possible. Having established this (apparently) verifiable context, it describes out-of-the-ordinary phenomena experienced by these individuals. And it combines a tone of dispassionate reportage with a mood of the uncanny.

The main protagonists seem to have been prominent figures in the monastic life of their era (although I have not been able to find further references to them in the standard records of that time). Huizang was abbot of the White Horse Monastery in Luoyang, which was famed as the very first Buddhist monastery established in China, and he was sufficiently skilled—that is, he likely had sufficient connections with Tang aristocratic families and, as hinted in the brief profile, the emperor himself—that he was able to carry out a campaign to renovate and rebuild portions of the complex. He was well known for meditative attainment and thus appears to be rather more than an affable fund-raiser or shrewd political calculator of the sort who sometimes rises to these prominent monastic positions. That these strange experiences were reported by such a man and members of his party gives the report credibility within the circles of this text's readership. And at the same time, the report lends greater weight and luster to the reputation of Huizang and his circle. As I will discuss later, it is fully expected within Chinese Buddhist milieus that eminent practitioners will be met by supernatural responses, so in this context the juxtaposition of such persons and experiences is logical and reasonable.

The emphasis on precise identification of the protagonists in these tales of experience is not peculiar to this single brief narrative. It accords with the pattern set by Huixiang throughout his monograph on Wutai shan and is seen in all the later works on the site, down to contemporary oral narratives told by present-day residents. This element also holds in narratives found in monographs on other Chinese sites, and indeed is a basic characteristic of Chinese "miracle tales" found in a wide variety of text types.[9]

While the lead figure in our story is a man of stature, sometimes the protagonist is not eminent at all (although she or he may become famous as a result of a tale's circulation). This especially is true in many of the earlier narratives from Wutai shan, in which ordinary folk such as woodcutters and hunters recount their experiences. For example, Huixiang begins one narrative with the following introduction: "At the side of the Luminous Cloud Monastery within the walls of Fanzhi xian, there lives an old man who makes his living by gathering medicinal herbs. His family name is Wang, personal name Xiang'er. I once went to his house to eat, and I had the opportunity to converse with the old man. This is what he said to me."[10]

One reason for the presence of so much biographical detail in these accounts, I think, is the powerful strength of biographical writing as a genre in China from the Han period onward. At the time that Huixiang composed his Wutai shan monograph, for example, one could readily find accounts of lives in such places as the extensive biographical sections of the official histories; elaborate, stylized accounts inscribed on stone at tomb sites; and special collections of biographies (often derived from the funerary inscriptions), exemplified in a Buddhist context by the successive editions of the *Biographies of Eminent Monks.* All of these works memorialize the lives of individuals distinguished by such factors as wealth, accomplishment (within certain well-defined parameters), prominence, power, or in some cases infamy. Because many tales collected in works such as the Wutai shan monographs were gathered from such sources, naturally they retain their biographical emphasis. (Of course, a deeper question remains: *why* is the genre of biography so developed in medieval Chinese writing? An answer to that question is complex and lies beyond the scope of this essay.)

Not only are individuals identified in such narratives as the tale of Huizang, but also time and place are fixed, sometimes down to the specific day and hour, as well as the number of paces distant from a landmark. This level of specificity anchors the narrative to a ground of credibility and helps to establish a tension between an utterly ordinary reasonability and the extraordinary phenomena that are described. Even today when one walks among the high peaks of Wutai shan with longtime residents, they often will begin stories by saying: "At this very place where we are standing now, at such-and-such time, Mr. So-and-So from such-and-such region (or, with considerably more impact, 'I personally') had the following experience."

In the Wutai shan narratives (and in those of many other sites), place is so strongly emphasized that it should be considered a principal protagonist in the narratives. I will return to this matter below. At this point, it is enough to assert that these narratives center on person, place, and phenomena, entirely intertwined.

The phenomena described in the Huizang narrative fit into two broad categories: natural phenomena interpreted as extraordinary, and what probably should be thought of as "supernatural" phenomena. In early tales from Wutai shan and other sites, many natural phenomena are invested with special meaning when they are seen or encountered in particular circumstances, as, for example, particular types of medicinal herbs growing in the wild. In the Huizang narrative, we meet with two natural phenomena often encountered in early Tang tales of this sort: auspicious birds and shining clouds.

Tang bird lore was specific. Certain birds were auspicious (or the opposite), and their appearances at particular times and places or directions were invested with meaning, as Edward H. Schafer so eloquently has made clear to us. In this context, white cranes, especially those with crimson-crested heads, were viewed with awe, as thousand-year-old beings who were intermediaries of the gods.[11]

Shining clouds also had meaning. The term *jingyun*, "luminous cloud," refers to an auspicious omen—sometimes multicolored—that manifests itself in response to great peace on earth. It is recorded that such clouds were significantly observed following the enthronement of the founder of the Tang dynasty, about seventy years prior to the recording of the Huizang narrative.[12] Earlier I quoted briefly from the introduction to one of Huixiang's tales, in which the protagonist lived next to a Luminous Cloud Monastery (Jingyun si) in Fanzhi xian. A long stone inscription found in this region dated to 634 tells of a certain immortal who ascended into a rosy cloud during the Kaihuang period (581–600) of the Sui dynasty. It is possible that the monastery was founded upon seeing such a sign, or was renamed based on tales of such an event.[13]

What is important to bear in mind here is that birds and clouds (and a wide range of additional items, such as medicinal plants) are part of the natural world. Anyone can see them. Within this particular realm of religious meaning, they are invested with significance.

It is easy enough to deal with birds and clouds—we see them all the time, at least where I live on the central coast of California. But the other feature of these tales is the supernatural side: bright, shining lights appear out of the night (or even daytime) sky, and they hover or move about, even following or surrounding persons. Sometimes these lights take on culturally recognizable forms, according to observers, such as the shape of a buddha image. At other times, they can be shapeless and amorphous, or precisely layered in a thousand hues. As we will see in further narratives, visions of these lights take on a myriad of forms. I will return shortly to further discussion of these lights and other supernatural phenomena, in the context of their Wutai shan appearances.

In concluding this brief survey of some characteristic elements of the early Wutai shan narratives, I would like to comment on their tone and mood. As is shown clearly in the Huizang tale, the tone of the early Tang narratives most commonly is that of straightforward, matter-of-fact reporting: "here is what happened—first x, then y, then z." In Huixiang's monograph, that tone is fairly consistent, but it does shift to a more animated and emotionally expressive approach when he presents eyewitness accounts, such as the tale recounted to him by Herbgatherer Wang. In the context of this reportorial tone, what is most striking is the distinct mood of uncanniness that permeates the early tales. The protagonists do not feel snug and safe in their homes (and indeed, for the most part they are in the wilds, not at home). Rather there is a sense of being ill at ease, of disconcerted unsettlement, sometimes of fear or even terror that may accompany encounters with such supernatural phenomena as the glowing lights. These glowing lights are not tame in the early accounts: they do unexpected things, in accordance with rules that are not understood. There is a wild quality to many of the incidents described by Huixiang, and people are deeply startled and upset by their experiences. These phenomena are manifestations of a wild, awesome, and even frightening power.[14]

One could suggest that this mood of the uncanny in his work derives from Huixiang's predilections, and that may be so, but I think there are other circumstances or cultural forces at work. The wild quality of the incidents seems to be a characteristic of the Chinese mountain cults at their early stage of development, when these remote areas were still little explored. Also, and very important, a significant influence was the genre of *zhiguai* tales, or "tales of the strange," a literary tradition of several centuries' extent that Huixiang specifically draws from in some sections of his monograph (he quotes from several collections of these works). Here again the prevailing mood often is that of the uncanny.[15]

Ordinary country folk often appear in the early narratives, because they are the mainstay of the population at or near Wutai shan, and they are the folk who constantly are exploring the hills, valleys, and caves in search of resources and shelter from inclement weather. As the population of monks, nuns, and pilgrims swells in the mid- to late Tang (eighth and ninth centuries) with the opening up of mountain territories for pilgrimage and religious occupation, these villagers are pushed out of the story to make way for the tales of believers. The villagers don't leave the Wutai area, they simply lose their voice in the Buddhist compendiums of tales. (And they have yet to regain it some twelve centuries later.)

The qualities that I have highlighted above as features of the early narratives, especially of the early Tang, are carried over in narratives composed in the late eighth through eleventh centuries and on to the present. What becomes more apparent in the later narratives, however, is a recession of ordinary (non-Buddhist) folk from visibility, a taming of the impression made by phenomena, and narratives that often are far longer, more descriptive and discursive, more consciously composed as tales. Also, there is a smoothening out of form as time goes on: certain narrative types emerge, and the tales are set into these molds.

Let us return now to the subject of place in the Huizang narrative. While the initial lines of the text focus on the protagonists, and their names are repeated throughout the report, the phenomena that they experienced did not happen at random, but occurred in a specific region (the Wutai Mountains) at specifically identified sites there. We need to be aware that although the narratives focus on identified individuals, they are about place and power as much as they are about anything else: a great pile of such reports from Wutai shan creates a powerful impression about the special qualities of that mountain region. Indeed, this report—one among many—is found in a substantial compendium of lore about Wutai shan, and we should consider that mountain center a primary subject of the tale.

GREAT BALLS OF FIRE

Medieval Buddhist records suggest that Wutai shan was associated with strangely luminous phenomena from very early times. According to an unnamed Daoist text (a so-called *xian jing*, or "scripture of the immortals") cited in Huixiang's early monograph on the site, "The Wutai Mountains are named

'Purple Palace.' There is always a purple emanation. Immortals dwell there."[16] This purple haze appears to be a kind of pneuma that is exhaled by the body of the mountainous region. Buddhists lay no interpretive claim to this haze. It is part of the intrinsic power of the place that predates their occupation.

There also are numerous accounts of shining five-colored clouds that appear out of nowhere in a clear blue sky. But more significant to Buddhists in the hierarchy of strange phenomena are the radiant nighttime lights, sometimes white and sometimes multicolored, that appear from time to time in the region. They call these *foguang,* or "buddha lights," and understand them as manifestations of spirit power, either generalized or specified as the power of Wenshu pusa, the prevailing Buddhist deity of the Wutai Mountains. Early in the Buddhist history of the place, a concentration of light experiences within a bowl-like ridge in a southern sector of the range led to the creation of a monastery at that site, named Foguang si, "Buddha's Radiance Monastery." We can see in this simple example the economic power of these manifestations. This site continued to be famous for dramatic manifestations of light through much of the medieval period.[17] Architectural complexes that are associated with tales of manifestations of light, such as the Buddha's Radiance Monastery, serve as a particular type of narrative of power, one that has three-dimensional presence and emphatically occupies territory, claiming that territory for a particular explanation of reality. While the light manifestations are intermittent and of relatively short duration (usually an evening at most), buildings last for centuries and serve as a site to receive an economic response to the feelings and emotions generated in the experience of seeing (or hearing about) the lights.

These buddha lights became known as a feature of the sacred mountain, indeed, an element that made it sacred or confirmed the presence of invisible power. There are many accounts to be found in the literature about Wutai shan, most especially from the seventh century onward. By the time of the Japanese pilgrim Ennin (793–864), the learned monk whose detailed travel diary is a marvelous source of medieval Wutai shan lore, it was clear that one of the goals of travelers was to experience this phenomenon personally. In his entry for the second day of the seventh lunar month of 840, Ennin provides his eyewitness account:

> Today atop the Southern Terrace, with the ascetic monk [Yiyuan] and others numbering several tens, we sought the manifestation of the Great Sage. By nightfall we had not seen it, so we returned to our cloister lodgings [just below the summit]. In the first period of the night, in the sky above a ridge separated from the terrace to the east by a valley, we saw a sacred lamp. The assembled persons saw it together and venerated it. The glowing light of this lamp at first was about as large as an alms bowl. Later it grad-

ually grew as large as a small house. The great assembly with utmost sincerity chanted with loud voice the name of the Great Sage. Then another lamp appeared near the valley. It also was like a rainhat [in size] at first and then gradually grew larger. From our distant gaze, it appeared that the two lamps, with blazing light, were some ten *zhang* [a hundred feet] apart. Then at midnight they disappeared.[18]

Manifestations such as these are significant in visual representations of Wutai shan, such as the tenth-century mural at Dunhuang cave 61 and other less famous paintings and prints (to be discussed in the section "Visual Representations" below). The physical site thus became utterly entangled with such narratives of strange possibilities, and these narratives—verbal and visual—created powerful expectations among pilgrims, who were drawn to Wutai shan from all over the Asian Buddhist world. Like Ennin, many hoped to view the lights as an integral part of their Wutai shan experience.

Here is a report many centuries later by the famed Chan master Xuyun, from his visit to Wutai shan in 1885 (his forty-fifth year):

After the Great Prayer meeting [held at Xiantong Monastery in the sixth month], I climbed the Great Compass Peak to worship the wisdom lamps. The first night there was nothing to be seen. The second night I saw a fireball on the Northern Terrace summit. It flew to the Central Terrace, where it fell, and in a brief instant it split into some ten balls of varying size, large and small. On the second night I also saw three fireballs fly up and down in the sky at the Central Terrace, and fireballs appeared at four or five places on the Northern Terrace. They also were large and small—not at all the same in size.[19]

Xuyun's use of the term "wisdom lamp" (*zhideng*) makes clear the explicit connection between Wenshu, the bodhisattva closely associated with wisdom, and the fireball phenomena.

Pilgrims' expectations and reports have continued on into the modern era, such as the account of John Blofeld, an English resident in China who traveled to Wutai shan in the 1930s:

We reached the highest temple [of the Southern Terrace] during the late afternoon and gazed with interest at a small tower built upon the topmost pinnacle about a hundred feet above us. One of the monks asked us to pay particular attention to the fact that the windows of this tower overlooked mile upon mile of empty space. . . . Shortly after midnight, a monk carrying a lantern stepped into our room and cried: "The bodhisattva has appeared!" . . .

The ascent to the door of the tower occupied less than a minute. As each one entered the little room and came face to face with the window beyond, he gave a shout of surprise, as though all our hours of talk had not sufficiently prepared us for what we now saw. There in the great open spaces beyond the window, apparently not more than one or two hundred yards away, innumerable balls of fire floated majestically past. We could not judge their size, for nobody knew how far away they were, but they appeared like the fluffy woolen balls that babies play with seen close up. They seemed to be moving at the stately pace of a large, well-fed fish aimlessly cleaving its way through water; but, of course, their actual pace could not be determined without a knowledge of the intervening distance. Where they came from, what they were, and where they went after fading from sight in the West, nobody could tell. Fluffy balls of orange-colored fire, moving through space, unhurried and majestic—truly a fitting manifestation of divinity![20]

When I carried out repeated field studies at Wutai shan in the mid-1980s through mid-1990s, I had the opportunity to hear many longtime residents discuss their experiences, and they provided a wide variety of descriptions of the many types of light phenomena that can be seen there. Perhaps the most idiosyncratic report came from an eminent senior monk, who spoke of being surrounded one evening by a mass of flitting bits of light that resembled butterflies.[21] The most recent eyewitness account heard was reported by two senior monks from the Bamboo Grove Monastery (Zhulin si), a relatively isolated site. I met these two men in October 2000, when we shared guest lodgings for a week at the Monastery of the Pagoda of the Thousand Buddhas (Qianfo ta si) in the small northern Guangdong city of Meizhou. They reported that one night in the previous winter numerous fireballs had appeared and the entire sky opposite the monastery had been ablaze with light. All present at the monastery had seen this. With deep roots in history, these manifestations of light remain an ongoing phenomenon.

Some written accounts make clear that anyone can see these manifestations of light, but for the most part the medieval records link these experiences to the presence of special persons. The light manifests itself because such persons are there, or the event is worth recording because of its proximity to a person of power. Beyond the larger narrative that speaks to the power of the place, these tales also say something about the observer. Great numbers of stories about such persons create powerful impressions about their special qualities and cause a bright spotlight to be fixed on the heroes of the tales.

SHINING IN THE LIGHT: HIGHLIGHTED HUMANS

The first extract from Huizang's report, given above, and the accounts of the fireballs just discussed juxtapose person, place, and phenomena. Wutai shan records also occasionally focus on persons who glow. That is, rays of light conspicuously highlight these historical figures at a potent moment, or such persons appear to be surrounded by the kinds of lights especially associated with these mountains. For example, Ennin met an eminent hundred-year-old monk named Lingjue at Wutai shan. He was told that when three learned monks from the Buddhist monastic university at Nalanda in India came to Wutai shan on pilgrimage the previous year and paid a call on that venerable master, they saw light in the form of a five-colored cloud nimbus shining from his body.[22]

The following excerpt from a long medieval account (preserved in the monk Yanyi's mid eleventh century compendium of Wutai shan lore) relates how an individual's special qualities are revealed to others by the phenomena that occur around him. Both birds and light appear:

> The next day, after noon, Wuzhu was seated in front of the Scripture Repository Tower of the Wisdom Cloister when two auspicious birds fluttered about directly over his head. They circled him many times and then left toward the northeast. Three days later, when Wuzhu was seated inside the room at the hour when the sun was directly east, two rays of white light extended to the very crown of his head and then disappeared. All the monks present in the room—Faxian and others—saw this in its entirety. Wuzhu was greatly startled and said: "What is this auspicious sign?" Praying that it again appear, the disciples became firmly enmeshed in a net of doubt. But they stopped speaking, for the light again appeared and remained for a long time before it vanished.[23]

I should note that these phenomena are preliminary elements of a long and complex tale involving extensive visionary experience and revelatory transmission of teachings. Reports of these phenomena serve to presage the larger event, and they give the visionary a legitimate, "verifiable" position.

In all the narratives discussed so far, the events have been public. That is, there are multiple witnesses, and the phenomena thus are verifiable. The light comes from the outside, and persons have sensory engagement with it. Now we can turn to reports of a different category of experience.

INDIVIDUAL EXPERIENCE

Early accounts, such as those in Huixiang's seventh-century monograph, often focus on brief descriptions of strange phenomena that are publicly experienced, that is, by more than one person. Huixiang also recounts a number of individual or private experiences. Many of these are reports by hunters, woodcutters, and herb gatherers, who roam about alone in the mountains in pursuit of their sources of economic sustenance. There are some reports of individual experiences of monks, but most often they are public or group experiences.

By the late Tang and Song (by the late ninth through eleventh centuries), as seen in such works as the *Song Gaoseng zhuan* and Yanyi's *Guang Qingliang zhuan*, a considerable shift has taken place that registers in two ways. First (as remarked earlier), the voices of the non-Buddhist mountain folk have been muted in Yanyi's monograph. Their experiences are rarely recounted. I suspect that this is due to the thorough Buddhist inhabitation of the region that has been achieved by this time (there were at least seventy-two monastic establishments worthy of mention by Yanyi when he completed his work in the 1060s,[24] and surely there were additional smaller hermitages and other such sites), as well as the highly assertive Buddhist devotional-propagandistic aims of this text. Second, there now are many reports of individual experiences claimed by monks, which are highlighted in the texts and appear to take on considerable strategic importance both for the careers of those clerics and for the burgeoning reputation of the mountain center. In the most elaborate of these later narratives, we see that a means of intercourse and process is established between the deity (and his manifestations of light) and selected humans.

Encounters with balls of light continue, briefly described or mentioned in passing as a kind of baseline experience. Roughly sketched out, these baseline experiences often are multisensory and consist of perceiving a fragrant smell (often of rare incense), hearing the deep sound of bells or the clinking of stone chimes, and seeing bright lights. These experiences are not rare at Wutai shan, particularly as time goes on, and descriptions of them accordingly are brief.

In addition, long and complex narratives appear. These extended tales of individual experience often highlight striking inner transformations of the protagonists. One kind of tale found repeatedly in Huixiang's early compendium recounts entrance into a strange world where wild animals are tame and trees bear fruit in winter, a world of immortals or spirits incarnate, who dwell in villages or sometimes caves hidden away in secret sectors of the mountain region. By the late Tang and Song, this narrative type has been thoroughly Buddhicized and extended in length. Not only do worthy monks see the kinds of lights characteristic of Wutai shan that already have been discussed, but they may see bright, shining humanlike beings—sometimes from a distance, sometimes at conversational range. They also may see the habitations of these luminous ones: buildings made of golden or silver light, often accessible by crossing a shining bridge, led by a young guide. In the most complex versions of these tales, a worthy monk is led across the bridge to gain entrance to radiant monasteries that are inhabited by shining beings in monastic dress: Wenshu pusa and his retinue of sages. There the individual has remarkable experiences, receives teachings directly from the bodhisattva, and finally is sent back to the ordinary world (not permitted permanent residence in this extraordinary monastic compound, an experience some monks know all too well from their attempts to gain entry to well-funded earthly establishments), where he lives to tell his tale.

Several very important Tang-period monasteries were built at Wutai shan based on such reports, following sketches produced by the protagonists in a kind of visionary architecture. Most often the visionary became founding abbot. Long after the founders' deaths, these monastic complexes remained as three-dimensional, inhabitable narratives of memory. Several of them still stand.[25]

To complement translated accounts that I already have published about some learned, high-status monks and their experiences, I would like to provide a tale of a somewhat different kind of man. Here we can turn to a more humble sort, a dim-witted fellow nicknamed Oxcloud, whose mind becomes illumined. The text forms a brief chapter in Yanyi's mid-eleventh-century monograph on Wutai shan, *Extended Records of the Clear and Cool Mountains* (*Guang Qingliang zhuan*, T. 2099: 51, 120c-121a); the indented sentences and phrases marked by an asterisk reflect significant variants on the tale as earlier told by Zanning in his *Records of Eminent Monks Compiled in the Song* (*Song Gaoseng zhuan*, T. 50, 2061, 843bc). Again, as in the long passage cited earlier from Huixiang's monograph, rather than providing pithy excerpts I have included a translation of the full account of Niuyun's experiences so that one can survey the wider field in which light phenomena take place.

Venerable Oxcloud Seeks Intelligence

The monk Niuyun [Oxcloud] was a native of Yanmen [Goose Gate, a city near the Wutai Mountains in present-day Shanxi Province]. His lay family name was Zhao. *In his childhood years, he seemed like a simpleton. His parents sent him to a village school, but he never spoke nor did he regard anything with interest.

> *In his childhood years, it appeared that his intelligence was incomplete. When he was sent to enter the village school, by the end of the day he still could not recognize a single character. It is only when he saw monks or nuns that he would raise up his hands and kneel in veneration.

At the age of twelve, his family sent him to the Cloister of the Good Dwelling Pavilion at [Wutai shan's] Huayan Monastery, where he became a monk, taking Jingjue as his master. Every day he was ordered to draw water and collect firewood. *Everyone ridiculed his simple and dull qualities. When he reached the age to accept the complete monastic precepts [twenty years old], he was utterly unable to memorize [scriptures and liturgies].

> *At that time the assembly made light of his dullness, and in return for his efforts they mocked and reviled him. As he reached the age for taking the full precepts, it became increasingly difficult for him to memorize [scriptures and liturgies].

When he reached his thirty-sixth year, in the last month of winter he gave rise to a sincere inner intention and reflected to himself: "I have heard people say that on the terraces there is always the manifestation body of Wenshu. Now I will go there barefoot. If I see Wenshu, I will seek only intelligence, so that I can study and recite the scriptures and rites." Just at this moment the weather turned to snow and intense cold, but in his heart there was no turning back, no aversion.

He first reached the summit of the Eastern Terrace. Suddenly he saw an old man who had lit a fire and was seated beside it. Yun asked him: "Where have you come from in this snow and cold?" The old man replied: "I've come from down below." Yun said: "On what path? There's not a single footprint!" The old man said: "I came before the snow began to fall."

He in turn questioned Yun: "Master, what heart-resolve did you make such that you withstand the cold to reach here barefoot through the snow? How could you not have suffered?" Yun said: "Even though I am a monk, I despair at my stupidity. I can't recite scriptures and rites." The old man said: "Why have you come here?" He replied: "I seek a vision of Wenshu Bodhisattva for the sole purpose of begging him for intelligence." The old man said: "This is rare!"

The old man questioned him further: "If you don't see Wenshu Bodhisattva here, then what will you do?" Yun said: "I'll climb up the Northern Terrace." The old man said: "I, too, intend to go there." Yun said: "Shall we go together?" The old man said: "Please, master, you go first."

Yun then circumambulated the terrace summit, took leave of the old man, and went off to the west [toward the Northern Terrace]. He reached the Northern Terrace just at sunset, and again he saw the old man seated by a burning fire. Oxcloud was startled and *suspicious,

*felt strange,

and he asked the old man: "When we left the Eastern Terrace, we separated and I came first. How could you already have reached here?" The old man said: "Master, you don't know the shortcuts. That's why you came more slowly."

Even though Yun accepted these words, *in his heart he said: "This old man is no other than a response form of Master Wenshu." And so he immediately began to prostrate himself before him.

*his heart had been prepared, and he thought: "Isn't this old man the response form of Wenshu?" Yun then prostrated himself before him, crying at his feet.

The old man said: "I am a common man [or layman?], you shouldn't prostrate yourself to me." *Yun merely continued to worship—his feelings did not falter.

*He was only eager to engage in prostration, and his emotions were gathered without waver.

After a long time the old man said: *"Wait until I enter *samādhi* [meditative concentration],

*"Stop these prostrations. Wait until I enter *samādhi,*

and I will investigate the karmic acts of your past life that have led to your present dullness." The old man seemed to close his eyes, and then he suddenly *said these words:

*smiled and said:

"In your previous life you were an ox, and because you transported the canon of scriptures to a monastery, now you have been reborn as a monk. From that time as an ox to the present, you have been dull witted. Bring me a mattock from beside the Dragon Hall and I will chop off that silted-up flesh on your heart and head, and make you bright and keen."

Yun followed just as he was told and went over to the side of the hall, where he took hold of a mattock. He crossed over to the old man, who said: "Just close your eyes. Wait for me to tell you to open them, and then you can do so."

Yun relied on his instructions. He felt then as if his very heart were cut, but his body experienced no pain or suffering. His mind then cleared: it was like encountering a bright lamp in a darkened room, as if the sun and moon were disclosed to the dark night. The old man ordered him to open his eyes, and when the master's eyes opened, he saw that the old man was transformed into an image of Wenshu. He said to Yun: "From now on, you will recite the scriptures and rites, and gradually you will not forget or lose what you have seen or heard. You have great causes and conditions at the Huayan Monastery's East of the Torrent Cloister. You will not fall back."

Overcome by emotion, Yun prostrated himself on the ground in veneration. He had not raised his head up for an instant when the bodhisattva already had vanished. The master then descended the mountain. His limbs and trunk seemed especially light. He was able to memorize scriptural texts. His eyes could see; his ears could hear. There was nothing that he did not understand and retain.

In the summer of the following year, in the fifth month, as Yun circumambulated the King Aśoka Stupa,[26] reciting a *sūtra* as he paced the path, at the moment when the *ergeng* evening hour [9:00 p.m.] began, Yun suddenly saw a ray of straight light. This light ray went from the summit of the Northern Terrace and connected to the base of the auspicious stupa. It remained for a long time without dispersing. Within this radiance, atop the present pavilion there appeared a manifested pavilion with a single altar from which radiant colors flamed and glittered. Before it there was a signboard inscribed in golden characters: *"Pavilion of Stability."

*"Stability."

The master then thought of the prophetic words of the bodhisattva, and accordingly he had a building constructed based on the pavilion that had appeared in the midst of the radiance.*

*Because the transformations of the Way ordained it to be so, the people united to donate their valuables.

In the twenty-third year of the *kaiyuan* reign period of Emperor Ming of the Tang [735], when the master was in his sixty-third year, in the summer of his forty-fourth year since ordination, he died without illness.*

*As to Yun's [original monastic] name, the first character has been lost. Because he received Wenshu's prophecy and explanation of his past life as an ox, from that time on for this reason he was called "Niu" [Ox].

The medieval records from Wutai shan emphasize visions of light that take form, reveal form, or illuminate form. In the narrative about Oxcloud, light plays a significant metaphorical role in describing a process of awakening. Having awakened from a kind of walking sleep, Oxcloud then is able to see the normally unseeable: forms illuminated by divine light.

One of the most striking elements of this account, and others from the same era, is the transformative power of these particular, individualized experiences in which light plays a role. In all these complex narratives surviving from medieval times, the person who has an extraordinary, private experience is changed from that moment onward; the heroes of the Wutai shan vision narratives come into their own as a result of their pivotal experiences. This at least is a key element of the narrative structure.[27]

The visionaries also gain extraordinary influence within religious and secular communities, such that the radiant building complexes seen or entered in visionary experiences are replicated full-scale, using more earthly materials (usually at tremendous expense). Records make clear that in some significant cases the funding for construction and maintenance of these complexes comes from members of the imperial family and high officials.[28]

This can and should be read as an intricate example of power responding to power, imperial power responding to and interacting with expressions of religious power. From a very standard medieval point of view, the auspicious vision reflects well on the auspicious qualities of the ruler, who is responsible for the territory in which this vision has occurred. The ruler's auspicious qualities are further made evident by his sponsorship of good works, by his assistance in realization of the vision by sponsoring actual construction. It should not be ignored that one of the responsibilities borne by such sponsored monasteries was the obligation to perform regular rites and prayers to benefit the imperial family. And what of the visionary? Usually he became abbot of the newly constructed monastery. Thus, one can imagine that reports of such visions were both exciting and highly problematic for all concerned.

VISUAL REPRESENTATIONS

In addition to written narratives about light at Wutai shan, some based on oral tales and others consciously composed, there also is a substantial body of visual representations. Again, some of these visual representations clearly are based on tales and surviving written accounts, while others exist on their own. Here I would like to focus on two types of visual expression: two-dimensional works (paintings, drawings, and blockprints) and architectural complexes. This discussion is limited to a brief survey of these materials in the context of some of the issues raised here, as I discuss these representations and their functions at considerable length in *Buddhist Encounters with the Wutai Mountains.*

The body of two-dimensional representations can be set in a tentative historical progression. This progression is tentative because it is based on surviving works, which surely constitute only a small fraction of the total number of works originally produced. From the ninth century, there are wall paintings at the Dunhuang caves, a Buddhist site located in China at the northwestern terminus of the "silk route." These wall paintings show the natural environment of Wutai shan dominated by great balls of light (some with recognizable images within) and thus emphasize the numinous qualities of the mountain locale (cave 159, west wall; plate 8). Wenshu appears above one of the peaks, while a few scattered structures—especially stupas—superimpose a Buddhist built environment on the natural terrain. From a somewhat later date, the tenth century, there are works that develop this visual statement and place Wenshu prominently above the mountains as the presiding deity who has descended on a radiant multicolored trail. Here the mountains clearly are subordinated to Wenshu's bodily appearance, and thus, we see this place indisputably as a Buddhist site. (One example of this depiction is a Liao-period painting on paper kept in the Musée Guimet)[29] Finally, there are comprehensive depictions of the physical territory, built environment, numinous events, and bodily manifestations of the deity. The most famous of these, and perhaps the earliest, is a mural in Dunhuang cave 61, dated to 947–957 (plates 9–12).[30]

The cave 61 mural is an extraordinary work, large and intensively detailed, with cartouches that identify most of the principal scenes and landmarks. In my reading, it is divided into three horizontal registers. At the lowest level is the ordinary world of China, with pilgrims on the road passing scenes of daily life. The Wutai territory is set apart by great gates, and when the pilgrims enter these gates, they move into the middle register. This is a physical realm where laypersons and monks meet and confer, where the built environment is identified as Buddhist (named monasteries, stupas, thatched huts where hermit monks meditate), and where all these humans—clerics and laypersons—encounter the strange manifestations of spirit forces. We see auspicious birds and strange waters, but very prominently we also see numerous manifestations of light that take a wide range of forms and colors. There is a sense here that the key mode of interaction between humans and the spirits in this middle realm, this realm of sanctified physical territory, is through the medium of light. And one sector of this middle realm is labeled the "world of blue-green lapis lazuli radiance" (*qing liuli guang shijie*), testifying to its mysterious light-filled quality and perhaps also derived from the shimmering blue-green intensity of Wutai's forests and grasslands. Looming above all of this is the third register. It teems with spirits, who appear on auspicious five-colored clouds—first the five hundred dragon kings who are local spirits of the place, and then Wenshu and his retinue of Buddhist saints, who float above them in a position of clear dominance.

This painting is strikingly similar to the medieval compendiums of Wutai shan lore compiled by Huixiang and Yanyi. It is filled with detail, is carefully organized (according to its own logic), and subordinates all this detail to represent a Buddhist reading of the site in totality, a reading that establishes the site under Buddhist control. Unlike the texts, the painting also probably functioned as an icon. It drew the power of the site from afar to bring blessings to the prominent family, at that time rulers of the Dunhuang region, which sponsored construction and decoration of cave 61 (this cave's program of decorations most especially is dedicated to Wenshu). And in contrast to the texts, which carefully establish historical moments for strange phenomena such as light-filled visions, the painting presents the various discrete events all at once. Thus, history lingers here. In this pictorial notion of Wutai shan, powerful manifestations are not episodic, but strangely and evocatively are permanently embedded in the landscape.

I have put these modes in a sequence of apparent development, but I also must emphasize that new versions of each type have been produced fairly continuously up to the present day, both as portable works (prints and paintings) and as murals painted at places such as the courtyard walls of Luohou Monastery at Wutai shan.[31]

The two-dimensional works described above focus on place, and they make certain kinds of interpretive statements about the mountain locale. While many historical individuals are shown in comprehensive works such as the Dunhuang cave 61 mural, they are thoroughly subordinated to the larger narrative. In addition, there also are works that focus especially on an individual's experiences. For example, there are Ming-period woodblock prints, such as those included in a 1556 edition of Baocheng's *Shishi yuanliu.* This book provides an illustrated biography of Śākyamuni Buddha and also a variety of tales from the great body of Chinese Buddhist lore. Texts and illustrations are closely integrated on the same page. Among the many episodes found in this work, there are several from Wutai shan, including a depiction of dragons appearing before the Tang monk Chengguan as he sits at a writing table (fig. 8.1). Chengguan's mind was illumined in a series of visionary experiences, thus enabling

澄觀造疏 一百五十二
高僧傳云唐釋澄觀徧尋名山旁求秘藏
梯航既具壺奧必臻後游五臺一一巡礼
仍往峨嵋備覩聖像却還五臺居華嚴寺
專行方等懺法時寺主賢林請講大經因
慨舊疏文繁義約惙然長想況文殊主智
普賢主理二聖合為毘盧遮那万行兼通
即是華嚴之義也吾既游普賢之境界消
妙吉之鄉原不疏毘盧有辜二聖矣觀將
撰疏俄於寤寐之間見一金人當陽挺立
以手迎抱之無何咀嚼都盡覺即汗流自
喜吞納光明徧照之徵遂著疏一十卷後
常思付授忽夜夢身化為龍矯首于南臺
蟠尾于山北拏攫碧落鱗鬣耀日須臾蜿
蜒化為千數小龍騰耀青冥布散而去蓋
取象乎教法支分流布也製疏時堂前池
生五枝合歡蓮花一花皆有三節洎至長
安朝臣歸向則齊相国常太常武元衡李
逢吉鄭絪李吉甫等咸慕高風俱從戒訓

FIGURE 8.1. The Tang monk Chengguan (738–840) sitting at his writing table in the Wutai Mountains and composing his famous commentary on the *Huayan Sūtra*, while a dragon appears in an auspicious cloud, perhaps as a memory of his potent dream-vision. (After a Ming-period (1556) blockprint collection of illustrated Buddhist stories: Baocheng, *Shishi yuanliu* [photolithographic reprint, Beijing: Zhongguo shudian, 1993].)

him to roam freely through the vast reaches of the *Huayan Sūtra,* which he then explored in a lengthy and highly influential commentary. What we have here in visual form is a relative of the textual category of "highlighted humans," in which the spotlight turns on individuals.

Earlier we looked at textual narratives of monks who saw fully realized architectural assemblages as light-filled visions. Sometimes they entered these structures, according to the accounts, and sometimes they sketched out these buildings based on memories of the vision. At least four of the major Tang-period monasteries at Wutai shan are said to have been built under such circumstances, and pavilions or other structures have been raised at existing monasteries based on reports, such as that of the monk Niuyun. The intent was to replicate with earthly materials the buildings made of light. These structures, then, were not only places for inhabitation and religious activity, but also solid testimony to the immanence and power of Wenshu, testimony that he is present at Wutai shan, that one stands within his buildings under his protection, that he could appear at any moment. And it never should be forgotten that these immovable structures take Buddhist possession over the formerly wild mountain territories.

AN INTERJECTION

So far in this essay we have examined a variety of narratives, mainly about persons who see light or are highlighted themselves, for others to see. The events in these narratives all take place in the Wutai Mountains. Some of them, such as the Dunhuang cave 61 mural, as well as the two medieval compendiums taken as complete entities rather than chapter by chapter, have as their subject not only many discrete experiences, but also the totality of these experiences, and thus the larger subject of these narratives points to the extraordinary qualities of the site, of the Wutai Mountains.

Chinese Buddhists, of course, are not non-Chinese for being Buddhist. The indigenous evidentiary traditions of Chinese state religion are significant for understanding one principal mode by which these unusual light phenomena have been interpreted. That is, such unusual, benign phenomena traditionally have been interpreted as flashes of natural cosmic resonance that appear in spontaneous response to the rectitude of the ruler. In this regard, it is important to note that there are clear historical relations between reports of such light phenomena and the periodic support of the imperial family for Buddhist religious enterprises at Wutai shan. This support began at least as early as the sixth century (perhaps even earlier) and continued through to the late Qing, the last imperial dynasty.

The evidentiary mode also is crucial for Buddhist interpretations of these phenomena. Displays of light—associated with special places and beings of great purity—play a major role in many of the Buddhist scriptures most popular in China. In this context of understanding, light associated with Wutai shan lends credibility to the powerful narrative put forth by Chinese Buddhists that these mountains are the earthly residence of a key figure of the Buddhist pantheon, Wenshu pusa. Narratives about these extraordinary phenomena thus are an important factor in the great shift in attitude that takes place in the mid-Tang period (by the mid-eighth century), in which Buddhists reconceive religious geography and begin to see China not as a borderland subordinate to the Indian Buddhist heartland, but as a central territory within the Buddhist world.[32]

Furthermore, light associated with Wutai shan's special persons testifies to the extraordinary spiritual resonance of these men and women, to the deep level of their pure cultivation. Extensive reports of these various types of light phenomena, brought together, create a narrative that testifies to the living reality, specifically in China, of the world of the scriptures. The light-filled vision records of individuals testify to the possibility of attaining the goals set forth in those scriptures.

One further point from another angle. The phenomena at Wutai shan and their interpretations form part of a larger preoccupation with light that is basic to Chinese Buddhist notions of effective religious practice. Having thought about balls of light and highlighted humans, we need to ask further, in order to gain a sense of some broader contexts: What else glows in the Chinese Buddhist world? (This question also is relevant to thinking about internal illumination, one of the key issues of the final section of this essay.) The simplest answer is that buddhas and other highly developed beings glow, and things associated with them are radiant. Not only are buddhas and bodhisattvas described in a wide range of texts as brilliant, light-producing beings, with luminous and radiant minds, but also their realms are characterized by pure light. (And thus, a rare place on earth where light constantly flashes forth, such as Wutai shan, may be understood as a materialization of a celestial pure land or as a portal to that realm.) Here in our muted, dusty world, some things may shine out through the ordinary haze: images of the deities, relics (or the stupa structures in which they are housed) of the buddhas and persons of great accomplishment, and scriptures (which are physical objects that give body to the words and thoughts of the buddhas).

The living bodies of buddhas and great sages may glow or emit flashes of light, and the replica bodies—the images made to represent these beings, to recreate their bodily forms—will do the same. In Chinese Buddhist traditions, basic formal elements of imagery usually are highly standardized, although one way in which radical changes may occur is based on narratives of visionary experience.

It is important that the images are not ready for ritual use until they are formally consecrated. In this present era of Buddhist revival in China, which follows a long period of intense religious persecution, it is not uncommon to see red cloth over the faces of newly constructed sculptures in ritual halls. This indicates that the consecration ceremony has not yet occurred. One does not perform ritual prostrations before these sculptures, because the force of the deity is not yet "there" in the image. The consecration rite, called *kaiguang*, or "opening the light," activates these images by linking them directly to that which they represent, so that flows of light pass freely from the buddhas and bodhisattvas through the images.

Those who engage sincerely in the daily rituals before these images are not strangers to this flow of light. On occasion it is strikingly evident to all present, and leads to various types of human response, including economic responses such as generous donation. It is clear that these experiences of light (at Wutai shan and elsewhere) are read as the manifestation of presence, a flow of pure power that registers as visible light. Here we recognize light as a principal means of communication and response, with bursts of data sent forth in a bright stream of flowing radiance.

COUNTERARGUMENTS: NO LIGHT, INTERNAL LIGHT

So far we have considered narratives of experience—verbal and pictorial—that describe light which streams in from the outside. That is, according to the descriptions and depictions the faculty of sight responds to what is perceived as an external stimulus. In some cases, this stimulus is independently verifiable by multiple witnesses, while in other cases it is a private experience. But in all these cases, it seems clear that from the point of view of those who do the seeing (at least as represented in the narratives), there is an external force or phenomenon that is registered, observed, and taken very seriously.

In contrast, some views, most especially associated with the various Chan practice lineages, are not concerned with external phenomena such as luminous visions. They emphatically reject such phenomena as dangerous because dwelling on such matters fosters attachment to what are considered transient illusions. It diverts focus from the real work at hand.

Linji Yixuan (d. 866), the formidable Chan master who lived for many years beside the Hutuo River on a pilgrimage route to Wutai shan, is said once to have growled: "There are some types of students who go off to Mount Wutai looking for Mañjuśrī. They're wrong from the very start! Mañjuśrī isn't on Mount Wutai. Would you like to get to know Mañjuśrī? You here in front of my eyes, carrying out your activities, from first to last never changing, wherever you go never doubting—*this* is the living Mañjuśrī!"[33]

For Linji, at that particular teaching moment, light phenomena and spectacular apparitions have little to do with real accomplishment. That accomplishment is seen in the pure state of mind that has no waver and is expressed consistently in all human endeavors.

But some Chan masters have been interested in light-filled consciousness. Tales about internal light form a counternarrative to concerns about the seductive allure of external phenomena. The perfection of insight texts of Indian Mahāyāna are a principal source tradition for Chan approaches, and there we can find representations of internally generated radiance, the light that emanates from a pure mind. For example, consider the description of the sage Vimalakīrti's room, which is "constantly flooded with rays of golden light that never change, day or night. It is not lit by the shining of the sun or moon."[34] This image, in which a bright habitation represents an illuminated mind, was picked up by Buddhist monk-poets such as Hanshan (c. late eighth to early ninth centuries):

I have a cave of my own
a cave with nothing inside
spotless and spacious
bright and clear everyday
vegetables feed a frail body
a cloth robe masks a mirage
let your thousand sages appear
I have the Real Buddha[35]

This approach of Linji and Hanshan, which points to the illumined mind and its activities in daily life, is not recorded in the medieval chronicles of Wutai shan, which among their many functions served to legitimize and propagate the cult of the mountain and its presiding deity. But in independent works we do find Chan-associated narratives of formless experience in which the consciousness is flooded with light.

A classic account of this type of experience at Wutai shan is found in the autobiography of the Ming master Hanshan Deqing (1546–1623). This event occurred in 1575, when Deqing was in his thirtieth year and lived in seclusion on Wutai shan's Northern Terrace. Deqing was a Chan practitioner who had a particular interest in the *Huayan Sūtra.* During this period he was working hard to purify his sense faculties, following some techniques of the *Lengyan Sūtra,* so that he could perceive all phenomena with imperturbability. Deqing wrote:

One day after preparing rice porridge, I was circumambulating when suddenly I stood still. I perceived neither body nor mind, only a great radiant treasury, perfectly clear and still, like a huge round mirror, which reflected in its center the mountains, rivers, and great earth. When I awakened from this experience, in this bright state I searched for my body and mind, but they were not to be found. I composed this verse:

> In the flash of a single thought,
> the wild mind is put to rest;
> The sense organs within and the dust without
> are fully comprehended.
> The tumbling body strikes
> and breaks the great void;
> I observe the majesty of the ten thousand forms
> from their arising to disappearance.

From this time on all was clear within and without. Sounds and sights never again were obstacles. The collected doubts of the past disappeared. When I inspected my cooking pot afterwards, I saw that it had become covered with dust. Since I was alone without companion, I don't know how long this experience lasted.[36]

This type of experience is not intrinsic to Wutai shan. That is, the experience of pure consciousness or luminous mind, framed within Buddhist terms (here drawn from Deqing's Chan practice and study of the *Huayan Sūtra*), may occur at any place. It is not dependent on a particular locale because the potential for this experience is intrinsic to all sentient beings, including humans, wherever they may be, according to a wide range of statements in the Chan literature available to Deqing. But in fact, according to this testimony, it did occur at Wutai shan, which is a place that by the Ming period was well established as a site for rigorous cultivation practices, a place where some serious individuals went in order to make progress. And various factors established conditions that ultimately were conducive to the result. At his remote site, Deqing was able to dedicate himself to rigorous practice without concern that he might be interrupted by others, and at this site he first worked to disengage from automatic sensory responses by spending many days seated in meditation upon a small bridge over a roaring stream, until the sound no longer had any distracting effect on his mind. So we have a result that theoretically is not dependent upon a site, but in actual fact, according to Deqing's report, was tied to practices and experiences at a specific site and eventually by the power of the narrative became interwoven with understandings of the site, so that one might climb to the Northern Terrace and say: "Here is where Deqing was illumined."

Deqing's report of his experience, set against the brilliantly colored backdrop of the totality of Wutai shan visionary narratives, produces a peculiar tension: the contrast between form and formlessness in visionary experiences of light. Why do so many medieval narratives focus in great detail on the myriad illuminated forms revealed in visionary experience, while it is only later narratives, such as Deqing's, that speak to vast oceanlike illumination of consciousness? (While elements of his experience speak to form, the ultimate result is an enduring, illumined, formless state.) It is not simply a matter of the rise of Chan traditions, since formless meditations were well established in medieval times and were practiced at Wutai shan as well as other Chinese sites in that era, but it may be that the more insistent spread of Chan throughout Chinese practice traditions, as was seen by Deqing's era, helped to produce his kind of narrative.

At heart, I think, Wutai shan vision narratives are dominated by form because Wutai shan is the seat of manifestation of a particular deity, who takes form there. Devotees go to Wutai shan to have direct experience with this deity. That is what is on their minds and in their prayers, and when they have experiences or produce narratives about experience, the discourse is expressed in terms of form.

CONCLUDING COMMENTS

Chinese Buddhist worlds constitute a "culture of visions."[37] Ethnographic experience suggests that many contemporary religious professionals experience heightened sensory perceptions that are interpreted in ways associated with the aims and fruits of their religious path. That is, it is not unusual for accomplished monks and nuns to see and hear what they interpret as the deities and their realms. This occurs in the midst of daily liturgies in the worship hall and in the standard practices of the meditation hall, as well as during more specialized and intensive practice sessions. In addition, unusual experiences are reported at sites of power, such as the great pilgrimage mountains, and in the presence of objects of power, such as relics of accomplished persons of the past. Comments in literature from a wide range of time periods and genres suggest that the narratives of experience of present-day practitioners in China, tales that usually are recounted privately and are not for publication, reflect a texture of lived religious experience that extends back without break to the early days of Buddhist practice in China.

But in each generation only a few of these many tales are preserved in texts (or in visual representations) that have survived to the present day. Because we do not have access to the full range of possibilities, it is difficult to determine precisely why certain tales survived and others were never recorded, or were set in texts or paintings that now are lost. What we can study historically is what remains within our reach. In this essay I have set out some representative examples of tales of visions of light across a broad swath of time at one famous site, the Wutai Mountains. I have sought to show some of the larger semantic fields within which reports of visions of light should be considered in Buddhist China, and I have tried to show that while certain themes arise historically, and thus one can discern changes over the *longue durée,* these themes have not necessarily been discarded in succeeding narratives, but are retained in a cumulative process. There is of course far more to say about these narratives and their many contexts, but this is a beginning, which has emphasized aspects that may be useful for those concerned with comparison across cultures.

NOTES

1. For an extended discussion of sound and engagement of the senses in monastic practice, as well as discussion of Chinese Buddhist methods to purify the sense faculties, see "Soundscapes in Buddhist China," chapter 4 of my *Body and Practice in Buddhist China,* in preparation. For some relevant considerations of fragrance in an Indian Buddhist context, see John S. Strong, "Gandhakuṭī: The Perfumed Chamber of the Buddha," *History of Religions* 16 (1977): 390–406.

2. See Tang Yongtong, *Han Wei liang Jin nanbeichao fojiao shi* (Shanghai: Commercial Press, 1938), pp. 24–26.

3. For detailed discussion, see chapter 1, "Signs of Power in the Natural World," of my *Buddhist Encounters with the Wutai Mountains,* in preparation.

4. Huixiang, *Gu Qingliang zhuan,* T. 2098.51.1098a. (T. is the conventional abbreviation for *Taishō Shinshū Daizōkyō,* ed. Takakusu Junjiro and Watanabe Kaigyoku [Tokyo: Taishō issaikyō kankōkai, 1924–32], 100 vols.)

5. Ibid., 1099c. All months are given in accordance with the traditional lunar calendar, which begins approximately one month later than the modern calendar's new year.

6. Ibid., 1094a.

7. Located on Wutai shan's Southern Terrace.

8. Huixiang, *Gu Qingliang zhuan,* T. 2098.51.1100a. The branding practice and its contexts are discussed at length in chapter 3, "Offerings of Flesh and Blood," of my *Body and Practice in Buddhist China.*

9. For an overview of Chinese Buddhist examples of this form, see Donald Gjertson, "The Early Chinese Buddhist Miracle Tale: A Preliminary Survey," *Journal of the American Oriental Society* 101 (1981): 287–301.

10. Huixiang, *Gu Qingliang zhuan,* T. 2098.51.1100c. This tale is fully translated and discussed in chapter 1 of my *Buddhist Encounters with the Wutai Mountains.* Fanzhi ("Abundant Peaks") is north of Wutai shan, according to the geography section of Huixiang's text, T. 2098.51.1093c. The relevant map (#46/7) in the Tang series of *Zhongguo lishi ditu ji,* vol. 5 (Shanghai: Ditu chubanshe, 1980), places Fanzhi xian northwest of Wutai shan, on the banks of the Hutuo River.

11. Two works by Edward H. Schafer set forth the general range of bird auguries in the Tang, as well as medieval traditions centered on cranes. See his "The Auspices of T'ang," *Journal of the American Oriental Society* 83 (1963): 197–225, and "The Cranes of Mao Shan," in *Tantric and Taoist Studies in Honour of R. A. Stein,* ed. Michel Strickmann (Brusells: Institut Belge des Hautes Études Chinoises, 1983), 2:372–93. See also Peter C. Sturman, "Cranes above Kaifeng: The Auspicious Image at the Court of Huizong," *Ars Orientalis* 20 (1990): 34–68.

12. For concise references on *jingyun,* see *Zhongwen dacidian* (Taipei: Zhonghua xueshu yuan, 1982), 4:1367c. On the enthronement omens, see Howard J. Wechsler, *Offerings of Jade and Silk* (New Haven, CT : Yale University Press, 1985), pp. 68–69.

13. The inscription is found in the 1899 collection by Hu Pinzhi, *Shanyu shike congbian, juan* 4, pp. 1a–3a.

14. My notions of homeliness come from Gaston Bachelard, *The Poetics of Space,* trans. Maria Jolas (Boston: Beacon Press, 1969), and my understandings of its opposite, uncanniness, were sparked by Anthony Vidler's *The Architectural Uncanny: Essays in the Modern Unhomely* (Cambridge, MA: MIT Press, 1992). The source for these concepts so eloquently elaborated upon by Bachelard and Vidler ultimately goes back to Sigmund Freud, but of course the moods existed long before Freud articulated them.

15. On the earliest examples of this genre, see Kenneth DeWoskin, "The Six Dynasties *Chih-kuai* and the Birth of Fiction," in *Chinese Narrative, Critical and Theoretical Essays,* ed. Andrew H. Plaks (Princeton, NJ: Princeton University Press, 1977), pp. 21–52; and Robert Ford Campany, *Strange Writing: Anomaly Accounts in Early Medieval China* (Albany: State University of New York Press, 1996).

16. Huixiang, *Gu Qingliang zhuan,* T. 2098.51.1093a.

17. See Marylin Rhie, *The Fo-kuang ssu: Literary Evidences and Buddhist Images* (New York: Garland, 1977). On its oldest standing buildings, see Liang Ssu-ch'eng, *A Pictorial History of Chinese Architecture* (Cambridge, MA: MIT Press, 1984), pp. 43–49.

18. Ennin, *Nittō guhō junrei gyōki,* in *Dainihon bukkyō zenshō* (Tokyo: Suzuki Research Foundation, 1972), 72:116a. For a somewhat different translation, see *Ennin's Diary,* trans. Edwin O. Reischauer (New York: Ronald Press, 1955), p. 260.

19. Cen Xuelu, ed., *Xuyun heshang nianpu* (Hong Kong: Xianggang foxue shuju, 1969), p. 17. The summit of Great Compass Peak is no more than an hour's walk north-

east from Xiantong Monastery, and it rises high enough to afford a panoramic view of all the five terraces.

20. John Blofeld, *The Wheel of Life* (Boulder, CO: Shambhala, 1972), pp. 149–50.

21. Field notes, 1986.

22. Ennin, *Nittō guhō junrei gyōki*, p. 112a; *Ennin's Diary*, p. 228.

23. Yanyi, *Guang Qingliang zhuan*, T. 2099.51.1112bc.

24. Ibid., 1105c–1106b.

25. I have written elsewhere about such narratives in some detail, although not from the angles presented here. See "The Manifestation of a Monastery: Shenying's Experiences on Mount Wutai in Tang Context," *Journal of the American Oriental Society* 106 (1986): 119–37, and also chapter 1 of *Studies on the Mysteries of Mañjuśrī* (Boulder, CO: Society for the Study of Chinese Religions, 1983). On the related theme of entrance to luminous caves, see my "Secret Halls of the Mountain Lords: The Caves of Wutaishan," *Cahiers d'Extrême-Asie* 5 (1989–90): 115–40.

26. A monument said to contain genuine bodily relics of Śākyamuni Buddha, eighty-four thousand of which were said to have been distributed by the Indian king Aśoka. There were several of these stupas at Wutai shan in medieval times. One remains, at the center of Tayuan si (Monastery of the Stupa Cloister), located next to Xiantong Monastery (formerly known as Huayan Monastery, the home temple of Niuyun).

27. In contemporary China, I have observed informally that claims to significant experience are evaluated in part through examination of a person's behavior, understanding, and general way of being. Senior members of the tradition look for significant ascertainable changes in a person as clear testimony to the depth and efficacy of an experience. I suspect that this informal method has deep roots in the history of Chinese Buddhist practice. The emphasis on change in the medieval narratives thus testifies to the significance of the recorded experiences.

28. One such case, the Monastery of the Golden Pavilion, is discussed in chapter 1 of my *Studies on the Mysteries of Mañjuśrī*.

29. Musée Guimet EO 3588.

30. On the dating of the cave and a comprehensive descriptive view of the mural, see Dorothy C. Wong, "A Reassessment of the *Representation of Mt. Wutai* from Dunhuang Cave 61," *Archives of Asian Art* 46 (1993): 27–52. The best source for a full range of illustrations of the mural and the entire decorative program of cave 61 is Zhao Shengliang, *Dunhuang shiku yishu: Mogaoku di liushiyi pian* (n.p.: Jiangsu meishu chubanshe, 1995).

31. Among two-dimensional representations of Wutai shan, there also are illustrated route books for pilgrims and commercial travelers. I have examined several examples in the collection of the Library of Congress; these date from the late Ming and early Qing periods. While these works set forth in a horizontal, linear fashion stages of travel both to and within the Wutai Mountains, they depict the natural and built environment without reference to supernatural phenomena.

32. This argument is developed at some length in my *Buddhist Encounters with the Wutai Mountains.*

33. *The Zen Teachings of Master Lin-chi,* trans. Burton Watson (Boston: Shambhala, 1993), pp. 38–39.

34. *The Vimalakirti Sutra,* trans. Burton Watson (New York: Columbia University Press, 1997), p. 89.

35. *The Collected Songs of Cold Mountain,* trans. Red Pine (Port Townsend, WA: Copper Canyon Press, 1983), poem 163. The translations of Red Pine (Bill Porter) at times are very free (for example, the first line of this poem might read more literally: "In my house there is a cave"), but they seem to capture the spirit of the Hanshan poems in a way that finds no equal.

36. *Zixu nianpu* [Chronological Autobiography], in *Hanshan laoren mengyu ji* [Collected Dream Journeys of Old Man Hanshan], (Putian: Guanghuasi Fojing liutongchu, n.d.), pp. 2908–9. Many thanks to Shi Jueguan of Nanputuo Monastery (Xiamen) for the timely gift of Deqing's writings. I have borrowed a few phrases from three earlier and very different translations. See Pei-yi Wu, *The Confucian's Progress* (Princeton, NJ: Princeton University Press, 1990), p. 153; Charles Luk, *Practical Buddhism* (London: Rider, 1971), p. 81; and (for the verse) Sung-peng Hsu, *A Buddhist Leader in Ming China* (University Park: Pennsylvania State University Press, 1979), p. 70. The divergences in all four translations attest to the cryptic qualities and highly contextualized meaning of Deqing's apparently plain words.

37. The term is taken from the works of William A. Christian, Jr., especially his *Local Religion in Sixteenth Century Spain* (Princeton, NJ: Princeton University Press, 1981), and *Apparitions in Late Medieval and Renaissance Spain* (Princeton, NJ: Princeton University Press, 1981).

CHAPTER NINE

The Eyes of Michinaga in the Light of Pure Land Buddhism

Mimi Hall Yiengpruksawan

When the Indian queen Vaidehī asks Buddha to show her the purified realm where she will be born again free of sorrow and affliction, she gains a revelation. In it Vaidehī catches a glimpse of Amitāyus, the Buddha of the Pure Land that she desires to perceive. So bright is the light emitted from Amitāyus that Vaidehī cannot see him clearly.[1] This episode, from the *Guan Wuliangshou jing* (*Sūtra on Contemplating the Buddha of Measureless Life*),[2] speaks to a fundamental need given voice throughout the Mahāyāna canon. It is the aspiration not only to be in the presence of Buddha and to encounter him directly, but above all to see him before the very eyes. Daniel B. Stevenson describes this "resonantal" interaction as the "archetypal Buddhist decorum of the sacred."[3] But as the experience of Vaidehī suggests, seeing Buddha involves an encounter with sometimes blinding light. Indeed, to proceed with the cycle of contemplation prescribed by Buddha to allow her to see the Pure Land, she must stare into the sun (T.12.342a2–4).

In general it is the process of seeing, or visualization, that has tended to occupy the attention of commentators with an interest in understanding how Buddha comes to be perceived through mental evocation or in ritual. This has been especially the case in study of the "visualization sūtras" that by the fourth century CE were becoming a prominent part of the Central Asian and Chinese Mahāyāna literature. As epitomized by the *Guan Wuliangshou jing,* these texts provide vivid descriptions of encounters with Buddhist deities during which everything is seen in utmost detail from each leaf and jewel of a pure land to the radiant face of Buddha.[4]

Alan Sponberg has defined as "eidetic" the class of visualization exercises that developed around such texts. The goal is to mentally construct "an eidetic image of some specific object or scene" in order to envision it "in the most minute detail." By so doing the practitioner is able to access an "alternative sensorium" where it is possible to enter the presence of a Buddha and to have the experience "in all of its sensual and affective detail."[5] Thus, the first nine of the sixteen contemplations expounded by Buddha in the *Guan Wuliangshou jing*—exercises that Vaidehī must master if she is to see Amitāyus in his Pure Land—construct piece by piece the exact physical features of what she desires to envision. There is a fractal logic to the process, with the colossal form of Amitāyus immanent in the tiniest clusters of leaves and jewels stirring in the fragrant breeze.

The role of the visual arts in Mahāyāna tends to be understood in terms of the need to see Buddha and to enter into his presence whether ritually or through didactic narrative. This is especially true for the Pure Land teaching that emerged as a distinctive discourse within Chinese Tiantai Buddhism. The object of the Pure Land teaching, in doctrine and practice, is the Buddha variously and interchangeably called Amita (Measureless), Amitāyus (Measureless Life), and Amitābha (Measureless Light). This Buddha has purified and now lives in a cosmic realm—a "Buddha field"—far to the west of the imperfect world that humans inhabit. It is called Sukhāvatī (Bliss); it is perfect; its inhabitants know only boundless happiness, beauty, and purity. What Vaidehī seeks from Buddha is perception of Sukhāvatī and, ultimately, rebirth there in the presence of Amitāyus.

In general terms Amitāyus is central to Tiantai philosophy and ritual. He is the Buddha who serves as the object of the visualization exercise set out in the *Pratyutpannasamādhi sūtra* (*The Sūtra Wherein the Buddhas Stand before One;* Chinese *Panzhou sanmei jing*). This sūtra is the principal text of the second of the four forms of Tiantai religious exercise, "constantly walking samādhi," during which the practitioner chants the name of Amitāyus, visualizes him and his Pure Land, and circumambulates an altar with his image upon it. The *Mohe zhiguan* (*The Great Calming and Contemplation*), a treatise on meditation by the Tiantai patriarch Zhiyi (538–597), gives the following instruction: "One should mentally recollect the Buddha Amitābha ten trillion Buddha lands to the west in a jeweled pavilion, under a jeweled tree, on an island in a jeweled pond in a jeweled land, expounding sūtras while sitting among a congregation of bodhisattvas."[6]

In more specific terms Amitāyus is the central figure of a Tiantai movement based on the teachings of the *Wuliangshou jing* (*Sūtra on Amitāyus*) and *Amituojing* (*Sūtra on Amita*), which are the Chinese translations of the longer and shorter versions of the *Sukhāvatīvyūha sūtra* (*Sūtra on the Display of the World of Bliss*), and on the *Guan Wuliangshou jing*, with its story about Vaidehī. Because these texts expound the Pure Land of Amitāyus, and provide instructions on how to gain rebirth there, they are known as the Pure Land teaching. Although closely related to the texts and practices of the "constantly walking samādhi" of basic Tiantai practice, this teaching strongly emphasizes the objectives of visionary experience of Amitāyus and rebirth in Sukhāvatī. It is highly visual in nature and offers what Luis O. Gómez calls "revelatory descriptions" of Amitāyus and Sukhāvatī in such detail as to call to mind the classical Greek rhetorical device of *ekphrasis.* Such descriptions, as Gómez points out, are consistent with the word *vyūha,* "magnificent display," in the Sanskrit sūtra title.[7] Basically the texts provide a template for the eidetic visualization of Amitāyus in his Pure Land.

The Pure Land teaching is conducive to extensive interpretation and representation in the plastic arts due to its focus on Amitāyus and the especially visual orientation of the *Guan Wuliangshou jing.* Visual cultures around Pure Land texts and themes have been well developed in Central and East Asia since at least the sixth century CE, with some of the most elaborate examples seen in Japan of the eleventh and twelfth centuries. Such art forms range in iconography from paintings of Amitāyus in his palace in Sukhāvatī to architectural programs that seek to replicate on earth the very structures and luxury of that Pure Land. The representations generally involve extensive use of precious materials such as gold, silver, mother of pearl, and crystal or glass. In tandem with the texts these corporeal embodiments of the Pure Land teaching achieve, in very concrete terms, the type of visionary encounter promoted in the sūtras. The need to see Amitāyus in his purified realm is met through art in concrete ways that lend support to the mental evocations that are at the crux of the process. It becomes possible to render visible to the somatic eye that which is not so easily seen.

The attention that many commentators have paid to the processes of seeing and visualization in how Buddha comes to be perceived is understandable in view of the visual orientation of movements such as the Pure Land teaching. Nonetheless, it bears consideration that one central and paradoxical component has tended to be left outside the general discourse on seeing. This is the property of light. It can be addressed in two ways: in terms of the Buddha body and as the basic substance of a purified Buddha realm. That the body of Buddha radiates light is attested throughout the Mahāyāna literature. One of the primary characteristics of a Buddha body is the sheen of its golden color. It is often described as emitting beams of light. There is a memorable passage in the *Avataṃsaka sūtra* where the Cosmic Buddha Vairocana, "the Illuminator," speaks, not in words, but by rays of light streaming from his teeth (T.10.26b-c,

26c11–12). Alexander C. Soper made note of the light symbolism "suffusing the Buddha idea." He described the Buddha of the *Guanfo sanmei hai jing* (*The Sūtra on the Oceanlike Samādhi of the Visualization of the Buddha*), a visualization sūtra closely related to the *Guan Wuliangshou jing*, as "an enormous electrical display, acting only by the emission of rays that cross the universe."[8]

The Buddha who is the object of the Pure Land scriptures—Amita, Amitāyus, Amitābha—is similarly a figure of light and radiance. Vaidehī sees Amitāyus with rays of light streaming from his pores (T.12.343b20). In the Chinese version of the longer *Sukhāvatīvyūha sūtra* the Buddha gives other titles for Amitāyus "because of his majestic and celestial radiant light." Among these other names are Buddha of Measureless Light, Buddha of Boundless Light, Buddha of Unimpeded Light, Buddha of Unopposed Light, Buddha Monarch of Flaming Lights, Buddha Pure Light, and so on (T.12.270a23–25, 270a26–270b3).[9] In the *Guan Wuliangshou jing*, when Vaidehī is instructed to visualize Sukhāvatī, she is told that her body will be illuminated by hundreds of colorful rays of light (T.12.342a11–13, 342b2–19). That it is with the sun that the visualization of Amitāyus begins is in keeping with the solar imagery by which the Buddha body tends to be figured (T.12.341c29–342a5).

The Pure Land texts describe Sukhāvatī as suffused with brilliant light emanating from Amitāyus. The light is reflected from the countless jewels strung from trees made of gold and silver, from the icelike deep blue ground shot with gold, from every fixture and every object. There is a hallucinatory and kaleidoscopic aspect to so emphatic a language of light and reflectivity. A representation of this may have been the intention at Konjikidō, consecrated in 1124 as the Pure Land worship hall and mausoleum of a twelfth-century Japanese patron (fig. 9.1). The ethereal white of the mother-of-pearl inlay and the reflective surfaces of gold and shining black lacquer give off a strange and uncanny light. Like J. G. Ballard's crystal world the space seems a prismatic realm of light mirrored by light.[10] It is consistent with what seems to be a fundamental notion in the Pure Land scriptures, that the approach to Sukhāvatī is a journey into light itself. For those with ordinary eyes, like Vaidehī at the beginning of her quest, the glare is such that nothing can be seen at first glance (T.12.341c23–24, 342c17–18). But it is also the point at which the process of seeing begins.

This chapter is a case study in how one famous Japanese aristocrat of the eleventh century, gone suddenly blind, turned to the light of Amitāyus in a quest to see that ultimately resembled that of Vaidehī. This is not in any sense the way this man and his activities have ever been understood in the scholarship on Pure Land visual culture in Japan. Indeed, it marks a radical departure of considerable scope when the assumptions surrounding early Pure Land

FIGURE 9.1. Konjikidō, Chūsonji, Hiraizumi, Iwate Prefecture, 1124, interior.

teaching and practice in Japan are taken into critical consideration. What drives the thesis is a perspective that can only have been reached by thinking as much about light as about seeing.

MICHINAGA BUILDS MURYŌJUIN

In the eleventh and twelfth centuries there emerged among aristocrats in the capital region of Kyoto a devotional culture around Amitāyus and Sukhāvatī as expounded in the Pure Land scriptures.[11] Central to this culture was the production of architecture, statuary, and painting intended to represent, and embody, the beautiful realm of Amitāyus and its material luxury. One of the celebrated products of this Pure Land visual culture is the Amitāyus hall (Amidadō)—popularly known as the Phoenix Hall—at Byōdōin in the village of Uji in what is now Kyoto Prefecture (fig. 9.2). Consecrated in 1053, the hall can be understood as an adaptation of the *Guan Wuliangshou jing* (Japanese *Kanmuryōjukyō*) in three dimensions. The chief patron of the hall, Fujiwara no Yorimichi (990–1074), and his designer, Jōchō (d. 1057), sought to communicate through this built environment the principal object of the Pure Land teaching. Their goal was to represent Amitāyus in the palace of Sukhāvatī.[12]

In keeping with the *Guan Wuliangshou jing*, which describes the colossal, golden-bodied Amitāyus inside his magnificent palace like a resplendent king, the sanctuary of the Phoenix Hall houses a large gilt-wood statue of Amitāyus—almost three meters in height—that dominates the room (fig. 9.3). On the doors and walls of the room are remnants of painted scenes that show the arrival of Amitāyus to welcome the dying to paradise after they have chanted his name in good faith. The scenes are based on the last three of the sixteen contemplations explained in the *Guan Wuliangshou jing*. The building itself follows continental conventions for the pictorialization of the palace of Amitāyus in his land of bliss. As in the sūtra there is a lake in front of the building where Amitāyus is enshrined. Lotuses grow in the water, as described in the sūtra. The hall faces east over the lake. It is to be viewed from the eastern bank, looking westward into the sun and toward the light-filled realm of Amitāyus (fig. 9.4). Everything is completely consistent with the Pure Land teaching of the *Guan Wuliangshou jing*.

Through the end of the twelfth century a large number of statues, paintings, and buildings appeared in and around Kyoto as the projects of men and women who took inspiration from the Pure Land teaching. In most cases it is apparent that such patrons wished to bring into their world a likeness of

FIGURE 9.2. Amitāyus hall (Phoenix Hall), Byōdōin, Uji, Kyoto Prefecture, 1053, aerial view from northeast.

FIGURE 9.3. Amitāyus hall, Byōdōin, interior.

Amitāyus and his Pure Land that they could experience physically as part of their devotions. Consequently there was much construction of halls for the worship of Amitāyus as understood in the Pure Land teaching.[13] Few of these buildings have survived, but enough remains to provide a clear indication of the goals and occasionally astounding luxury of Pure Land visual culture.

For example, Jōruriji was commissioned toward the end of the eleventh century on what is now the border of Nara and Kyoto prefectures. Its principal structure, aside from a pagoda, is a large Amitāyus hall that houses nine monumental gilt-wood statues of Amitāyus (fig. 9.5) and opens eastward over a lake. Architectural historians refer to this type of building as a nine-image Amitāyus hall (Kutai Amidadō). The figures of Amitāyus symbolize the nine hierarchical levels of rebirth possible for those who aspire to be born in Sukhāvatī specifically as detailed for Vaidehī in the *Guan Wuliangshou jing.* Shimizu Hiroshi has reported that, by the end of the twelfth century, some thirty nine-image Amitāyus halls had been built in the capital region around Kyoto. He has also shown that Amitāyus halls of square plan and more compact size were even more numerous.[14] Konjikidō is a particularly good example of such buildings. There is little doubt that the Pure Land teaching, and the plastic arts it inspired, was central to the intellectual and devotional aspirations of the Kyoto nobility in the eleventh and twelfth centuries.

One of the most intriguing factors in the emergence of this Pure Land visual culture is the sudden appearance of its distinctive iconographical program in 1020. The basic elements of that program had been around much longer, for at least fifty years, but they had not been combined in quite the way that they were in 1020. In the third lunar month of that year the aristocrat Fujiwara no Michinaga (966–1027) brought them together in a unique way with the completion of Muryōjuin, or Hall of Amitāyus. Nine months earlier, in 1019, he had ordered the hall built across the street to the east of his main residence, Tsuchimikado Mansion, in the elite northeastern section of Kyoto along East Kyōgoku Boulevard (Higashi Kyōgoku Ōji) between Tsuchimikado Boulevard (Tsuchimikado Ōji) and Konoe Boulevard (Konoe Ōji). As one of the most influential men of his time, loved and hated by many, Michinaga cuts a mythic figure in Japanese history and has been portrayed for hundreds of years—and accurately so—as a conniving politician who wielded enormous power at the imperial court and whose aesthetic tastes set the standard for Japanese high culture for generations to come. Muryōjuin is assigned a similarly formative role in the development of Japanese cultural norms especially in art and religion. Indeed it is impossible to understand a site such as the Phoenix Hall without

FIGURE 9.4. Amitāyus hall, Byōdōin, view from east.

FIGURE 9.5. Amitāyus hall, Jōruruiji, Nara Prefecture, late eleventh century.

some reference to Muryōjuin, and not only because Yorimichi was the son of Michinaga.

Muryōjuin was destroyed in a fire in 1058 and never reconstructed. Moreover, Michinaga dismantled and rebuilt it in 1025. What is know of Muryōjuin today derives for the most part from brief notations in several contemporary diaries and, most important, from two sources written well after the building had disappeared. One of the sources, *Eiga monogatari* (*A Tale of Flowering Fortunes*), is believed to have been completed around the last decade of the eleventh century by palace aristocrats, probably women, who had been in service to Minamoto no Rinshi (964–1053), the principal wife of Michinaga, or otherwise knew his family well. It presents a romanticized history of the Kyoto court from the reign of Emperor Uda (r. 887–897) through the early years of Emperor Horikawa (r. 1086–1107), with emphasis on the efflorescence of culture around Michinaga in his interconnected roles of statesman, father to three empresses, aesthete, and devout Buddhist. The other source, *Fusō ryakki* (*Abbreviated Annals of Japan*) was completed in the early twelfth century as a record of Buddhist events from earliest times through the reign of Horikawa. It contains a description of Muryōjuin and its consecration. There is also a considerable amount of information on Muryōjuin in *Shoji kuyō ruiki* (*Records of Temple Consecrations*), a seventeenth-century collation of temple documents and related primary materials.

On the basis of these sources it is estimated that Muryōjuin measured eleven bays across (approximately fifty meters) and three bays deep (twenty meters). It stood on the western bank of an artificial lake that had been excavated specifically for it. The plan was similar to that of the Amitāyus hall at Jōruriji, for which it was the prototype. The hall opened eastward over the lake. It had gold fixtures and floral designs in mother of pearl and probably resembled Konjikidō in decoration. Its polished wood floor shone like a mirror. On the east-facing doors, to the north and south, were paintings of the nine levels of rebirth. Gold and silver pigment glowed from the depictions of Amitāyus on a cloud coming to welcome the devout to his Pure Land. Nine huge golden statues of Amitāyus, of a size and technique probably comparable to that of the Phoenix Hall Amitāyus, filled the length of the hall one to a bay. The statues, "all nine in a row," were covered in gold. At the center of the building, in the bay directly in front (and to the east) of the central bay with its statue of Amitāyus, was a worship chamber used exclusively by Michinaga. Here he secluded himself behind screens to chant the name of Amitāyus and pray. When he did so, he grasped in his hands a braided string leading to the hands of the central Amitāyus and, from there, to those of the other statues.[15]

Michinaga went on to expand the Muryōjuin precinct across from Tsuchimikado into a large temple complex that included a pagoda and belfry, eight major halls, quarters for monks, private quarters for himself, and a lake with an extensively landscaped rock garden. In 1022 the complex was named Hōjōji.[16] Some likened it to Sukhāvatī.[17] Sightseers would gather along East Kyōgoku Boulevard to catch a glimpse of Hōjōji over its retaining wall. Especially famous was the main hall with its lustrous white walls, encrustation of colorful gems, and sparkling green roof.[18] After 1022 it was more common to hear Muryōjuin referred to as the Amitāyus hall, as Michinaga and his family apparently preferred. The hall remained important to him despite the newer and more elaborate buildings that made up Hōjōji. Over the ensuing years it was used for a variety of rituals for Michinaga and his immediate family. In 1027 Michinaga died there. According to *Eiga monogatari* Michinaga faced west, fixed his eyes on the Amitāyus statues, and expired grasping the braid that lead to the central figure.[19] In time this death scene, and the hall at which it occurred, would be understood as the defining moment in the development of Pure Land visual culture in Japan.

In its day Muryōjuin appears to have been an anomaly. On architectural and iconographical grounds it departed considerably from earlier structures dedicated to the worship of Amitāyus, such as the eighth-century halls at Tōdaiji and Hokkeji. Its apparent focus on the *Guan Wuliangshou jing* gave it an unusual scriptural framework and devotional program. There were also no obvious antecedents for the extraordinary floor plan that accommodated nine statues of Amitāyus arranged in a row. This makes it the first known example of the nine-image Amitāyus hall as seen at Jōruriji (fig. 9.5). In this sense the Muryōjuin can be understood as a prime object. Even the concept of the Amitāyus hall appears to have been redefined with its appearance.

Prior to the construction of Muryōjuin there had been two types of hall devoted to the worship of Amitāyus. The earlier type was seen occasionally at eighth-century monasteries in the old capital of Nara. An example would be the Amitāyus hall at Hokkeji, which enshrined a monumental statue of Amitāyus in a square hall with images of celestial beings on the walls.[20] The second and more recent type was the circumambulation hall (Jōgyō Zanmaidō, "constantly walking Samādhi hall"). In Michinaga's day three halls of this type existed at Enryakuji, the monastic seat of the Tendai (Tiantai) sect on Mount Hiei northeast of the city of Kyoto, one in each of the temple's three precincts.

The oldest Enryakuji circumambulation hall, consecrated in 851, stood in the East Pagoda (Tōtō) precinct near the summit of Mount Hiei and enshrined an Amitāyus triad—Amitāyus accompanied by the bodhisattvas Avalokiteśvara (Japanese *Kannon*) and Mahāsthāmaprāpta (Japanese *Dai Seishi*)—with paintings of the nine levels of rebirth on the interior walls. In 894 the next circumambulation hall was built in the neighboring West Pagoda (Saitō) precinct; although the primary record is somewhat unclear, the hall is believed to have housed an Amitāyus triad with paintings of Sukhāvatī on the pillars of its sanctuary. A century later, around 970, another circumambulation hall was constructed in the more newly developing Yokawa precinct some distance away on the northern flank of Mount Hiei. It enshrined an Amitāyus triad along with figures of Kṣitigarbha (Japanese *Jizō*) and Nāgārjuna (Japanese *Ryūjū*).[21]

These halls were square in plan and intended for use as sites for the "constantly walking samādhi" set out by Zhiyi in *Mohe zhiguan* (Japanese *Maka shikan*) using the *Pratyutpannasamādhi sūtra* (Japanese *Hanju zaṇmai kyō*) as a guide. Practitioners circumambulated the Amitāyus triad while chanting the name of Amitāyus and visualizing his body. In keeping with the teachings of Zhiyi the circumambulation hall was typically paired with a lotus hall (Hokke Zanmaidō, "lotus Samādhi hall"), where the "part walking, part sitting samādhi" took place around a copy of the *Lotus Sūtra* (*Saddharmapuṇḍarīka sūtra;* Japanese *Myōhō renge kyō*) and an image of the bodhisattva Samantabhadra (Japanese Fugen). Whereas the "constantly walking samādhi" focused on visualization of Amitāyus, here the emphasis was on repentance through recitation of incantations accompanied by visualization of Samantabhadra.[22] It was in this Tendai setting of visualization, recitation, and penitence that there developed on devotional grounds a lasting connection between Amitāyus and the *Lotus Sūtra.*

By the turn of the eleventh century, when Michinaga was emerging as the dominant personality at court, the circumambulation hall had begun to be used for several activities at some remove from the original monastic function. One such activity was the practice of *fudan nenbutsu,* or "nonstop [*fudan*] calling to mind of Buddha [Amitāyus] [*nenbutsu*]." It had its origin in the "constantly walking samādhi" with its three-month program of concentration, vocalization of the name of Amitāyus, and walking around an altar as inspired by the *Pratyutpannasamādhi sūtra.* In time the practice attracted a significant lay following as men and women of the aristocracy began to stage *fudan nenbutsu* sessions under the supervision of Tendai monks for short periods of time (usually overnight). Many such meetings were held to memorialize some person recently deceased and had a strongly soteriological orientation. To accommodate this new trend a number of circumambulation halls were built at the tutelary temples of Kyoto aristocrats. Hōkōin, the memorial temple of Michinaga's father Kaneie (929–990), had a circumambulation hall by 1000; Michinaga's sister, Empress Senshi (961–1002), sponsored a *fudan nenbutsu* session there in 1001. Shortly before Senshi's death in 1002 a circumambulation hall was built at her own temple, Gedatsuji.[23]

Another new use to which the circumambulation hall was being put at the turn of the eleventh century was as a site for meetings of the Twenty-five Meditations Society (Nijūgo Zanmaie). A recent study by Sarah Johanna Horton has illuminated much about the fellowship.[24] It was formed in 986 by a group of Tendai clerics and some middle-ranking Kyoto courtiers such as Yoshishige no Yasutane (d. 1002). Members convened once a month, at the circumambulation hall in Yokawa, to spend a night reciting the *nenbutsu,* chanting the Kōmyō Shingon (Mantra of Light), and reading from the *Amituojing* (Japanese *Amida-kyō*). One of the aims of the society, as specified in its various charters, was to prepare for death and, through chanting and prayer, earn the spiritual merit to achieve rebirth in Sukhāvatī. This was entirely in keeping with the teaching of the *Amituojing,* their favored text, on how to achieve rebirth through the practice of *nenbutsu.*

The shift in focus in circumambulation hall function, away from meditation based primarily on the *Pratyutpannasamādhi sūtra* toward greater emphasis on the soteriological benefit of *nenbutsu* recitation as stipulated in the *Amituojing,* was part of a larger trend in the Tendai community that gained impetus with the abbacy of Ryōgen (912–985) and his disciples Jinzen (943–990) and Genshin (942–1017). Ryōgen was an accomplished Tendai thinker and rhetorician who placed greater emphasis on the Pure Land scriptures than had most of his predecessors. Using the Yokawa precinct as his base, he inculcated the Pure Land in Tendai monks and in the lay community. As a result the practice of *nenbutsu,* long a staple of Tendai meditation exercises, became strongly associated with the specific goal of visualizing and achieving rebirth in the Pure Land of Amitāyus. In this context *nenbutsu* recitation began to take on a mortuary dimension.

Jinzen succeeded Ryōgen as abbot in 985. His colleague Genshin had withdrawn from administrative affairs at Enryakuji several years earlier, opting instead for a life of seclusion in the Yokawa precinct. The aristocratic Jinzen appears to have been the favorite of Ryōgen, and the disciple chosen to continue his legacy, but in the long analysis it would be Genshin who gained the most credit for the success of the Pure Land teaching in Japan. In 985 he completed a manual on rebirth entitled *Ōjō yōshū* (*Essentials of Salvation*), for which he is now best known, although he was an expert in other areas of doctrine as well. The manual consists of Genshin's commentary and instructions interspersed with extensive citations from a variety of Mahāyāna texts. Most prominently featured are the *Pratyutpannasamādhi sūtra, Amituojing, Wuliangshou jing* (Japanese *Muryōjukyō*), *Guan Wuliangshou jing,* and *Guanfo sanmei hai jing* (Japanese *Kanbutsu zanmai kai kyō*). Using these texts Genshin makes a compelling case for *nenbutsu* recitation as the way to achieve rebirth in Sukhāvatī. In so doing he emphasizes the role of visualization as central to the proper practice of *nenbutsu.* The reward will be a visionary experience of Amitāyus at the moment of death.

Ōjō yōshū is justifiably famous for its riveting imagery and argumentation. One of the best-known sections outlines the proper way to die and the reward for doing so. According to the procedure a death site—ideally a building—must be prepared in advance by setting aside a special space and installing there an image of Amitāyus holding a five-colored braid in his hands. As death approaches the patient must chant the *nenbutsu* without stopping (or listen to others doing so), look westward at the figure of Amitāyus, and grasp the braid. In this way it is possible to achieve what Genshin, quoting the venerable Shandao (613–681), describes as *shōju raigō,* "welcoming by the sacred multitude," when Amitāyus with his retinue appears before the person awaiting death.[25]

That such death preparations were actually carried out is known from records of the activities of the Twenty-five Meditations Society, to which Genshin belonged. Horton provides an exhaustive account of the charters and their contents.[26] Members pledged to help one another through the process of dying, including arrangement of the place of death and nonstop chanting of the *nenbutsu.* It is commonly assumed that the society used *Ōjō yōshū* as a manual, but there is no evidence that this was the case.[27] A more likely explanation would be a common Tendai culture, and commonly held beliefs, around the Pure Land teaching in its mortuary dimension. That Genshin frequently cites Daochuo (562–645) and Shandao in *Ōjō yōshū*—in fact basing the instructions on death almost entirely on the views of these Pure Land masters—suggests strongly that there was already in place, at least within the Tendai community in Kyoto, a long-standing association of the Pure Land teaching and its rituals with death and deathbed procedures.

These mortuary aspects are clearly evident in the funerary practices of Kyoto aristocrats from the end of the tenth century. There was widespread memorializing of the dead through services focusing on Pure Land imagery and texts in combination with recitation and celebration of the *Lotus Sūtra.* In a typical example Michinaga's paternal aunt, Empress Anshi (927–964), was memorialized at Enyūji in 987 with an embroidered image of Sukhāvatī and a copy of the *Lotus Sūtra* as the objects of the service. Similarly, her son Emperor

Reizei (950–1011) was memorialized in 1011 and 1012 with a statue of Amitāyus, a painting of Sukhāvatī, and a transcription of the *Lotus Sūtra* on the altar.[28] It was common to hold such services in a private home, but the more likely sites were the circumambulation hall followed by the lotus hall. There was also a deathbed practice along the lines of what Genshin specified in *Ōjō yōshū*. For example, one of the imperial princesses died in 999 while reciting the *nenbutsu* and facing west. Michinaga's nephew and son-in-law, Ichijō (980–1011), died in a similar fashion in 1011.[29]

It is likely that *Ōjō yōshū* was the inspiration for such funerary practices with their focus on the Pure Land teaching. Judging from Horton's study of Genshin, which questions his prominence at the turn of the eleventh century, the most likely source was the century-old religious culture of Tendai, going back to the abbacy of Ennin (794–864), who had been responsible for the introduction and promotion of Pure Land texts including the commentaries of Shandao. By Michinaga's day a distinctive Pure Land subculture had developed around Ryōgen and his disciples, whose doctrinal roots lay with Ennin. This Yokawa-based culture—which included the activities of the Twenty-five Meditations Society—emphasized the Pure Land teaching and attached particular significance to *nenbutsu* recitation as the primary means to visualizing Amitāyus and ultimately achieving rebirth in Sukhāvatī. The functional transformation of the circumambulation hall, from Tendai meditation to Pure Land visualization, was a product of this culture and gave impetus to the eventual development of the Amitāyus hall proper.

Michinaga would have been well connected with the Yokawa circle of clerics. His grandfather, Morosuke (908–960), had been close to Ryōgen and sponsored much of the development of the Yokawa precinct; Morosuke's son Koretada (924–972), or Michinaga's granduncle, would later provide financing for the Yokawa circumambulation hall. Morosuke also retained Ryōgen as ritualist to the Fujiwara family. After Morosuke's death Empress Anshi, Michinaga's aunt, became Ryōgen's primary patron. Jinzen, who succeeded Ryōgen as abbot, was Michinaga's paternal uncle. After Jinzen many Enryakuji abbots came from the "northern" Fujiwara family branch into which Michinaga had been born.[30] Michinaga's own son Akinobu (994–1027), by his second wife Minamoto no Meishi (d. early eleventh century), took the tonsure at Enryakuji in 1012.[31] There is some evidence that Michinaga knew Genshin. In the sixth lunar month of 1004 Michinaga and Rinshi, staying at Gedatsuji, sent a messenger to Genshin to inquire about his health on hearing that he was ill.[32] About a year later Michinaga asked his close friend Fujiwara no Yukinari (972–1027), an accomplished calligrapher, to make him a new copy of *Ōjō yōshū*. Yukinari noted in his diary, *Gonki* (*Diary of the Provisional Major Counselor*), that he returned the original to Michinaga.[33]

Michinaga was not a member of the Twenty-five Meditations Society and said nothing about it in his diary, *Midō Kanpaku ki* (*Diary of the Muryōjuin Regent*). However, he was certainly familiar with the practice of *fudan nenbutsu*. In the fall of 1004 Michinaga joined a *fudan nenbutsu* session in the circumambulation hall of the Tōtō precinct at Enryakuji. He attended the event with the Tendai monks Kakukyo (926–1014), who was then the abbot, and Ingen (951–1028), who would become one of Michinaga's closest advisers and eventually abbot in 1020.[34] Michinaga also participated in *fudan nenbutsu* sessions at Hōkōin, the temple of his father, Kaneie, in 1005 and 1006, and at Gedatsuji in memory of his sister Senshi in 1002, 1004, and 1005.[35] He certainly knew what a circumambulation hall entailed, possibly sponsoring the one built in Kaneie's memory at Hōkōin. Moreover, Michinaga would have been well exposed to the mortuary dimension of Pure Land belief and practice by the time he was prominent at court. The circumambulation hall at Gedatsuji, where services were held in memory of his sister Senshi, contained a sandalwood statue of Amitāyus which was the focus of *nenbutsu* recitation. Michinaga also witnessed the death of Ichijō in 1011 and attended the memorial services for Emperor Reizei in 1012.[36]

Although Michinaga rarely mentioned Pure Land texts in his diary, instead favoring the *Lotus Sūtra*, it is clear that early in his life he developed a thorough grasp of the basic features of the Pure Land teaching as it mattered to people of his circle and their Tendai advisers. It is not clear how Michinaga got from this early exposure to Tendai doctrine and practice surrounding Amitāyus to the unique Pure Land iconography of Muryōjuin some twenty years later. The relevant sections are missing from his diary. Michinaga's associate and frequent critic Fujiwara no Sanesuke (957–1046) surprisingly has little to say about Muryōjuin in his own meticulously kept diary, *Shōyūki* (*Diary of the Ononomiya Minister of the Right*). The diaries furthermore indicate that Michinaga, already little interested in Pure Land belief, became less attentive to the practice of *nenbutsu* after the first decade of the eleventh century. It is true that in 1011 Michinaga commissioned a life-sized statue of Amitāyus along with one hundred copies of the *Amituojing* so that his family could achieve "rebirth in Sukhāvatī" (*ōjō gokuraku*), but this was an isolated case. Moreover, it coincided with the illness and decline of Ichijō—a member of Michinaga's family—who would die a few months later.[37]

Michinaga sometimes has been portrayed as a man without much interest in religion. By comparison with Sanesuke, who fervently staged various rituals, Michinaga was indeed on the cool and calculating side when it came to worship and devotion. But he was in reality a rather devout man, as shown in studies by G. Cameron Hurst III and others.[38] It is evident from Michinaga's diary that, from an early period in his life, he was much interested in the *Lotus Sūtra* and over time developed a firm devotion to it. He was also a consistent student of Tendai texts at least in his younger years. For example, in 1002 he took instruction from the monk Kakuun (953–1007) on *Mohe zhiguan* and probably attended Kakuun's lectures on the subject at the residence of the retired emperor Kazan (968–1008). Kakuun also tutored Michinaga in the *Lotus Sūtra.* Eventually the task would fall to Ingen as well.[39]

It is certain that the *Lotus Sūtra* was extremely important to Michinaga throughout his life for personal reasons but also in connection with his political aspirations and ideology.[40] In his diary he referred to it as his tutelary sūtra (*jikyō*).[41] So strong was Michinaga's commitment to the *Lotus Sūtra* that he promoted its study and worship by regularly holding, at great expense, elaborate multiday services to recite, hear lectures on, and celebrate the sūtra. These services were called the Eight Lectures on the Lotus (Hokke Hakkō) and the Thirty Lectures (Sanjikkō). Although Michinaga did not invent the services, he is credited with making them a prominent part of the religious life of the Kyoto aristocracy. Throughout his life Michinaga would hold these services at family temples or, even more frequently, at Tsuchimikado Mansion, often in memory of his sister Senshi or other members of his clan.[42] There is no question that the *Lotus Sūtra* was a beloved and critically important scripture for Michinaga from the 990s through his death in 1027.

If there was a Pure Land aspect to Michinaga's faith and devotions in the period directly leading up to Muryōjuin, it is not readily apparent. It is very difficult to get a clear picture of what Michinaga had in mind for the construction and iconography of the hall, and why. There is no alternative but to approach Muryōjuin through sites such as Jōruriji Amitāyus hall and sources such as *Eiga monogatari,* which postdate it by at least fifty years and thus offer an explanation only in hindsight. This approach has encouraged the several assumptions that now govern how Muryōjuin is understood and Michinaga's motives in building it. The assumptions are reasonable but deserve scrutiny as potentially misleading.

The first assumption is that Michinaga knew Genshin and was familiar with his views on the practice of *nenbutsu,* visualization of Amitāyus in Sukhāvatī, and deathbed ritual. That Michinaga sent a messenger to Genshin in 1004 is regarded as evidence for Michinaga's having known Genshin. The second assumption is that Michinaga was especially interested in the teachings of Genshin as presented in *Ōjō yōshū*. This is based on Michinaga's having asked Yukinari to make a copy of the manual in 1005. Third is the assumption that Michinaga, deathly ill in 1019, built Muryōjuin as the place where he planned to die. That Michinaga did die there, in 1027, lends credibility to this view. It is also consistent with contemporary practice as seen in the deathbed scene of Ichijō in 1011. Consequently, it is now widely accepted that Michinaga, worried about the afterlife and influenced by Genshin to devote himself to Amitāyus through *nenbutsu* recitation, conceived of Muryōjuin in response to the teachings of *Ōjō yōshū* particularly as manifested in the section on deathbed ritual.[43] The nine figures of Amitāyus, the braid attached to them, and the paintings of Sukhāvatī seem to support this view. It is further encouraged by the wording of *Eiga monogatari*, which quotes *Ōjō yōshū* in reference to Muryōjuin and Hōjōji. The authors even note that Michinaga intended to grasp the braid "at the hour of his death in order to ensure his rebirth in the Pure Land."[44]

What is surprising about this theory, that Michinaga commissioned Muryōjuin for his own death according to the instructions of Genshin as stipulated in *Ōjō yōshū*, is the lack of sustainable evidence for any of the three assumptions. Michinaga mentions Genshin only a few times in his diary, as having received a messenger from Michinaga and Rinshi twice in the same week in the sixth lunar month of 1004 and as having his name listed at court among those receiving ecclesiastic appointments in 1004 and 1007.[45] In none of these cases did Michinaga actually meet with Genshin. The diarist Sanesuke, a close and often critical observer of Michinaga, never mentions any contact between Michinaga and Genshin. Neither does Yukinari, a member of Michinaga's most intimate circle of family and friends, who died suddenly on the same day as Michinaga in 1027 and was rarely without his company for more than twenty years.[46] Even the authors of *Eiga monogatari* make no connection between Genshin and Michinaga.

Presumably the social climate around Mount Hiei at the turn of the eleventh century would have posed problems for an association between Michinaga and Genshin. Michinaga did not join the Twenty-five Meditations Society, and, given his inborn hauteur, he was probably not inclined to befriend its constituency. On political grounds as well the association would not have been easy. Kinship ties linked Michinaga firmly to the Tendai leadership that Genshin had apparently abandoned for a life of seclusion in Yokawa when Jinzen—Michinaga's uncle—was named successor to Ryōgen as abbot. Genshin appears to have been involved only peripherally with the prominent Tendai clerics, among them Kyōen (d. 1019) and Ingen, who had been associated with Ryōgen.

Ingen is occasionally described as a disciple of Genshin, but given his career, it might be more reasonable to see him as part of the Yokawa circle—later called the "Eshin [Genshin] school" (Eshinryū)—but not exclusively defined by it.[47] He came to have an important role in Michinaga's affairs and is mentioned very frequently in the diary. When Michinaga's son Akinobu took the tonsure and became a Tendai monk in 1012, it was Ingen who officiated. Ingen must have been close to Genshin, his senior by a decade, and certainly shared his devotion to the Pure Land teaching. But Ingen went on to a career that put him at the heart of palace society as one of the most popular clerics of his time. He remained close to Michinaga despite their occasional differences. He sat with Michinaga through many an illness and was at his side when he died.

The assumption that Michinaga was very familiar with the contents of *Ōjō yōshū* is based on a single reference in Yukinari's diary. Michinaga himself makes no mention of *Ōjō yōshū* in his own diary. The lack of citation is especially noteworthy in that Michinaga frequently mentioned texts important to him, such as the *Lotus Sūtra* and *Mohe zhiguan* among many others. The very thorough Sanesuke similarly makes no reference to *Ōjō yōshū* or to Michinaga's having had access to it. In fact there is no convincing way to establish that Michinaga, some fifteen years after an apparently passing interest in *Ōjō yōshū* in 1005, was thinking about it when he commissioned Muryōjuin. As Horton has recently demonstrated, *Ōjō yōshū* was not especially well known to either clerics or lay people in the early eleventh century. Indeed, it was only toward the close of the twelfth century, around the time that *Eiga monogatari* was being written, that *Ōjō yōshū* began to have a widespread following.[48]

That Michinaga was deathly ill when he commissioned Muryōjuin is plausible but not entirely convincing. Although he is sometimes described as a man of strong constitution, he was seriously ill for much of his life with a variety of ailments aside from the epidemics of smallpox, measles, and mumps that were a devastating presence in Kyoto in his day. Michinaga almost certainly suffered from diabetes compounded by stress and probably poor nutrition as well.[49] He also had a volatile temper and was prone to sudden rages. His cruelty toward Emperor Sanjō (967–1017), who went slowly blind over a period of several years, was duly noted by a disgusted Sanesuke.[50] Those who found Michinaga's behavior intolerable took some comfort from his susceptibility to disease. By his midforties Michinaga was experiencing severe headaches, weakness, thirst, fainting spells, and general malaise. In 1012 he became so ill that he expected to die and asked Sanesuke to care for his daughters.[51] Michinaga recovered but suffered attacks of sickness in 1013, 1015, 1016, and 1017. His illness in 1016, when visitors to Tsuchimikado Mansion heard him crying with pain, was so serious that there were predictions that he would die soon.[52] He admitted to Sanesuke that his greatest fear was disease.[53]

In none of these cases did Michinaga practice *nenbutsu* recitation or otherwise avail himself of Pure Land belief as specified in *Ōjō yōshū*. Rather, he and members of his family—led by his wife Rinshi and their daughter Empress Shōshi (988–1074)—staged readings of the *Lotus Sūtra* and services such as the Thirty Lectures.[54] On several occasions Michinaga was moved into the family chapel at Tsuchimikado Mansion, where statues of Amitāyus, Śākyamuni (Japanese *Shaka*), Bhaiṣajyaguru (Japanese *Yakushi*), and Avalokiteśvara were enshrined and worshiped.[55] During extreme illness, as in 1012 and 1013, Michinaga was taken to Hosshōji, the temple of his great-grandfather Tadahira (880–949) and placed inside its Five Wisdom Kings hall (Godaidō).[56] This was common practice for invalids, since the Wisdom Kings (Vidyārāja)—and especially Acala (Japanese *Fudō*)—were believed to combat disease by vanquishing the evil spirits that caused it. Michinaga was very fearful of curses and angry ghosts (not surprising for someone with many enemies) and tended to blame them for his illnesses. His attempts to placate spirits by posthumous appointments to high office occasionally met with exasperation, as when Kyōen demanded to know from Michinaga why people should do as ghosts bid.[57] This was not a man, in other words, who turned to the Pure Land teaching for solace.

In the fourth lunar month of 1018 a new and terrifying symptom developed. Michinaga began to experience chest pains that grew so violent at times that he fainted. He was gravely ill for several months, often lapsing into unconsciousness. The symptoms were blamed on the ghost of his older brother Michikane (961–995), with whom he had at one time feuded, and on that of Sanjō.[58] Treatment involved seclusion in the Wisdom Kings hall at Hosshōji and other measures.[59] By the end of the sixth lunar month Michinaga had gone back to his normal activities. He became obsessed with the landscaping underway for the new garden at Tsuchimikado Mansion, ordering huge boulders dragged from other sites in Kyoto.[60] But his illness returned at the end of the year with worsening chest pains and general debilitation including severe diarrhea. He was also beginning to have difficulty with his vision.

Michinaga's condition deteriorated through the spring and summer months of 1019. He could no longer see well, it became hard for him to keep a diary, and he curtailed most of his activities. Visitors described how strange it was to see Michinaga sleeping in the middle of the day.[61] He was so sick by the third lunar month of 1019 that he took the tonsure. Ingen served as the officiating master and gave Michinaga the monastic name Gyōkan, "Practice Vision."[62] After several more months of illness so terrible that Michinaga told Sanesuke that it was difficult to stay alive, in the sixth lunar month of 1019, he participated in a session of *nenbutsu* recitation at his residence.[63] Six weeks later Michinaga pledged to build an eleven-bay hall east of Tsuchimikado Mansion that would enshrine ten colossal statues of Amitāyus.[64] In the third lunar month of 1020, with Ingen officiating, the hall was consecrated with the title Muryōjuin.[65] Michinaga moved into the private residence built for him to the east of the building.

Shortly thereafter Michinaga went back to his former routine and remained in fairly good health for several years despite the epidemics of plague (1020–21) and measles (1025) that killed many of his associates and left the streets of Kyoto piled with the dead.[66] What is known about Michinaga at this time comes from the diary of Sanesuke, for Michinaga no longer kept a regular record of his activities and stopped writing entirely in 1021. During this period Michinaga took greater interest in Pure Land practice. The last entries in his diary are for hundreds of thousands of *nenbutsu* recitations performed over five days.[67] Thereafter Michinaga occasionally attended more sessions of *nenbutsu* recitation. He also obtained a copy of the *Amituojing* in the hand of the ninth-century patriarch Kūkai (774–835) and showed some concern about the afterlife.[68]

Muryōjuin was put to a variety of uses in these years, including *nenbutsu* sessions, New Year's celebrations, and the tonsure of Rinshi.[69] It became known as the Amitāyus hall after 1022, when Hōjōji was dedicated. There is no evidence that the hall was understood to have a mortuary connotation involving deathbed preparation according to *Ōjō yōshū*. That there were such buildings constructed in Kyoto is evident from Sanesuke's mention of one in 1029. He calls it a rebirth hall (Ōjōin), a term not used in reference to Muryōjuin.[70] Indeed, after Michinaga's daughter Empress Kishi (1007–25) was memorialized in the Amitāyus hall shortly after her death in childbirth of measles in 1025, Michinaga had it dismantled and rebuilt to the south and west of its original site as if in purification.[71]

Michinaga reached the end of his life in the winter of 1027 after a year of physical and mental torment. His chronic illness—diabetes—had returned with severe consequences in the third month of 1027. He was intermittently bedridden, often delirious, and so weak that he could not eat or drink. In the fourth month his daughter Empress Kenshi (994–1027) became desperately ill and remained so for five months until she died, her body swollen to grotesque proportions. Services were held in her behalf at the Amitāyus hall in an attempt to keep her alive, but all was for naught.[72] Sanesuke describes Michinaga resentfully complaining to an image of Buddha about her intense suffering.[73]

The authors of *Eiga monogatari* gave Michinaga a dignified and elegant deathbed scene of his own choosing within a cocoon of *nenbutsu* recitation and concentration on Amitāyus.[74] What Sanesuke describes is not at all the same. Michinaga had lain in his private quarters for several days covered in excrement because he could no longer control his bowels. There was a tremendous abscess on his back. His attempts to recite the *nenbutsu* were unsuccessful due to fainting spells. Visitors were shocked at his bad state, which included dementia, and a rumor made the rounds that he was dead. Ingen insisted that Michinaga be moved into the Amitāyus hall. Doctors finally lanced the abscess while Michinaga shrieked and then lost consciousness. He was pronounced dead a few days later, although Sanesuke and others were not sure he had actually expired because his body was still warm to the touch.[75] Michinaga was quickly cremated and the ashes transported to the family burial ground at Kohata. Empress Shōshi initiated memorial services for Michinaga several weeks after his death. The first was held in the Amitāyus hall with a painting of Sukhāvatī and copies of the *Lotus Sūtra* as the focus of the service, as had been done for deceased members of the family for some fifty years. According to Sanesuke it was as Michinaga would have wished.[76]

The complexity of Muryōjuin as a cultural production is well demonstrated by the place it occupied in the world of Michinaga and the role it was given. It grows difficult, when that context is scrutinized, to accept without question the many assumptions and expectations in the exegesis of Muryōjuin that have been in place since the end of the twelfth century on account of the persuasive rhetoric of *Eiga monogatari* and *Ōjō yōshū*. Without any doubt Muryōjuin had fundamental features in common with what Genshin presented in *Ōjō yōshū*. There is good sense in linking the one to the other. Both emerged out of a widespread Tendai subculture that put stock in Amitāyus as a savior and in the liberating effects of visualization and *nenbutsu* recitation as the means of access to him. What must be kept in mind, however, and what needs to be further elaborated, is the very special circumstance that forced Michinaga and his advisers, most prominently Ingen, to conceive of so unique—and in their context so utterly logical—a resolution to their needs. That this circumstance may well have been a product of chance, and its resolution a matter of improvisation rather than predictability, draws attention to the often random nature of cultural developments. It also returns the argument to the question of light as opposed to seeing.

MICHINAGA'S BLINDNESS

There is much about Muryōjuin that can be explained by keeping in mind the basic goals of the Pure Land teaching as it was known to Michinaga and his contemporaries. The hall drew on the same reservoir of imagery and expectation as did the circumambulation hall and, by extension, the rebirth hall. But its singularity is also evident. It housed nine monumental statues of Amitāyus—the first example of such an arrangement—with only the central figure provided with accompanying images of Avalokiteśvara and Mahāsthāmaprāpta. There were paintings of the nine levels of rebirth on its walls with the figures of Amitāyus rendered in gold and silver pigment. From what documentary sources have to say it is likely that the only other known examples of such paintings at that time were found in the circumambulation halls at Enryakuji. On structural grounds Muryōjuin was also unusual. It was rectangular rather than square in plan, of very large size to accommodate the enormous statues, and extravagantly decorated. Equally important, a complex of lake and gardens had been landscaped precisely to accommodate it in its westerly orientation.

There is enough specificity to the iconography and program to identify the possible source. In general terms the connection to the *Amituojing* is fairly obvious. A thousand copies of the sūtra had even been offered as part of the Muryōjuin consecration ceremony.[77] It was perhaps the best-known Pure Land scripture of Michinaga's day, although as noted he was not as interested in it as he was in other sūtras. Early on he had made copies of the *Amituojing*, once as part of a group of sūtras for ritual burial on the sacred mountain Kinpusen,[78] and then in 1011 most likely with the ailing Ichijō in mind. He mentions the *Amituojing* only once more in his diary, when he reports that he had it recited at Tsuchimikado Mansion in the twelfth lunar month of 1018.[79] Certainly the *Amituojing* was a feature of the *fudan nenbutsu* sessions that Michinaga had attended over the years. Its brevity—one fascicle—made it ideal for use in chanting and other devotional services, and its simplicity has always allowed for a quick grasp of the fundamentals of the Pure Land teaching. But absent from the text is mention of the nine levels of rebirth. Nor are the levels mentioned in the much longer and more elaborately argued *Wuliangshou jing*, of which the *Amituojing* is a succinct version.

The nine levels do appear in detail in the *Guan Wuliangshou jing*. Indeed, they are central to the story of Vaidehī and represent the final stages of her quest for a vision of Amitāyus in Sukhāvatī. For many reasons, not least the extended descriptions of the welcoming deathbed manifestations of Amitāyus in the latter half of the sūtra, the *Guan Wuliangshou jing* has tended to be understood in terms of what it offers as a guide to salvation through *nenbutsu* recitation with Amitāyus in mind. Julian Pas has made a good case that this emphasis on salvation and rebirth has "somehow obscured the original intention" of the sūtra.

That intention—assuming that such agency can be reconstructed—is rather a "vision quest," as Raoul Birnbaum would put it, and more precisely, a quest for "how to obtain a vision of this Buddha Amita in this life."[80] Even a general reading of the first nine contemplations that Vaidehī must successfully complete underscores the logic of what Pas has to say. Through them she is brought, detail by eidetic detail, to an encounter with the brilliantly gleaming body of Amitāyus. From that point, having seen his form (or sensed it through the dazzling light), Vaidehī can proceed through the next four contemplations to the final three that yield, at last, the nine levels of rebirth in three grades of spiritual qualification.

Whatever else it may be—the story of a devout queen seeking Buddha, a description of Sukhāvatī, a primer for *nenbutsu*—the *Guan Wuliangshou jing* is first and foremost a text about seeing Amitāyus and Sukhāvatī. It deploys a variety of terms for seeing from *guan,* "visualizing," and *jian,* "physically seeing," to *nian,* "recollecting." The words appear repeatedly, in phrase after phrase that emphasizes how, with proper practice, it will be possible to see Amitāyus and Sukhāvatī "whether the eyes are open or shut" (T.12.342a3–4). Rebirth itself involves the ocular aspect. Those born at the top of the hierarchy, in the highest grade, are granted sight more or less immediately. Those in the middle and lowest grades, although they have occasional sight, must make do with hearing the voices and sounds of Sukhāvatī.[81]

Michinaga had little to do with the *Guan Wuliangshou jing* until shortly before he decided to construct Muryōjuin. By comparison with the *Lotus Sūtra* it was not an especially popular text in the early eleventh century. However, there are sporadic references to it in connection with the family and friends of Michinaga. Yukinari records making a copy of it in 1000, along with other sūtras, and in 1002 he attended a memorial service for Michinaga's sister Senshi, at the Gedatsuji circumambulation hall, that featured a transcription of the *Guan Wuliangshou jing* in sixteen fascicles.[82] The only time that Michinaga himself mentions the *Guan Wuliangshou jing* is in the fifth lunar month of 1018, when he had Ingen punctuate a copy that he was using for the consecration of a sandalwood statue of Amitāyus.[83] Nonetheless, it is reasonable to assume that Michinaga probably had enough general knowledge of the sūtra to have been inspired to build Muryōjuin. But under the circumstances it seems more than coincidental that Michinaga's apparently sudden interest in the *Guan Wuliangshou jing* followed by a pledge to build Muryōjuin occurred just as he was going blind.

In the last months of 1018 Michinaga began to complain to Sanesuke that he was having trouble seeing. It was difficult for him to make out people across a room, and everything appeared as if in twilight. The problem had begun a year before.[84] In an attempt to heal his eyes Michinaga held the Eye of the Buddha service (Butsugen Hō) with the monk Shinyo (d. ca. 1029) officiating.[85] A week later he initiated the readings of the *Amituojing* at Tsuchimikado Mansion noted earlier. By the second lunar month of 1019 Michinaga was visually impaired to a significant degree. He reported—and the edge of fear still registers in his words these many centuries later—that he could barely see the faces of his friends and was no longer able to read. He could not see statues or monks. "How will I be able to see my garden?" he wrote. "What will I do if this gets worse?"[86] About a month later Michinaga took the tonsure as Gyōkan, "Practice Sight." Four months after that, in the seventh lunar month of 1019, as he suffered from chest pains and weakness, he pledged to build Muryōjuin.

The full extent of Michinaga's vision problems, and whether he remained impaired after 1019, is difficult to determine with any precision. Circumstantial evidence points to lasting loss of eyesight. This would be consistent with cataracts or retinopathy resulting from diabetes.[87] There are sporadic references to Michinaga's blindness after 1020. In the eighth month of 1021 he went to pray at Ishiyamadera, a day's journey away in nearby Ōmi Province, in the hope that his eyes would be healed.[88] In 1027 Sanesuke mentions that Michinaga had not been able to make a copy of the *Amituojing,* to be used in services for Kenshi, because he was unable to see clearly.[89] That he stopped writing his own diary in 1021, after years of faithfully keeping it, further suggests lasting visual impairment. In this context there is something poignant about the hundreds of thousands of *nenbutsu* recitations with which the diary ends.

Commentators have had surprisingly little to say about the blindness of Michinaga. It is not mentioned at all in *Eiga monogatari,* which raises important questions about how this much-cited text figures in historical writing. Modern historians have noted Michinaga's blindness but do not explore the ramifications of so debilitating a turn of events for so domineering a personality. Only Hurst has addressed directly both the blindness and the stress involved.[90] Most astonishing of all is the silence among art historians in regard to Michinaga's blindness. This is especially noteworthy because the period of his most avid patronage of Buddhist imagery, from 1020 through his death at the end of 1027, was also one of debilitating visual impairment.

It may well be that such lacunae have resulted from Michinaga's own wish to keep his affliction a secret. His was not the public drama that ensued as Sanjō went slowly blind from 1014 through 1015. Michinaga had behaved abominably toward Sanjō, as Sanesuke noted with distaste, complaining angrily about his inability to see and forcing him to abdicate as a result.[91] Five years later it is easy to understand that Michinaga might not have wanted to publicize his own loss of sight. He had also watched as Sanjō was treated with various medicines and Buddhist rituals, none of which had had any effect. Possibly this indicated to Michinaga that other therapies needed to be explored.

Following the consecration of Muryōjuin in 1020 Michinaga took up residence in the private quarters built for him just east of the hall. Within weeks he began an ambitious campaign to build up the land around Muryōjuin into the impressive complex that would become Hōjōji. Over several years Michinaga supervised the expansion of the Muryōjuin site well beyond anything Sanesuke, ever disapproving, had seen in thirty years of service. The area of the complex doubled to the huge size of two *chō*, or approximately 2.5 hectares, far in excess of the normal standard allowed courtiers under the law.[92] Laborers throughout the city were conscripted to drag more boulders to the site.[93] An extraordinary amount of wood was delivered for the construction of three huge halls and upwards of twenty-six colossal statues, some of it brought from homes of Kyoto courtiers ordered dismantled by Michinaga.[94] The smallest of these sculptures were equivalent in size—nearly three meters in height—to the Phoenix Hall Amitāyus. Michinaga also ordered hundreds of similarly enormous paintings. Sanesuke was beside himself at Michinaga's extravagance and lack of consideration for the Kyoto populace. These were times of epidemic, he wrote in his diary; people were dying. He described Michinaga as heartless in the face of so much suffering around him.[95]

Michinaga's relentless determination to build a temple complex at Muryōjuin—the only period in his life when he was so single-mindedly devoted to such a project—suggests several motivating factors. He may well have come to the conclusion, on going blind after months of serious illness including heart problems, that he was being punished for his sins. On the one hand there was the ever-present menace of angry ghosts. Sanjō, to whom Michinaga had been exceedingly mean, had died only recently. Many others now dead surely bore him a grudge as well. On the other hand there was the teaching of Michinaga's own tutelary scripture, the *Lotus Sūtra,* which in its twenty-eighth chapter threatens sinners with poor health and loss of eyesight.[96] It is certainly possible that Michinaga sought to regain both spiritual merit and good health by building Buddha worship halls and making Buddha statues as stipulated in the sūtra.

The importance of the *Lotus Sūtra* to the project is apparent in Sanesuke's comments to Michinaga on the day of the consecration of the main hall at Hōjōji in 1022. He had found Michinaga weeping at the main gate as the entourage of his grandson and son-in-law, Emperor Go Ichijō (1008–36), made its way into the compound. Sanesuke was moved enough to paraphrase the

Lotus Sūtra to Michinaga as he praised him for having built the temple. He said its goodness recalled the purifying white light that shone from Buddha's forehead as he began to teach the sūtra. It was a goodness of such merit that it would help bring salvation to all as it illuminated the universe.[97]

That Sanesuke spoke of light is telling in view of the strong possibility that Michinaga could not see much of what was being consecrated that day. It is important to keep in mind that the Hōjōji complex, including the temple's main hall, came after the construction of Muryōjuin and not before. Not only was this an inversion of standard practice, with what would typically have been a subsidiary hall built before the principal hall, but it also marked a departure from custom in the primacy of the Amitāyus hall. This points strongly to a specific agenda, and need, in the initial conceptualization and construction of the hall. After all, it is the *Guan Wuliangshou jing* that provides the iconographical framework for Muryōjuin, as seen in the nine statues, with their references to the nine visualizations that precede the encounter with Amitāyus, and the paintings of the nine levels of rebirth in Sukhāvatī. Muryōjuin on the west bank of its lake seems itself to stand for the palace of Amitāyus in Sukhāvatī, again as described in the *Guan Wuliangshou jing.*

For a man going blind at the height of his career the *Guan Wuliangshou jing* may have had a special resonance. As a sūtra about finding a way to see "whether the eyes are open or shut," and one that furthermore promises sightedness to those who follow its instructions, the *Guan Wuliangshou jing* must have appealed to Michinaga as his sight began to diminish. It is noteworthy that his interest in the sūtra dates to the period when he had begun to have difficulty seeing. That the sūtra was new to him is suggested by the need for Ingen to punctuate a copy for him. Why Michinaga was drawn to the *Guan Wuliangshou jing,* as opposed to the more commonly known *Amituojing,* is impossible to know. But it bears consideration that there possibly existed in Michinaga's day a connection between visualization sūtras and the blind. Indeed, Sanesuke records a blind recluse reciting the *Guanfo sanmei hai jing* in 1015, the only time this text is mentioned in his diary.[98] It could be that Michinaga's growing interest in the Pure Land teaching after around 1018 was not entirely due to fear of death. On the contrary, he was attracted to the teaching, and its texts, because he wanted to see.

Muryōjuin was the extraordinary result of Michinaga's quest for vision. As an improvisation it drew upon the past to arrive at an iconographical and architectural solution that was traditional but also innovative and even radical. It would make sense that Ingen played a part in guiding Michinaga toward that goal. His roots were in the Yokawa community that Michinaga had known as a young man, when at the turn of the eleventh century he had attended *fudan nenbutsu* sessions at Enryakuji and become acquainted with the circumambulation hall and its rituals. In earlier times Michinaga had also studied *Mohe zhiguan* and other works by Zhiyi. Given this background, it is likely that Michinaga knew the *Pratyutpannasamādhi sūtra* and remembered its emphasis on seeing Buddha, and specifically Amitāyus, through *nenbutsu* recitation. In later life, as the crisis of blindness engulfed him, Michinaga—no doubt bolstered by the advocacy of Ingen—brought together this earlier foundation of knowledge with a more recent and personal commitment to the *Guan Wuliangshou jing*. The result was a worship hall and conceptual program—Muryōjuin—the likes of which he might never have considered had he not gone blind.

It is significant that the main hall of Hōjōji, consecrated some twenty-eight months after Muryōjuin,[99] had as its primary object of worship a colossal statue—more than fifteen meters in height—of Mahāvairocana (Japanese *Dainichi*). There is nothing unusual in this choice, as images of Mahāvairocana, like those of Śakyāmuni, were typically installed in the main halls of temples in Michinaga's day. Nonetheless, the juxtaposition of Amitāyus and Mahāvairocana, setting aside (but not dismissing) their complex shared identity in the esoteric teaching of emanation that would have been well known to Michinaga, is provocative in the context of his blindness. For Mahāvairocana is the absolute *Buddha solaris* whose blazing light illuminates the cosmos, just as Amitāyus shines on Sukhāvatī and gives life to its inhabitants. Ultimately Hōjōji takes on a special dimension as a temple, inhabited by Michinaga, where the light of Buddha is the determining conceptual framework to which all else—the halls for penitence and protection, the chapels for the private devotions of Rinshi and Shōshi—is subordinated.

Over the centuries and through history one of the fundamental features of Muryōjuin, ironically enough, has been obscured. Because it has been understood in terms of *Ōjō yōshū* and *Eiga monogatari*, and because it holds much in common with the Pure Land worldview of those texts, Muryōjuin has been explained as meaning one thing when it most probably means something rather different. To say that it was intended as a site for Michinaga to achieve salvation through *nenbutsu* recitation, as stipulated by Genshin and other Pure Land advocates with whom Michinaga demonstrably had no contact, is to stop far short of the complete picture. It was certainly that to some degree, but Muryōjuin—in its anomaly and idiosyncrasy—also looked back to the venerable Tendai tradition that linked *nenbutsu* to seeing. Michinaga may have wanted to be reborn in Sukhāvatī, but first he wanted to be able to see.

SEEING THE LIGHT

It is useful to consider what there was for Michinaga to see at Muryōjuin on the day of its consecration and in the years that followed. Inside the structure stood nine gigantic statues covered in gold leaf. They occupied a space with polished floors, golden fixtures, and ample mother-of-pearl and glass or crystal inlay. It would have looked much like the interior of Konjikidō (fig. 9.1). Illuminated by the light of a lamp, or with sunlight entering from the east with the doors thrown open to receive it, the hall and its statues would have offered a glittering "magnificent display" that well suits the notion of Sukhāvatī. *Eiga monogatari* describes the light festival that Michinaga held at Muryōjuin in 1023. At sunset thousands of lanterns were lit around the complex and inside the hall as courtiers gathered bringing their own lamps with them. It seemed as though a million lights flickered in the night air to illuminate the ten worlds of the cosmos. The radiance was such that the blind began to gather outside the gates.[100]

This environment provides clues about what Michinaga might have wanted to see as his eyes began to fail him. It seems reasonable to suppose that it was light. The array of large statues in their immensity was possibly visible to him as indistinct forms, but their golden glow may well have offered something far more meaningful. Just as Vaidehī felt the illuminating power of Amitāyus as a body of light, so Michinaga gained a form of insight through the sheer experience of a light-filled space given over to the celebration of Amitāyus and Sukhāvatī. The tendency to understand Muryōjuin in terms of *Ōjō yōshū* has meant that a pivotal feature of the *Guan Wuliangshou jing*, the connection of vision to light, has been downplayed in favor of vision and salvation. In the circumstances of Michinaga's blindness it is well worth considering that the quest for salvation was secondary. He had come to know the *Guan Wuliangshou jing* late in life and in the crisis of his visual impairment. Through Muryōjuin he gave form to what the sūtra meant to him as a blind man who, like Vaidehī with her as yet ordinary eyes, wanted to see the light of Amitāyus.

In many ways the story of Michinaga, layered upon that of Vaidehī, calls to mind that archetypal journey from darkness into light, and toward redemption, that has been told over the millennia. It is found when Dante and Beatrice turn toward the noonday sun as they start the quest that will take them to the heaven of pure light called the Empyrean, a quest during which Dante, too, loses his sight after looking into a brilliant point of light but is finally granted vision; or when the resplendent image inside the Buddha Shadow Cave appears to Xuanzang and other monks out of the elemental darkness of its grotto. The stories point to an ancient awareness of the mystery of light and its nuclear powers. These words of a modern quantum physicist, Arthur Zajonc, are a reminder that the mystery still holds. Zajonc speaks of light as "a very specific thing" that cannot be anything in particular, whether polarization, wavelength, direction, or intensity. "What are the primary qualities of light that vouchsafe its unambiguous existence?" he asks. "The extraordinary response given by quantum realism is that there are none. Light, as an enduring, well-defined, local entity, vanishes. In its place a subtle, entangled object evolves, holding all four of its quantum qualities suspended within itself, until the fatal act of measurement."[101]

It bears thinking about that light is the property around which the *Guan Wuliangshou jing* is structured in its most basic sense. Light frames and sets in motion the vision quest; light is the body of Amitāyus; it is also the insight that grants access to it. There is much to be said for the possibility that Michinaga, in his attraction to this text in the context of his own blindness, initiated Muryōjuin, and ultimately Pure Land visual culture, in effect as a matter of chance. In this sense Muryōjuin did not follow logically from any particular Pure Land teaching and was in fact a product of unpredictability and improvisation. It was a specific, and stochastic, event—a mutation—that yielded the means, and the opportunity, for a process of cultural development that led to Pure Land visual culture but did not itself predict it. The lesson to be learned is that cultural historians may not always see what they are looking at.

NOTES

1. *Guan Wuliangshou jing*, in *Taishō shinshū Daizōkyō* [Newly Revised Tripitaka of the Taishō Era], ed. Takakusu Junjirō, Watanabe Kaikyoku, and Ono Genmyō (Tokyo: Daizō Shuppan, 1924–32), 100 vols., 12:342c17–18 (T.12.342c17–18). Hereafter citations from *Taishō shinshū Daizōkyō* will appear in the text in the abbreviated format noted in parentheses.

2. There is no Sanskrit equivalent. Names, terms, and titles are given in Sanskrit, when known, or in Chinese when that is the original language. Japanese equivalents are provided when relevant.

3. Daniel B. Stevenson, "The Problematic of the *Mo-ho chih-kuan* and T'ien-t'ai History," in *The Great Calming and Contemplation: A Study and Annotated Translation of the First Chapter of Chih-i's* Mo-ho chih-kuan, ed. Neil Donner and David B. Stevenson (Honolulu: University of Hawaii Press, 1993), p. 78. He finds this "decorum" manifested, for example, in the invocatory structure of ritual and visualization in the four forms of meditation (*samādhi*) in Tiantai monastic practice as presented by Zhiyi (538–97) in *Mohe zhiguan* [The Great Calming and Contemplation].

4. For a comprehensive discussion of visualization sūtras, see Nobuyoshi Yamabe, "*The Sūtra on the Ocean-Like Samādhi of the Visualization of the Buddha:* The Interfusion of the Chinese and Indian Cultures in Central Asia as Reflected in a Fifth Century Apocryphal Sūtra" (Ph.D. diss., Yale University, 1999).

5. Alan Sponberg, "Meditation in Fa-hsiang Buddhism," in *Traditions of Meditation in Chinese Buddhism,* ed. Peter N. Gregory (Honolulu: University of Hawai'i Press, 1986), pp. 22, 25, 27.

6. Neil Donner and David B. Stevenson, "An Annotated Translation of the First Chapter of the *Mo-ho chih-kuan,*" in Donner and Stevenson, *The Great Calming and Contemplation,* pp. 234–35, 239. For the *Pratyutpannasamādhi sūtra,* see Paul Harrison, *The Samādhi of Direct Encounter with the Buddhas of the Present: An Annotated English Translation of the Tibetan Version of the Pratyutpanna-Buddha-Sammukhāvasthita-Samādhi-Sūtra* (Tokyo: International Institute for Buddhist Studies, 1990).

7. Luis O. Gómez, *The Land of Bliss, The Paradise of the Buddha of Measureless Light: Sanskrit and Chinese Versions of the* Sukhāvatīvyūha Sūtras (Honolulu: University of Hawai'i Press, 1996), pp. 3, 223 n. 1.

8. Alexander C. Soper, "Aspects of Light Symbolism in Gandhāran Sculpture, Part III," *Artibus Asiae* 13, no. 1–2 (1950): 73.

9. Gómez, *Land of Bliss,* p. 177. The titles are after Gómez.

10. J. G. Ballard, *The Crystal World* (New York: Farrar, Straus and Giroux, 1988), pp. 200–203.

11. In classical Japan the most common designations for Amitāyus were Amida, after Amita ("Measureless"), and Muryōju (Amitāyus, "Measureless Life"). The designation for Amitābha ("Measureless Light"), Muryōkō, was not common.

12. For a study of the Phoenix Hall and its Pure Land scheme, see Mimi Hall Yiengpruksawan, "The Phoenix Hall at Uji and the Symmetries of Replication," *Art Bulletin* 77, no. 4 (December 1995): 647–72.

13. For an exhaustive study of Pure Land temple architecture, see Shimizu Hiroshi, *Heian jidai bukkyō kenchikushi no kenkyū* [Researches on Buddhist Architecture of the Heian Period] (Tokyo: Chūō Kōron, 1992).

14. Ibid., pp. 244–49, 255–56.

15. Ibid., pp. 45–46. *Fusō ryakki,* in *Shintei Zōho kokushi taikei* [A Library of Japanese History], rev. ed., ed. Kuroita Katsumi, 60 vols. (Tokyo: Yoshikawa Kōbunkan, 1929–64), 12:274 (Kannin 4/1020.3.22); *A Tale of Flowering Fortunes,* trans. William H. McCullough and Helen Craig McCullough, 2 vols. (Stanford, CA: Stanford University Press, 1988), 2:564–69; *Eiga monogatari,* ed. Yamanaka Yutaka, Akiyama Ken, Ikeda Naotake, Fukunaga Susumu, 3 vols. (Tokyo: Shōgakukan, 1997), 2:299–306; *Shoji kuyō ruiki,* in *Kōkan bijutsu shiryō, Jiinhen* [Published Exchange of Primary Historical Sources on Art, Temples and Monasteries Edition], ed. Fujita Tsuneyo, 3 vols. (Tokyo: Chūō Kōron, 1975), 2:464–66.

16. Shimizu, *Heian jidai bukkyō kenchikushi no kenkyū,* pp. 42–68; *Shoji kuyō ruiki,* pp. 467–78.

17. *A Tale of Flowering Fortunes*, 2:564; *Eiga monogatari*, 2:299.

18. *A Tale of Flowering Fortunes*, 2:545, 554; *Eiga monogatari*, 2:264–65, 276. *Sakeiki* [Diary of Tsuneyori, Major Controller of the Left], in *Zōho shiryō taisei* [Historical Materials], rev. ed., ed. Zōho Shiryō Taisei Kanseikai, 43 vols. (Kyoto: Rinsen Shoten, 1965), 6:91 (Kannin 4/1020.3.20). Eventually Michinaga posted a "no trespassing" sign; see *Shōyūki* [Diary of the Onomiya Minister of the Right], in *Dai Nihon kokiroku* [Records of Japan], ed. Tokyo Daigaku Shiryō Hensansho, 20 vols. (Tokyo: Iwanami Shoten, 1952–91), vol. 10, pts. 1–11, vol. 5, p. 251 (Kannin 4/1020.11.13).

19. *A Tale of Flowering Fortunes*, 2:760, 762–63. *Eiga monogatari*, 3:155, 162–66.

20. Shimizu, *Heian jidai bukkyō kenchikushi no kenkyū*, p. 279.

21. Ibid., pp. 230–34; Hamada Takashi, *Gokuraku e no dōkei* [Yearning for the Pure Land] (Tokyo: Bijutsu Shuppansha, 1975), pp. 111–16.

22. Donner and Stevenson, "Annotated Translation," pp. 248–69.

23. For circumambulation halls, see Shimizu, *Heian jidai bukkyō kenchikushi no kenkyū*, pp. 23–26, 235; and *Gonki* [Diary of the Provisional Major Counsellor], in *Dai Nihon kokiroku*, vols. 4–5, vol. 1, p. 236 (Chōho 3/1001.12.14), p. 271 (Chōho 4/1002.9.17). For *fudan nenbutsu*, see *Shōyūki*, 1:151 (Eien 2/988.12.17); *Gonki*, 2:196 (Kankō 1/1004.Intercalary 9.15).

24. Sarah Johanna Horton, "The Role of Genshin and Religious Associations in the Mid-Heian Spread of Pure Land Buddhism" (Ph.D. diss., Yale University, 2001).

25. *Ōjō yōshū*, in *Genshin* Ōjō yōshū [Genshin's *Ōjō yōshū*], ed. Ishida Mizumarō (Tokyo: Iwanami Shoten, 1991), p. 376a8–20.

26. Horton, "The Role of Genshin," pp. 127–49.

27. Ibid., pp. 73–74, 92–93, 128–37.

28. *Shōyūki*, 1:129 (Eien 1/987.4.29); *Midō Kanpaku ki* [Diary of the Muryōjuin Regent], in *Dai Nihon kokiroku*, vol. 1, pts. 1–5, vol. 2, p. 170 (Chōwa 1/1012.10.6).

29. *Gonki*, 1:94 (Chōho 1/999.12.5), 2:162 (Kankō 8/1011.6.22).

30. Neil McMullin, "The *Lotus Sutra* and Politics in the Mid-Heian Period," in *The Lotus Sutra in Japanese Culture*, ed. George J. Tanabe, Jr., and Willa Jane Tanabe (Honolulu: University of Hawai'i Press, 1989), pp. 123–29; Jacqueline I. Stone, *Original Enlightenment and the Transformation of Medieval Japanese Buddhism* (Honolulu: University of Hawai'i Press, 1999), p. 111.

31. *Shōyūki*, 3:3 (Chōwa 1/1012.4.5–6), 3:26–27 (Chōwa 1/1012.5.22–24).

32. *Midō Kanpaku ki*, 1:96 (Kankō 1/1004.6.22, 6.26).

33. *Gonki*, 2:39 (Kankō 2/1005.9.17).

34. *Midō Kanpaku ki*, 1:103 (Kankō 1/1004.8.17).

35. *Midō Kanpaku ki*, 1:111 (Kankō 1/1004. Intercalary 9.17), 1:161 (Kankō 2/1005.10.12), 1:200 (Kankō 3/1006.12.22); *Gonki*, 1:271 (Chōho 4/1002.9.17), 2:47 (Kankō 2/1005.12.23).

36. *Gonki*, 1:271 (Chōho 4/1002.9.17), 2:162 (Kankō 8/1011.6.22); *Midō Kanpaku ki*, 2:111 (Kankō 8/1011.6.22).

37. *Midō Kanpaku ki,* 2:98 (Kankō 8/1011.3.27); *Shōyūki,* 2:174 (Kankō 8/1011.3.27); *Gonki,* 2:153 (Kankō 8/1011.3.27).

38. G. Cameron Hurst III, "Michinaga's Maladies: A Medical Report on Fujiwara no Michinaga," *Monumenta Nipponica* 34, no. 1 (Spring 1979): 109–11.

39. *Midō Kanpaku ki,* 1:98 (Kankō 1/1004.7.8), 1:107 (Kankō 1/1004.9.8, 9.19), 1:144 (Kankō 2/1005.5.4), 2:229 (Chōwa 2/1013.6.22); *Gonki,* 1:243 (Chōho 4/1002.1.4), 1:244 (Chōho 4/1002.1.18), 1:245 (Chōho 4/1002.2.6), 1:260 (Chōho 4/1002.5.13).

40. For the ideological importance of the *Lotus Sūtra* in the later mythologizing of Michinaga, see William E. Deal, "The *Lotus Sutra* and the Rhetoric of Legitimization in Eleventh-Century Japanese Buddhism," *Japanese Journal of Religious Studies* 20, no. 4 (December 1993): 216–95.

41. *Midō Kanpaku ki,* 3:16 (Chōwa 4/1015.*6.22).

42. Shimizu, *Heian jidai bukkyō kenchikushi no kenkyū,* p. 324; Willa Jane Tanabe, "The Lotus Lectures: *Hokke Hakkō* in the Heian Period," *Monumenta Nipponica* 39, no. 4 (Winter 1984): 401–3.

43. Shimizu, *Heian jidai bukkyō kenchikushi no kenkyū,* pp. 43, 68 (no. 28); Yamanaka Yutaka, *Fujiwara no Michinaga* (Tokyo: Kyoikusha, 1988), pp. 245, 253, 268–69.

44. *A Tale of Flowering Fortunes,* 2:569, 573–74; *Eiga monogatari,* 2:306, 314; Horton, "The Role of Genshin," pp. 75–76.

45. *Midō Kanpaku ki,* 1:91 (Kankō 1/1004.5.24), 1:244 (Kankō 4/1007.12.16).

46. *Shōyūki,* 8:45 (Manju 4/1027.12.4).

47. Yamanaka, *Fujiwara no Michinaga,* p. 245. See also *Shōyūki,* 4:60 (Chōwa 4/1015.7.21), where Sanesuke describes Ingen as a disciple of the past abbot Gakukyō (d. early eleventh century).

48. Horton, "The Role of Genshin," pp. 36–38, 68–70, 90.

49. Hurst, "Michinaga's Maladies," pp. 104–8.

50. *Shōyūki,* 4:7 (Chōwa 4/1015.4.13), 4:30 (Chōwa 4/1015.5.19).

51. *Shōyūki,* 3:36 (Chōwa 1/1012.6.9).

52. *Shōyūki,* 4:187 (Chōwa 5/1016.5.10), 4:190 (Chōwa 5/1016.5.18).

53. *Shōyūki,* 4:39 (Chōwa 4/1016.6.13).

54. *Shōyūki,* 3:34 (Chōwa 1/1012.6.6), 4:187 (Chōwa 5/1016.5.10).

55. *Shōyūki,* 3:35 (Chōwa 1/1012.6.8). For statues in the chapel, see *Gonki,* 1:249 (Chōho 4/1002.3.1).

56. *Midō Kanpaku ki,* 2:238 (Chōwa 2/1013.8.14).

57. *Shōyūki,* 4:32 (Chōwa 4/1015.5.22).

58. *Shōyūki,* 5:22 (Kannin 2/1018.*4.20), 5:26 (Kannin 2/1018.5.2).

59. *Midō Kanpaku ki,* 3:160 (Kannin 2/1018.*4.16); *Shōyūki,* 5:21 (Kannin 2/1018.*4.16).

60. *Shōyūki,* 5:45 (Kannin 2/1018.6.26).

61. *Shōyūki,* 5:141 (Kannin 3/1019.4.28).

62. *Shōyūki,* 5:128 (Kannin 3/1019.3.21).

63. *Shōyūki,* 5:152 (Kannin 3/1019.6.1).

64. *Shōyūki,* 5:171 (Kannin 3/1019.7.17). The citation lists "ten" and not "nine" statues, but nine statues were dedicated in 1020. Possibly at the outset Michinaga considered ten statues in connection with the ten worlds illuminated by Buddha as he instructs Vaidehī in her quest.

65. *Midō Kanpaku ki,* 3:220 (Kannin 4/1020.3.22); *Sakeiki,* 91 (Kannin 4/1020.3.22).

66. *Shōyūki,* 6:13 (Jian 1/1021.2.21), 7:113 (Manju 2/1025.7.27), 7:118 (Manju 2/1025.8.8).

67. *Midō Kanpaku ki,* 3:228 (Kannin 5/1021.9.1–5).

68. *Shōyūki,* 6:124 (Jian 2/1022.10.13), 6:168–169 (Jian 3/1023.5.28).

69. *Shōyūki,* 6:1 (Jian 1/1021.1.1), 6:15 (Jian 1/1021.2.29), 7:108 (Manju 2/1025.7.15).

70. *Shōyūki,* 8:159 (Chōgen 2/1029.9.8).

71. *Shōyūki,* 7:150 (Manju 2/1025.10.24–25).

72. *Shōyūki,* 8:30 (Manju 4/1027.9.14).

73. *Shōyūki,* 8:26 (Manju 4/1027.9.6).

74. *A Tale of Flowering Fortunes,* 2:760, 762–63; *Eiga monogatari,* 3:155, 162–66.

75. For these scenes, see Hurst, "Michinaga's Maladies," pp. 106–8; and *Shōyūki,* 8:37–45.

76. *Shōyūki,* 8:53 (Manju 4/1027.12.16), 8:57 (Manju 4/1027.12.28).

77. *Shoji kuyō ruiki,* p. 465.

78. *Midō Kanpaku ki,* 1:229 (Kankō 4/1007.8.11).

79. *Midō Kanpaku ki,* 3:188 (Kannin 4/1018.12.2).

80. Julian F. Pas, *Visions of Sukhāvatī: Shan-Tao's Commentary on the* Kuan Wu-Liang-Shou-Fo Ching (Albany: State University of New York Press, 1995), p. x.

81. See T.12.344c24–25 (highest grade, first level), 345a15–16 (highest grade, second level), 345a29–345b1 (highest grade, third level), 345b15–16 (middle grade, first level), 345b27–29 (middle grade, second level), 345c5–7 (middle grade, third level), 345c21–25 (bottom grade, first level), 346a8–11 (bottom grade, second level), and 345a22–25 (bottom grade, third level).

82. *Gonki,* 1:179 (Chōho 2/1000.12.8), 1:271 (Chōho 4/1002.9.17).

83. *Midō Kanpaku ki,* 3:164 (Kannin 2/1018.5.29).

84. *Shōyūki,* 5:56 (Kannin 2/1018.10.17), 5:88–89 (Kannin 2/1018.12.22–24).

85. *Midō Kanpaku ki,* 3:187 (Kannin 2/1018.11.24).

86. *Midō Kanpaku ki,* 3:192 (Kannin 3/1019.1.15), 3:194–95 (Kannin 3/1019.2.6).

87. Hurst, "Michinaga's Maladies," pp. 104, 108.

88. *Shōyūki,* 6:34 (Jian 1/1021.8.1).

89. *Shōyūki,* 8:20 (Manju 4/1027.8.23).

90. Hurst, "Michinaga's Maladies," pp. 103–4. For a typical treatment of Michinaga's blindness, see Yamanaka, *Fujiwara no Michinaga,* pp. 233–34, 236–37, 253.

91. *Shōyūki,* 4:68 (Chōwa 4/1015.8.20).

92. Shimizu, *Heian jidai bukkyō kenchikushi no kenkyū,* p. 58. For regulations, see Yamada Kunikazu, "Jōkō no gosho: Goin" [Palaces of Retired Emperors: Retirement

Temples], in *Yomigaeru Heiankyō* [Bringing Ancient Kyoto Back to Life], ed. Murai Yasuhiko (Tokyo: Tankōsha, 1995), p. 36.

93. At one point Sanesuke wondered whether there would be any boulders left in Kyoto; see *Shōyūki,* 6:172 (Jian 3/1023.6.11).

94. *Shōyūki,* 7:80 (Manju 1/1024.12.27).

95. *Shōyūki,* 6:23 (Jian 1/1021.3.29).

96. I am grateful to William Bodiford for reminding me of this passage.

97. *Shōyūki,* 6:119 (Jian 2/1022.7.14).

98. *Shōyūki,* 4:72 (Chōwa 4/1015.9.10).

99. Possibly this relates to the twenty-eight chapters of the *Lotus Sūtra.* Matthew Kapstein, personal communication, has suggested a connection with the twenty-eight constellations.

100. *A Tale of Flowering Fortunes,* 2: 587–89; *Eiga monogatari,* 2:342–45.

101. Arthur Zajonc, *Catching the Light: The Entwined History of Light and Mind* (New York: Bantam Books, 1993), p. 315.

PART FOUR

Concluding Reflections

CHAPTER TEN

Rethinking Religious Experience: Seeing the Light in the History of Religions

Matthew T. Kapstein

There is in God (some say)
A deep, but dazling darkness.

Henry Vaughan, *Silex Scintillans*

INEFFABILITY AND CONTENT

Throughout this book we have examined religious experiences of light in a variety of cultural-historical settings and from several distinct disciplinary perspectives. Inevitably the question arises, whether these varied investigations, scattered like so many independent points of light, cohere to form a single beam, illuminating the study of religious experience in general. One's initial response to this challenge will in large measure turn on the presuppositions one brings to the discussion, as the readers commissioned by the Press to review this book in manuscript demonstrated in their remarks: while one referee stated that "the thematic focus [on light] does work to structure the essays and give the work noticeable coherence," another commented that "despite the fact that they all deal *in some sense or another* with the themes of light and vision, they simply do not of themselves form a coherent whole" (emphasis original).[1] What we see here, of course, is a division that runs right through the contemporary study of religious experience, between those who hold that phenomena or themes common to diverse traditions can reasonably be isolated and studied comparatively and those who maintain that, when we give historical and cultural context their due, apparent similarities tend to dissolve into a kaleidoscopic field of culturally specific constructions.

To begin to address the aporetic impasse in which we find ourselves here, we must clarify our conception of "religious experience" to the extent possible, and this is no easy matter. Religious experience has been an intensively contested category in recent years, and much of the contestation turns on some puzzling assumptions about the more general category of "experience." In the space available here, it will not be possible to disentangle all the yarn that has been spun about these matters, and I must apologize to readers if, on occasion, we must review familiar territory in elementary terms. Nevertheless, I hope at the very least that by the end of this chapter I shall have proposed some ways of thinking about experience that will prove useful to the contemporary study of religion, and to illustrate something of their utility in connection with our present theme of light.

There is currently a broad consensus that the concept of religious experience is not old: its development belongs to the nineteenth century; it finds clear expression in the pietism of Schleiermacher and matures under the sign of the Hegelian phenomenological revelation of Spirit.[2] This is not to say that experience is nowhere referred to in traditional religious texts; for descriptions of particular, religiously valued experiences are abundantly present in mystical and devotional literatures, and, though perhaps less common, general categories approximating our category of experience are sometimes encountered in traditional sources as well.[3] The claim, rather, is that the concept of properly *religious* experience, taken as a sui generis type of internal, personal, cognitive, or affective event, occurring in similar ways to persons in many different cultural and historical settings, and providing a warrant for religious adherence while remaining immune to external criticism, is a relatively modern invention. Such a notion of religious experience has been much criticized in recent years as having arisen largely as the expression of a protective strategy,[4] an effort to locate secure foundations for faith in an age in which traditional theological assurances were shaken by the relentless advances of science, technology, and humanism, an age during which a newly enlightened world left off its childhood fairy tales to become at last disenchanted.

The paradigm case of religious experience has often been identified as mystical experience, frequently understood to be an ineffable, transcendental absorption in oneness.[5] Mystical experience, thus detached from any particular religious tradition, was thought to have the delightful property of ubiquity, which indeed seemed to flow from its very characterization. Nevertheless, the strong claim made in this context was that mystical experiences of this type (or of a small number of similarly identifiable types)[6] could literally be found everywhere—at least throughout the "great traditions" of Christianity, Islam, Hinduism, and so on—so that such experiences seemed to disclose the universal bedrock grounding religious intuitions. As such, mystical experience could be taken to be an experiential correlate to Hegel's concept of *Geist*.[7] Furthermore, toward the end of the nineteenth and the beginning of the twentieth centuries, in a world in which colonial encounters and displacements urged persons of goodwill to seek some hope for the future in notions of our common humanity, the concept nicely offered a basis for affirming there to be a common core to human religious life. The comparative study of religious experience in this way proved to be edifying, and for some it offered an apologetic foundation for the so-called perennial philosophy.[8]

The conception of religious or mystical experience as privileged and private access to an ineffable, transcendent reality or sphere of being has, however, now generally fallen out of favor.[9] On purely formal grounds, as many of the so-called constructivists have argued, the very notion of "ineffable experience" turns out either to depend upon misdescription[10] or to be conceptually incoherent. For a literally "ineffable" or "inconceivable" experience must be taken as one that is at bottom devoid of propositional content: it must be ineffable through and through.[11] Descriptions of it issue after the experience in question has passed; they represent the mystic's—or worse, the hagiographer's—way of talking about the experience once it is over, and thus are discursive memory-events, interpretations, or imaginative reconstructions, not phenomenological transcriptions.[12] What we must recognize, therefore, is that when comparing the teachings of mystics who are claimed to have been the subjects of ultimately ineffable experiences, it is not even in principle possible for us to determine whether or not they "experienced the same thing."[13] In other terms, apophatic religious discourses may be fruitfully compared only in relation to their positive features as discursive constructions, but not with reference to the final ends to which they are supposed to conduce, precisely because the game of apophatic discourse itself places such matters off the board. It has been one of the systematic errors running right through the modern study of religious experience to attempt to understand apophatic religious discourses—such as are found in the works of thinkers like Nāgārjuna, Śaṅkara, and Eckhart—in terms of experience at all.[14]

Nevertheless, once we have put aside the logically self-contradictory concept of contentless experience, that is, the concept of experiencing literally nothing, can we not still speak of religious or mystical experiences that are amenable to phenomenological determination of one kind or another? One response is just to concede this point, and to turn from the paradoxes and puzzles of supposedly ineffable experience to compare instead experiences that are characterized by phenomenologically contentful descriptions. So-called pure consciousness experience and the perception of God are two examples that have recently been much discussed;[15] the religious experiences of light considered in the present book may suggest others.

In contrast to the common emphasis on the nonsensorial and even ineffable character of certain religious experiences, experiences of light—except where "light" is used in a purely metaphorical fashion—belong in the first instance to the phenomenology of vision.[16] As such, they remind us that there is an important, and certainly underemphasized, class of religious experiences which do engage the senses and are thus amenable to phenomenological description in sensorial terms, at least in large part; experiences of light may be euphemistically described as "ineffable" in order to accentuate their magnificence, but they are certainly not contentless. What is more, in the case of light, it is not merely a sensory *phenomenology* that concerns us; for in many cases the *physical perception* of light is literally intended. As Sarah Iles Johnston shows us (chap. 1), in Neoplatonic mysticism it was precisely solar light that was often thought to be divine. And the physical perception of light is stressed in other chapters as well (see especially the contributions of Catherine Asher [chap. 7] and Raoul Birnbaum [chap. 8]). In the ninth chapter of this book, Mimi Yiengpruksawan introduces us to the medieval Japanese courtier Michinaga, whose religious devotion to the Buddha of Boundless Light, Amitābha, she argues, was related to the onset of his blindness and his fear of thus being deprived of the perception of physical light. Because light is in the first instance experienced sensorially, religiously valued experiences of it may be engendered by attending to the natural environment in particular ways (as occurs in some of the accounts discussed by Birnbaum), or through ascetic practices inducing visionary perception (as referred to in Hossein Ziai's contribution, and throughout chapters 3–6 as well), or by means of artistic and architectural constructions (as emphasized by Asher and Yiengpruksawan; but see also the stunning image of Hagia Sophia given by Andrew Louth in fig. 4.1). As illustrated by these and other examples, such experiences of light, whether in the physical world or interior vision, contribute to the formation of religious agents in accord with the projects underwritten by the specific traditions concerned.

To be sure, we can and do speak of all sorts of experiences in terms of their phenomenal, cognitive, and affective properties, and our ability to articulate contentful experiences in this way offers prima facie ground for holding that inner experience is not really private, as it is often supposed to be. Whether or not there is a distinct class of properly *religious* or *mystical* experiences that have phenomenal or affective properties distinguishing them systematically from other types of experience remains, however, far less clear. It was indeed for this reason that in earlier generations some scholars converged on ineffability as a mark of the mystical, though, as we have seen, ineffability in truth marks nothing at all. If the phenomenal character of the experiences of light we are considering establishes their credentials as experiences, it remains nevertheless uncertain that they possess determinate phenomenal properties marking them as particularly religious.

SKEPTICISM AND SCIENCE

In an outstanding essay on our topic, Robert H. Sharf argues that the modern rhetoric of religious experience arose in part as a response to empiricism, which he defines as "the notion that all truth claims must be subject, in theory if not in fact, to empirical or scientific verification." Sharf regards the emphasis on experience in connection with the study of religion as a means "to forestall scientific critique. Religious truth claims were not to be understood as pertaining to the objective or material world, which was the proper domain of science, but to the inner spiritual world, for which the scientific method was deemed inappropriate."[17] Thus, he holds, "the term 'experience' . . . is often used to thwart the authority of the 'objective' or the 'empirical,' and to valorize instead the subjective, the personal, the private." Sharf's views here have been warmly endorsed by others writing recently on religious experience, notably by Russell T. McCutcheon.[18]

I would suggest, however, that those familiar with the history of Western science and philosophy treat Sharf's remarks in the spirit of a game of "what's wrong with this picture." For as is very well known, empiricism is nothing other than the valorization of experience in philosophy and in the sciences. (The Greek word *empeiria,* after all, is rendered *experientia* in Latin.)[19] As a distinct philosophical movement, empiricism is usually associated with the line of British philosophers, from John Locke on, who opposed themselves to the rationalism of Descartes by insisting that the foundations of our knowledge are to be found solely in experience, including our apperceptive experience of our own minds, and not in supposed certainties of reason.[20] Thus, Schleiermacher himself characterized his project as "empirical," in contrast to the speculative dogmatics he rejected.[21] Though Sharf is no doubt correct to hold that there was some connection between empiricism and the emergence of the modern rhetoric of religious experience, I therefore suspect that he errs in his assessment of the precise relationship between them: the impulse underlying the post-Kantian experiential turn in the philosophy of religion was perhaps not in the first instance intended to remove religion from the domain of scientific reflection so much as it was to modernize religious thought by harmonizing it with a dominant trend in the rhetoric of the positive sciences themselves. What was strange about invoking "experience" as a protective strategy in this way was not the turn to experience per se; it was rather the emerging conceit that in the context of religious life experience belongs solely to the subject and so is immune to the criticism or even, in the final analysis, the understanding of others.[22] My experience alone, in other words, comes to be regarded as an incorrigible epistemic authority.[23] What is so odd about this is the ready acceptance such a paradigm requires of what is at root a skeptical, and not an empiricist, view of experience. Though Schleiermacher in part adopted the rhetoric of empiricism, his legacy to the later discussion of religious experience was thus an uneasy mix of that rhetoric with the post-Cartesian quest for apodictically certain grounds.[24]

When we conceive of experience as inevitably private and inscrutable to others, a sort of magic lantern show in a Cartesian theater with seating for one, we have adopted the skeptic's perspective.[25] For it is with precisely this view of experience in mind that the traditional skeptical puzzles—how can I be certain that I am not being deceived by a devil? how can we know that we are not just brains floating in a nutriment bath, enjoying "experiences" that have no relation to the external world?—seem so forceful in their ability to undermine common assurances regarding intersubjective experience and knowledge.[26] Once under the spell of such conundrums, it becomes easy to accept the skeptical picture of experience as if it were entailed by our normal experience of the world. But it is not. To see this, let us consider briefly the manner in which "experience" becomes involved in the progress of science and in aesthetic judgment, two domains about which it is difficult to think coherently without some relatively well-formed, if problematic, assumptions relating to experience and to the intersubjectivity thereof.

The skeptical view of experience assumes that experience is strictly private, or subjective, and thus stands apart from the public, objective sphere. Experience, on this view, enjoys a troubled relationship with scientific knowledge, which aims always at objectivity; science, unlike subjective experience, so it is held, belongs to the domain of our shared reality. Such notions, however, are strikingly at odds with the actual procedures of the knowledge-building enterprise that is "science," and wholly ignore the historical role of experience in the foundation and ongoing elaboration of the modern scientific enterprise. For one of the primary points of departure for the modern sciences, over and against the Aristotelian traditions of the medieval schools, was the renewed valuing precisely of "experience."[27] The new scientist was an empiricist, one who relied in the first instance upon the data gleaned through direct observation, and not just the texts.[28] The French lexicon reminds us at once that our modern notion of experience is inextricably tied to this scientific project; for in French a "scientific experiment" is "une *expérience* scientifique," while "someone experienced" is "quelqu'un *expérimenté*."

Nonetheless, the exact role of observation and experience in the development of the sciences is something that raises a great many puzzles and problems in its own right. Consider Galileo in this context. When he observed the phases of Venus and the moons of Jupiter through the lens of his telescope, were these reliable observations, or distortions, akin to hallucinations or optical illusions, induced by his use of a man-made, vision-altering instrument? It was not unreasonable for some of his contemporaries to have raised such questions. In time, as we all know, the greater mass of educated persons came to accept that telescopes and similar optical devices, when manufactured according to exacting standards and correctly manipulated, do yield dependable visual information. Galileo's use of his "subjective" observational data was in this way historically vindicated.[29]

As this much simplified retelling of the story illustrates, science makes use not only of individual experience, but also of historically changing judgments on the part of both small numbers of experts and a more loosely conceived "educated public" as to just what counts as reliable experience. Scientific knowledge is in this sense historically and culturally constructed,[30] precisely as is, on some accounts, "religious experience." It seems clear, therefore, that constructedness need not be taken by itself to entail want of truth value, though Katz may nonetheless be correct to insist that "religious experience is irrelevant in establishing the truth or falsity of religion in general or any specific religion in particular."[31]

Our reflections on religious experiences of light serve further to underscore the porousness of the barriers we might erect to distinguish "religious" from "scientific" experience. As Johnston shows us, "the observable properties of light, especially sunlight, underlay the theurgists' metaphysical doctrines." In Ziai's examination of the Persian mystical philosopher Suhrawardī the "certitude obtained by the movement from sense data . . . to demonstration based on reason, which is the basis of discursive scientific knowledge, is said to obtain when visionary data upon which the philosophy of Illumination rests are 'demonstrated.'" The divinatory qualities of light may equally illustrate the merging of religious and scientific modes of reflection. Thus, following Birnbaum's discussion of the evidentiary roles of light in Chinese religions, we learn that particular observable phenomena were interpreted in relation to "indigenous Chinese discourses on natural responses to the moral power of the ruler, whose body extends to controlled physical territory and the social-political space of a state; and the luminous world of the Mahāyāna Buddhist scriptures that were introduced to China from Central Asia and India. In both of these cultural complexes the appearance of bright light signifies appropriate power, and on this matter at least, in actual practice in China, these two interpretive modes merged without great conceptual collisions."

Moreover, just as scientific experience is contestable, so too the experiences of light we are examining in religious contexts. Andrew Louth introduces us to the Calabrian monk Barlaam, who, in contrast to those within the Orthodox Catholic tradition for whom the mystical experience of light was of key importance, argued that "no experience, and certainly no experience mediated by the senses, as a vision of light must be, could be an experience of the ineffable God. To experience light not emanating from normal created sources, such as the sun, was to have a hallucination." And within the Tibetan Buddhist world, studied in chapter 6, the disappearance of some adepts in a "body of light" was widely believed to occur on some occasions, while the religious significance of such occurrences was itself much debated. That religious experience, like other types of experience, is subject to contestation supports the contention that it is not in fact taken to be private, and that within specific historical traditions no particular authority stems from claims based upon the supposed incorrigibility of private experience alone.

THE ANALOGY OF AESTHETIC RESPONSE

Some rumination on aesthetic response may help us to further clarify our ideas about this. Imagine that we are listening together to an Andalusian Sephardic song. Assuming that we are not audially impaired, we will believe ourselves to be hearing similar sequences of sound, whose characteristics of pitch, rhythm, and so forth, we experience in common. If called upon to explain how, in this case, common experience is possible, we will no doubt elaborate a tale about the isomorphisms holding among patterns of disturbance in the air—which constitute the music's physical reality—and sensory responses in the inner ear, the effects of those responses in the central nervous system, and so forth. In short, physics and physiology together seem to ground our supposition that perceptual experiences may be shared, that is to say, that we may experience the same things and reasonably presume our experiences of those things to be phenomenally similar. The skeptical challenges to this are fun to wrestle with in philosophy class, but in ordinary circumstances we just don't worry about them. Should you tell me that the Sephardic song sounds to you to be a lot like Little Richard's *Lucille,* I will politely suggest that you should have your ears examined, and only if you return with a clean bill of health will your observation incline me to epistemological, or perhaps psychological, puzzlement.

But now do you hear the beauty of the song? As soon as we raise this question we remember Protagoras, and all the old adages return to mind: man is the measure of all things; beauty is in the eye of the beholder; there's no accounting for taste; only a mother could love a face like that; and more. Our common wisdom urges us to hold that the aesthetic response is ineluctably personal and private, just as some suppose religious experience to be. But this, as some have rightly argued, is also untrue.[32]

Consider: there are a great many of us who, when we hear the Sephardic song, hear its beauty. We do not hear the song on the one hand and then hear its beauty besides. (I use "beauty" here and in what follows solely as a placeholder to refer to the positive aesthetic value, of whatever kind, that we attribute to an aesthetically valued object.) This is not to deny that there are also those who do not hear the beauty of the song when listening to it, a fact that conduces us to the Protagorean conclusion that to hear the beauty of the song is not in fact to hear anything at all, but rather to have a particular type of purely subjective response to what is heard.

As this objection is raised, my train of thought is briefly broken. The gentle melody of the song has been interrupted by a lively instrumental interlude, with the rattle of tambourines and brassy harmonies. We glance over at one another and smile. I know that you find this instrumental passage to be delightful, and I know that you know that I do as well. Our aesthetic responses, therefore, are not merely subjective; they are intersubjective.[33] They can be communicated to and apprehended by others. We have the ability to participate in aesthetic experiences together and to discover when it is that we don't. If this were not the case, it would be difficult to explain the appeal of specific arts to variously constituted collectivities, large and small. If this were not the case, it would be difficult to explain how taste could ever be educated; it would be difficult to explain our notions of judging rightly in aesthetic matters, of connoisseurship, and the like. In short, a purely subjectivist account of aesthetic response seems inadequate. If we do not wish to conclude beauty to be among the primary objective properties of the song that the receptive auditor hears in much the same manner that she hears the middle C plucked on the lute, then we shall nevertheless have to open up a space that embraces both what we hold to be clearly objective and what we regard as purely subjective; we shall have to acknowledge, in other words, the intersubjectivity of our aesthetic responses, and perhaps also the reality—if only the abstract or imaginal reality—of aesthetic values.

For the constructivist none of this is really a problem. The constructivist will argue that the common aesthetic responses of persons usually reflect a whole range of common background conditions owing to which certain groups of persons will respond to particular aesthetic inputs in similar ways.[34] Persons who enjoy medieval Spanish music probably share certain features of education and cultural background that have at least enabled their cultivation of this particular preference. And we know that persons of widely different backgrounds, or during different historical periods, often cannot easily appreciate the same things. Eighteenth-century European travelers in India, for instance, usually found Hindu religious sculptures to be hideous monstrosities,[35] a response famously shared by the first critics to behold Picasso's *Les Desmoiselles d'Avignon.*[36] Similar examples of culturally conditioned aesthetic evaluation are legion, despite the vagaries of individual judgment. So, one may urge, although aesthetic response may not be *purely* subjective, it is nevertheless *largely* a matter of cultural construction. And the same, it will be argued, holds true for religious experience.

I do not think this to be wrong, so far as it goes, but the picture is far too narrow. It does not address, for example, the apparent historical truth that differing cultures have been always learning to appreciate things aesthetically valued by others, and that this capacity, to find beauty in what one has not been conditioned to see as aesthetically valuable, but which others do, has generally played a great role in motivating relations of exchange and cultural appropriation. Consider in this regard the medieval spread of Hindu story literature throughout the Islamic world and the West, the vogue of chinoiserie in seventeenth- and eighteenth-century Europe, the adoption of Western classical music in nineteenth-century Japan, Chicago's embrace of Thai cooking. One may object, of course, that the Arab enjoyment of a Hindu story may not be the same as the Hindu enjoyment thereof, but this objection turns on a mistake. For there is no such thing as *the* Hindu enjoyment or *the* Arab enjoyment of the tale.[37] There are only the millions of individual acts of enjoyment, but these, far from being events in hermetically sealed Cartesian theaters, are interrelated by their intersubjectivity, whose possibilities may be actualized both within and across cultural boundaries. Perhaps these possibilities do not facilitate understanding across those bounds as well as within them, but the question of degree is not at all what is at issue here. To this we might add that the common (though by no means universal) human love of novelty exerts continual pressure upon cultural systems, forcing us to transcend ourselves by appropriating new materials with which to continue the ongoing constructive enterprise.

The intersubjectivity of experience is pertinent to our efforts to understand the religious experiences of light with which this book is fundamentally concerned. Because light is a matter of perception for us, its symbolic value is frequently related to a shared phenomenology of light perception. Light is almost universally associated with the heavens and high places, and with the warmth and power of the sun. The lights of fire, of the stars and moon, and of peculiar phenomena such as rainbows and reflective surfaces may also be evaluated in relation to specific religious interests. The common association of celestial and solar light with power and elevation in particular seems often to issue in the emergence of symbolic codes that are remarkably similar even in altogether different cultural and historical settings. Frequently, for instance, solar symbolism becomes tied to ideologies of male power, of patriarchy, or, as some would have it, phallocracy. In this respect, there is an unmistakable resonance between Elliot Wolfson's discussion of the "'hardened spark' . . . identified . . . as the aspect of the divine mind that corresponds to the phallus," and an image encountered early on in Paul Muller-Ortega's investigations, that of the *jyotirliṅga,* Śiva's "liṅga of light." A reading of the cross-cultural interpretations of religious experiences of light that emphasizes these and other androcentric valuations, moreover, is reinforced by the persistent connection between religiously charged light symbolism and monarchal power—if saints have their halos, so too emperors and kings. The contributions of Asher and Birnbaum, among others, provide excellent examples of the intersections between sacred and imperial luster.

At the same time, we should resist insisting too one-sidedly upon the association between light and masculine symbolism; light plays a role in the religious experience of women and in the formation of a feminine religious symbolism as well: consider, for instance, the light-saturated symbolism of the Marian cult, or the myth of the descent of the Japanese imperial line from a solar goddess, or the light imagery suffusing the writings of Saint Teresa of Avila.[38] If the light tends often to be a male attribute, it is an attribute whose telos, in many contexts, seems to be the dissolution of dichotomies, including the dichotomy of gender. That the light cannot thus be thought of reductively is best illustrated by its quality not of bright radiance, but of self-occlusion. As Wolfson describes it, "there is no darkness set in opposition to light, for the most brilliant light is the most impenetrable darkness. In this moment, there is no difference between lucidity and obscurity, translucence and opaqueness."

The religious phenomenology of light is therefore not uniform; but we may affirm nevertheless that the varied roles played by light in the construction of religious experience, and the religious themes associated with light, are recurrent throughout widely divergent cultural settings.[39]

* * *

Let us review briefly the argument up to this point as it applies to religious experience in general. Following the arguments of the constructivist critics of perennialism, I have asserted that treating religious or mystical experience as ineffable private experience is doubly mistaken, because the literal notion of "ineffable experience" is conceptually incoherent, while that of "private experience" depends on our taking seriously a skeptical view of experience that we ought not to take seriously, at least not in this context. Hence, any meaningful discussion of experience, religious or otherwise, must concern itself with contentful and hence essentially effable experiences, experiences that may be engaged intersubjectively and so are not, in any relevant sense, private. As the short example of experience in scientific practice showed us, questions regarding what kinds of experience we may attend to and treat as authoritative, and the ways and modes in which we may do so, are adjudicated not by individuals acting without any context or framework, but by communities of discourse, so that experience is enmeshed in culturally engendered regimes of interpretation and thus is in this sense culturally constructed. But I hold this to be true across the board, for religious and scientific experience alike, so that the mere fact of cultural construction has no particular bearing on matters of truth, facticity, and so on. The upshot for religion, of course, is that, were experiences of the divine within a given community such as to disclose the true order of things, they would be no less constructed for that, but also no less true.[40] It must be emphasized, however, that while culture and experience are thus inextricably interwoven—and this I do take to be a perennial truth—experience in itself is incapable of determining any truth beyond its specific, self-evident disclosures.[41] The history of scientific practice, once again, offers ample evidence in support of this assertion.[42] Finally, I turned to aesthetic experience in order to suggest that even in those areas in which subjectivist accounts of experience may initially seem plausible, they are seen on closer inspection not really to be so. Aesthetic experience, like religious experience, is a puzzling phenomenon, but it seems nevertheless to be correctly characterized as intersubjective, amenable to communication even across cultural boundaries, so that, tentatively at least, we may assume this to be possibly true of religious experience as well. To say this, however, presupposes that it still makes some sense to speak of "religious experience," though this has yet to be shown.

STATES AND OBJECTS

It will be worthwhile now to expand upon the neglected analogy between aesthetic and religious experience;[43] for the close relationship between religion and art, a relationship that does approach cultural universality, certainly warrants further scrutiny of their many resemblances in respect to the category of experience.[44]

The Sephardic song has now long since ended and it is the Bach Passacaglia in C minor that is playing. I find this to be a profoundly moving composition, mysteriously dark and luminous at the same time. It seems in fact a trivialization to call it "beautiful" or even "sublime," though it is sublimely beautiful. The sounds of the organ sweep over me like a great wave of terrible power, threatening to cause me to lose my bearings altogether, indeed, to lose myself. If I permit myself to become wholly absorbed in this experience, I readily find that I am brought to tears by this music, though I have no idea really why it is that I am crying, or even if I am the one who weeps.

There are other works of art that I find induce similar experiences. Some are religious works, others not; and sometimes this experience of emotionally overpowering transport is also aroused by remarkable beauty or grandeur in nature. I could characterize the experience in question as a type of religious awe, but I am not at all certain that it would be meaningful to do so. One of the works that affects me in this way, for instance, is Hieronymus Bosch's magnificent *Christ Mocked (The Crowning with Thorns)* in the National Gallery in London, a painting that I have at times gazed at for so long that it has become engraved like a photograph in memory. I can speculate that, if I were a Christian, and if I were to experience Bosch's work as I do, I would not hesitate to think of my experience as being in some sense religious. But I am not a Christian, and, so far as I am consciously aware, my experience of the painting has nothing at all to do with either feelings of faith or particular religious beliefs.

These thoughts suggest to me that aesthetic experience, when suitably intense and characterized by a sense of awe and of self-transcendence, may resemble some types of religious experience, and that under certain circumstances we may be very much inclined to think of such experiences religiously. The similarity to some types of religious experience that we plausibly find here is reflected in the role religions have always played in inspiring art, and equally in the use of art to arouse, structure, and intensify religious feeling. Religious art is both part and product of the religious disciplines of the person.[45]

Similar observations are warranted in connection with certain of our experiences of light. Ordinary or unusual physical light may be regarded as the literal presence of the divine, but, more often, light may be taken as a sign, as evidence of the divine presence, or of sanctity. The lights perceived by pilgrims in China's Wutai Mountains (chap. 8) are indicative of the presence of the bodhisattva Wenshu (Mañjuśrī), while the light released and publicly witnessed at the deaths of some Tibetan adepts (chap. 6) is seen as proof of their spiritual attainment. Light may be architecturally or otherwise enhanced, as in the construction of Mughal-era saints' tombs and royal palaces (chap. 7), to instill in the devotee or spectator a sense of religious awe, whether verifying saintly blessing or the emperor's divinity. In all of these cases the perceiver is presumed to be religiously moved in the course of the experience of light in question. The experience both reflects and contributes to the formation of the religious agent. One learns to perceive light in particular ways that are sanctioned by the authority of tradition. One learns, in short, to see the light religiously. This seeing may resemble the seeing that takes place when one is aesthetically moved by the light and overawed by it. But, as the example of my response to the Bosch masterpiece illustrates, religious experience cannot be reduced to aesthetic experience alone.[46] So we must inquire now as to just what it is that distinguishes them.

The object of aesthetic experience, we may affirm tautologically, is whatever there may be, natural or artificed, whether perceptible to the senses or object of thought, to which aesthetic value, or beauty, is attributed. For the most part, within the limits of our education and cultural background, we have no difficulty identifying such objects, and we are often able, too, to articulate the features in virtue of which we ascribe aesthetic value to them, though we don't all do this equally well. Be that as it may, it is precisely when we speak of religious experience in analogous terms that we find ourselves getting into trouble. For what, exactly, is the object of religious experience, and just what is the peculiarly religious value that we ascribe to it?[47]

There is, of course, an answer to this question about religious value, one associated with the early-twentieth-century phenomenology of religion as articulated by Otto and van der Leeuw, among others, that perhaps merits continuing reflection: religious value is the value attributed to whatever is deemed holy, or, in somewhat different terms, sacred, divine, sanctified, or blessed.[48] Any object or state, be it physical, mental, or ideal, to which holiness, and so on, is attributed in this way is an object or state of religious value. We may say, then, that experiences involving the religious value of any such object or state are a fortiori religious experiences. The pronounced analogy with the characterization of aesthetic experience will be obvious (as indeed it was obvious to Otto),[49] not least thanks to an analogous reliance on tautology; where aesthetic and religious experience differ, on this account, is just in holding beauty and sacrality, respectively, to be the proper characteristics attributed to the objects of concern.[50]

I find this approach to the general definition of religious experience attractive for a number of reasons, but it is also deeply problematic. Some, no doubt, will vehemently object that I have lured them into the constructivist tent only to perform the cheap trick of pulling a perennialist rabbit from my hat. (And to add insult to injury, you may exclaim, the rabbit's name was Otto!) Let me assure you, then, that things are not as bad as all that.

We may return briefly to our musings on musical beauty: the Sephardic song and the Bach passacaglia were both beautiful, but now I am listening to Katie Webster singing *Pussycat Moan* and that is beautiful too, perhaps even sublime. Precisely what is the property in virtue of which the very different musical paradigms I have mentioned are similarly characterized? Is the beauty they seem to share the same, or different? If different, why do we call it "beauty" in all these cases? Indeed, is the beauty of the Bach passacaglia the same as or different from the beauty of the Fourth Brandenburg Concerto, and is the beauty of the first movement of that concerto the same as or different from the beauty of its third? In short, beauty, O Subhūti! is emptiness and emptiness is beauty! To attempt to define the beautiful on the model of phenomenological definitions of the holy, surely, seems absurd.[51] Modern writers on aesthetics, accepting the impossibility of essentialist definitions of beauty, have generally been content to drop the effort altogether, making do with an unavoidable vagueness and complexity to the category of aesthetic value.[52] In the case of religion, I would say that something similar should obtain—in short, that while Otto and company were right to focus upon the category of the holy, they went wrong in seeking to define it terms of a phenomenological analysis of ideal essences. At best, such definitions can play a heuristic role here, introducing a messily constructed category by signaling just some of its typical members.

Accordingly, just as the aesthetic object may be anything to which aesthetic value is ascribed—be it Yosemite Valley, *Hamlet,* or a Campbell's soup can—so too the object of religious experience.[53] For while in some cases it may be the abstract object of mystical contemplation that is deemed sacred, the same may be true in other contexts of rocks, human remains, serpents, or songs. What makes the aesthetic object an aesthetic object is just a subject's attribution of aesthetic value to it, and the case of religiously valued objects is analogous. Further, we may say that religious experience, far from requiring definition in terms of phenomenologically distinctive states of the subject—ineffable oneness, pure consciousness experience, the feeling of dependence, the perception of God, what have you—may be virtually any possible state of the subject: my joy may be valued religiously, but also my sorrow; my silence may be valued religiously, but so too my frenzy; hence, the experiences of joy, sorrow, silence, or frenzy may all be religious experiences, sharing equal claim to this title with ineffable, transcendental states or perceptions of God.[54] Of course, the subjectivism and arbitrariness that seem entailed by these assertions are limited, once again, by the restrictive role of human culture: almost anything *may* be perceived as meriting aesthetic interest, but in any given community, on any given occasion, only some things *will* be;[55] analogously, almost any experience may be spiritually valued, but in our actual life-worlds the possibilities are variously delimited. Religiously creative individuals, like creative artists, may sometimes challenge these limits, transgress them, and succeed in initiating their reconstruction, but such creativity derives its power in part from its relation to pregiven cultural frameworks and can never be entirely dissociated from them.

It seems clear, then, that religious experience may in principle supervene upon any kind of experience: fetch water, chop wood. Mystics like al-Hallāj and Sri Ramakrishna are sometimes taken as exemplars of the possibility of literally transmuting all experience into religious experience, but these examples also suggest the impossibility of such universal illumination determining the concrete, historical forms of religious life. These are best taken as limiting cases, pointing to the end of religion, pun intended. Al-Hallāj's persecutors may be said in some sense to have known this and to have acted accordingly.[56] Ramakrishna's disciples, as we know, took great care to clean up his act.[57] Within any particular religious life-world, specific types of experience come to be valued religiously, while others are not, and the transgressions of the great mystics can be reappropriated only if suitably redescribed.

In relation to the experiences of light studied here, the creative appropriation of experience for religious ends is evident. Light is a favorite color in the religious palate, a preferred key in the music that is mysticism. Iamblicus exemplifies this artistry in his employment of light; so too do Suhrawardī, Abhinavagupta, Maximos the Confessor, and the author(s) of the *Zohar.* All are joined by a common fascination with light and its properties, and in particular with the light that arises within, in the course of ascetic or ritual practice. But each one equally produced his own distinctive creation, differing absolutely from all the others mentioned and embodying in its overall scheme the symbols, meanings, and values of a particular tradition.

The foregoing arguments support a general conception of experience according to which widespread, underdetermined human capacities are dialectically related to the determinations engendered by ongoing constructive cultural, historical, and linguistic activity. (Indeed, the ability to engage in such types of constructive activity must be counted among our widespread human capacities.) Expression, interpretation, and understanding are among the intersubjective dimensions of such activity that are at once experienced and productive of experience. It is the intersubjective face of experience that allows us to know the pains, pleasures, values, and tastes of our fellows and to elaborate in concert with them the shared domains of our culture, including our religious culture. Within the capacious, dynamic system that unfolds here, religious experiences are whatever experiences are imbued with religious value for the subjects of the experiences in question, and their objects are the objects, of whatever kind, to which such value is attributed.[58]

One conclusion that is warranted is that the study of religious experience cannot be reasonably separated from the study of the varied religious life-worlds in which such experiences are cultivated and articulated. What Robert Gimello has wisely urged in respect to the study of mysticism in particular applies equally, in my view, to religious experience in general: "Ecstasies, intuitions, sudden insights, epiphanies, transports of union, disenthralments, and the like may be necessary to the definition of mysticism, in the sense that there is nothing which can reasonably be called mystical that does not include such things, but there is much more to the matter than that. The mysticism of any particular mystic is really the whole pattern of his life. The rare and wonderful 'peaks' of experience are a part of that pattern, but only a part, and their real value lies only in their relation to the other parts, to his thought, his moral values, his conduct towards others, his character and personality, etc. The modern study of mysticism has, I believe, tended to overlook those relations."[59] In short, we must study religious experiences in relation to the total formation and discipline of the religious agents to whose formation *as* religious agents they contribute. Philosophical reflection on religious experience goes wrong when it treats its topic primarily as the concern of a denaturalized epistemology; religious experience should be considered, rather, in its connection with the ways of "spiritual exercise," or of the "technologies of the self," as elaborated within specific life-worlds.[60]

The cultivation of the characteristic, tradition-specific modes of religious experience contributes to the formation of the religious agent, so that religious experience marks not so much the final goal of the path (which, as we have seen, is often placed outside of all marking by the game of apophatic discourse) as the religious techniques of the self. The experiences of receiving the sacraments for Christians, of rendering homage to one's guru in Hindu traditions, of Buddhist circumambulations, of ritual prayer for Muslims, and of Torah study for Jews may be mentioned as typical examples. The experience, it must be stressed, is in these cases not identical to the outward act alone, and hence, as part of the formation of the religious agent, great attention is paid to just how one ought to understand these acts and to feel while performing them. Religious culture thus forms experience even as experience informs religious culture.

CONSTRUCTIONS AND PERENNIAL POSSIBILITIES

You may now be reassured that the perennialist rabbit has been returned to his hutch, banished from this particular performance. But perhaps we have not yet seen the last of him. Let us consider some of the more extreme claims made on behalf of the constructivism with which my argument so far has been in broad accord. Some of these are evident in the remarks of Hans Penner, who asserts, for example, that "mystical languages cannot be thought of as referring to the same Reality, because Reality is relative to a language system. Different mystical languages, therefore, represent or express different mystical worlds."[61] Because, on this view, differing systems must be radically incommensurable, meaningful comparison becomes effectively impossible; we may undertake the contextually rich investigation of particular historical-cultural life-worlds only in order to describe their specific religious languages, but we cannot directly compare them.

Earlier, I referred briefly to historical instances of cross-cultural exchange and understanding. I believe that the cultural atomization that seems to flow from an extreme adherence to the constructivist-contextualist view has the unfortunate result of rendering such cross-cultural currents counterintuitive, if not altogether unintelligible. An example from the history of early Christian relations with paganism, the two of which may be taken as representative of "different language systems" about as well as anything can, will illustrate this point. Consider these words from the closing paragraph of Thomas Mathews's superb study of early Christian art, *The Clash of Gods:* "The modern historian is necessarily cautious about venturing beyond the physical to reconstruct the emotional reactions of the ancients to their art. Yet what evidence exists must be acknowledged, and it points to the strong parallel between the pagan and the Christian reactions to their icons. . . . The icon carried the same effect as the statue; to experience it was to quiver under the gaze of the god who peered out at you. . . . Like his pagan predecessors, the devout Christian trembled in awe of the divine presence that looked out through the eyes of the icon, while he offered flowers and candles in veneration."[62]

It is not difficult to find other examples of apparent intersection among religious modes of experience in the history of religions. Instances might be drawn from the Jewish and Muslim cult of the saints in medieval North Africa, Sufi and Bhakti devotionalism in North India, Buddhist and Taoist esotericism in China, "interfaith" worship in the contemporary United States. One may object that in such cases it is false to speak of differing religious worlds and languages, that one ought to speak instead of a world of medieval North African spirituality and the like. But against this, it seems clear that no one ever thought of himself as an adherent of "medieval North African spirituality," and that sixteenth-century pilgrims seeking blessings at Moroccan saints' tombs would have identified themselves as Jews or as Muslims, whose sacred languages were the languages of Torah or Qur'ān.[63] "Medieval North African spirituality" perhaps typifies the modern religionist's constructs, but it is not at all a construct of the communities it purports to describe. In short, the radical contextualist must decide between a counterintuitive atomization of human cultural history and recourse to redescriptions of a kind that contextualism, ironically, generally intends to avoid.[64]

Given this, it may be worthwhile to inquire whether perennialism might not hold some positive lessons that we might still retrieve. As we have already seen, perennialism has been much criticized, and I think rightly so, for staking its claims on putative experiences that, on closer inspection, proved to be conceptually incoherent, or entirely inscrutable. Elsewhere, perennialist projects have faltered by tacitly introducing theological presuppositions into their analysis and thus falling into circular argumentation.[65] Very recent attempts to revive perennialism, notably those of Robert Forman and his collaborators, have sought to avoid these pitfalls by focusing upon definable psychological states or capacities, whose definitions in principle can be elaborated without religious preconceptions of any kind. "Pure consciousness experience" has, in this way, been offered as a common core underlying a very broad range of mystical traditions. Though pure consciousness experience may sometimes be spoken of as "ineffable" or "contentless," it is in fact amenable to highly abstract phenomenological description, as well as to precise specification in relation to standard tables of ideal typical psychological experiences. In short, it can in principle be accurately picked out from among our effable mental states.[66]

I shall assume now that Forman and his collaborators are correct to assert that there are such pure consciousness experiences, that we can identify them, and that we can reasonably identify descriptions of them in some traditional accounts.[67] Our ability to pick out pure consciousness experiences, and indeed many other sorts of psychological experience, in this way parallels our ability to pick out standard colors, as famously documented in the work of Brent Berlin and Paul Kay.[68] This suggests that we are entitled to call into question the extreme relativism that follows from some forms of constructivism, as noted above.

The analogy to color perception invites a further proposal. It appears plausible to hold that the story we should tell ourselves about colors will be one in which the facts of color perception are shown to be all and only facts about the physical world—chiefly, in this case, light, optics, and the anatomy and neurophysiology of vision—supervenient upon which are a variety of cognitive, linguistic, cultural, and affective facts, which are in various ways constructed and highly variable. Color perception, it has been well argued, may be quite constant from the perspectives of physics and physiology, but our languages and aesthetics of color demonstrate that such constants as there are leave radically underdetermined our cultural constructions and interpretations of the colors we see.[69]

Returning to consider pure consciousness experience, the analogy seems compelling. For even if we assume this to be a widespread phenomenon, which we find described in traditional texts emanating from varied religious sources, it is clear that in some cases, owing to great differences of language and culture, this identification will be doubtful, and that even where this is not so, pure consciousness experiences are seldom assessed and interpreted in identical ways.[70] Furthermore, there are religious traditions that do not recognize this to be a particularly significant type of experience at all, and it seems entirely possible to imagine pure consciousness experiences occurring without any religious value being attributed to them. So, while Forman and company may be correct to hold that such experiences are very widespread, and even to hold that they represent the actualization of a perennial human capacity, they do not convince me that this, or for that matter anything else, is indeed the universal common core of mystical experience. Their positive contribution lies just in arguing, pace some forms of constructivism, that we can reasonably aspire to identify certain religiously valued types of experience across cultural and historical bounds, and to do so without theological presupposition.

The question we should pose, then, concerns the convergences and divergences among different religious ways of deploying identifiable types of experience in the formation of the agent. Concurring with Robert Gimello's view, cited above, we should emphasize not so much the particular culminating experiences that are characterized as ends as the ways in which experience is woven into the tissue of specific religious life-worlds. It is with this perspective in mind that we may return once more to religious experiences of light. The investigation of light in this context cooperates with the "soft perennialism" entertained here precisely because, despite the great variety of cultural-historical constructions under discussion, we cannot doubt that in a great many cases they are correctly described as concerned with experiences of light. Light, under one description or another, is a universal religious symbol if anything is, and most religions make literal or metaphoric reference to experiences of light in various contexts. Nevertheless, it is striking that spiritual techniques focusing upon light became particularly accentuated in a number of particular religious movements, often described as "mystical," in late antiquity and the medieval period. Historically speaking, these movements were often but not exclusively formed under influences stemming from Neoplatonism, old Iranian religions, or Indian esotericism. (In some cases—Mughal courtly religion under Akbar is a likely example—all three of these traditions may be seen to converge.) The exact twists and turns of the streams of thought and practice emanating from these fonts in most cases have yet to mapped with precision, though some suggestions may be found in the preceding chapters (and in the earlier works referred to in n. 39).

It is in the context of such movements that "light" often figures metaphorically to refer to the modality of mind's awareness of itself. Thus, for the fourth-century Byzantine monk Evagrios, the state he calls *apatheia* occurs "when the intellect begins to see its own light, and remains calm during the visions of sleep, and can look at things with serenity." For the eighth-century Indian Buddhist philosopher Haribhadra, the essence of mind "is far removed from the nature of the one and the many [and] being unoriginated, *is clear light.*" In examples such as these, our topic apparently begins to merge with pure consciousness experience. This may occur in connection with the cultivation of experiences of light in interior vision, experiences catalyzed by ritual, devotional, and ascetic techniques. These, however, ensure that the experience of inner light is framed and interpreted in contextually determinate ways. In the Neoplatonic sources discussed by Johnston, "divinities direct their light so that it shines upon the theurgist, which causes his soul to ascend," while the Buddhist Tantric adept may regard the object of contemplation as "in its nature a divinity embodying the essence of mind, radiating light" (chap. 6). At its uppermost limits, the interior vision of light may expand to disclose the highest theological principle: the Light of Lights in the system of the Persian philosopher Suhrawardī (chap. 2), or the Kashmiri Śaivite Light that is the union of existence and consciousness (chap. 3), or the Orthodox Catholic's Taboric Light of the Transfiguration (chap. 4). It seems clear, however, that while the visionary experience of phenomenal light may propel the mystic to the zenith of realization, the word "light," at such heights of abstraction, is by no means being used uniformly to refer to phenomenal experience at all.

We have seen earlier that, in discussing mysticism, one wants to distinguish between instances of "pseudoineffability" and the "genuine ineffability" said to characterize real mystical experience, which derives, we are told, from the complete breakdown of all normal categorial schemes of place, time, and so on, during the experience, and the misrepresentation of that same experience which thus inevitably results, should one attempt to describe it in language using those same categorial schemes (as indeed one must) afterward. In other words, the ineffability of these experiences is supposed to derive from a formal constraint on the use of language. For this reason, I have argued that possible "experiences" whose phenomenological character does not in any respect conform to the categorial structures of language as we have it are not really experiences. Whether or not we agree to restrict the use of the word "experience" in this way, it is widely agreed that some major trends in mysticism insist that the path culminates where language and thought can no longer take us, and for this reason, phenomenological description is often abandoned in favor of apophatic or paradoxical discourse.

Light lends itself to religious symbolism in part owing to the manner in which it bridges the physical and the spiritual. Light may be thought to disclose the essential nature of all that reveals religious value: light is light, but Torah is also light, as are the sacraments, as is the Buddha's word. Interestingly, light also bridges the difficult gap between apophatic and cataphatic discourses; for while light is phenomenally experienced, light also represents a clearing; it is what is perceived when all else is removed. The idea of light, therefore, may be taken to resolve the apparent paradox that results from affirming both apophasis and cataphasis in a common system of theological discourse. The divine nature can be approached positively and negatively, but usually we seem unable to get our minds around both at once, and light offers a path whereby we might transcend this apparent dilemma. In the words of a celebrated Hindu text, the *Kaṭha Upaniṣad:*

"This is that"—so they think, although
　　the highest bliss can't be described.
But how should I perceive it?
　　Does it shine?
　　Or does it radiate?

There the sun does not shine,
    nor the moon and stars;
There lightning does not shine,
    of this common fire need we speak!
Him alone, as he shines, do all things reflect;
    this whole world radiates with his light.[71]

And in the words of Plotinus: "The Intelligence is beautiful—of all things the most beautiful. Dwelling in pure light and 'stainless radiance,' it envelops everything with its own light. The realm of sense, so beautiful, is only its reflected shadow. It abides in full resplendence because it contains nothing dark to the mind or obscure or indefinite. It knows beatitude."[72]

In the systems we have considered in this book—Platonic mysticism, the Byzantine hesychast tradition, medieval Kabbalah, Suhrawardī's Illuminationism, and Buddhist and Hindu esotericism—it is the task of the adept to ascend by paths of phenomenal light to arrive at the light beyond all lights. Who are we to say whether that light is in all these cases the same or different? For sameness and difference are excluded from its very nature. Each of the traditions considered here engages the light while maintaining its proper identity, its specific universe of discourse, practice, symbol, understanding, and interpretation. So we may ponder whether their intersecting phenomenologies and theophanies of light disclose their experiential core to be the same, different, both, or neither? I will leave it to thinkers much wiser than myself to decide.

* * *

It will be useful now to summarize our general conclusions.

1. So-called "contentless" experiences and the like are not in fact experiences at all, and it is a confusion to attempt to discuss them in terms of the phenomenology of experience.[73]

2. Contentful experiences, owing to our capacity for intersubjectivity and understanding, are not properly private and can in principle be accessible to any qualified agent.

3. There is no universal, paradigmatic type of "religious experience." As in the case of aesthetic experience, any experience may be in principle a "religious experience" if only it is valued as such. Religious experiences, like aesthetic experiences, are thus second-order experiences, constituted by our interpretations and judgments of primary phenomenal experiences of sound, sight, and so on, and of mental and abstract phenomena as well.

4. The acts of evaluation and judgment, whereby religious experiences are properly constituted, always belong to a cultural context. They are engendered by and inform the acts of culturally embedded agents. However, cultural construction neither fully determines such experience nor precludes possibilities of intersubjectivity extending even across cultural boundaries. Cultural construction, though playing a significant role in the constitution of religious experience, is thus an underdetermining condition.

5. Despite the pronouncedly constructivist-contextualist orientation of these assertions, some concessions to perennialism nevertheless may be in order. Careful phenomenological characterization, psychometric classification, and the like may plausibly be invoked to define suitably clear types of experience that may reasonably be compared across cultural and historical boundaries.[74] Moreover, we may aspire to identify experiential capacities of human agents that approach universality, although the capacities in question will seldom be actualized universally, or in precisely similar ways. One such capacity may well be the ability to evaluate our experiences and their contents religiously, just as we have a capacity for their aesthetic evaluation.

Before closing these general reflections on religious experience, I wish to offer a very tentative sketch of one further argument. In the foregoing discussion, aesthetic and religious experiences alike have been treated as "second-order experiences," acts of interpretation and evaluation that may supervene, in principle, on primary experiences of any kind, as well as on other second-order experiences. I may, for instance, understand there to be religious value in an experience of great pain, or I may find religious value in experiencing aesthetic wonder with respect to an object of great beauty. (It goes without saying that while undergoing the experience itself one lives it as an organic whole.) These acts of valuation are possibly intersubjective, and thus, they may be experienced collectively and made subject to public criticism and scrutiny. As in the case of aesthetic judgment, the attribution of religious value may itself be evaluated: within our social and historical worlds, we may exercise good taste or bad, or make sound or unsound ascriptions of religious value. And some, at least, of these judgments will be culturally and historically transitive. A number of observations now seem warranted.

The constituents of our world, including ourselves as living beings, are at present often conceived as physical systems, which may be reduced to primitive physical events of various kinds. Given recent investigations of religious experience in relation to the brain, and especially the conception of "innate capacities" as it has been recently endorsed by some perennialists, it may well be that the arguments outlined above are all consistent with the project of physical reduction.[75] Paradoxically, one may therefore conclude, both constructivism and some of the leading varieties of contemporary perennialism seem to accord in their common prospects for harmonization with a physicalist ontology.[76] However, although the approach advocated here may be construed as *consistent* with some varieties of physicalism, by itself it neither implies nor entails this. Our capacities for religious experience reflect something about our functioning as neurophysiological systems, but equally something about the way the world is, such that religious experience, like aesthetic experience, and indeed like consciousness itself, is among the capacities of some kinds of physical system. That is to say, we experience the values, including the religious or the aesthetic values, of things precisely because what things there are have potential properties of value. And we, in turn, can evaluate our experiences of things religiously or aesthetically because we are beings who have the capacity to experience religious and aesthetic values. Thus, our world, which is constituted by the things we experience and ourselves as experiencers, is such that values are among its potentialities, and these potentialities, in turn, are actualized whenever a conscious agent experiences an object religiously, aesthetically, and so on. Although religious and aesthetic values may well be in a significant sense culturally and historically constructed upon the ground of material systems, these same values as potentialities of those systems in this way belong to the very fabric of our world. The apparently immediate awareness of religious value, or religious experience, finds its basis in the objective universe, in ourselves as subjects, and in the cultural worlds in which we are formed. But none of these is by itself a determining condition. Religious experience, like aesthetic experience, emerges from a complex skein of conditions, each element of which is underdetermining with respect to the experience in question.

Read in this way, the argument put forth here comports not so much with pure physicalism, but rather with some form of dual aspect theory, that rather puzzling view which holds the physical and the mental to be identical, without one's being reduced to the other.[77] As quanta of light, according to physics, may be understood in differing contexts to be either particles or waves, so mind and matter are two ways in which a single reality discloses itself. In connection with our present concerns, we may say that religious experience reveals to us not only something about our innate brain capacities, but equally something about the real possibilities of the world in which we live and of ourselves as conscious agents, possibilities that cannot be reduced to the purely physical phenomena in which they are grounded, and with which they may be ontologically, though not phenomenologically, identical. And because light, the main topic of this book, belongs prominently both to physics and to spiritual worlds of meaning, this perspective is particularly attractive here. In the effulgence of the light, we may say, the secrets of the kingdom stand revealed.

NOTES

1. I take this opportunity to thank the Press's two referees—Professor William Darrow and one anonymous reader—for their many critical and constructive comments, contributing in particular to the development of the present chapter.

2. On Schleiermacher's contribution to the formation of the modern conception of "religious experience," see in particular Wayne Proudfoot, *Religious Experience* (Berkeley: University of California Press, 1985), chap. 1. The role of Hegelianism in the background of nineteenth- and early-twentieth-century discussions of religious experience has not, to my knowledge, been very well explored. Rudolf Otto, whose phenomenology certainly owes much to the Hegelian milieu, was nevertheless inclined to regard Hegel's notion of Spirit as "absolute reason" as contrasting fundamentally with his own idea of the "numinous," the distinctive feature, in Otto's view, of all religious experience (*The Idea of the Holy* [New York: Oxford University Pres, 1958], p. 92). Nevertheless, refer to William James's opinion, cited in n. 7 below.

3. Robert H. Sharf, "Experience," in *Critical Terms for Religious Studies,* ed. Mark C. Taylor (Chicago: University of Chicago Press, 1998), pp. 94–116, argues that "the valorization of experience in Asian thought can be traced to a handful of twentieth-century Asian religious leaders and apologists" (p. 99). Wilhelm Halbfass, *India and Europe: An Essay in Understanding* (Albany: State University of New York Press, 1988), chap. 21, convincingly demonstrates the relative unimportance of "experience" for many streams of classical Indian religious thought, including the *advaitavedānta* of Śaṅkara. (Though I concur with him regarding the cases he considers, one might object that Halbfass directs little attention to those traditions, like Bengali Vaiṣṇava devotionalism and the religio-aesthetic philosophy it spawned, for which experience does seem a significant category.) For a rebuttal of Sharf's position that seeks to demonstrate the importance of the category of experience for an Asian religious tradition, see Janet Gyatso, "Healing Burns with Fire: The Facilitations of Experience in Tibetan Buddhism," *Journal of the American Academy of Religion* 67, no. 1 (1999): 113–47.

4. Proudfoot, *Religious Experience,* p. xv: "The autonomy of religious life is defended in order to preclude inquiry and to stave off demands for justification from some perspective outside of that life. The result is a combination of genuine insights into the ways in which religion ought to be studied and protective strategies that serve apologetic purposes." Proudfoot amplifies his concept of "protective strategies" in pp. 199–209 and passim. Cf. Russell T. McCutcheon, *Critics Not Caretakers: Redescribing the Public Study of Religion* (Albany: State University of New York Press, 2001), esp. chap. 1.

5. I concur with Sharf, "Experience," p. 95, that the terms "religious experience" and "mystical experience" lack clear definition and are not well distinguished from one an-

other in the literature. The problems of defining "mystical experience" in particular are reflected throughout the three useful collections edited by Steven T. Katz: *Mysticism and Philosophical Analysis* (Oxford: Oxford University Press, 1978), *Mysticism and Religious Traditions* (Oxford: Oxford University Press, 1983), and *Mysticism and Language* (Oxford: Oxford University Press, 1992).

6. For a summary of such typologies, as elaborated by Zaehner, Stace, and Smart, among others, see Steven T. Katz, "Language, Epistemology, and Mysticism," in Katz, *Mysticism and Philosophical Analysis,* esp. pp. 24–25. A recent effort to treat the great diversity of mystical experiences while nonetheless retaining the common rubric "mysticism" may be found in Jess Byron Hollenbach, *Mysticism: Experience, Response, and Empowerment* (University Park, PA: Pennsylvania State University Press, 1996).

7. William James, *The Varieties of Religious Experience* (New York: Modern Library, 1902), p. 389 n. 1, goes so far as to say: "What reader of Hegel can doubt that that sense of a perfected Being with all its otherness soaked up into itself, which dominates his whole philosophy, must have come from the prominence in his consciousness of mystical moods like this, in most persons kept subliminal? The notion is thoroughly characteristic of the mystical level, and the *Aufgabe* of making it articulate was surely set to Hegel's intellect by mystical feeling." On this remarkable passage, see further John E. Smith, "William James's Account of Mysticism: A Critical Appraisal," in Katz, *Mysticism and Religious Traditions,* p. 255. Walter T. Stace, *Mysticism and Philosophy* (Philadelphia: Lippincott, 1960), represents in some respects a contemporary Hegelian reflection on mysticism.

8. For a judicious review of the formation of modern religious perennialism, see J. J. Clarke, *Oriental Enlightenment: The Encounter between Asian and Western Thought* (London: Routledge, 1997), chaps. 7–8. On the related topic of the influences of esotericism on the contemporary study of religion, refer to Steven M. Wasserstrom, *Religion after Religion: Gershom Scholem, Mircea Eliade, and Henry Corbin at Eranos* (Princeton, NJ: Princeton University Press, 1999).

9. Part of the difficulty here flows, of course, from well-known conceptual problems surrounding "privacy" in general, on which see, for instance, the following articles all reproduced in George Pitcher, ed., *Wittgenstein: The Philosophical Investigations* (Notre Dame, IN: University of Notre Dame Press, 1968): A. J. Ayer, "Can There Be a Private Language?" pp. 251–66; R. Rhees, "Can There Be a Private Language?" pp. 267–85; John W. Cook, "Wittgenstein on Privacy," pp. 286–323.

10. Some, for instance, would maintain that there is a queer sense in which all experience is ineffable: I can never say anything that would allow you to see, as it were, my world "from the inside." Whether there is anything nontrivial to such assertions seems at least very dubious, and the assertion itself may well be ill formed, a point to which we shall have occasion to return below, in considering privacy. More often, we are led to speak of awe-inspiring experiences, or experiences which move us to use heightened superlatives, as being somehow uncommunicable in language.

11. Bimal Krishna Matilal, "Mysticism and Ineffability: Some Issues of Logic and

Language," in Katz, *Mysticism and Language,* pp. 143–57, thus argues that paradoxical mystical language may be used indirectly to *show* what cannot be directly referred to: "The emptiness of all metaphysical theses can be *shown,* not *stated* in language" (p. 155).

12. See especially Steven T. Katz, "Language, Epistemology, and Mysticism," pp. 22–74; Frederick J. Streng, "Language and Mystical Awareness," pp. 141–69; and Renford Bambrough, "Intuition and the Inexpressible," pp. 200–213; all in Katz, *Mysticism and Philosophical Analysis.*

13. As Steven Collins once trenchantly put it: "It is, perhaps, as if entering a room full of people sitting in peaceful (or exasperated!) silence, one were to be able to conclude that they were all thinking 'the same thing'" (*Selfless Persons* [Cambridge: Cambridge University Press, 1982], p. 10).

14. Cf. Proudfoot, *Religious Experience,* pp. 124–36. As he rightly argues, "Many of the terms employed in the literature of the history of religions to capture a universal feature of religious experience or practice also appear to function as placeholders. Though purportedly descriptive, they are lifted out of their original meanings and employed in ways that empty them of their original meanings and suggest that they are undefinable" (p. 131). The problem is exemplified by Rudolf Otto's eccentric comparative essay on Śaṅkara and Eckhart, *Mysticism East and West: A Comparative Analysis of the Nature of Mysticism,* trans. Bertha L. Bracey and Richenda C. Payne (New York: Meridian, 1957), which generally steers clear of the difficulties involved in seeking to compare directly negative discourses. While he mentions negation and silence several times (e.g., pp. 7, 31), his analysis is based almost entirely upon the comparison of the positive theological assertions of oneness and being.

15. On pure consciousness experience see Forman, *The Problem of Pure Consciousness.* Discussions of the perception of God have been prominent throughout the work of recent "reformed" epistemologists, but note in particular William P. Alston, *Perceiving God: The Epistemology of Religious Experience* (Ithaca: Cornell University Press, 1991).

16. Though it would take us beyond our present concerns, it may be noted that our theme thus dovetails with an interest in the role of ocularity and vision in Western philosophy that has become prominent since the publication of Richard Rorty's celebrated *Philosophy and the Mirror of Nature* (Princeton, NJ: Princeton University Press, 1980). More recently, see in particular David Michael Levin, ed., *Sites of Vision: The Discursive Construction of Sight in the History of Philosophy* (Cambridge, MA: MIT Press, 1997); idem, *The Philosopher's Gaze* (Berkeley: University of California Press, 1999).

17. Sharf, "Experience," p. 95.

18. McCutcheon, *Critics Not Caretakers,* p. 7.

19. On the terms "empical" and "experience" in the main languages of Western philosophy, refer to D. W. Hamlyn, "Empiricism," in *The Encyclopedia of Philosophy,* ed. Paul Edwards (New York: Macmillan, 1967), 2:499–505; André Lalande, *Vocabulaire technique et critique de la Philosophie,* 16th ed. (Paris: Presses Universitaires de France, 1988), pp. 280–81, s.v. "empirique, empirisme, empiriste," and pp. 321–23, s.v. "expéri-

ence"; and Johannes Hoffmeister, *Wörterbuch der Philosophischen Begriffe* (Hamburg: Felix Meiner, 1955), p. 198, s.v. "Empirie."

20. John Locke, *An Essay Concerning Human Understanding,* ed. Peter H. Nidditch (Oxford: Clarendon Press, 1974), bk. 2, chap. 1, par. 2: "Our Observation employ'd either about *external, sensible Objects; or about the internal Operations of our Minds, perceived and reflected on by our selves, is that, which supplies our Understandings with all the materials of thinking*" (emphasis original). The conception of empiricism as including within its purview our apperceptive experience of our own minds was never lost, and in the mid-nineteenth century underlies, for instance, Franz Brentano's usage in his *Psychology from an Empirical Standpoint,* trans. Antos C. Rancurello, D. B. Terrell, and Linda L. McAlister (New York: Humanities Press, 1973).

21. Of course, in this way he replicated the rationalist-empiricist dichotomy in the sphere of theology. B. A. Gerrish, "Friedrich Schleiermacher," in *Nineteenth Century Religious Thought in the West,* ed. Ninian Smart, John Clayton, Patrick Sherry, and Steven T. Katz (Cambridge: Cambridge University Press, 1985), 1:123–56. Cf. Proudfoot, *Religious Experience,* p. 16, representing Schleiermacher's views: "The theologian is an empiricist, and his aim is to provide an accurate account of the religious affections within a particular community." We must note as well that, besides the appeal to empiricism, Schleiermacher's experiential turn reflects the emphasis, common to a broad range of early Protestant traditions, on the need of the individual to experience divine grace for herself.

22. Cf. McCutcheon, *Critics Not Caretakers,* p. 4, on what he calls the "private affair" tradition in the study of religion, which conceives "religion as an inherently meaningful, nonempirical, uniquely personal experience that transcends historical difference and evades rational explanation."

23. Thus James's famous analysis of the authority of the mystical experience for the subject of the experience in question: *The Varieties of Religious Experience,* pp. 422–29.

24. Otto Pfleiderer, *The Philosophy of Religion on the Basis of Its History,* trans. Alexander Stewart and Allan Menzies (London: Williams and Norgate, 1886), 1:322, clearly reflects this tension: "But the truth is, that feeling [as posited by Schleiermacher] is a mere psychological form of consciousness, and so little essentially divine or the being of God in us, that it is, on the contrary, quite indifferent with regard to its contents, and can have for its contents what is lowest and meanest, just as well as what is highest."

25. The metaphor is due to Daniel C. Dennett, *Consciousness Explained* (Boston: Little, Brown, 1991).

26. For a forceful contemporary defense of epistemological skepticism, see Peter Ungar, *Ignorance: A Case for Scepticism* (Oxford: Clarendon Press, 1975); and for an equally forceful critique of "brains in a vat" and similar puzzle cases, Hilary Putnam, *Reason, Truth, and History* (Cambridge: Cambridge University Press, 1981), chap. 1.

27. Nevertheless, there was, of course, a prominently empirical dimension of Aristotle's own method, and some Western medieval thinkers did accentuate this. See, e.g.,

Sir William Cecil Dampier, *A History of Science and Its Relations with Philosophy and Religion* (Cambridge: University Press, 1971), pp. 90–93, on Friar Roger Bacon.

28. Cf. ibid., p. 129: "Medieval Scholasticism . . . worshipped the human reason acting within the bounds of authority; [modern science] accepts brute facts whether reasonable or not."

29. Refer to Stillman Drake, *Discoveries and Opinions of Galileo* (Garden City, NY: Doubleday-Anchor, 1957). Note the opinion (p. 75) of "the eminent Jesuit astronomer Father Cristopher Clavius [who] had previously been reported as saying that in order to see such things [as Galileo had observed] one would first have to put them inside the telescope." Galileo, for his part, was very sensitive to criticism of this sort, as may be seen in his insistence in *The Starry Messenger* (Drake, *Discoveries and Opinions of Galileo*, p. 30) that "it is necessary to prepare quite a perfect telescope."

30. This has been widely accepted since the publication of Thomas S. Kuhn, *The Structure of Scientific Revolutions* (Chicago: University of Chicago Press, 1962), and subsequent editions.

31. Katz, "Language, Epistemology, and Mysticism," p. 22. Katz's assertion seems in principle correct, though there may be counterexamples to even this formulation. If a goal of a particular religion, say Buddhism, is a state of peace of mind and emotional tranquility, and if by adhering to the course of personal discipline recommended by the tradition one comes to experience this for oneself, then it would seem reasonable to adduce such experience as one bit of evidence supporting the truth of the general claim made by Buddhism that by living in a certain way one comes to realize a particular end. The kinds of truth claim that cannot be verified by religious experience are metaphysical, not practical, and I assume that this is primarily what Katz had in mind.

32. As Mary Mothersill puts it: "if there are experiences that characteristically arise from the apprehension of 'works of art,' then, on the one hand, works of art *do* have something in common, and, on the other, 'aesthetic experience' has a straightforward application"(*Beauty Restored* [Oxford: Clarendon Press, 1984], p. 53).

33. Cf. Hans-Georg Gadamer, *Truth and Method* (New York: Crossroad, 1982), pp. 219–21, on Husserl's view that "we cannot conceive subjectivity as an antithesis to objectivity" (p. 220).

34. For a relatively clear parallel to constructivism in contemporary aesthetics, see Arthur Danto, "The Artworld," *Journal of Philosophy* 61, no. 19 (1964): 571–84. Danto's position is not, it must be emphasized, to be identified with cultural constructivism as we usually understand it; for the constructed world with which he is concerned—the artworld—is conceived here as a peculiar domain of value production in its own right, apart from any one cultural sphere: "The greater the variety of artistically relevant predicates, the more complex the individual members of the artworld become; and the more one knows of the entire population of the artworld, the richer one's experience with any of its members" (pp. 583–84). There is no reason, then, that the "artworld" should not be populated by artifacts drawn from many cultures: Sienese frescoes, Jackson Pollocks, Japanese *netsuke*, and Congolese masks all now people the artworld.

35. P. J. Marshall, ed., *The British Discovery of Hinduism in the Eighteenth Century* (Cambridge: Cambridge University Press. 1970), p. 3.

36. Joseph Margolis, *What, after All, Is a Work of Art?* (University Park, PA: Pennsylvania State University Press, 1999), chap. 2, "Relativism and Cultural Relativity," which concludes (p. 66): "I find the Western emblem of the world's diversity displayed, however problematically, in Picasso's *Les Desmoiselles d'Avignon.* For, within that interrupted painting, one sees the impossibility of avoiding the spontaneous urge to bend the Intentional forms of one society to the art and criticism of another."

37. The seems often a tendency in recent work on religious experience, among constructivists no less than perennialists, to speak of cultures monolithically: Christian mystics experience God, Buddhists *nirvāṇa,* Hindus *brahman,* and the like. But this is clearly too crude and fails to do justice to the remarkable diversity we find within any one of these traditions.

38. It is a matter of some regret that such examples of feminine religious radiance were among the topics that could not be explored within the limitations of the present volume.

39. With regard to the phenomenology of light in the histories of differing religious traditions, one may note, in addition to the references given elsewhere in this book, the contributions of participants in the Eranos meetings, several of whom were especially interested in this topic. See, for instance, in *Papers from the Eranos Yearbooks,* ed. Joseph Campbell (Princeton, NJ: Princeton University Press), Max Pulver, "The Experience of Light in the Gospel of St. John, in the 'Corpus hermeticum,' in Gnosticism, and in the Eastern Church," in vol. 4, *Spiritual Disciplines* (1985), pp. 239–66; Henry Corbin, "Divine Epiphany and Spiritual Birth in Ismaili Gnosis," in vol. 5, *Man and Transformation* (1980), pp. 69–160; Jean Daniélou, "The Dove and the Darkness in Ancient Byzantine Mysticism," ibid., pp. 270–96; and Henri-Charles Puech, "The Concept of Redemption in Manichaeism," in vol. 6, *The Mystic Vision* (1982), pp. 247–314. Further investigations along these lines include Henry Corbin, *The Man of Light in Iranian Sufism,* trans. Nancy Pearson (Boulder, CO: Shambhala, 1978); Mircea Eliade, *Mephistopheles and the Androgyne: Studies in Religious Myth and Symbol,* trans. J. M. Cohen (New York: Sheed and Ward, 1965), chap. 1; and Mircea Eliade, "Spirit, Light, and Seed," *History of Religions* 11 (1971): 1–30.

40. Cf. Alston, *Perceiving God,* chap. 4 on "doxastic practices."

41. This, of course, is a point that Karl Barth and others have urged against Schleiermacher. Refer to Gerrish, "Friedrich Schleiermacher," p. 148: "From merely human experience you cannot get either to God or to the real Christ."

42. As Carl G. Hempel once argued, "the cognitive meaning of a statement in an empiricist language is reflected in the totality of its logical relationships to all statements in that language and not to observation sentences alone." From "The Empiricist Criterion of Meaning," in *Logical Positivism,* ed. A. J. Ayer (New York: Free Press, 1959), p. 123.

43. Philosophical theology, no less than the investigation of religious experience, reflects this. As Patrick Sherry, writing in *A Companion to Philosophy of Religion,* ed.

Philip L. Quinn and Charles Taliaferro (Oxford: Blackwell, 1997), p. 279, affirms, "Beauty is probably today the most neglected of the divine attributes."

44. Refer to Etienne Gilson, *The Arts of the Beautiful* (New York: Charles Scribner's Sons, 1965), esp. chap. 8, "Art and Christianity."

45. This is reflected in the remarks of Gilson, *The Arts of the Beautiful,* p. 173: "The image makes me look within myself for the object of my piety, to which I am directed through my apprehension of the work."

46. Once again, Gilson, *The Arts of the Beautiful,* p. 167, says it well: "Modern art galleries are full of works, Egyptian, Greek, European and African, that once served religious purposes and are now reduced to the condition of artistic masterpieces devoid of all religious meaning and no longer exercising any religious function. Everybody realizes this when looking at a statue of Zeus, because, as a god, Zeus has lost his worshipers, but the countless representations of Christ, of the Virgin and of the saints that crowd our art galleries are just as innocent of religious meaning as any Greek or Roman divinity."

47. Of course, for a broad range of current work on religious epistemology, the object of religious experience is "God." But, unless we are limiting our inquiry to claims within a particular tradition with a clear and consistent understanding of "God," this is clearly inadequate for the larger purposes either of the study of religion in general or of even the diverse traditions that are sometimes lumped together under the rubric of "theism."

48. Otto, *The Idea of the Holy;* G. van der Leeuw, *Religion in Essence and Manifestation,* trans. J. E. Turner (Princeton, NJ: Princeton University Press, 1986).

49. Otto, *The Idea of the Holy,* chap. 7.

50. Cf. Wasserstrom, *Religion after Religion,* pp. 56–57, on the "tautegorical sublime."

51. Consideration of some of the better efforts to formally define "beauty" readily convinces us of the shortcomings of the enterprise:

"Beauty is pleasure regarded as the quality of a thing" (George Santayana, "The Nature of Beauty," in *Critical Theory since Plato,* ed. Hazard Adams [New York: Harcourt Brace Jovanovich, 1971], p. 706).

"It appears probably that the beautiful should be *defined* as that of which the admiring contemplation is good in itself" (G. E. Moore, *Principia Ethica* [Cambridge: Cambridge University Press, 1968], p. 201; emphasis original).

Franz Brentano, adopting a less rigorous formulation, perhaps comes closer: "In ordinary life we use 'beautiful' with reference to any phenomenon which can be rightly preferred for its own sake to ordinary phenomena and which presents itself in such a manner that it in fact arouses love and delight in a particularly high degree in the man of proper disposition—the man endowed with good taste" (Franz Brentano, *The Foundation and Construction of Ethics,* ed. Franziska Mayer-Hillebrand, trans. Elizabeth Hughes Schneewind [New York: Humanities Press, 1973], p. 177).

52. R. G. Collingwood, *The Principles of Art* (New York: Oxford University Press, 1958), p. 40: "When . . . aestheticians want to use the word ['beauty'] as a name for the quality in things in virtue of which we enjoy an aesthetic experience in connexion with

them, they want to use it as a name for something non-existent. There is no such quality. The aesthetic experience is an autonomous activity."

53. Van der Leeuw, *Religion in Essence and Manifestation,* pt. 1, "The Object of Religion," reflects this very well.

54. It remains one of the great merits of William James's pioneering investigations that he sought to emphasize the *varieties* of religious experience. He affirms (*The Varieties of Religious Experience,* p. 27) that when "we are willing to treat the term 'religious sentiment' as a collective name for many sentiments which religious objects may arouse in alteration, we see that it probably contains nothing whatever of a psychologically specific nature. There is religious fear, religious love, religious awe, religious joy, and so forth."

55. Cf. Ian Hacking, "Five Parables," in *Philosophy in History,* ed. Richard Rorty, J. B. Schneewind, and Quentin Skinner (Cambridge: Cambridge University Press, 1985), pp. 103–24, esp. pp. 104–7 on the style of porcelain known as "the green family."

56. Of course, it must be recalled that the charge of "pantheism" leveled against Hallāj probably misrepresented his teaching. Nevertheless, the misrepresentation is itself a type of response to the mystic's transgressions. The classic study remains Louis Massignon, *The passion of al-Hallāj: Mystic and Martyr of Islam,* trans. Herbert Mason (Princeton, NJ: Princeton University Press, 1982), 4 vols.

57. Jeffrey J. Kripal, *Kālī's Child: The Mystical and the Erotic in the Life and Teachings of Ramakrishna* (Chicago: University of Chicago Press, 1995).

58. Note that this formulation agrees only in part with the position criticized by Proudfoot, *Religious Experience,* pp. 233–35, that "religious experience, emotion, action, belief, and practice must each be identified under a description that is available to and can plausibly be ascribed to the subject of that experience. To identify an experience from a perspective other than that of the subject is to misidentify it." But no two perspectives on an experience can be identical. It is for this reason that, as indicated earlier, contestation over the interpretation of experience has been possible, and indeed is often encountered, within religious traditions. Religious traditions never needed to wait for the contemporary critique of "experience as a protective strategy" in order to adopt a critical perspective on their own.

59. Robert M. Gimello, "Mysticism in Its Contexts," in Katz, *Mysticism and Religious Traditions,* p. 85.

60. Refer, in this context, especially to Pierre Hadot, *Philosophy as a Way of Life,* ed. Arnold I. Davidson, trans. Michael Chase (Oxford: Blackwell, 1995); and Luther H. Martin, Huck Gutman, and Patrick Hutton, eds. *Technologies of the Self: A Seminar with Michel Foucault* (Amherst: University of Massachusetts Press, 1988). Also relevant in this context is Pierre Bourdieu, *Outline of a Theory of Practice,* trans. Richard Nice (Cambridge: Cambridge University Press, 1977), esp. pp. 87–95, on "the dialectic of objectification and embodiment."

61. Hans H. Penner, "The Mystical Illusion," in Katz, *Mysticism and Religious Tradi-*

tions, p. 93. Penner's views are clearly indebted to the linguistic relativism ultimately stemming from the work of Benjamin L. Whorf, *Language, Thought and Reality* (Cambridge, MA: MIT Press., 1956). See further Martin Hollis and Steven Lukes, eds. *Rationality and Relativism* (Cambridge, MA: MIT Press, 1982).

62. Thomas F. Mathews, *The Clash of Gods: A Reinterpretation of Early Christian Art* (Princeton, NJ: Princeton University Press, 1995), p. 190.

63. Refer to Issachar Ben-Ami, "Folk Veneration of Saints among Moroccan Jews," in *Studies in Judaism and Islam*, ed. Shelomo Morag (Jerusalem: Hebrew University, 1981).

64. For a critical review of contextualism, see Ben-Ami Scharfstein, *The Dilemma of Context* (New York: New York University Press. 1989).

65. McCutcheon, *Critics Not Caretakers*, p. 86: "much of the current scholarship on religion deviates dramatically from my position, for it presumes that religious experiences . . . are somehow privileged and either originate from, or gain meaning by reference to, something that lies outside historical change."

66. Forman, *The Problem of Pure Consciousness*, pp. 5–9.

67. There are, of course, strong objections that can be raised here. See n. 70 below.

68. Brent Berlin and Paul Kay, *Basic Color Terms: Their Universality and Evolution* (Berkeley: University of California Press, 1969).

69. John Gage, *Color and Meaning: Art, Science, and Symbolism* (Berkeley: University of California Press, 1999), pp. 29–30, 105–7, reviews the main objections to Berlin and Kay's work. For an example of an effort to make use of Berlin and Kay's results in connection with anthropological research, see M. E. Combs-Schilling, *Sacred Performances: Islam, Sexuality, and Sacrifice* (New York: Columbia University Press, 1989), pp. 39–41. In the light of Gage's critical remarks (which reflect and refer to a wide range of earlier critical comment on Berlin and Kay), Combs-Schilling's discussion seems not sufficiently attuned to the marked limitations to any real-world applications of the scheme of "basic color terms."

70. Thus, referring to the contributions to Forman, *The Problem of Pure Consciousness*, even if we grant that the "concept of nothingness in Jewish mysticism" discussed by Daniel C. Matt (pp. 121–59) and the Indian Buddhist notions of pure consciousness investigated by Paul J. Griffiths (pp. 71–97) both do involve notions of pure consciousness experience as defined by Forman, it is still very difficult to make out that they are in any significant respect saying the same things about it.

71. Patrick Olivelle, *The Early Upaniṣads: Annotated Text and Translation* (New York: Oxford University Press, 1998), p. 399.

72. Elmer O'Brien, *The Essential Plotinus*, 2nd ed. (Indianapolis: Hackett, 1981), p. 175.

73. In a rather different context, it is of interest to note that the Tibetan philosopher Sa-skya Paṇḍita (1182–1251), in his *Tshad-ma rigs-gter* (Beijing: Mi-rigs-dpe-skrun-khang, 1989), pp. 56–57, states that *buddhajñāna*, the Buddha's gnosis, being "inconceivable," cannot be discussed on analogy to ordinary cognition at all.

74. Or as Richard A. Shweder, *Thinking through Cultures: Expeditions in Cultural Psychology* (Cambridge, MA: Harvard University Press, 1991), p. 69, writes: "As for

those who fear that if truth is not unitary, then nihilism will reign and that polytheism is merely a code word for anarchy, it is comforting to remind ourselves, again and again, that the fact that there is no uniform reality (God, foundation, truth) does not mean that there are no realities (gods, foundations, truths) at all."

75. Some examples of recent work exploring aspects of religious experience from the perspective of the cognitive sciences include: Francisco J. Varela, Evan Thompson, and Eleanor Rosch, *The Embodied Mind: Cognitive Science and Human Experience* (Cambridge, MA: MIT Press, 1991); Robert K. C. Forman, ed. *The Innate Capacity: Mysticism, Psychology, and Philosophy* (Oxford: Oxford University Press, 1998); James H. Austin, *Zen and the Brain: Toward an Understanding of Meditation and Consciousness* (Cambridge, MA: MIT Press, 1999); Jensine Andresen, ed., *Religion in Mind: Cognitive Perspectives on Religious Belief, Ritual, and Experience* (New York: Cambridge University Press, 2001).

76. I should note here that I do not regard there to be any plausible argument from religious experience to the existence of God, so that, because the topic at hand has no bearing on the question, the possible truth of theism is neither affirmed nor denied by these limited remarks on physicalism. Despite my doubts regarding the "argument from experience," I concur with the so-called reformed epistemologists (for instance, William P. Alston and Alvin Plantinga) that the subjects of theistic religious experiences may rationally judge their experiences to be among the warrants for their faith. Note, too, that God, if she exists, might have created a thoroughly physical universe.

77. Thomas Nagel, *The View from Nowhere* (Oxford: Oxford University Press, 1986), esp. chap. 3.

CONTRIBUTORS

CATHERINE B. ASHER is associate professor in the Department of Art History at the University of Minnesota. She is the author of *The Architecture of Mughal India* (2nd ed., Cambridge University Press, 2001), coeditor of *Perceptions of South Asia's Visual Past* (American Institute of Indian Studies, 1994), and also author of many articles on the art and architecture of India from the twelfth century to the present time.

RAOUL BIRNBAUM studies Buddhist practice traditions in China and their worlds of representation, from medieval times to the present. He has written *The Healing Buddha* (Shambhala, 1979), *Studies on the Mysteries of Mañjuśrī* (Society for the Study of Chinese Religions, 1983), and numerous articles. He is professor of Buddhist studies at the University of California, Santa Cruz, where he also holds the Patricia and Rowland Rebel Chair in History of Art and Visual Culture.

MATTHEW T. KAPSTEIN is Numata Professor of Buddhist Studies in the Divinity School of the University of Chicago and directeur d'études at the École Pratique des Hautes Études, Paris. His publications include *The Tibetan Assimilation of Buddhism: Conversion, Contestation, and Memory* (Oxford University Press, 2000), *Reason's Traces: Identity and Interpretation in Indian and Tibetan Buddhist Thought* (Wisdom, 2001), and, with the anthropologist Melvyn C. Goldstein, *Buddhism in Contemporary Tibet: Religious Revival and Cultural Identity* (University of California Press, 1998).

SARAH ILES JOHNSTON is professor of Greek and Latin and an associate of the Religious Studies Program at the Ohio State University. She specializes in the religions of ancient Greece and Rome. Her publications include *Restless Dead* (University of California Press, 1999), *Hekate Soteira* (Scholars' Press, 1990), and *Medea* (with James Clauss; Princeton University Press, 1997).

ANDREW LOUTH is professor of patristic and Byzantine studies at the University of Durham. He is the author of several books, including *Origins of the Christian Mystical Tradition: Plato to Denys* (Oxford University Press, 1981), *Denys the Areopagite* (Geoffrey

Chapman, 1989), *Maximus the Confessor* (Routledge, 1996), and *St John Damascene: Tradition and Originality in Byzantine Theology* (Oxford University Press, 2002).

PAUL E. MULLER-ORTEGA is professor of religion at the University of Rochester. He received his Ph.D. from the University of California, Santa Barbara (1985). He is the author of *The Triadic Heart of Śiva: Kaula Tantricism of Abhinavagupta in the Non-dual Shaivism of Kashmir* (State University of New York Press, 1989) and a coauthor of *Meditation Revolution: A History and Theology of the Siddha Yoga Lineage* (Agama, 1997), as well as the author of a number of articles on topics in the study of the Śaivism of Kashmir.

ELLIOT R. WOLFSON is the Abraham Lieberman Professor of Hebrew and Judaic Studies at New York University. He is the author of several books on the history of Jewish mysticism, including *Along the Path: Studies in Kabbalistic Myth, Symbolism, and Hermeneutics* (State University of New York Press, 1995), *Circle in the Square: Studies in the Use of Gender in Kabbalistic Symbolism* (State University of New York Press, 1995), and *Through a Speculum That Shines: Vision and Imagination in Medieval Jewish Mysticism* (Princeton University Press, 1996).

MIMI HALL YIENGPRUKSAWAN is professor of art history at Yale University. Her publications include *Hiraizumi: Buddhist Art and Regional Politics in Twelfth-Century Japan* (Harvard University Asia Center, 1998), *Buddhist Art Treasures from Nara* (with Michael Cunningham and John Rosenfield; Cleveland Museum of Art, 1998), and numerous articles.

HOSSEIN ZIAI is professor of Islamic and Iranian studies at UCLA, where he has taught since 1988. His books include *Anwāriyya: An 11th Century A.H. Persian Translation and Commentary on Suhrawardī's Ḥikmat al-Ishrāq* (Amir Kabir, 1984), *Knowledge and Illumination: A Study of Suhrawardī's Ḥikmat al-Ishrāq* (Scholars' Press, 1990), *The Ball and the Polo Stick; or, the Book of Ecstasy* (with Wheeler Thackston; Mazda, 1999), *The Book of Radiance* (Mazda, 1998), and *The Philosophy of Illumination* (with John Walbridge; Brigham Young University Press, 2000).

INDEX